Celebrating Irving Fisher: The Legacy of a Great Economist

Made in the USA
Monee, IL
19 October 2026

66036449R00262

Celebrating Irving Fisher: The Legacy of a Great Economist

Edited by
Robert W. Dimand and John Geanakoplos

Blackwell Publishing

350 Main Street, Malden, MA 02148-5020, USA
9600 Garsington Road, Oxford OX4 2DQ, UK
550 Swanston Street, Carlton, Victoria 3053, Australia

First published 2005 by Blackwell Publishing Ltd.

Library of Congress Cataloging-in-Publication Data

Celebrating Irving Fisher : the legacy of a great economist / edited by Robert W. Dimand and John Geanakoplos.
p. cm.
Includes bibliographical references and index.

ISBN:978-1-4051-3307-4

1. Fisher, Irving, 1867–1947. 2. Economists—United States. 3. Economics–United States—History. I. Fisher, Irving, 1867–1947. II. Dimand, Robert W. (Robert William) III. Geanakoplos, John, IV. Title.

HB119.F5C45 2005
330.1—dc22

2004065957

A catalogue record for this title is available from the Library of Congress.

For further information on
Blackwell Publishing, visit our website:
http://www.blackwellpublishing.com

Dedication

To the Memory of
JAMES TOBIN
Great Economist, Inspiring Teacher and Friend,
and Admirer of Irving Fisher

Irving Fisher. Courtesy of Professor George Fisher.

Irving Fisher and his wife Margaret Hazand Fisher with their three children in 1902. Courtesy of Professor George Fisher.

Irving Fisher and Margaret Hazand Fisher, celebrating their fortieth wedding anniversary, 1933. Courtesy of Professor George Fisher.

Irving Fisher on television with his world map, 1945. Courtesy of Professor George Fisher.

Acknowledgements

We wish to thank the following organizations for permission to reprint materials that now appear in this volume.

James Tobin's encyclopedia entry "Fisher, Irving (1867–1947) is reprinted from Eatwell, J., M. Milgate and P. Newman (eds.) *The New Palgrave: A Dictionary of Economics.* 1987, 2: 369–376. United Kingdom, London and Basingstoke: The Macmillan Press Limited; New York, N.Y. The Stockton Press and Japan, Maruzen Company Limited. The essay is reproduced with the kind permission of Palgrave Macmillan.

The essay by Robert E. Hall entitled "Controlling the Price Level," originally appeared as an electronic article in a series Contributions to Macroeconomics 2 (1), Article 5. See *http://www.bepress.com/bejm/contributions/vol2/iss1/art5.* Reprinted with kind permission of The Berkeley Electronic Press.

James Tobin's essay, "Fisher's *The Nature of Capital and Income,*" was first published in German translation in Bortram Schefold Editor, "*Vadernecum zu Einem Klassiker dir Amerikianischen Nationalö Konomie: Irving Fisher's "The Nature of Capital and Income.*" Duesseldorf Verlag Wirtschaft und Finanzen GmbH, 1991, pp. 59–68. Printed in English in William Barber ed. *Works of Irving Fisher,* 14 Vols. London. Pickering & Chatto, 1997, 2:1–5.

James Tobin's essay, "Fisher's Introductory Text" This Tobin essay was first published in the *American Economic Review: Papers and Proceedings,* 87 (May 1997): pp. 430–432. We are grateful to the American Economic Association for its permission to republish this essay.

Dr. George Fisher supplied the pictures of Irving Fisher and his family and we are grateful to him for allowing us to reproduce them as frontispieces to this volume.

Contents

Foreword

I'm delighted to be able to add a few words to this volume that celebrates the work of my grandfather, Irving Fisher, and explores the major themes of his life. The papers collected here naturally focus on his professional contributions, which I am not equipped to address. My words must be more personal.

I was not quite 10 when my grandfather died, and so never had a chance to know him as an academic, only as a kindly gentleman who visited our home on important occasions. But a few threads of my grandfather's professional life seem to have been woven into my own, nevertheless.

The papers in this volume show that many of my grandfather's contributions involved using equilibrium concepts to model the complex interactive behavior of economic systems. That approach clearly owed much to the work of his mentor J. Willard Gibbs, who had earlier published the definitive treatment of the mathematical conditions governing equilibrium in heterogeneous chemical systems. Much of my early geological work involved using equilibrium models to explain the dynamic patterns recorded by mineral assemblages in rocks found in the eroded cores of mountain ranges. Because the simplified treatment of chemical equilibria in most of the standard texts of physical chemistry is unable to cope with the complexities of geological systems, I had to return to Gibbs's original papers for a more complete treatment. So in an odd sense Gibbs became my mentor, as well as my grandfather's. And in a way it was my grandfather who introduced me to our joint mentor by financing the publication of Gibbs's collected works, which taught me the thermodynamics that I needed to know.

I am deeply indebted to my grandfather for the profound epistemic humility that he displayed when the Depression of the 1930s undermined both his personal and his professional fortunes. How galling it must have been to hear his ill-timed remark about the stock market's permanently high plateau repeated over and over! But my grandfather hardly seemed to notice. Instead, he returned to his office and quickly published two books on the market crash—books intended not to bolster his pre-1929 ideas, but to explore the lessons of the crash. That example has several times helped me to see new possibilities when my own ideas have begun to unravel, and will always stand as a reminder that new paradigms emerge from the ashes of the old.

But my grandfather's most important gift was his deep personal commitment to using economics to address concrete problems facing the nation and the world. The sense that science (in my case, earth science) had something important to say about how to live came later to me than to my grandfather, but it did come. Most of my work in the last decade has been devoted to learning how to live sustainably in an ever more crowded world, one in which the fate of all humans is increasingly connected by the many strands of globalization. When pressured to return to more traditional geological work, I am grateful that he showed me the importance of using science to live wisely. I hope that his example will also encourage the next generation of scholars to move beyond the narrow disciplinary boundaries within which most academics are trained, and to respond imaginatively to the needs of an increasingly complex world.

George W. Fisher
Professor of Geology
Johns Hopkins University

Celebrating Irving Fisher: The Legacy of a Great Economist

By ROBERT W. DIMAND and JOHN GEANAKOPLOS*

Introduction[1]

Irving Fisher made seminal contributions across an astonishing spectrum of economic science: monetary policy rules, the neoclassical theory of capital and interest, expected inflation as the difference between real and nominal interest, the Fisher "ideal" index number, indexed bonds, correlation analysis, distributed lags, the "Phillips curve," the debt-deflation process, taxing consumption rather than income, the value of human capital and improvement in health, even the computation of general equilibrium. On May 8 and 9, 1998, economists gathered at Fisher's university, Yale, to celebrate his contributions and to examine themes in economics suggested by his work. The publication of William Barber's 14-volume edition of *The Works of Irving Fisher* in 1997, the 50th anniversary of Fisher's death, provided a suitable occasion for reflecting on Fisher's legacy and inspiration for economics. This volume contains revised versions of the papers and comments presented on that occasion, together with other writings on Fisher by James Tobin.

No other American economist working before World War II has had anything close to the influence that Irving Fisher has on modern economics. James Tobin (1985: 29–30) reports that Fisher led his contemporaries Wesley Clair Mitchell, John Bates Clark, and Frank W. Taussig in column inches in the *Social Sciences Citation Index* for 1976–1980 by the ratio 9:3:1:1 (with Fisher's lead growing over time), "[m]uch more than the others, moreover, Fisher is cited for substance rather than for history of thought."

In the early 20th century, Fisher was the most cited economist in

*We thank Nora Wiedenbach, a member of the Cowles Foundation staff for her prodigious efforts in helping us organize the conference of 1998 and to edit this volume.

[1]Parts of this Introduction draw on Robert W. Dimand, "Irving Fisher and Modern Macroeconomics," *American Economic Review: Papers and Proceedings* 87:2 (May 1997).

The American Journal of Economics and Sociology, Vol. 64, No. 1 (January, 2005).

the world. George Stigler and Claire Friedland (1979) have calculated that Fisher was the economist cited most often in journal articles published in English in all fields of economics in the period 1886 to 1924, but Jeff Biddle (1996: 150–151), who eliminates self-citations, places Alfred Marshall first (and Fisher fourth) for 1904–1924.

In the money and fluctuations literature, Fisher was the most-cited economist in the 1920s (with Mitchell second, and the young Keynes tenth). By the 1940s, Fisher vanished completely from citation lists as John Maynard Keynes captured the profession's attention (Deutscher 1990). Yet contemporary macroeconomics builds largely upon Fisher's foundations. Once remembered primarily for his spectacular misprediction of stock prices in October 1929 and for eccentric crusades (reform of the calendar, a new world map projection, Prohibition, the use of mathematics in economics), Fisher emerges in retrospect as a major figure in the development of economics—not least for those innovations his contemporaries found most ludicrous, such as building a hydraulic model to simulate the determination of prices in a general equilibrium system.

What Were Fisher's Contributions?

FISHER'S CONTRIBUTIONS TO THE MODERN THEORY of capital, income, interest, and saving, discussed by John Geanakoplos and James Tobin in this volume, have proved of central importance. The two-period consumption diagram of Fisher's *The Rate of Interest* ([1907] 1997, Vol. 3: 409) put intertemporal choice on the same footing as contemporaneous choice among goods (and was promptly extended to international exchange by Enrico Barone in 1908). Fisher's diagram brought together impatience (the marginal rate of time preference, represented by the slope of the indifference curve) and expected rate of return on investment (reflected in the slope of the budget constraint). Like Marshall's supply and demand diagram, Fisher's diagram brought together key concepts of economics and made their interaction conveniently and memorably visible for analysis and teaching. Fisher's diagram is the basis for permanent-income and life-cycle consumption theories, with the simple Keynesian absolute-income hypothesis restricted to cashflow-constrained consumers in imperfect credit markets. Fisher's rate of return over costs, developed in *The Rate of Interest* and *The Theory of Interest* ([1930] 1997, Vol. 9), was recognized by John Maynard Keynes as equivalent to his marginal efficiency of capital (Keynes 1937; Kregel 1988; Dimand 1995), so modern theories of investment, saving, and consumption all have roots in Fisher's analysis of impatience and opportunity to invest.

The elements of Fisher's analysis were brilliantly anticipated in 1834 by John Rae (to whom Fisher dedicated *The Rate of Interest* and, jointly with Eugen von Böhm-Bawerk, *The Theory of Interest*) and developed by Böhm-Bawerk. Fisher was the first to draw them together, using his two-period diagram, and the first to show how they interacted to determine equilibrium. Fisher (1907) even anticipated the Cambridge capital controversies over reswitching of techniques, with a numerical example of multiple solutions for Böhm-Bawerk's average period of production (without noticing that his own rate of return over costs could be similarly subject to multiple roots).

An implication of Fisher's two-period consumption diagram was that, given the possibility of borrowing or saving, the relevant budget constraint for consumption decisions is the discounted present value of expected lifetime after-tax income. Fisher expounded his view of the stock of wealth or capital as the capitalized value of a stream of expected receipts (so that the flow of income rather than the stock of capital is the fundamental concept) in *The Nature of Capital and Income* ([1906] 1997, Vol. 2), discussed by James Tobin in this volume. Tobin brings out the importance of Fisher's insistence upon the then-unfamiliar concepts of discounting and net present value.

Since the market value of the assets acquired with savings is the discounted present value of the expected receipts to be received from owning the assets, Fisher held that it would be double-counting to include as income both the savings and the subsequent stream of earnings from the assets. As John Shoven and John Whalley discuss in this volume, Fisher redefined income to exclude net savings, so as to avoid double taxation and a tax-induced bias against saving. Instead of the income tax, Fisher proposed an expenditure tax. In recent years, Fisher's concern about a tax bias against capital accumulation has again come to the fore in public finance.

Fisher emphasized that human capital, the discounted present value of the stream of income from human skills and abilities, far exceeds the value of physical capital. He cited an estimate stating that human capital in the United States was worth five times as much as physical capital. Accordingly, he advocated investment in improving health, co-authored a best seller on *How to Live* (1915), and devoted his two presidential addresses to the American Association for Labor Legislation to proposals for a national department of health and for health insurance. Fisher's guide to a healthy life sold 400,000 copies in 21 editions in his lifetime, far more than any of his other books, while insurance companies distributed 12 to 15 million copies of an abridgement. Papers by William Nordhaus and Victor Fuchs in this volume, with comments by Robert Dimand, the late Alvan Feinstein, T. N. Srinivasan, and Richard Zeckhauser, follow Fisher in their concern with the economic value of the health of nations.

Fisher's American Economic Association monograph *Appreciation and Interest* ([1896] 1997, Vol. 1) was the first substantial study of expected inflation as the difference between nominal interest and real interest, a distinction whose recognition Fisher credited to earlier writers, especially Alfred Marshall. This relationship has become known as the Fisher equation. Considering rates of interest in different monetary standards, Fisher (1896) pioneered the uncovered interest parity theorem that nominal interest rates in two countries will differ by the expected rate of change of the exchange rate between the currencies of the countries. Attributing differences among money rates of interest for different terms to expectations about the future course of prices, Fisher offered an expectations theory of the term structure. He is often misremembered as asserting that real interest is independent of inflation and monetary shocks. This was true only for comparison of equilibria; his theory of economic fluctuations stressed the effect of monetary shocks on real interest during transition periods (see Dimand 1999a, 1999b). In *The Theory of Interest* (1930), Fisher used a distributed lag of past price level changes to represent expected inflation in correlations between nominal interest and expected inflation, an anticipation of the adaptive expectations hypothesis. Given Fisher's role as a pioneer of distributed lags and correlation analysis and as the founding president of the

Econometric Society, it is highly appropriate that Peter C. B. Phillips applies new methods of data description for nonstationary time series to an "Econometric Analysis of Fisher's Equation" in this volume.

Fisher's compensated-dollar proposal for stabilizing the cost of a basket of commodities, advanced in *The Purchasing Power of Money* ([1911] 1997, Vol. 4) and *Stabilizing the Dollar* ([1920] 1997, Vol. 5), advocated a policy rule (varying the dollar price of gold to target a commodity price index, not a monetary aggregate) instead of discretion. Advocacy of monetary policy rules (other than the gold standard) was unusual in Fisher's day (see Robert Hall in this volume), as was Fisher's preference for internal stabilization over exchange stability.

Fisher's monetary theory of economic fluctuations, first presented in Chapter IV of *The Purchasing Power of Money* (1911), anticipated later developments such as the Phillips curve and adaptive expectations. Indeed, Fisher's "A Statistical Relation Between Unemployment and Price Changes" (1926) was reprinted in 1973 as "Lost and Found: I Discovered the Phillips Curve—Irving Fisher," a title devised by George Stigler, then editing the *Journal of Political Economy* (although the direction of causality in Fisher's article ran from price changes to unemployment, while that of A. W. H. Phillips ran from unemployment to wage changes). Fisher's rejection of the belief of W. Stanley Jevons, Wesley Mitchell, William Beveridge, Henry L. Moore, and Nikolai Kondratieff that economic fluctuations reflect the summation of truly periodic cycles has carried the field so completely that "business cycles" as the name of a field no longer implies that fluctuations are cyclical—even though David Hendry and Mary Morgan (1995: 45–48) find that Fisher erred in claiming that his own monthly data for U.S. trade for 1915–1923 showed no cyclical tendencies (Fisher 1997, Vol. 8). Like Milton Friedman and Anna Schwartz (1963), Fisher attributed the onset and severity of the Great Depression to a contraction of the money supply that the Federal Reserve could have prevented (Cargill 1992). Going beyond a monetary theory of fluctuations, Fisher ([1933] 1997, Vol. 10) developed a debt-deflation theory of depressions, stressing the consequences for stability of changes in the real value of nominal-valued inside debt that had not been anticipated when the debts were incurred. This analysis, which influenced Hyman Minsky's theory of financial-system fragility, is only now being absorbed by the mainstream (see Tobin 1980, Ch. 2; Minsky 1982; King 1994; Robert Dimand in this volume). Fisher (1935) assembled a 27-country data set to study the role of the gold standard in the international transmission of the Depression, anticipating a post-1980 wave of similar studies (see Dimand 2003).

Fisher took the equation of exchange from the work of Simon Newcomb, to whom he dedicated *The Purchasing Power of Money*, and expressed it as $MV = PT$, where M is the stock of money, V the velocity of circulation, P the price level, and T an index of transactions. Fisher then expanded the equation of exchange to $MV + M'V' = PT$, to take account of demand deposits M' as well as currency M, and attempted an independent measurement of the velocities of circulation of currency and deposits, drawing on a survey of cash-holding and spending by his Yale students and on David Kinley's (1897, 1910) studies of bank clearings. Although Fisher expounded the quantity theory of money in terms of the velocity of circulation of money rather than of a stable money demand function, Bennett McCallum and Marvin Goodfriend (1987) credit Fisher's *Theory of Interest* (1930: 216) with the first correct and unambiguous account of the marginal opportunity cost of holding money.

Fisher's 1891 Yale doctoral dissertation, published the following year as *Mathematical Investigations in the Theory of Value and Prices* ([1892] 1997, Vol. 1), introduced general-equilibrium analysis into American economics (with some unnecessary originality, as he wrote much of the thesis before discovering the writings of Léon Walras and Francis Ysidro Edgeworth). In his dissertation, Fisher presented his hydraulic model to simulate price determination (see William Brainard and Herbert Scarf in this volume, and the comments by Donald Brown and Felix Kubler and by K. R. Sreenivasan). Though that machine was destroyed in transit to the Columbian Exhibition in Chicago, it and a later version by Fisher were ancestors of A. W. H. Phillips's hydraulic macro-model (Leeson 2000) and forerunners of today's computable general equilibrium modeling.

Fisher's commitment to making his theory empirically meaningful led to *The Purchasing Power of Money*'s attempted statistical verification of the quantity theory of money, to annual articles in the *American Economic Review* (1911–1919) on the equation of exchange, to his massive *The Making of Index Numbers* ([1922] 1997, Vol. 7) and the Fisher "ideal index" (the geometric mean of the Paasche and Laspeyres indexes), and to Fisher's Index Number Institute, whose *weekly* commodity price index was accompanied by weekly articles by him. Fisher's exhaustive test approach to index numbers, searching for the formula that best satisfied a set of statistical tests (see W. Erwin Diewert in this volume), has borne belated fruit: in 1995, the U.S. Department of Commerce's Bureau of Economic Analysis switched to a chain-weighted index approximating Fisher's ideal index. A reliable price index was crucial for Fisher's proposed monetary-policy rule (the compensated dollar plan), for his campaign to educate the public against what he termed *The Money Illusion* ([1928] 1997, Vol. 8), and for his proposal to index transactions against monetary instability (see John Geanakoplos in this volume). Fisher persuaded Rand Kardex (later Remington Rand) to issue the first indexed bonds in the 1920s: the U.S. government followed only in 1996.

Fisher was notorious for an empirical failure: his excessive optimism about stock prices in October 1929. While he could not have been expected to predict when a stock price bubble would burst, he was overly sanguine in denying any such bubble and insisting that soaring stock prices reflected the sound fundamentals of a "New Economy" based on new technologies. Fisher's public reputation and personal finances were devastated by the Wall Street crash. However, Kathryn Dominguez, Ray Fair, and Matthew Shapiro (1988) argue that the severity and duration of the Depression could not have been forecast even with modern statistical techniques and data sets because unpredictable policy mistakes were responsible. In addition, Fisher's claims for a high rate of return on owning common stocks over the long term may be viewed as an early discovery of what is now known as "the equity premium puzzle."

These varied contributions in the many publications listed in Irving Norton Fisher's vast bibliography of his father's writings (I. N. Fisher 1961–1972) have a breadth unmatched by Fisher's contemporaries. John Bates Clark, paired with Fisher in James Tobin's article on the

American Economic Association's centenary (Tobin 1985), is remembered primarily as a favorite straw man of the Cambridge capital controversies. Fisher's contributions closely parallel much of modern macroeconomics, yet his role was long neglected. References to him vanished from macroeconomics in the 1940s. The "Mark I" monetarism of Milton Friedman and his Chicago students had many Fisherian features: the quantity theory of money, a monetary-policy rule, domestic price stability rather than fixed exchange rates, adaptive expectations, the permanent-income consumption function (based on Fisher's two-period consumption diagram), and Federal Reserve responsibility for the Great Depression. Friedman often placed less emphasis on links with Fisher than with Chicago oral tradition. However, Friedman (1972: 12) paid a handsome tribute to Fisher when, addressing the American Economic Association on the question "Have Monetary Policies Failed?," he quoted at length from Fisher's exchange with J. Laurence Laughlin on the quantity theory of money at the 1910 AEA meetings and then stated: "And now I must cease quoting from Fisher, with whom I am in full agreement, and proceed instead to plagiarize him—albeit with modifications to bring him down to date."

James Tobin (1985: 36–37) concluded that Fisher's "insights contain the making of a theory of the determination of economic activity, prices, and interest rates in short and medium runs. Moreover, in his neo-classical writings on capital and interest Fisher had laid the basis for the investment and savings equations central to modern macroeconomic models. Had Fisher pulled these strands together into a coherent theory, he could have been an American Keynes." Fisher never pulled the strands of his economics together in a grand synthesis. His monetary economics, from the equation of exchange through index numbers to the compensated dollar, was united by a concern with the consequences of imperfectly expected monetary shocks but was not set in the context of either the general equilibrium analysis of his dissertation or his capital theory.

This failure to draw his monetary theory of fluctuations, his general equilibrium analysis, and his theory of interest and capital together into a coherent synthesis was one of three reasons for Fisher's inability to hold the attention of his audience in the 1930s and 1940s. The second reason was that Fisher did not deal with the macroeconomic coordination problem that Keynes and Friedrich von Hayek tackled in very different ways in the 1930s. Fisher offered no explanation of how a drop in nominal income and spending led to mass unemployment in that decade. He did go beyond his monetary theory of economic fluctuations to investigate the debt-deflation process, but he presented no explicit theory of unemployment and the labor market. Fisher correlated output and unemployment with distributed lags of past price level changes, but in the Great Depression of the 1930s, the public and the economics profession demanded an explanation of mass unemployment that focused on what had gone wrong with adjustment in the labor market.

The third reason for Fisher's eclipse was the wreckage of his public reputation and personal finances by his misjudgment of stock prices, compounded by his misfortune in providing in October 1929 a memorable and quotable remark about stock prices reaching a permanently high plateau. Fisher could not have predicted the subsequent monetary, fiscal, and tariff policies that turned the slump into a deep depression, and although the equity premium literature suggests that he was right about common stocks as an investment for the long term, his reputation was shattered.

For these three reasons, Fisher found no contemporary audience for his debt-deflation theory of depressions, his explanation of the spending collapse. Even his monetary theory of economic fluctuations was forgotten as introductory textbooks attached his name to a constant-velocity, constant-output version of the quantity theory of money. With historical perspective, however, Fisher can now be recognized as among the most fruitful builders of modern economics. It is not at all unusual for a once-renowned scholar to fade in the collective memory of his or her discipline. There are also numerous instances of unnoticed precursors such as Gossen being belatedly discovered. What is remarkable is that Fisher, having achieved eminence and then been ignored by his professional peers, is once again seen as a crucial figure in the development of economics.

Overview of the Volume

JAMES TOBIN'S *NEW PALGRAVE* ARTICLE on Fisher has become a classic, an evaluation of a great Yale monetary economist by another great

Yale monetary economist. Tobin, the 1981 Nobel laureate in Economic Science, was consulting editor for William Barber's edition of *The Works of Irving Fisher* and has long recognized Fisher as America's outstanding scientific economist of the first half of the 20th century.

William J. Barber, the editor of the 14-volume edition of *The Works of Irving Fisher*, draws on his unrivaled knowledge of Fisher's writings and papers to reflect on Fisher's life and career, and especially on Fisher's often-troubled relationship with Yale University, where Fisher was an undergraduate and graduate student and spent his entire teaching career.

The modern study of computation of general economic equilibrium begins with the fixed-point algorithm from Herbert E. Scarf's "On the Computation of Equilibrium Prices," appropriately in *Ten Economic Studies in the Tradition of Irving Fisher* (Fellner et al. 1967), published to celebrate the centenary of Fisher's birth. Now, William C. Brainard and Herbert E. Scarf examine "How to Compute Equilibrium Prices in 1891," sorting out how the hydraulic machine outlined in Fisher's 1891 dissertation (published as Fisher 1892) actually worked. Brainard and Scarf use Matlab to simulate the path of adjustment in Fisher's hydraulic model for a variety of preferences, endowments, and initial conditions. Donald Brown and Felix Kubler apply a different method of solving nonlinear systems of equilibrium equations, the homotopy method suggested by Eaves, to the adjustment path of Brainard and Scarf's digital version of Fisher's hydraulic machine. The physicist and mechanical engineer K. R. Sreenivasan looks to the mathematical tools available in 1891 to understand why Fisher turned to a hydraulic simulation of general equilibria rather than attempting a mathematical solution of his system of equations describing general competitive equilibrium.

A group of three papers and three comments considers Fisherian themes in monetary economics and macroeconomics. Robert E. Hall examines Chile's experiment with the Unidad de Fomento as an implementation of Fisher's compensated-dollar plan, under which the resource content of the unit of account is varied to stabilize the cost of a bundle of commodities. James Tobin argues that the present multiplicity of available stores of values reduces the importance of stabilizing the real value of currency, and concludes: "At the end of the century, monetary and economic stability does not seem to be as daunting a challenge as it appeared to Fisher. Fisher himself deserves considerable credit for this happy result." Martin Shubik raises several questions that need to be answered before Hall's proposed indexed unit of account can be a practical policy rather than a theoretical possibility. He draws attention to ongoing work on stochastic strategic game process models as a source of insights into the microeconomics of money, financial institutions, efficiency, and inflation.

Peter C. B. Phillips's "Econometric Analysis of Fisher's Equation" applies new econometric techniques to "Fisher's equation," which equates the nominal interest rate to the sum of real interest and expected inflation. Phillips's new methods of data description for nonstationary time series provide a nonparametric mechanism for modeling the spatial densities of a time series that displays random wandering characteristics (like interest rates and inflation) and an estimation procedure called modified log periodogram regression to obtain semiparametric estimates of long range dependence in U.S. real interest rates. John Rust summarizes Phillips's key theoretical results "for the benefit of readers who may not be familiar with advanced stochastic processes," identifies empirical puzzles that remain unresolved, and doubts whether some of the empirical questions are well posed. Fisher was a pioneer in the use of distributed lags and correlation analysis and was a crucial figure in the creation of both the Econometric Society and the Cowles Commission (now the Cowles Foundation), so the application of novel econometric techniques to the Fisher equation is particularly apt as part of a celebration of Fisher's legacy.

Robert Dimand suggests that the debt-deflation process of Fisher (1933), which was also briefly mentioned independently by Keynes, provides a way of introducing a corridor of stability into macroeconomic models, so that the models would be self-adjusting for small shocks but not for shocks large enough to push the economy beyond the threshold of stability. Such models could explain why the classical adjustment mechanism would usually work but occasionally break down, as in the Great Depression.

Two papers by James Tobin discuss Fisher's innovative *Elementary*

Principles of Economics (1912) and *Nature of Capital and Income* (1906). Tobin describes Fisher's elementary textbook, which has been almost entirely forgotten, as a brilliant attempt to make advanced economic theory accessible to students in introductory classes. Tobin's essay on *The Nature of Capital and Income* was first published in German, in a collection of essays accompanying a facsimile reprint of Fisher's book, and was reprinted as an introduction to the reprint in *The Works of Irving Fisher.* Tobin emphasizes the simplicity and comprehensiveness of Fisher's concept of capital and praises Fisher's book for its careful attention to the distinction between stocks and flows and to the dimensionality of concepts used in economic discourses. However, Tobin finds that Fisher's concept of income (equated to current consumption) remains controversial and suggests that some notion of sustainable consumption (such as the hypothetical intact-capital rate of consumption that Fisher termed "standard income") would be preferable.

John B. Shoven and John Whalley, and their discussants Alan J. Auerbach and Michael J. Graetz, offer a modern perspective on Fisher as a founding father of public finance and on Fisher's proposal to substitute a consumption tax for an income tax, which was most fully expounded by Fisher in the 1930s and 1940s (Fisher 1997, Vol. 12) but derived from the distinctive concept of income presented in *The Nature of Capital and Income.* Rounding out the group of papers on Fisher's theories of capital, interest, and public finance is John Geanakoplos's paper on "The Ideal Indexed Bond and Irving Fisher's Impatience Theory of Interest with Overlapping Generations," with a comment by Robert J. Shiller. Fisher long advocated inflation indexed bonds. Geanakoplos shows that, in the context of a multicommodity Capital Asset Pricing Model (CAPM) world, the best welfare-improving bond pays the minimum money needed to achieve the same utility, rather than the minimum needed to buy the same commodity bundle. Geanakoplos also shows that in stationary overlapping generations (OLG) economies with land, the real interest rate at the stationary state depends on impatience (as in Fisher's impatience theory of interest).

Consideration of Fisher's innovation in indexed bonds leads naturally to Fisher's test approach to index theory in *The Making of Index*

Numbers (1922). W. Erwin Diewert develops an alternative branch of index number theory, using differences rather than ratios, that had its origins around the time that Fisher developed his test approach. In his comment, Matthew D. Shapiro reflects on Fisher's contribution to index number theory.

The last group of papers and comments follows from Fisher's concern with the economic value of improving public health. William D. Nordhaus examines "Irving Fisher and the Contribution of Improved Longevity to Living Standards" (with comments by Robert Dimand and T. N. Srinivasan), and Victor R. Fuchs writes on "Health, Government, and Irving Fisher" (with comments by the late Alvan R. Feinstein and by Richard Zeckhauser). As these papers show, this subject was of central importance to Fisher, a lifelong crusader for health reform.

These papers celebrate the life, contributions, and legacy of Irving Fisher, a great scientific economist and outspoken social crusader, a man of brilliance, integrity, and eccentricity who did much to advance theoretical and empirical economics.

References

Barone, Enrico. (1908). *Principi di economia politica.* Rome: Athenaeum.

Biddle, Jeff. (1996). "A Citation Analysis of the Sources and Extent of Wesley Mitchell's Reputation." *History of Political Economy* 28(2): 137–169.

Cargill, Thomas F. (1992). "Miscellany: Irving Fisher Comments on Benjamin Strong and the Federal Reserve in the 1930s." *Journal of Political Economy* 100 (December): 1273–1277.

Deutscher, Patrick. (1990). *R. G. Hawtrey and the Development of Modern Macroeconomics.* Ann Arbor: University of Michigan Press.

Dimand, Robert W. (1995). "Irving Fisher, J. M. Keynes and the Transition to Modern Macroeconomics." In *New Perspectives on Keynes,* Annual Supplement to *History of Political Economy.* Eds. Allan Cottrell and Michael S. Lawlor. 27: 247–266.

——. (1999a). "Fisher's Monetary Macroeconomics." In Loef and Monissen (1999): 35–58.

——. (1999b). "Irving Fisher and the Fisher Relation: Setting the Record Straight." *Canadian Journal of Economics* 32(3): 744–750.

——. (2003). "Irving Fisher on the International Transmission of Booms and Depressions Through Monetary Standards." *Journal of Money, Credit and Banking* 35(1): 49–90.

Dominguez, Kathryn M., Ray C. Fair, and Matthew D. Shapiro. (1988). "Forecasting the Depression: Harvard Versus Yale." *American Economic Review* 78(4): 595–612.

Fellner, William, et al. (1967). *Ten Economic Studies in the Tradition of Irving Fisher*. New York: John Wiley & Sons.

Fisher, Irving. (1892). *Mathematical Investigations in the Theory of Value and Prices, Transactions of the Connecticut Academy of Sciences*. Rpt. in Fisher (1997). *The Works of Irving Fisher*, vol. 1. Ed. William J. Barber. London: Pickering and Chatto.

——. (1896). *Appreciation and Interest*. New York: Macmillan for the American Economic Association. Rpt. in Fisher (1997). *The Works of Irving Fisher*, vol. 1. Ed. William J. Barber. London: Pickering and Chatto.

——. (1906). *The Nature of Capital and Income*. New York: Macmillan. Rpt. in Fisher (1997). *The Works of Irving Fisher*, vol. 2. Ed. William J. Barber. London: Pickering and Chatto.

——. (1907). *The Rate of Interest*. New York: Macmillan. Rpt. in Fisher (1997). *The Works of Irving Fisher*, vol. 3. Ed. William J. Barber. London: Pickering and Chatto.

——. (1912). *Elementary Principles of Economics*. New York: Macmillan. Rpt. in Fisher (1997). *The Works of Irving Fisher*, vol. 5. Ed. William J. Barber. London: Pickering and Chatto.

——. (1920). *Stabilizing the Dollar*. New York: Macmillan. Rpt. in Fisher (1997). *The Works of Irving Fisher*, vol. 6. Ed. William J. Barber. London: Pickering and Chatto.

——. (1922). *The Making of Index Numbers*. Boston: Houghton Mifflin. Rpt. in Fisher (1997). *The Works of Irving Fisher*, vol. 7. Ed. William J. Barber. London: Pickering and Chatto.

——. (1926). "A Statistical Relation Between Unemployment and Price Changes." *International Labour Review* 13(6): 785–792. Rpt. in Fisher (1997). *The Works of Irving Fisher*, vol. 8. Ed. William J. Barber. London: Pickering and Chatto and as "Lost and Found: I Discovered the Phillips Curve—Irving Fisher." *Journal of Political Economy* 81 (1973): 496–502.

——. (1928). *The Money Illusion*. New York: Adelphi. Rpt. in Fisher (1997). *The Works of Irving Fisher*, vol. 8. Ed. William J. Barber. London: Pickering and Chatto.

——. (1930). *The Theory of Interest*. New York: Macmillan. Rpt. in Fisher (1997). *The Works of Irving Fisher*, vol. 9. Ed. William J. Barber. London: Pickering and Chatto.

——. (1933). "The Debt-Deflation Theory of Great Depressions." *Econometrica* 1:3 (October): 337–357. Rpt. in Fisher (1997). *The Works of Irving Fisher*, vol. 10. Ed. William J. Barber. London: Pickering and Chatto.

——. (1935). "Are Booms and Depressions Transmitted Internationally Through Monetary Standards?" *Bulletin de l'Institut International de Statistique* 28(2): 1–29. Rpt. as appendix to Dimand (2003). "Irving Fisher on the International Transmission of Booms and Depressions Through Monetary Standards." *Journal of Money, Credit and Banking* 35(1): 49–90.

——. (1997). *The Works of Irving Fisher*, 14 vols. Ed. William J. Barber. London: Pickering and Chatto.

Fisher, Irving, assisted by Harry Gunnison Brown. (1911). *The Purchasing Power of Money*. Rpt. in Fisher (1997). *The Works of Irving Fisher*, vol. 4. Ed. William J. Barber. London: Pickering and Chatto.

Fisher, Irving, and Eugene Lyman Fisk. (1915). *How to Live*. New York: Funk & Wagnalls.

Fisher, Irving Norton. (1961–1972). *A Bibliography of the Writings of Irving Fisher*, with supplement. New Haven: Yale University Library.

Friedman, Milton. (1972). "Have Monetary Policies Failed?" *American Economic Review* 62(2): 10–18.

Friedman, Milton, and Anna J. Schwartz. (1963). *A Monetary History of the United States, 1867–1960*. Princeton: Princeton University Press.

Gayer, Arthur D., Ed. (1937). *Lessons of Monetary Experience*. New York: Farrar & Rinehart.

Hendry, David F., and Mary S. Morgan. (1995). "Introduction." In *The Foundations of Econometric Analysis*. Eds. David F. Hendry and Mary S. Morgan. Cambridge, UK: Cambridge University Press.

Keynes, John Maynard. (1937). "The Theory of the Rate of Interest." In *Lessons of Monetary Experience*. Ed. A.D. Gayer. New York: Farrar & Rinehart.

King, Mervyn. (1994). "Presidential Address: Debt-Deflation: Theory and Evidence." *European Economic Review* 38(3/4): 419–445.

Kinley, David. (1897). "Credit Instruments in Business Transactions." *Journal of Political Economy* 5: 157–174.

——. (1910). *The Use of Credit Instruments in Payments in the United States*, Senate Document No. 399 (National Monetary Commission), 61st Congress, 2nd Session. Washington, DC: Government Printing Office. Rpt. Fairfield, NJ: Augustus M. Kelley.

Kregel, Jan A. (1988). "Irving Fisher, Great-Grandparent of the *General Theory*: Money, Rate of Return Over Cost, and Efficiency of Capital." *Cahiers d'Economie Politique* 14/15: 59–68.

Leeson, Robert, Ed. (2000). *A. W. H. Phillips: Collected Works in Contemporary Perspective*. Cambridge: Cambridge University Press.

Loef, Hans-E., and Hans-George Monissen, Ed. (1999). *The Economics of Irving Fisher*. Cheltenham, UK, and Northampton, MA: Edward Elgar Publishing.

McCallum, Bennett T., and Marvin S. Goodfriend. (1987). "Demand for Money: Theoretical Analysis." In *The New Palgrave: A Dictionary of Economics*, vol. 1. Eds. John Eatwell, Murray Milgate, and Peter Newman. London: Stockton Press.

Minsky, Hyman. (1982). *Can "It" Happen Again? and Other Essays*. Armonk, NY: M. E. Sharpe.

Rae, John. (1834). *New Principles of Political Economy*. Boston. Rpt. in R. Warren James (1965). *John Rae, Political Economist*. Toronto: University of Toronto Press.

Stigler, George J., and Claire Friedland. (1979). "The Pattern of Citation Practices in Economics." *History of Political Economy* 11(1): 1–20.

Tobin, James. (1980). *Asset Accumulation and Economic Activity*. Chicago: University of Chicago Press.

——. (1985). "Neoclassical Theory in America: J. B. Clark and Fisher." *American Economic Review* 75(6): 28–38.

Irving Fisher (1867–1947)

By James Tobin*

Abstract. This essay is reprinted from Eatwell, J., M. Milgate and P. Newman (eds.) *The New Palgrave: A Dictionary of Economics*. 1987, 2: 369–376. United Kingdom, London and Basingstoke: The Macmillan Press Limited; New York, N.Y. The Stockton Press and Japan, Maruzen Company Limited. The essay is reproduced with the kind permission of Palgrave Macmillan.

Irving Fisher was born in Saugerties, New York, on 27 February 1867; he was residing in New Haven, Connecticut at the time of his death in a New York City hospital on 29 April 1947.

Fisher is widely regarded as the greatest economist America has produced. A prolific, versatile and creative scholar, he made seminal and durable contributions across a broad spectrum of economic science. Although several earlier Americans, notably Simon Newcomb, had used some mathematics in their writings, Fisher's dedication to the method and his skill in using it justify calling him America's first mathematical economist. He put his early training in mathematics and physics to work in his doctoral dissertation on the theory of general equilibrium. Throughout his career his example and his teachings advanced the application of quantitative method not only in economic theory but also in statistical inquiry. He, together with Ragnar Frisch and Charles F. Roos, founded the Econometric Society in 1930; and Fisher was its first President. He had been President of the American Economic Association in 1918.

Much of standard neoclassical theory today is Fisherian in origin, style, spirit and substance. In particular, most modern models of

*Professor James Tobin (1918–2002) received the Nobel Prize in economics in 1981. He served as the Sterling Professor of Economics at Yale University and served on the Yale faculty from 1950 until his retirement from teaching in 1988. For additional biographical information about Tobin, see p. 113 below. This article is reprinted from Eatwell, J., M. Milgate, and P. Newman, eds., *The New Palgrave: A Dictionary of Economics*, 1987, 2:369–376, reproduced with permission of Palgrave Macmillan.

The American Journal of Economics and Sociology, Vol. 64, No. 1 (January, 2005).

capital and interest are essentially variations on Fisher's theme, the conjunction of intertemporal choices and opportunities. Likewise, his theory of money and prices is the foundation for much of contemporary monetary economics.

Fisher also developed methodologies of quantitative empirical research. He was the greatest expert of all time on index numbers, on their theoretical and statistical properties and on their use in many countries throughout history. From 1923 to 1936, his own Index Number Institute manufactured and published price indexes of many kinds from data painstakingly collected from all over the world. Indefatigable and innovative in empirical research, Fisher was an early and regular user of correlations, regressions and other statistical and econometric tools that later became routine.

To this day Fisher's successors are often rediscovering, consciously or unconsciously, Fisher's ideas and building upon them. He can be credited with distributed lag regression, life cycle saving theory, the 'Phillips curve', the case for taxing consumption rather than 'income', the modern quantity theory of money, the distinction between real and nominal interest rates, and many more standard tools in economists' kits. Although Fisher was not fully appreciated by his contemporaries, today he leads other old-timers by wide and increasing margins in journal citations. In column inches in the *Social Sciences Citation Index* (1979, 1983) Fisher led his most famous contemporaries, Wesley Mitchell, J. B. Clark, and F. W. Taussig in that order, by rough ratios 5:3:1:1 in 1971–5 and 9:3:1:1 in 1976–80. Much more than the others, moreover, Fisher is cited for substance rather than for history of thought.

For all his scientific prowess and achievement, Fisher was by no means an 'ivory tower' scholar detached from the problems and policy issues of his times. He was a congenital reformer, an inveterate crusader. He was so aggressive and persistent, and so sure he was right, that many of his contemporaries regarded him as a 'crank' and discounted his scientific work accordingly. Science and reform were indeed often combined in Fisher's work. His economic findings, theoretical and empirical, would suggest to him how to better the world; or dissatisfaction with the state of the world would lead him into

scientifically fruitful analysis and research. Fisher's search for conceptual clarity about 'the nature of capital and income' led him not only to lay the foundations of modern social accounting but also to argue that income taxation wrongly puts saving in double jeopardy. Fisher turned his talents to monetary theory because he suspected that economic instability was largely the fault of existing monetary institutions. His 'debt-deflation theory of depression' was motivated by the disasters the Great Depression visited upon the world.

Economics was not the only aspect of human and social life that engaged Fisher's reformist zeal. He was active and prolific in other causes: temperance and Prohibition; vegetarianism, fresh air, exercise and other aspects of personal hygiene; eugenics; and peace through international association of nations.

Fisher was an amazingly prolific and gifted writer. The bibliography compiled by his son lists some 2000 titles authored by Fisher, plus another 400 signed by his associates or written by others about him. Fisher's writings span all his interests and causes. They include scholarly books and papers, articles in popular media, textbooks, handbooks for students, tracts, pamphlets, speeches and letters to editors and statesmen. They include the weekly releases of index numbers, often supplemented by commentary on the economic outlook and policy, issued for thirteen years by Fisher and assistants from the Index Number Institute housed in his New Haven home.

Fisher was the consummate pedagogical expositor, always clear as crystal. He hardly ever wrote just for fellow experts. His mission was to educate and persuade the world. He took the trouble to lead the uninitiated through difficult material in easy stages. Whenever he was teaching or tutoring students, he wrote handbooks or texts for their benefit—in mathematics and science when he was still a student himself, in the principles of economics when he was the professor responsible for the introductory course. Fisher's economics text was published in 1910 and 1911. Its graceful exposition of sophisticated theoretical material will impress a modern connoisseur, but it was too difficult for widespread adoption. Some of it survived in a leading introductory text of the 1920s and 1930s, by the younger Yale economists Fairchild, Furniss and Buck (1926).

A Brief Biography

IRVING FISHER GREW UP AND attended school successively in Peace Dale, Rhode Island; New Haven, Connecticut; and St. Louis, Missouri. His father, a Congregational minister, died of tuberculosis just when Irving had finished high school and was planning to attend Yale College, his father's *alma mater*. Irving was now the principal breadwinner for himself, his mother and his younger brother. He did have a $500 legacy from his father for his college education. The family moved to New Haven, and together managed to make ends meet. Irving tutored fellow students during term and in summers.

Fisher was a great success in Yale College, ranking first in his class and winning prizes and distinctions not only in mathematics but across the board. He was also determined to make good in the extra-curricular college culture so important in those days. His efforts won him election to the most prestigious secret senior society, Skull and Bones, the ultimate reward senior campus leaders bestowed on members of the class behind them.

Awarded a scholarship for graduate study, he stayed on at Yale. Graduate Studies were not departmentalized in those days, and Fisher ranged over mathematics, science, social science and philosophy. His most important teachers were Josiah Willard Gibbs, the mathematical physicist celebrated for his theory of thermodynamics, William Graham Sumner, famous still in sociology but at the time also important in political economy, and Arthur Twining Hadley, a leading economist specializing in what is now known as Industrial Organization.

As the time to write a dissertation approached, Fisher had still not chosen his life work. Young Fisher's interests and talents were universal. In the seven years at Yale before he finished his doctorate, he had written and published poetry, political commentary, book reviews, a geometry text together with tables of logarithms, and voluminous notes on mathematics, mechanics and astronomy for the benefit of students he was teaching or tutoring. If he had specialized in anything in six years at Yale, it was mathematics, but even in his graduate years he had spent half his time elsewhere.

Sumner put him on to mathematical economics, and in his third

year of graduate study, he finished the dissertation that won him worldwide recognition in economic theory. Fisher's 1891 PhD was the first one in pure economics awarded by Yale, albeit by the faculty of mathematics. Although the university, thanks to Sumner, Hadley and Henry W. Farnum, was strong in 'political economy', there was no distinct department for the subject, let alone for 'economics'. This was generally the case in American universities. Venturing into mathematical economic theory, Fisher was very much on his own; and his route into economics was quite different from that of most American economists of his era.

The dominant tradition in American political economy was imported from the English classical economists, mainly Smith, Ricardo and John Stuart Mill; it was just beginning to be updated by Marshall. This tradition Fisher's mentors at Yale had taught him well. But the neoclassical developments on the European continent from 1870 on, the works of Walras and Menger and Böhm-Bawerk, or even those of their English counterparts Jevons and Edgeworth, had been little noticed at Yale or elsewhere in America.

At the time, the main challenge in America to classical political economy was coming from quite a different direction. The American Economic Association was founded in 1886 by young rebels against Ricardian dogma and its *laissez-faire* political and social message. They included Richard T. Ely, J. B. Clark, Edwin R. A. Seligman and other future luminaries of American economics. Many of them had pursued graduate studies in Germany. In the German emphasis on historical, institutional and empirical studies they found welcome relief from implacable classical theory, and in the German faith in the state as an instrument of socially beneficial reform they found a hopeful antidote to the fatalism of economic competition and social Darwinism. Sumner was prominent among several elders who refused to join an Association born of such heresy; he did not relent even though the AEA very soon became sufficiently neutral and catholic to attract his Yale colleagues and other initial holdouts. Fisher, a bit younger than the founding rebels and educated solely at one American university, was not involved. It was his reconstruction, rather than their revolution, that was destined eventually to replace the classical tradition in the mainstream of American economics.

Fisher stayed at Yale throughout his career. He started teach mathematics, evidently even before he received his doctorate and was appointed Tutor in Mathematics. His first economics teaching was under the auspices of the mathematics faculty, an undergraduate course on 'The Mathematical Theory of Prices'. In 1894–5 during his Wanderjahr in Europe, this young American star was welcomed by the leading mathematically inclined theorists in every country. On his return he became Assistant Professor of Political and Social Science and began teaching economics proper. He was appointed full Professor in 1898 and retired in 1935.

Fisher was struck by tuberculosis in 1898. He spent the first three years of his professorship on leave from Yale and from science, recuperating in more salubrious climates. His lifelong crusade for hygienic living dates from this personal struggle to regain health and vigour. The experience powerfully reinforced his determination to gain 'a place among those who have helped along my science' and his ambition 'to be a *great* man', as he wrote to his wife (I. N. Fisher, 1956, pp. 87–8). After his recovery the books and articles began flowing from his pen, never to stop until his death at the age of 80.

Fisher participated actively in teaching and in university affairs until 1920. Thereafter his writings and his myriad outside activities and crusades preoccupied him. He taught only half time and had little impact on students, undergraduate or graduate. Thus Fisher had few personal disciples; there was no Fisherian School. The student to whom Fisher was closest, personally and intellectually, was James Harvey Rogers, a 1916 PhD who returned to Yale as a professor in 1930. His career was prematurely ended by his tragic death in a plane crash in 1939 at the age of 55.

Fisher was, on top of everything else, an inventor. His most successful and profitable invention was the visible card index system he patented in 1913. In 1925 Fisher's own firm, the Index Visible Company, merged with its principal competitor to form Kardex Rand Co., later Remington Rand, still later Sperry Rand. The merger made him wealthy. However, he subsequently lost a fortune his son estimated to amount to 8 or 10 million dollars, along with savings of his wife and her sister, when he borrowed money to exercise rights to buy additional Rand shares in the bull market of the late 1920s.

More than money was at risk in the market. Fisher had staked his public reputation as an economic pundit by his persistent optimism about the economy and stock prices, even after the 1929 crash. His reputation crashed too, especially among non-economists in New Haven, where the university had to buy his house and rent it to him to save him from eviction. Until the 1950s the name Irving Fisher was without honour in his own university. Except for economic theorists and econometricians, few members of the community appreciated the genius of a man who lived among them for 63 years.

Irving Fisher's marriage to Margaret Hazard in 1893 was a very happy one for 47 years. She died in 1940. They had two daughters and one son, his father's biographer. The death of their daughter Margaret in 1919 after a nervous breakdown was the greatest tragedy of her parents' lives. Their daughter Carol brought them two grandchildren.

General Equilibrium Theory

FISHER'S DOCTORAL DISSERTATION (1892) is a masterly exposition of Walrasian general equilibrium theory. Fisher, who was meticulous about acknowledgements throughout his career, writes in the preface that he was unaware of Walras while writing the dissertation. His personal mentors in the literature of economics were Jevons (1871) and Auspitz and Lieben (1889).

Fisher's inventive ingenuity combined with his training under Gibbs to produce a remarkable hydraulic-mechanical analogue model of a general equilibrium system, replete with cisterns, valves, levers, balances and cams. Thus could he display physically how a shock to demand or supply in one of ten interrelated markets altered prices and quantities in all markets and changed the incomes and consumption bundles of the various consumers. The model is described in detail in the book; unfortunately both the original model and a second one constructed in 1925 have been lost to posterity. Anyway Fisher was a precursor of a current Yale professor, Herbert Scarf (1973) and other practitioners of computing general equilibrium solutions. In his formal mathematical model-building too, Fisher was greatly impressed by the analogies between the thermodynamics of his mentor Gibbs and economic systems, and he was able to apply Gibb's innovations in vector calculus.

Fisher expounds thoroughly the mathematics of utility functions and their maximization, and he is careful to allow for corner solutions. He uses independent and additive utilities of commodities in his first mathematical approximation and in his physical model; later he was to show how this assumption could be exploited to measure marginal utilities empirically (1927). But the general formulation in his dissertation makes the utility of every commodity depend on the quantities consumed of all commodities. At the same time, he states clearly that neither interpersonally comparable utility nor cardinal utility for each individual is necessary to the determination of equilibrium. Fisher's list of the limitations of his analysis is candid and complete. The supply side of Fisher's model is, as he acknowledges, primitive. Each commodity is produced at increasing marginal cost, but neither factor supplies and prices nor technologies are explicitly modelled.

Finally, Fisher shows his enthusiasm for his discovery of mathematical economics by appending to his dissertation as published an exhaustive survey and bibliography of applications of mathematical method to economics.

General equilibrium with intertemporal choices and opportunities. The distribution of income and wealth, and in particular the sources, determinants and social rationales, of interest and other returns to private property, were obsessive topics in economics, both in Europe and North America, at the turn of the century. One important reason, especially in Europe, was the Marxist challenge to the legitimacy of property income. Answering Marx was a strong motivation for the Austrian school, in particular for the capital theory of Böhm-Bawerk and his followers. Neoclassical economics was in a much better position than its classical precursor to respond to the Marxist challenge. The labour theory of value, which Marx borrowed from the great classical economists themselves, neither explains nor justifies functionally or ethically incomes other than wages.

These topics engaged the two leading American economists of the era, John Bates Clark and Fisher. Clark (1899) set forth his marginal productivity theory of distribution, arguing that a generalized factor of production, capital, the accumulation of past savings, has like labour a marginal product that explains and justifies the incomes of its owners.

Fisher attacked these problems in a more elegant, abstract, mathematical, general and ethically neutral manner than Clark, and than Böhm-Bawerk. At the same time, his approach was clearer, simpler and more insightful than that of Walras.

The general equilibrium system of Fisher's dissertation was a single-period model. No intertemporal choices entered; hence the theory was silent on the questions of capital and interest. But Fisher took up these subjects soon after.

His first contribution, one that should not be underestimated, was to set straight the concepts and the accounting. This he did in (1896) and (1906) with clarity and completeness that have scarcely been surpassed. It's all there: continuous and discrete compounding; nominal versus real rates; the distinction between high prices and rising prices, and its implications for observations of interest rates; the inevitable differences among rates computed in different *numéraires*; rates to different maturities and consistency among them; appreciation, expected and unexpected; present values of streams of in-and out-payments; and so on. Schumpeter calls this work 'the first economic theory of accounting' and says 'it is (or should be) the basis of modern income analysis' (1954, p. 872).

Perhaps the most remarkable feature is Fisher's insistence that 'income' is consumption, including of course consumption of the services of durable goods. In principle, he says, income is psychic, the subjective utility yielded by goods and services consumed. More practically, income could be measured as the money value, or value in some other *numéraire*, of the goods and services directly yielding utility, but only of those. Receipts saved and invested, for example in the purchase of new durable goods, are not 'income' for Fisher; they will yield consumption and utility later, and those yields will be income. To include both the initial investment and the later yields as income is, according to Fisher, as absurd as to count both flour and bread in reckoning net output. This view naturally led Fisher to oppose conventional income taxation as double taxing of saving, and to favour consumption taxation instead. His views on these matters are loudly echoed today.

Fisher published his theory of the determination of interest rates in *The Rate of Interest* (1907). A revised and enlarged version was published in 1930 as *The Theory of Interest.* One motivation for the revision was that Fisher's many critics apparently did not understand the 1907 version. They typically concentrated on the 'impatience' side of Fisher's theory of intertemporal allocation and missed the 'opportunities' side. It was there in 1907 already; the theory is much the same in both versions.

In 1930 Fisher is at pains to label his theory the 'impatience and opportunity' theory. 'Every essential part of it', he acknowledges, 'was at least foreshadowed by John Rae in 1834.' He does claim originality for his concept of 'investment opportunity'. This turns on the 'rate of return over cost, [where] both cost and return are differences between two optional income streams' (1930, p. ix). As Keynes acknowledged, this is the same as his own 'marginal efficiency of capital' (Keynes, 1936, p. 140).

In these books Fisher extended general equilibrium theory to intertemporal choices and relationships. This strategy was different from Walras. Walras tried to extend his multi-commodity multi-agent model of exchange to allow for production, saving and investment. This maintained his stance of full generality but was also difficult to expound and to understand. Fisher saw that intertemporal dependences were tricky enough to justify isolating them from the intercommodity complexities that had concerned him in his doctoral thesis. Therefore he proceeded as if there were just one aggregate commodity to be produced and consumed at different dates. This simplification enabled him to illuminate the subject more brightly than Walras himself.

The methodology of Fisher's capital theory is very modern. His clarifications of the concepts of capital and income lead him to formulate the problem as determination of the time paths of consumption—that is, income—both for individual agents and for the whole economy. Then he divides the problem into the two sides, tastes and technologies, that are second nature to theorists today. One need only read Böhm-Bawerk's murky mixture of the two in his list of reasons for the agio of future over present consumption to realize that Fisher's procedure was not instinctive in those times.

Fisher's theory of individual saving is basically the standard model to this day. Undergraduates learn the two-period 'Fisher diagram', where a family of indifference curves in the two commodities consumption now c_1 and consumption later c_2 confront a budget constraint $c_1 + c_2/(1 + r) = y_1 + y_2(1 + r)$, where the y's are exogenous wage incomes in the two periods and r is the (real) market interest rate. From the usual tangency can be read the consumption choices and present saving or dissaving. This is indeed a Fisher diagram, but of course he went much beyond it.

He stated clearly what we now call the 'life cycle' model, explaining why individuals will generally prefer to smooth their consumption over time, whatever the time path of their expected receipts. But he was not dogmatic, and he allowed room for bequests and for precautionary saving. Where Fisher differed from later theorists, and especially from contemporary model-builders, was in his unwillingness to impose any assumed uniformity on the preferences (or expectations of 'endowments'—the latter term was not familiar to him though the concept was) of the agents in his economies, and in his scruples against buying definite results by assuming tractable functional forms. In general, many of the advances claimed in present-day theory appear to depend on greater boldness in these respects.

On the side of technology, Fisher's approach was the natural symmetrical partner of his formulation of preferences, equally simple, abstract and general. He assumed that the 'investment opportunities' available to an individual (not necessarily the same for everybody) and to the society as a whole can be summarized in the terms on which consumption at any date can be traded, with 'nature', for consumptions at other dates. In modern language, we would say that Fisher postulated intertemporal production possibility frontiers, properly convex in their arguments, consumptions at various dates.

All that remained for Fisher, then, was to assume complete intertemporal loan markets cleared by real interest rates, count equations, and show that in principle the equalities of saving and investment at every date determine all interest rates and the paths of consumption and production for all individuals and for the society. Like hundreds of mathematical theorists since, he set the problem up so that it conformed to a paradigm he knew, in this case the Walrasian paradigm of his own doctoral dissertation. A more rigorous proof of the existence of the equilibria Fisher was looking for came much later, from Arrow and Debreu (1954). As we know, the problems of infinity, whether agents are assumed to have infinite or finite horizons, are much more troublesome than Fisher imagined.

In any event, Fisher had an excellent vantage point from which to comment on the controversies over capital and interest raging in his day. His formulation of 'investment opportunities' seems to allow for no factor of production one could call 'capital' and enter as argument in a production function. For that matter, he doesn't explicitly model the role of labour in production either, or of land. Strangely, in Fisher's insistence that interest is *not* a cost of production, he seems to say that labour is the only cost, evidently because labour and labour alone is a source of disutility, the loss of utility from leisure, the opportunity cost of the consumption afforded by work. Proceeding in the same spirit, he postulates that, from a position of equality of present and planned future consumption a typical individual will require more extra future consumption than present consumption as compensation for extra work. The difference, the agio, is interest, whether or not it is a "cost". Fisher attributes the agio to 'impatience', at the same time scorning the notion that interest is the cost of securing the services of a factor of production called 'abstinence' or 'waiting'.

In the 1890s and 1900s Knut Wicksell, discovering marginal productivity independently of Clark, was modeling production as a function of labour and land inputs with the output also depending on the lags between those inputs and the harvests (Wicksell [1911], 1934, vol. I, pp. 144–66). This is an 'Austrian' formulation, akin to Böhm-Barwerk's examples of trees and wine, in which time itself appears to be productive. Fisher rightly objects to any generalization that waiting longer increases output. His own intertemporal frontiers are, to be sure, sufficiently general to encompass such technologies. They can also accommodate Leontief input–output tables and Koopmans–Dantzig activity matrices with lags, Hayekian triangular structures with inventories of intermediate goods in process, Solow technologies with durable goods and labour jointly yielding output contemporaneously or later. The only common denominator of these and other representations of technology is that they relate consumption opportunities at different dates to one another, though not necessarily always in the convex trade-off terms Fisher assumed. There does not appear to be any summary scalar measure to which the productivity of a process is generally monotonically related, whether roundaboutness, average period of production, or replacement value of existing stocks of goods.

Fisher describes himself as an advocate of 'impatience' as an explanation of interest, although he realizes there are two sides of the saving-investment market, and although he acknowledges that real interest rates can at times be zero or negative. He does appear to believe that in a stationary equilibrium with constant consumption streams, consumers will require positive interest, and that only those technologies and investment opportunities affording a 'rate of return over cost' equal to this pure time preference rate would be used. He does not face up to Schumpeter's argument in 1911 that in such a repetitive and riskless 'circular flow', rational consumers would not care whether a marginal unit of consumption occurs today or tomorrow (Schumpeter [1911], 1934, pp. 34–6). Like Böhm-Bawerk, Fisher appeals to the shortness and uncertainty of life as a reason for time preference. For life-cycle consumers, however, time preferences are entangled with age preferences, and it is hard to defend any generalization as their net direction. Fair annuities take care of the uncertainty.

Monetary Theory: The Equation of Exchange and the Quantity Theory

IRVING FISHER WAS THE MAJOR American monetary economist of the early decades of this century; the subject occupied him until the end of his career. Here especially Fisher combined theorizing with empirical research, both historical and statistical. The problems he encountered led him to invent statistical and econometric methods—index numbers and distributed lags in particular—to apply for the purposes at hand to the data he and his assistants compiled. (He even studied the turnover of cash and checking accounts of a sample of Yale students, professors and employees.)

Money was a big subject in American economic literature in the 19th century, before Fisher came on the scene. The monetary events of the times—the inconvertible greenbacks issued during the Civil War, their redemption in gold in 1879, the demonetization of silver, the rapidly increasing importance of banks—stimulated research and controversy. Nevertheless, monetary theory was relatively undeveloped and unsystematized, both in Europe and in America. Fisher's treatise (1911a) was an ambitious attempt to organize with the help of theory a large body of historical and institutional information.

Yet for all its theory, statistics and index numbers, *The Purchasing Power of Money* is a tract supporting Fisher's proposal for stabilizing the value of money. This came to be known as the 'compensated dollar', the gold-exchange standard combined with a rule mandating periodic changes in the official buying and selling of gold inverse to changes in a designated commodity price index. In 1911 Fisher proposed that the gold price changes be uniform and synchronous in the currencies of all countries linked by fixed exchange parities, in proportional amounts related to an international price index. Later he was willing to accept as second best that the United States adopt the scheme on its own. Keynes proposed a similar but less formal rule for the United Kingdom (1923).

The proposal is an early example of a policy *rule*, another Fisherian idea ahead of its time, more likely to be popular among economists today than it was with Fisher's contemporaries. Indeed, some rules recently proposed are quite Fisherian, for example Hall (1985).

The 'compensated dollar' is but one of several proposals Fisher advanced over the years for stabilizing price levels or mitigating the effects of their unforeseen variation. In the 1911 book he also writes favourably of the 'tabular standard', which meant no more operationally than facilitating price-indexed contracts. In the 1920s he launched a crusade for 100 per cent reserves against checkable deposits, culminating in *100% Money* (1935). This idea is also beginning to resurface in the 1980s as a preventive defence against the monetary hazards of bank failures. In Schumpeter's view, Fisher's zeal for monetary reforms lost him some of the attention and respect his scientific contributions to monetary economics deserved, and made him come across as more monetarist than his own analysis and evidence justified (Schumpeter, 1954, pp. 872–3).

The Purchasing Power of Money is a monetarist book. Fisher asserts the quantity theory as earnestly and persuasively as Milton Friedman. There are two species of quantity theories. One is a simple implication of the 'classical dichotomy': since only relative prices and real endowments enter commodity and factor demand and supply functions, the solution values for real variables in a general equilibrium are independent of scalar variations of exogenous nominal quantities. While Fisher mentions this implication of general equilibrium theory, he does not dwell upon it as one might expect. Anyway, it does not quite apply to a commodity money system like the gold standard, which Fisher was analysing. Fisher's theory is mainly of the second kind, based on the demand for and supply of the particular nominal assets serving as media of exchange.

Fisher is usually given credit for the Equation of Exchange, although Simon Newcomb, a celebrated figure in American astronomy as well as an economist, had anticipated him (1886, pp. 315–47). The Equation is the identity $MV = PT$, where M is the stock of money; V its velocity, the average number of times per year a dollar of the stock changes hands; P is the average price of the considerations traded for money in such transactions; and T is the physical volume per year of those considerations. It is an identity because it is in principle true by definition. Actually Fisher, of course, recognized the heterogeneity of transactions by writing also $MV = \Sigma p_i Q_i$, where the p_i and Q_i are individual prices and quantities. His interest in index numbers was substantially a quest for aggregate indexes P and T derived from the individual p_i and Q_i in such a way that the two forms of the equation would be consistent. Much of the book (1911a), both text and technical appendices, is devoted to this quest.

Here and in later writings, particularly (1921) and (1922), Fisher was looking for the 'best' index number formula. He postulated certain criteria and evaluated a host of formulas, investigating their properties both *a priori* and from applications to data. Since the criteria inevitably conflict, there can be no formula that excels on all counts. Although Fisher was mainly interested in measuring movements of the aggregate price level, naturally he wanted a price index P and a quantity index T to have the property that $P_1T_1/P_0T_0 = (\Sigma p_1Q_1)/(\Sigma p_0Q_0)$, where the subscripts represent two time periods at which observations of p's and Q's are available.

This and various other desirable consistency properties are not hard to meet. The difficult question is the choice of weights in the two indexes, especially when a whole series of consistent period-to-period comparisons is desired, not just one isolated comparison. For a price index, should the quantity weights be those of a fixed base year, yielding what we now call a 'Laspeyres' index $(\Sigma p_1Q_0)/(\Sigma p_0Q_0)$? Or should the weights be those of the ever-changing current period, yielding a 'Paasche' index $(\Sigma p_1Q_1)/(\Sigma p_0Q_1)$? The indicated correlate quantity indexes would be the opposites, respectively 'Paasche' and 'Laspeyres'. In 1911 Fisher opted for the Paasche price index. He also seemed to approve the idea of chain indexes, in which the period 0 of the above formulas is not fixed in calendar time but is always the prior period, even though these violate one possible desideratum, that the relative change between two periods should be independent of the base used. He also wrote favourably of the practical advantages of an entirely different procedure, namely taking the median of an expenditure-weighted distribution of percentage price changes from one period to the next.

In 1920, however, Fisher proposed as the 'Ideal Index' a candidate he had not ranked high in 1911, namely the geometric mean of the Laspeyres and Paasche formulas. This formula has the pleasant property that the correlate of an Ideal price index is an Ideal quantity index. Correa Walsh, another index number expert, on whose comprehensive treatise (1901) Fisher relied heavily from the beginning of his own investigations, reached the same conclusion independently at about the same time (Walsh, 1921).

These index number issues do not seem as important to present-day economists as they did to Fisher. Knowing that they are intrinsically insoluble, we finesse them and use uncritically the indexes that government statisticians provide. But Fisher's explorations have been important to those practitioners.

In Fisher's Equation of Exchange (1911a) the T and the Q_i are measures of all transactions involving the tender of money, intermediate goods and services as well as final goods and services, old goods as well as newly produced commodities, financial assets as well as goods. The corresponding velocity is likewise comprehensive, much more so than the 'income' or 'circuit' velocity preferred by some monetary theorists, notably Alfred Marshall and his followers in Cambridge (England), who count only transactions for final goods, for example for Gross National Product.

Fisher elaborated the equation to distinguish the quantities M and M' of the two media currency and checking deposits and their separate velocities V *and* V': $MV + M'V' = PT$. This was a bow to the rising importance of bank deposits relative to currency as transactions media. Previous practice counted only government-issued currency as money, in modern parlance high-powered or base money, and regarded bank operations as increasing its velocity rather than adding to a money stock.

How does the quantity theory come out of the Equation of Exchange? Fisher argues that the real volume of money-using transactions T is exogenous; that the velocities are determined by institutions and habits and are independent of the other variables in the equation; that the division of the currency supply, the monetary base in current terminology, between currency and bank reserves is stable and independent of the variables in the equation; that banks are fully 'loaned up' so that deposits M' are a stable multiple of reserves, determined by the prudence of banks and by regulation; that exogenous changes in currency supply itself are the principal source of shocks, which, given the preceding propositions, move price level P proportionately. The many qualifications for transitional adjustments are conscientiously presented, but the monetarist message is loud and clear.

The argument is familiar to modern readers, but certain features deserve notice:

(1) Fisher gives the most illuminating account available of the institutions and habits that generate the society's demand for transactions

media relative to the volume of transactions. He rightly emphasizes the fact that, and the degree to which, receipts and payments are imperfectly synchronized. He seeks the determinants of velocity in such features of social and economic structure as the frequency of wage and bill payments and the degree of vertical integration of firms. His belief that these institutions change only slowly supports his contention that velocities are exogenous constants.

(2) Much ink has been spilled on the difference between Fisher's velocity approach to money demand and the Cambridge (England) 'k' formulation. The latter, like Walras's *encaisse desiré*, directs attention to agents' portfolio decisions. To Fisher's critics that seems behavioural, while velocity is mechanical. The issue is overblown; the same phenomena can be described in either language. If the other variables in the equation are defined and measured the same way, then V and k are just reciprocals each of the other. Fisher himself discusses hoarding. Fisher's explicit attention, in discussing economy-wide demand for circulating media in distinction to other stores of value, to the fact that money 'at rest' soon takes 'wing' to fly from one agent to another seems to be a merit of his approach.

(3) As already noted, Fisher resolved a question current in his day, whether banks' creation of deposit substitutes for currency should be regarded as increasing the velocity of basic money or as enlarging the supply of money. His choice of the latter course compels attention to the structure, behaviour and regulation of banks. He could not be expected to foresee that the proliferation of future candidates for designation as 'money' would create the monetarist ambiguities we see today.

(4) For the most part later writers have not followed Fisher in his preference for a comprehensive concept and measure of transactions volume. It is hard to attach meaning to the *real* volume of financial transactions, and therefore to see why a T that includes them should be a constant or exogenous term in the equation. On the other hand, modern students of money demand tend simply to forget transactions other than those on final payments.

(5) Fisher ignores the possibility that other liquid assets can serve as imperfect substitutes for money holdings because they can be converted into means of payment as needed, though at some cost. Partly

for this reason, he ignores interest rate effects on demand for transactions media. In his day there may have been more excuse for these omissions than there was later. But they are still surprising for an author who elsewhere pays so much attention to the effects of interest rates and opportunity costs on behaviour.

(6) When Fisher was writing, the United States was on the gold standard; the exchange parities of the dollar with sterling and other gold-standard currencies were fixed. Fisher discusses in detail the implications of foreign transactions for the elements of the Equation of Exchange and for the quantity theory. He recognizes that tendencies towards purchasing-power parity, even though imperfect, make money supplies in any one country endogenous, tie prices to those of other countries and enhance quantity adjustments to monetary shocks in the short run. Much of the 1911 book applies, therefore, to the gold standard economies in aggregate. Indeed, Fisher finds the increase in gold production after 1896 to be the main cause of price increases throughout the world.

Macroeconomics: Business Fluctuations and the Great Depression

THE QUANTITY THEORY BY NO MEANS exhausts Fisher's ideas on macroeconomics. His views were much more subtle then straightforward monetarism, but they are scattered through his writings and not systematically integrated. Consider the following non-neutralities emphasized by Fisher:

(1) Probably Fisher's principal source of fame, especially among non-economists, is his equation connecting nominal interest i, real interest r and inflation π: $i = r + \pi$. It is frequently misused. Like the Equation of Exchange, it is first of all an identity, from which, for example, an unobservable value of r can be calculated from observations of the other two variables. More interesting, certainly to Fisher, is its use as a condition of equilibrium in financial markets; for this purpose π must be replaced by expected inflation π^e, another unobservable. In a longer run, as Fisher recognized, steady-state equilibrium would also be characterized by equality of actual and expected inflation: $\pi = \pi^e$.

The Fisher equation is frequently cited nowadays in support of complete and prompt pass-through of inflation into nominal interest rates. Fisher's view throughout his career was quite different. For one thing, neither Fisher's theory of interest nor his reading of historical experience suggested to him that equilibrium real rates of interest should be constant. Moreover, from (1896) on he believed that adjustment of nominal interest rates to inflation takes a very long time. This he confirmed by sophisticated empirical investigations, regressions in which the formation of inflation expectations was modelled by distributed lags in actual inflation. During the transition, inflation would lower real rates; nominal rates would adjust incompletely. The effect was symmetrical; he attributed the severity of the Great Depression to the high real rates resulting from price deflation.

Moreover, Fisher was quite explicit about the effects of these movements of real interest rates on real economic variables, including aggregate production and employment. In *The Purchasing Power of Money* these transitional effects are mentioned, but minimized in the author's zeal to convince readers of the importance of stabilizing money stocks. But in Fisher's writing on interest rates, the transitions turn out to be long. In his accounts of cyclical fluctuations in business activity, and especially of the Great Depression, they play the key role.

(2) An assiduous student of price data, Fisher knew that some prices were more flexible than others, that money wages were on the sticky side of the spectrum, and that the imperfect flexibility of the price level meant that the *T* on the right-hand side of his Equation of Exchange would absorb some of the variations of the left-hand side.

In the early 1930s he came to a very modern position. Real variables like production and employment are independent of the level of prices, once the economy has adjusted to the level. But they are not independent of the rate of change of prices; they depend positively on the rate of inflation. He even calculated a 'Phillips' correlation between employment and inflation (1926). He was just one derivative short of the accelerationist position (Friedman, 1968); in a little more time he would have made that step, aware as he was of the difference between actual and expected inflation. Anyway, his policy conclusion was that stabilizing the price level would also stabilize the real economy.

(3) During the Great Depression, observing the catastrophes of the world around him, which he shared personally, Fisher came to quite a different theory of the business cycle from the simple monetarist version he had espoused earlier. This was his 'debt-deflation theory of depression' (1932), summarized in the first volume of *Econometrica*, the organ of the international society he helped to found (1933). The essential features are that debt-financed Schumpeterian innovations fuel a boom, followed by a recession which can turn into depression via an unstable interaction between excessive real debt burdens and deflation. Note the contrast to the Pigou real balance effect, according to which price declines are the benign mechanism that restores full-employment equilibrium. The realism is all on Fisher's side. This theory of Fisher's has room for the monetary and credit cycles of which he earlier complained, and for the perversely pro-cyclical real interest rate movements mentioned above.

Fisher did not provide a formal model of his latter-day cycle theory, as he probably would have done at a younger age. The point here is that he came to recognize important non-monetary sources of disturbance. These insights contain the makings of a theory of a determination of economic activity, prices, and interest rates in short and medium runs. Moreover, in his neoclassical writings on capital and interest Fisher had laid the basis for the investment and saving equations central to modern macroeconomic models. Had Fisher pulled these strands together into a coherent theory, he could have been an American Keynes. Indeed the 'neoclassical synthesis' would not have had to wait until after World War II. Fisher would have done it all himself.

His practical message in the early 1930s was 'Reflation!' When his Yale colleagues and orthodox economists throughout the country protested against public-works spending proposals and denounced Roosevelt's gold policies, Fisher was a conspicuous dissenter. He was right. Characteristically, he crusaded vigorously for his cause—in speeches, pamphlets, letters and personal talks with President Roosevelt and other powerful policy-makers. Characteristically too, as his letters home (I. N. Fisher, 1956, p. 275) disclose, he saw clearly and unapologetically that in lobbying for what was good for the country he was also hoping to rescue the Fisher family finances.

Addressing the President of Yale shortly after Fisher's death, Joseph Schumpeter and eighteen colleagues in the Harvard economics department wrote, 'No American has contributed more to the advancement of his chosen subject . . . The name of that great economist and American has a secure place in the history of his subject and of his country.' According to his son, this is the eulogy that would have pleased Irving Fisher the most (I. N. Fisher, 1956, pp. 337–8) Today, four decades later, economics can confirm the judgement and prediction of that eulogy.

James Tobin

Author's Note: Fortunately Fisher's son, Irving Norton Fisher, preserved the memory of his father in two indispensable publications, a biography and a comprehensive bibliography (1956, 1961). I have also relied extensively on John Perry Miller's biographical essay (1967) and Professor William Barber's account (1986) of political economy at Yale before 1900. My review of Fisher's contributions to general equilibrium theory, the theory of capital and interest, monetary theory and macroeconomics draws heavily and often literally on a recent essay of my own (Tobin, 1985).

Selected Works

1892. *Mathematical Investigations in the Theory of Value and Prices*. New Haven: Connecticut Academy of Arts and Sciences, *Transactions 9*, 1892. Reprinted, New York: Augustus M. Kelley, 1961.

1896. Appreciation and interest. *AEA Publications* 3(11), August 331–442. Reprinted, New York: Augustus M. Kelley, 1961.

1906. *The Nature of Capital and Income*. New York: Macmillan.

1907. *The Rate of Interest*. New York: Macmillan.

1910. *Introduction to Economic Science*. New York: Macmillan.

1911a. *The Purchasing Power of Money*. New York: Macmillan.

1911b. *Elementary Principles of Economics*. New York: Macmillan.

1921. The best form of index number. *American Statistical Association Quarterly* 17, March, 533–7.

1922. *The Making of Index Numbers*. Boston: Houghton Mifflin.
1926. A statistical relation between unemployment and price changes. *International Labour Review* 13, June, 785–92.
1927. A statistical method for measuring 'marginal utility' and testing the justice of a progressive income tax. In *Economic Essays Contributed in Honor of John Bates Clark*, ed. J. H. Hollander, New York: MacMillan.
1930. *The Theory of Interest*. New York: MacMillan.
1932. *Booms and Depressions*. New York: Adelphi.
1933. The debt-deflation theory of great depression. *Econometrica* 1(4), October, 337–57.
1935. *100% Money*. New York: Adelphi.

Bibliography

Arrow, K. J., and G. Debreu. (1954). Existence of an equilibrium for a competitive economy. *Econometrica* 22(3): July, 265–290.

Auspitz, R., and R. Lieben. (1889). *Untersuchungen über die Theorie des Preises*. Leipzig: Duncker & Humblot.

Barber, W. J. (1986). Yale: the fortunes of political economy in an environment of academic conservatism. In William J. Barber, *Economists and American Higher Learning in the Nineteenth Century*. Middletown, Conn.: Wesleyan University Press.

Clark, J. B. (1899). *The Distribution of Wealth*. New York: Macmillan.

Fairchild, F. R., E. S. Furniss, and N. S. Buck. (1926). *Elementary Economics*. 2 vols, New York: Macmillan. 5th edn, 1948.

Fisher, I. N. (1956). *My Father Irving Fisher*. New York: Comet Press.

——. (1961). *A Bibliography of the Writings of Irving Fisher*. New Haven: Yale University Library.

Friedman, M. (1968). The role of monetary policy. *American Economic Review* 58(1). 1–17.

Hall, R. E. (1985). Monetary policy with an elastic price standard. In *Price Stability and Public Policy*. Federal Reserve Bank of Kansas City, 137–160.

Jevons, W. S. (1871). *The Theory of Political Economy*. London: Macmillan.

Keynes, J. M. (1923). *A Tract on Monetary Reform*. London: Macmillan.

——. (1936). *The General Theory of Employment, Interest and Money*. New York: Harcourt, Brace.

Miller, J. P. (1967). Irving Fisher at Yale. In *Ten Economic Studies in the Tradition of Irving Fisher*. Ed. William Fellner et al. New York: Wiley.

Newcomb, S. (1885). *Principles of Political Economy*. New York: Harper.

Rae, J. (1834). Reprinted as *The Sociological Theory of Capital*. New York: Macmillan, 1905.

Samuelson, P. A. (1967). Irving Fisher and the theory of capital. In *Ten Economic Studies in the Tradition of Irving Fisher.* Ed. William Fellner et al. New York: Wiley.

Scarf, H. (with T. Hansen.) (1973). *The Computation of Economic Equilibria.* New Haven: Yale University Press.

Schumpeter, J. A. (1912). *Theory of Economic Development.* Trans. from the 2nd German edn of 1926 by R. Opie, Cambridge, Mass.: Harvard University Press, 1934.

Schumpeter, J. H. (1954). In *History of Economic Analysis.* Ed. E. B. Schumpeter. New York: Oxford University Press.

Social Sciences Citation Index. (1979, 1983). *Five Year Cumulation,* 1971–5 and 1976–80. Philadelphia: Institute for Scientific Information.

Tobin, J. (1985). Neoclassical theory in America. *American Economic Review* 75(6): December, 28–38.

Walsh, C. M. (1901). *The Measurement of General Exchange Value.* New York and London: Macmillan.

——. (1921). *The Problem of Estimation.* London: King & Sons.

Wicksell, K. (1911). *Lectures on Political Economy.* Trans. E. Classen (from the 2nd Swedish edn), London: George Routledge & Sons, 1934.

Irving Fisher of Yale

By William J. Barber*

Abstract. An overview of the career and contributions of Irving Fisher.

Yale had difficulty in coming to terms with Irving Fisher during his lifetime. That phenomenon bears pondering. After all, Fisher was very much a son of Yale. All of his formal higher education—from his undergraduate years to the award of his Ph.D.—carried Yale's seal of approval. His Yale experience was crucial in shaping his professional trajectory. He was often to remark that his work in mathematical economics had been inspired by two Yale mentors: Willard Gibbs, the mathematical physicist, and William Graham Sumner, the political economist who was also the most outspoken Social Darwinist on the American scene. Fisher, it should also be noted, was based at Yale throughout his entire adult life. Only once did he seriously seek full-time employment outside New Haven. This occurred in 1906 when he lobbied hard, though unsuccessfully, to head the Smithsonian Institution in Washington, DC. (Excluded here is his brief flirtation with running for a seat in the U.S. Senate in 1934, an exercise that was quixotic from the start.)

Despite all this, Fisher experienced the fate of a prophet without honor at his own university. This gathering, convened roughly a half century after his death, marks only the second occasion on which his contributions have been systematically celebrated at Yale. The first was organized in 1967, two decades after his death. It generated a volume entitled *Ten Economic Studies in the Tradition of Irving Fisher*. All but one of the essays appearing in that work were written by members of the Yale Economics Department. The exception was a centennial appreciation prepared by Paul Samuelson, in which

*William J. Barber is Andrews Professor of Economics, Emeritus, at Wesleyan University. A past president of the History of Economics Society, he edited *The Works of Irving Fisher*. 14 vols. London: Pickering & Chatto, 1997.

The American Journal of Economics and Sociology, Vol. 64, No. 1 (January, 2005).

he saw fit to scold earlier generations of Yale economists for their failure to applaud the contributions to the discipline made by one of their own.

Discussion of the relationship between Fisher and his Yale contemporaries abounds with complexities. It may still be worth trying to unravel them. Such an exercise can throw instructive light on attributes of Fisher's style, on the academic culture of Yale in his day, and on the state of the art in American economics in the first half of this century.

I

Fisher and Yale in the 1880s

LET US BEGIN WITH a look at the Yale that Fisher encountered as a freshman in 1884. There had been revolutionary developments in American higher education in the post–Civil War decades—most notably, Harvard's decision under President Eliot to adopt an elective system and the launching of Johns Hopkins as an institution dedicated to postgraduate studies. At this time, Yale held out as a bastion of academic conservatism. The core of the institution, in the view of its administrative leadership, was Yale College, and top priority should properly be assigned to preserving its essentially lockstep curriculum. This involved compulsory studies of the ancient languages (Latin and Greek), mathematics, and the natural sciences, as well as some work in Biblical studies. The itemization of its curricular prescriptions afforded little room for modern subjects, though it had been standard practice for some time in the denominationally affiliated colleges (as Yale then was) for the president to lecture to seniors on themes in political economy. Just what that amounted to differed with the interests and tastes of the incumbent.

More by accident than by design, this peculiarity of the traditional pattern turned out to be a catalyst to some modest curricular reforms by the time Fisher arrived on the scene. The seeds of change were sown in 1872 when newly appointed President Porter—a Congregational clergyman, like all of his predecessors—elected to focus his required lectures to seniors on moral philosophy, metaphysics, and the "evidences of Christianity." The expected political economy component was then eligible to be spun off. To fill the empty space, Porter appointed William Graham Sumner, then an Episcopal minister in New Jersey, as a Professor of Political and Social Science. This was a remarkable turn of events. Sumner had no visible qualifications as a scholar in the social studies. He had done a stint of postgraduate study in Europe following his graduation from Yale in 1863, with attention primarily to church history and Biblical criticism. But he did possess what was then regarded as an essential qualification: he had the Yale blue in his blood.

Sumner's dynamism in the classroom soon attracted enthusiastic student audiences to political economy and prompted demands for more curricular space for this subject matter. Yale's administrators did their best at stonewalling. In the spring term, 1884—the semester before Fisher matriculated—Sumner and several faculty colleagues managed to break that resistance after sequestering the president in his office for several hours. As a result, half of the junior year and 80% of the senior year were liberated from requirements. These changes produced a dramatic increase in the demand for instruction in political economy. To satisfy it, three additions to the faculty with backgrounds in this subject matter were ultimately authorized. All appointees were graduates of Yale and each had done postgraduate work in German universities. (A word is in order about the individuals in this triumvirate. Two of its members—Henry W. Farnam, Yale B.A., 1874, and University of Strasbourg Ph.D., 1878, and Arthur T. Hadley, Yale B.A., 1876, with postgraduate study at the University of Berlin—had been eager to teach political economy before the curricular reform of 1884 afforded regular opportunity to do so. They had initially been obliged to settle for appointments as tutors in required subjects such as Latin and Greek. The third member—John C. Schwab, Yale B.A., 1886, University of Göttingen Ph.D., 1889—was the first to begin his teaching at Yale in the field of his preference.)

The developments noted above set the context for the fit between Fisher and his Yale contemporaries. As an undergraduate, mathematics had been his preferred subject and he was exposed to political economy only in an introductory course taught by Hadley. After graduating in 1888, he remained at Yale as a doctoral candidate in mathematics. Along the way, he was captivated by courses with Sumner. It was at Sumner's suggestion that he chose to combine mathematics and economics and to produce his pathbreaking dissertation on "Mathematical Investigations in the Theory of Value and Prices." Upon its completion, Fisher joined the Yale faculty as a tutor in mathematics. In his first year on the job, he offered an undergraduate course on the "Mathematical Theory of Prices"—described as open to students "who besides studying political economy have taken or are pursuing a course in calculus"—in the academic year 1891–1892. Mathematics remained Fisher's departmental affiliation until 1895 when his title became Assistant Professor of Political and Social Science. This changed in 1898 when he was promoted as Professor of Political Economy.

II

Fisher's Early Development

FISHER'S PROFESSIONAL DEVELOPMENT took a path quite different from the one traveled by most American economists who reached professional maturity in the last two decades of the 19th century. With but a few exceptions, the bulk of his contemporaries approached the discipline conditioned by postgraduate study in Germany. More often than not, they had developed a taste for the teaching of the "German Historical School," which spurned abstract theorizing and urged the intervention of the state to improve economic life. Some of the more enthusiastic among them—led by Richard T. Ely—were stimulated by this experience to form the American Economic Association in 1885, an organization designed originally to attack Sumner and like-minded advocates of unbridled *laissez-faire*. Fisher's perspective on the discipline was molded by quite distinct intellectual influences. His early work in mathematics had predisposed him toward the value of abstract reasoning and had persuaded him that mathematical tools were essential if economics were to attain genuine scientific standing.

Though Fisher was innocent of direct exposure to the doctrines of the German Historical School, he did have firsthand contact with European economists in his formative years. In the academic year

1893–1894, with a Yale Ph.D. in hand and after his thesis had been published, he took the grand tour. As he observed at the time, his "little book" amounted to "a letter of introduction to a great many people."[1] It opened the way for meetings with Pantaleoni in Rome, with Pareto and Walras in Lausanne, with Böhm-Bawerk and Menger in Vienna, and with Edgeworth in Oxford. Fisher's exposure to this subset of economists in Britain and on the Continent meant that he brought home views totally alien to those imported by young Americans influenced by the teachings of the German Historical School.

Fisher's background thus set him apart from the "Young Turks" who had mobilized as the American Economic Association. And it also differentiated him from colleagues at Yale when he began his instruction in political economy. Sumner had by then left economics in favor of sociology. Work in political economy was dominated by the triumvirate of the German-trained who had no natural affinity for Fisher's analytic style. Despite divergences in perspectives, it did not follow that an amicable *modus vivendi* could not be accomplished. A shared loyalty to Yale was a promising bonding agent, as was a common respect for Sumner as the "inspirer," even though—as individuals—they might distance themselves (as Fisher did) from the master's view on economic policy. In addition, Fisher's senior associates in political economy were genuinely impressed with the favorable reception of his work among the profession's luminaries in Europe.

There was still no disguising the fact that Fisher's vision for Yale as an institution and for the direction of its program in economics was not shared by the Yale establishment. This came through clearly in the late 1890s in discussions over the selection of a new president. Arthur T. Hadley was among the leading candidates and was ultimately chosen, thus becoming the first in that job who was not an ordained Congregationalist. Fisher thought well of Hadley personally, but had his doubts. Writing to Sumner, he observed: "If an equally good man of equally favorable age can be found who has been connected with some other university than Yale, I should think it better. Yale is too self-centered. It needs fresh blood."[2] When writing to Hadley, Fisher assured him that he was his choice among Yale faculty members mentioned for this post, but added:

> If no one from the faculty is to be chosen I wish the choice could be someone connected with another university. Our ruts of Yale tradition are very deep and hard. Yale begets Yale and we suffer from "in and in breeding." . . . If the Corporation is so mediaeval that it cannot break away from ecclesiasticism, or give us a young man, or a man who will study questions of curriculum, who will know the professors and their work, who will build up departments rather than dormitories, who will accommodate salaries to men we want and not men to the salary we fix, who will go for quality rather than quantity, who will coordinate the courses, then I say Yale is doomed. We cannot wait another quarter of a century when we are that much behind Harvard already.[3]

Another factor was to have a more formidable impact on Fisher's relationships with Yale. In mid-1898—shortly after his elevation to a full professorship—he fell victim to tuberculosis, the disease that had claimed his father's life some 14 years earlier.

III

The Early 1900s

TUBERCULOSIS PUT FISHER out of action for three years. When he resumed his teaching duties on a part-time basis in the fall term of 1901, he did so as a changed man. His successful recovery from an illness that was usually terminal had convinced him that life as a conventional academician would no longer satisfy him. The first manifestations of his newly acquired sense of mission were to be found in his extracurricular work on problems of health. As a TB patient, he had already designed (and patented) a tent for the treatment of victims of this disease, and it was awarded a prize by the New York Medical Association. This new enthusiasm was soon evident in New Haven when he recruited Yale students to participate in experiments on diet and endurance, the results of which were published in the *Yale Medical Journal*.

While Fisher's interests and activities extended over a range much broader than was typical for the Yale professoriate, he still did what was called for in an ordinary faculty member. He performed his share of teaching duties in the introductory sequence in economics and offered advanced courses that alternated between Economic Theory, the Theory of Capital, the Theory of Distribution, and the Theory of

Prices and Price Levels.[4] In addition, in the academic year 1902–1903, he served as chair of a university committee—designated as the Committee on Numbers and Scholarship—that was charged to investigate why Yale's competitive attractiveness (*vis-à-vis* Harvard) for the ablest students had suffered. The Committee concluded that Yale's "conservatism" and its "rather rigid curriculum" were responsible for this outcome. In the wake of its report, the compulsory study of Greek was eliminated.[5] Fisher also served on a Committee on the Course of Study in 1906 that called for reforms that would encourage greater concentration in student work. These committee services were singular: they marked the only occasions on which Fisher took a prominent part in the routines of academic governance.

By 1907, Fisher had embarked on a course that would progressively distance him from his Yale colleagues. A turning point was his decision to become a prime mover in launching a Committee of One Hundred under the aegis of the American Association for the Advancement of Science to lobby for the creation of a federal department of health. The notoriety he acquired thereby led shortly thereafter to an assignment through the hand of President Theodore Roosevelt to prepare a report on the "conservation of human life" for the National Conservation Committee. This project, in turn, brought him into close touch with the President of the University of Wisconsin, Charles R. Van Hise, a leading architect of the "Wisconsin Idea," which called for active collaboration between the state university and state government. With regard to Van Hise, Fisher observed in a letter to his wife: "He has more of my ideas of running a university than anyone else I ever met. I wish we had a man half as good as Pres. of Yale."[6] Such activities meant that Fisher was spending increasing amounts of time outside New Haven. Nevertheless, there was some spinoff at Yale. For a number of years, Fisher offered a course that drew on the expertise he had thus acquired. In the academic year 1909–1910, for example, it was entitled "National Efficiency" and described as follows: "A study of natural resources, racial vigor, and social institutions, as related to national efficiency, with special reference to the United States. Special topics: child labor, working hours, sanitation."[7]

Fisher's extra-economic crusades sparked some tensions in his relationships with fellow economists at Yale. But this was not the only source of strain. With the publication of *The Nature of Capital and Income* (1906) and *The Rate of Interest* (1907), the contrast between Fisher's style of economics and that of his Yale colleagues was prominently on display. One can surmise that the latter did not fully comprehend the novelty and ingenuity of Fisher's conceptual apparatus and his use of mathematical techniques. In practicing his brand of theorizing, Fisher was one of a kind in pre–World War I Yale. But for that matter, he would not have had that much intellectual company at any other American institution. His departmental associates in New Haven preferred to cultivate applied fields, teaching and writing on such topics as financial institutions, public finance, industrial combinations, labor problems, railroads, and so forth. They did, however, encourage Fisher to take charge of the introductory course, which he did for several years, writing his own textbook for that purpose. But he abandoned introductory teaching for good in the year after its publication in 1912. By then Fisher was busy campaigning for a "compensated dollar"—a monetary reform that promised to stabilize the cost of living and that he regarded as an application of the insights he had acquired when writing *The Purchasing Power of Money*, published in 1911.

IV

The 1920s

By 1920, Fisher had demonstrated that he was something less than an ideal team player as a member of the Yale faculty. From a departmental chairman's point of view, he could all too easily be carried away by his causes. At this point in his career, they included the promotion of a Life Extension Institute (and of a manual he had put together on rules for healthy living entitled *How to Live*), national prohibition of alcoholic beverages, eugenics, and world peace, as well as stable money. Fisher was altogether in character when he scratched his teaching assignments for the fall term of 1920, informing the Yale authorities that he was compelled to perform more important duties. He then barnstormed the country as a spokesman for the Pro-League of Nations Independents in support of the Cox-Roosevelt ticket.

During the decade of the 1920s, the links between Fisher and Yale became even more tenuous. It was no longer just a matter of his absenteeism for crusading. He was allocating substantial blocks of time to various business-related pursuits. One of them involved the manufacture and distribution of a unique filing device known as the Index Visible, which he patented in 1913. When this enterprise was taken over by Rand-Kardex (shortly to become Remington-Rand) in 1925, Fisher became independently wealthy and was rewarded by a seat on the parent corporation's board. A letter informing his son of this transaction is revealing about his priorities:

> The money itself is not needed greatly for added personal comforts and neither Mother nor I want it for swelling around. So it is dedicated primarily to the causes in which Mother and I are interested. . . . This added income will enable me to further the four chief causes which we have at heart, the abolition of war, disease, degeneracy, and instability of money.[8]

A decade later, when his financial circumstances were in ruins, he reported that he had "spent about a million dollars on prospects of health (including the alcohol problem and world peace and eugenics) and economic reforms, especially the stable money movement."[9]

Meanwhile, Fisher had developed another business interest as a follow-up to his studies in *The Making of Index Numbers*, which appeared in 1922. In 1923, he founded an Index Number Institute that he operated with a staff from his residence. This was intended as a vehicle for enlightening the public via the distribution of his calculations of index numbers that reflected the economy's recent performance. These data were reported in a weekly syndicated column, accompanied by Fisher's commentary on current events. At its peak, the Index Number Institute's weekly report reached a potential readership of about 7 million people.

Around Yale, Fisher's visibility diminished to the vanishing point. He cut back his teaching to one graduate course in one term per year and he tended to meet his handful of graduate students at his home, rather than on the campus. The Yale community was nonetheless mindful of his presence—indeed, it was reminded of it with some regularity through his frequent pronouncements to the press. It is reasonable to infer that Fisher did more to spread Yale's name throughout the land than did any other single person of the day. Not all of that publicity was welcome. On the contrary, there were many in New Haven who regarded his statements, particularly on lax enforcement of Prohibition and on eugenics, to be an institutional embarrassment. But the statements most damaging to his professional reputation as an economist were made in September and October 1929, when he asserted that the stock market had reached a permanently high plateau. Fisher's own confidence in the sustainability of "new era" prosperity was complete. Heavily in the market on margin, he paid dearly when his own portfolio was wiped out.

V

The 1930s

THE CHASM DIVIDING Fisher from the bulk of his Yale colleagues widened still further in the decade of the 1930s. This time there was an added complicating factor. Fisher's disastrous prognostician in 1929 prompted him to rethink his analyses to determine what had gone wrong. By 1932, he believed that he had found the answer. "As to the laws governing depressions," he wrote, "I did not then [in 1929] know, what since I have learned and embodied in my book, *Booms and Depressions*, the important role of over-indebtedness and its tendency to break down the price level through distress selling, contraction of deposit currency, and slackening of its velocity."[10] It thus appeared that the route to economic recovery was contingent on "reflation" of the general price level to its pre-Depression elevation. Fisher was persuaded that this could be accomplished through a combination of heterodox interventions (among them, abandonment of the gold standard; an increased price of gold, with the nominal "profit" arising from the incremental value of the Treasury's gold stock used to back a special currency issue of "yellowbacks"; and the introduction of a scrip that would lose 2% of its exchange value unless a two-cent stamp were affixed to it). Fisher was tireless in putting these messages before high officials in the executive branch, before congressional committees, and before the general public in his syndicated column and in letters to editors.

By late 1933, members of Yale's economics faculty had reached zero tolerance for Fisher's monetary "heresies." (There was one exception: James Harvey Rogers was sympathetic to Fisher's "reflationary" doctrines, but he was on leave in Washington as an official adviser.) On the initiative of R. B. Westerfield, Fred R. Fairchild, Hudson B. Hastings, and J. E. McDonough, those on the premises in New Haven were invited to sign a petition beginning as follows: "The undersigned, teachers of economics in Yale University, hereby express the grave concern with which we view the present consequences and tendencies of the Government's attitude toward the monetary system."[11] The petition then proceeded to denounce New Deal experimentations that Fisher had endorsed and called for an early return to the gold standard. Fisher's name was not mentioned in this document. But there could be no mistaking its target when the *New York Times* reported it, along with a letter from Fisher defending Roosevelt's monetary policies and dissenting from the gold standard suggestion of 15 Yale professors.[12]

In this company, Fisher was indeed the odd man out. He remained a member of the faculty until he reached mandatory retirement age in mid-1935, even though he was not around that much. Even so, a reader of the section of the Yale catalogues allocated to economics for the three academic years beforehand would have been unaware of his existence.

After taking emeritus status, Fisher remained active in promoting two reforms that were dear to his heart: the scrapping of the fractional reserve system of commercial banking in favor of "100 percent reserves" and the adoption of a spending tax (as opposed to an income tax as conventionally understood). Thanks to Yale, his circumstances in his final years were more comfortable than they might otherwise have been. The collapse of the stock market during the Depression had obliged him to sell his New Haven residence to Yale, with the understanding that he and his wife could remain there as life tenants. In 1939, however, he petitioned the treasurer of Yale to cancel notes he had given to the university in lieu of rental payments. Otherwise, he would be obliged to declare personal bankruptcy. Such a step would compromise his ability to earn and to discharge his debts. He still entertained the notion that another invention would repair his fortunes. The Yale Corporation agreed to this cancellation.

Fisher's Yale contemporaries never got the measure of the man. In the first instance, divergent conceptions of the direction economics should properly take, as well as differing readings of the course Yale should chart for itself, were obstacles to better understandings. Latterly, Fisher's post–World War I disengagement from university life, his idiosyncrasies, and his ultimate dependency on Yale stood in the way. Even with his death in 1947, comprehension of his contributions did not immediately improve in New Haven. There was something uncharitable about the tone of the memorial notice prepared for the *American Economic Review* by his Yale colleague, R. B. Westerfield. Though Westerfield acknowledged that Fisher was "known the world over as one of the leading mathematical economists," he added that "his liberal use of mathematics and physics not only delimited his audience but also led to many misunderstandings, for it minimized the psychological factor and his similes did not fit the facts too well." His advocacy of the "compensated dollar" was noted, with a side observation that he clung to it "despite its theoretical and practical weaknesses and its political impossibilities." Westerfield further observed that Fisher's "eagerness to promote his cause sometimes had a bad influence on his scientific attitude" and criticized him for "select[ing] his data to prove his position rather than to find the truth" in his writings on Prohibition.[13]

In 1967—the occasion on which Fisher was first systematically honored in New Haven—Paul Samuelson concluded his keynote address with the toast: "Twenty five years from now, again in New Haven!" We have allowed 31 years, rather than 25, to elapse. But we can still identify with Samuelson's forecast that by the time of a follow-up gathering "the contribution of Irving Fisher will be appraised at its true worth, and Schumpeter's prophecy will have come true that Irving Fisher's 'name will stand in history . . . as the name of this country's greatest scientific economist.'"[14]

Notes

1. Fisher to William Greenleaf Eliot, March 25, 1894. Fisher Papers, Yale University Manuscripts and Archives (hereafter YUMA).

2. Fisher to William Graham Sumner, n.d. (but apparently written during the winter of 1898–1899). Sumner Papers, YUMA.

3. Fisher to Hadley, December 6, 1898. President Arthur T. Hadley Papers, YUMA.

4. Course descriptions were as follows: Economic Theory: "This course will treat of (1) methods of economic study with especial reference to the use of mathematics in economics and statistics and (2) the applications of these methods to the more difficult problems of economic theory, such as value, prices, price levels, capital, interest, distribution and international trade." (Yale University Catalogue, 1902–1903.) Theory of Capital: "This course will treat of controverted points as to Capital and its relation to Interests and Distribution. Special attention will be given to the work of Böhm-Bawerk and John Rae." (*Ibid.*, 1908–1909.) Theory of Interest and Distribution: "A study of the causes governing the rate of interest and the significance of those causes in explaining the accumulation and dissipation of wealth among social classes." (*Ibid.*, 1906–1907.) Currency and Prices: "The relation of money and circulating credit to price levels; methods of constructing index numbers; inflation and its application to the crisis of 1907; statistics and history of prices." (*Ibid.*, 1908–1909.)

5. This matter is discussed in George Wilson Pierson (1952). *Yale College: An Educational History, 1871–1921.* New Haven: Yale University Press.

6. Fisher to Margaret Hazard Fisher, December 4, 1908. Fisher Papers, YUMA.

7. Yale University Catalogue, 1909–1910.

8. Fisher to Irving Norton Fisher, June 17, 1925. Fisher Papers, YUMA.

9. Fisher to Henry L. Stimson, July 4, 1935. Stimson Papers, YUMA.

10. Fisher, I. (1933). "Statistics in the Service of Economics." *Journal of the American Statistical Association* March: 9–10. This was delivered as the presidential address to the Association on December 29, 1932.

11. R. B. Westerfield et al., Mimeographed Petition, December 7, 1933.

12. *New York Times*, December 16, 1933, p. 2.

13. Ray B. Westerfield. (1947). "Memorials: Irving Fisher." *American Economic Review* September: 656–661.

14. Paul A. Samuelson. (1967). "Irving Fisher and the Theory of Capital." In *Ten Economic Studies in the Tradition of Irving Fisher*. Eds. William Fellner et al. New York: John Wiley and Sons.

How to Compute Equilibrium Prices in 1891

By WILLIAM C. BRAINARD and HERBERT E. SCARF*

ABSTRACT. Irving Fisher's Ph.D. thesis, submitted to Yale University in 1891, contains a fully articulated general equilibrium model presented with the broad scope and formal mathematical clarity associated with Walras and his successors. In addition, Fisher presents a remarkable hydraulic apparatus for calculating equilibrium prices and the resulting distribution of society's endowments among the agents in the economy. In this paper we provide an analytical description of Fisher's apparatus, and report the results of simulating the mechanical/hydraulic "machine," illustrating the ability of the apparatus to "compute" equilibrium prices and also to find multiple equilibria.

I

Introduction

IRVING FISHER'S Ph.D. thesis, submitted to Yale University in 1891, is remarkable in at least two distinct ways. The thesis contains a fully articulated general equilibrium model presented with the broad scope and formal mathematical clarity that we associate with Walras and his successors. But what is even more astonishing is the presentation, in the thesis, of Fisher's hydraulic apparatus for calculating equilibrium prices and the resulting distribution of society's endowments among the agents in the economy.

*William Brainard is the Arthur M. Okun Professor of Economics at Yale University. A graduate of Oberlin College and Yale University, his research is primarily in macroeconomics. He is a Fellow of the Econometric Society and co-editor of the *Brookings Papers on Economic Activity*. Herbert E. Scarf is the Sterling Professor of Economics at Yale University. He received his Ph.D. in Mathematics from Princeton in 1954. He was at the RAND Corporation from 1954 to 1956, and taught in the Department of Statistics at Stanford from 1956 to 1963. In 1963, Scarf joined the Department of Economics at Yale and the Cowles Foundation. He received the Lanchester Prize of the Operations Research Society of American in 1974 and the von Neumann Medal in 1983. He is a member of the National Academy of Sciences and the American Philosophical Society and is a Distinguished Fellow of the American Economic Society.

The American Journal of Economics and Sociology, Vol. 64, No. 1 (January, 2005).

Fisher's development of the general equilibrium model was done without any knowledge of the simultaneous achievement of Walras. In the introduction to his thesis, Fisher states that

> [t]he equations in Chapter IV, Sec. 10, were found by me two years ago, when I had read no mathematical economist except Jevons. They were an appropriate extension of Jevons' determination of the exchange of *two* commodities between *two* trading bodies to the exchange of *any number* of commodities between *any number* of traders. . . . These equations are essentially those of Walras.

Even though Fisher's construction of what we now call the Walrasian model of equilibrium was a fully original achievement, he did have contemporaries: the central ideas of equilibrium theory were independently discovered at several locations in the final decade of the last century. But the second theme of Fisher's thesis was entirely novel in conception and execution. No other economist of his time suggested the possibility of exploring the implications of equilibrium analysis by constructing specific numerical models, with a moderately large number of commodities and consumers, and finding those prices that would simultaneously equate supply and demand in all markets. The profession would have to wait until rudimentary computers were available in the 1930s before Leontief turned his hand to a simplified version of this computation.

Fisher's hydraulic machine is complex and ingenious. It correctly solves for equilibrium prices in a model of exchange in which each consumer has additive, monotonic, and concave utility functions, and a specified money income; the market supplies of each good are exogenously given. Both additivity and fixed money incomes make the model of exchange to which his mechanism is applied less than completely general. But we know of no argument for the existence of equilibrium prices in this restricted model that does not require the full use of Brouwer's fixed point theorem. Of course fixed point theorems were not available to Fisher and in that section of his thesis in which first-order conditions are presented for a general model of exchange, Fisher argues for consistency by counting equations and unknowns.

It is hard to discover the source of Fisher's interest in computation. He was a student of J. Willard Gibbs, and perhaps the theme of concrete models in mechanics was carried over to economics. But it is also possible that his hydraulic apparatus is simply an instance of an American passion for complex machinery that gets things done. Fisher, himself, had a passion for innovation. In the course of a long career, he invented an elaborate tent for the treatment of tuberculosis (described in the *Journal of the American Medical Association*, 1903), developed a mechanical diet indicator that permited easy calculation of the daily consumption of fats, carbohydrates, and proteins, copywrited (1943) an icosahedral world globe with triangular facets that when unfolded was allegedly an improvement on the Mercator projection, and patented an "*index visible filing system*" (1913) sold to Kardex Rand, later Remmington Rand, in 1925 for $660,000.

II

Fisher's Cisterns

LET US BEGIN by describing the special model of exchange that is solved by the Fisher machine. There are, say, m consumers, indexed by $i = 1, \ldots, m$ and n goods, indexed by $j = 1, \ldots n$. Consumer i has the utility function

$$u_i(x_1, \ldots, x_n) = \sum_{j=1,n} u_{ij}(x_j),$$

with each u_{ij} increasing and concave. Society's endowment of good j is E_j, and consumer i's income is Y_i.

At prices $p = (p_1, \ldots, p_n) \geq 0$, consumer i is assumed to maximize utility subject to his budget constraint

$$\max u_i(x_1, \ldots, x_n) \text{ subject to}$$
$$\sum_{j=1,n} p_j x_j \leq Y_i.$$

If the marginal utility of income for consumer i is λ_i, the demands, x_{ij}, will satisfy the first order conditions:

$$u'_{ij}(x_{ij}) \leq \lambda_i p_j \; (= \text{if } x_{ij} > 0).$$

A competitive equilibrium is given by a price vector p so that the market demands obtained by the summation of individual demands are equal, commodity by commodity, to the market supply. In other words, we are asked to find $p = (p_1, \ldots, p_n) \geq 0$, $\lambda = (\lambda_1, \ldots, \lambda_m) \geq 0$ and a matrix of commodities $[x_{ij}]$, such that

$$u'_{ij}(x_{ij}) \leq \lambda_i p_j, (= \text{if } x_{ij} > 0)$$

$$\sum_{i=1,m} x_{ij} \leq E_j \ (= \text{if } p_j > 0) \text{ and}$$

$$\sum_{j=1,n} p_j x_{ij} \leq Y_i \ (= \text{if } \lambda_i > 0).$$

These are Irving Fisher's equations.

To solve these equations on an electronic computer we would input the endowment vector E, the income vector Y, and provide a description of the mn marginal utilities $u'_{ij}(x_{ij})$ as functions of their arguments. Fisher invented a clever way to represent a typical marginal utility by an irregularly shaped cistern that is meant to receive varying amounts of water during the operation of the machine.

Imagine a cistern with a uniform thickness of unity, and with a shape shown in Figure 1.

The origin is placed at the northwest corner of the cistern, which has a vertical height of d units. For each $0 \leq \xi \leq d$, the width of the cistern is given by the function $f(\xi)$. If the cistern is filled with water up to ξ units below the top of the cistern, the volume of water it contains will be

$$\int_{\xi}^{d} f(t)dt.$$

Fisher designs the cistern so that the depth ξ is equal to the marginal utility, for that consumer and that good, of the volume of water it contains, i.e.,

$$\xi = u'\left(\int_{\xi}^{d} f(t)dt\right)$$

as an identity for all ξ. With this construction, the maximal depth d is equal to $u'(0)$, and one needs to select utility functions with a finite marginal utility at zero in order to have cisterns of finite depth. Another feature of this utility function is that the consumer is satiated

Figure 1

A Cistern

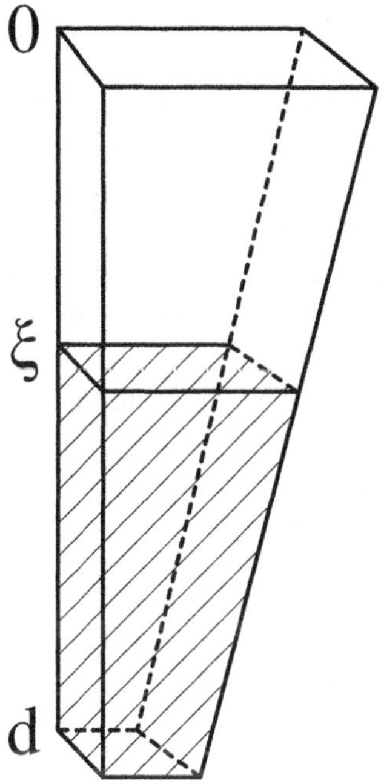

when the cistern is filled to its top and consumption is equal to $\int_0^d f(t)dt$.

The connection between the utility function $u(x)$ and the shape of the cistern $f(\xi)$ is unusual, and the reader may find it useful to calculate f for various well-known utility functions. For example, if $u(x) = -e^{-x}$, the shape function is $f(\xi) = 1/\xi$, and the depth, d, is unity. As a second example, if $u(x) = dx - \frac{1}{2b}x^2$, the shape function is $f(\xi) = b$ and the box is rectangular. And finally if $f(\xi) = b + at$, with $b + ad > 0$, the utility function is given by

$$u(x) = \frac{1}{12a^2}\left((b+2ad)^3 - 6bax - \left((b+2ad)^2 - 4ax\right)^{3/2}\right).$$

In order to see a way in which these cisterns can be used to solve an optimization problem, consider a single consumer with utility function

$$u(x) = \sum u_j(x_j).$$

Construct a cistern for each utility function $u_j(x_j)$ and let their tops be rigidly connected by a rod constrained to be horizontal, but free to move vertically, so that the cisterns will float in a tub of water without changing their relative positions. Insert a fixed amount of water, Y, into the right-most cistern, and let the interiors of the cisterns be connected by rubber tubes so that the water flows easily from one to another.

When the apparatus reaches an equilibrium, the input of water, Y, will be allocated among the n cisterns, with cistern j containing an amount x_j. The level of water will be the same in each cistern, say λ units below the top, so that

$$\sum x_j = Y \text{ and}$$

$$u_j'(x_j) = \lambda, \text{ for each } j.$$

We see that this assemblage of the Fisher cisterns solves the problem

$$\max \sum u_j(x_j) \text{ subject to}$$
$$\sum x_j = Y,$$

Figure 2

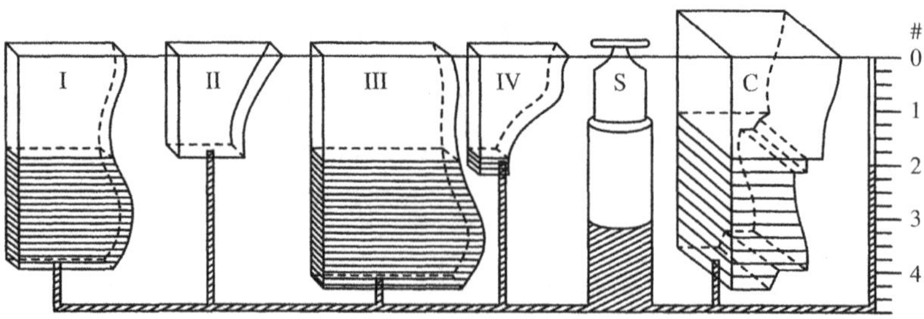

simply by using the fact that freely flowing water will seek a common level in the series of interconnected cisterns, thereby equating the marginal utility for each good to a common price of unity.

We have evaluated the demand functions of this consumer at income Y, and at prices $p = (1, \ldots, 1)$. In order to deal with general prices, and several consumers, we shall have to assemble the cisterns in a considerably more complex fashion.

III

A Preliminary Machine: Pareto Optimal Allocations

LET US CONSIDER a construction that is not quite the one used by Fisher, but that allows us to explore models of exchange with m consumers. Figure 3 depicts the case of two consumers (I, II) and two commodities (A, B). Construct a separate rod for each of the m consumers. On the rod for the ith consumer, we place n cisterns, one for each commodity, and for each such good we connect all of the m cisterns referring to that good by a tube in which water will flow. The west sides of the cisterns for each commodity are aligned parallel to a float F lying on the surface of the water. The left end of each rod is attached to this float, F. The ith rod will make an angle α_i with the water surface.

In this construction the float F is not permitted to move and the angles α_i are fixed in advance. What does move are the cisterns along each rod; but in the following precisely constrained way.

Constraining the Cisterns

All of the cisterns relating to good j have their northwest corners at the *same horizontal distance*, say p_j, from their attachment to float F.

The distances from F may shift during the functioning of the machine but all distances relating to the same commodity are constrained to be the same. These distances are determined by inserting, into the tube for good j, an amount of water equal to the market supply E_j of that good. The water levels for the m cisterns for good j reach a common level, and together the cisterns move along the rods so that this common level is equal to the water level in the

Figure 3

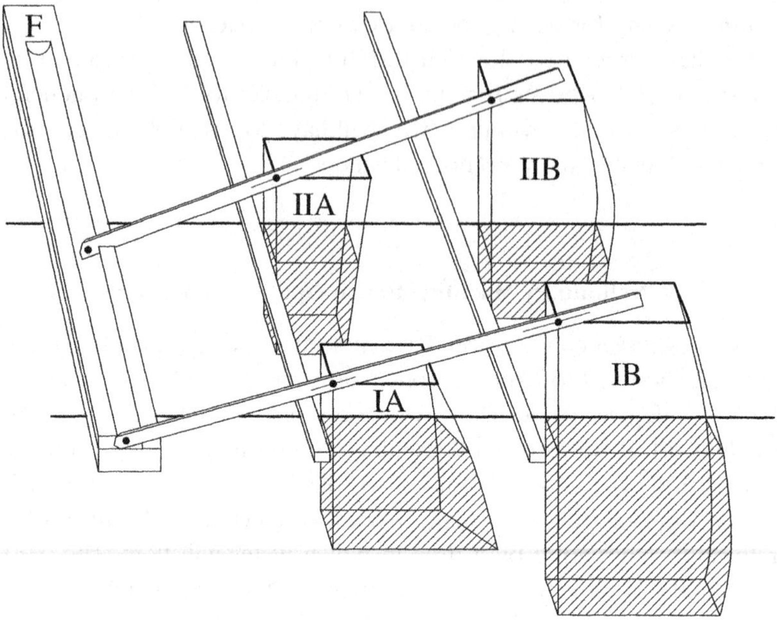

surrounding tub (let us not be concerned that a line of cisterns may very well have to pass through an adjacent line).

Let the volume of water in cistern *ij* be x_{ij}, and the horizontal distance of the cisterns for commodity *j* from the float *F* be p_j. We then have

$$\sum_i x_{ij} = E_j$$

$$u'_{ij}(x_{ij}) = p_j \tan(\alpha_i),$$

so that x_{ij} is the allocation of the market supplies E_j that maximizes the social welfare function

$$\sum_i \lambda_i \sum_j u_{ij}(x_{ij}),$$

when λ_i is given by $1/\tan(\alpha_i)$, and is therefore on the Pareto frontier. And conversely, concavity of the individual utility functions implies that any Pareto optimal allocation is obtained by some selection of λ_i and therefore by some selection of these angles α_i. Of course, Fisher wrote before Pareto and this concept does not appear in his thesis.

Typically this allocation will not satisfy the individual budget constraints $\Sigma p_j x_{ij} = Y_i$ and the angles of the rods must be systematically varied so as to find those angles for which the value of consumption equals income for each consumer. But at this point in our exposition, it is far from clear how to modify the apparatus so as to compare consumption and income. Nothing in this machine permits us to calculate the cost of the commodity bundle demanded by a particular consumer. At no place is a quantity multiplied by a price. We shall return to this issue after describing Fisher's somewhat different arrangement of these cisterns.

Fisher's Construction (Preliminary)

There are some substantial differences between the instrument described in the previous section and Fisher's use of these cisterns, rods, and floats to accomplish the same end. In Fisher's arrangement, the horizontal locations of the northwest corners of the cisterns are fixed; the only possible movement of these corners is strictly vertical. This would present a serious constraint for the mechanism described above, since it does not provide enough flexibility to determine the relative prices, p_j, if the number of goods is greater than two. As we shall see, Fisher's modification of the mechanism permits him to extend the number of goods to three, but no further extension is possible for him. The number of consumers is arbitrary, though the actual model constructed by Fisher has three consumers as well.

Let us introduce a coordinate system to describe the fixed horizontal positions of the three cisterns for each consumer along their common line. The cistern for good 1 will be at the point on its line with coordinate −1, good 2 at the point with coordinate 0, and good 3 at 1. In Fisher's machine the northwest corners of the cisterns are not placed on a single rigid rod as in the previous section; instead they are attached to a connected pair of rods that pivot above the middle cistern, as shown in Figure 4. The left rod for each consumer begins at the point on the line with coordinate $-1 - a$, passes through

Figure 4

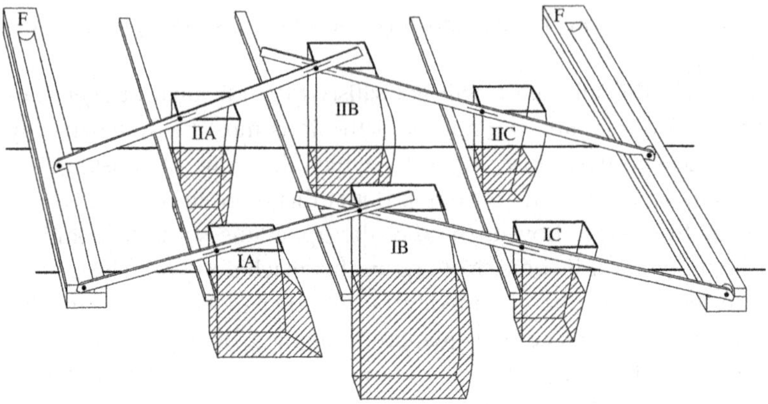

the corner of the cistern for good 1 at −1, and then through the corner of the middle cistern for good 2 at 0. The right rod begins at the point on the line with coordinate 1 + *c*, passes through the corner of the cistern for good 3 at 1, and then joins the left rod at the corner of the cistern for good 2.

The beginnings of these pairs of rods are secured on two floats, one to the left at coordinate −1 − *a* and the other to the right at coordinate 1 + *c*. The floats are permitted to move laterally, so that the values of *a* and *c* are arbitrary. Let us also assume for the moment that the northwest corners of the cisterns describing the same good, for the various consumers, are all connected by a rigid bar parallel to the surface of the water, so that all of these corners are forced to be at the same height. Movement of the floats implies sliding pivots.

As before, the cisterns for a common good are connected by tubing through which water will move freely. A quantity of water equal to the supply of that good is entered into the corresponding tube by setting the levels of certain plungers at the back of the tub. The water levels for the cisterns for each commodity will find a common level, and subsequently the floats to the right and left will move so that all of the cistern levels, for each consumer and for each good, will equilibrate at the water level of the tub. If the quantity of water in cistern

ij is x_{ij} then $\Sigma_i x_{ij} = E_j$ for each good. Moreover, the surface of the water in each cistern referring to good j is at the same depth below its northwest corner, so that for each j the marginal utilities $u'_{ij}(x_{ij})$ are identical for all consumers i.

If we set $p_j = u'_{ij}(x_{ij})$ we see that the apparatus has found an allocation x_{ij} and prices p such that

$$\sum_i x_{ij} = E_j$$

$$u'_{ij}(x_{ij}) = p_j.$$

As with the previous construction, the hydraulic instrument has produced a particular Pareto optimal allocation; in this case the allocation with the marginal utility of income equal to unity for all consumers. Other Pareto optimal allocations can be found by multiplying each utility function by a nonnegative constant, or by allowing the bars connecting the northwest corners of the cisterns to make an angle with the surface of the water different from zero.

But it is still not clear how to find an efficient allocation in which the value of consumption is equal to income for all consumers. A reasonable scholar might perfectly well have given up at this point, but Fisher persisted with an ingenious and intricate modification of the apparatus, designed to solve this problem.

It would be difficult to improve on Fisher's description of the final mechanism. The next section is taken directly from his thesis. He denotes the consumers by *I, II, III* and commodities by *A, B, C.* His statements about marginal utilities and their relationship to prices are only true at equilibrium.

Fisher's Construction (The Schematic Figure 5 and Text Taken from Section 4 of His Thesis)

The water in these cisterns must be subjected to two sets of conditions, first: the sum of all of the contents of *IA, IIA, IIIA*, etc., shall be a given amount (vis: the whole of the commodity *A* consumed during the given period) with a like given sum for the *B* row, *C* row, etc., secondly: the sum of *IA, IB, IC*, etc., each multiplied by a coefficient (the price of *A*, of *B*, of *C*, etc.), shall be given (vis: the whole income of *I* during the period) with a like given sum for the *II* row, *III* row, etc.

To realize these two sets of conditions each cistern is divided into two by a vertical partition of wood. The front compartments are all of unit thickness one inch (say). All front compartments belonging to the same front-and-back row are mutually connected by tubes (in the tank but not in connection with the water of the tank) thus fulfilling the first set of conditions.

The thickness of the back compartment is adjustable but is (as will soon appear) constrained to be always equal to the price, thus if the price of *A* is \$1, of *B* \$3 and *C* \$1.20, the thickness of all of the cisterns in the *A* row will be 1, in the *B* row 3 and in the *C* row 1.2 (inches).

Since the thickness of the front compartment is unity, the contents of each back compartment equals the contents of the front multiplied by the number of inches of thickness of the back cistern, that is the back compartment contains a volume of water equal the amount of the commodity multiplied by its price. It contains therefore the *money value* of the commodity. The double cistern represents the double light in which each commodity is commonly regarded—so many pounds, yards, etc. and so many dollars worth.

All back compartments of the same right and left rows are mutually connected by tubes—that is the sum of their contents is given—thus fulfilling the second set of conditions.

The back compartments can change their thickness, as the walls at the right, left and bottom are of flexible leather; the back plane is kept parallel to the wood partition by two double "parallel rules" not diagrammed.

There remains to be described the system of levers. The purpose of these levers is to keep the continuous ratio of marginal utilities, the same for all individuals and equal to the ratio of prices.

First there is a system of oblique levers [our Figure 5] connected by sliding pivots with the tops of the cisterns and having their lower extremities hinged to wooden floats *F*, the hinges being at the level of the water of the tank. The floats are free only to shift latterly. It is evident from . . . similar triangles in [our Figure 5] that the ordinates of the 2 cisterns *IA* and *IB* are proportional to the distances of the *A* and *B* rods . . . from the hinge in the left float *F*. Likewise in the row behind, the ordinates are proportional to each other and in general all of the ordinates of the front row are proportional to those of the row next behind and so on. Remembering that each ordinate is a marginal utility we have:

$$\frac{dU}{dA_1}:\frac{dU}{dB_1}=\cdots=\frac{dU}{dA_2}:\frac{dU}{dB_2}=\cdots\frac{dU}{dA_3}:\frac{dU}{dB_3}=\cdots=\cdots$$

which is the required condition that the marginal utilities must be proportional.

Secondly there are the horizontal levers (*F*34, etc., Figure 10 [our Figure 6]) lying on the surface of the water in the tank. These relate to prices. The sliding pivots 3, 4 are connected to the rods *RRR*, which in

Figure 5

Fisher's apparatus.

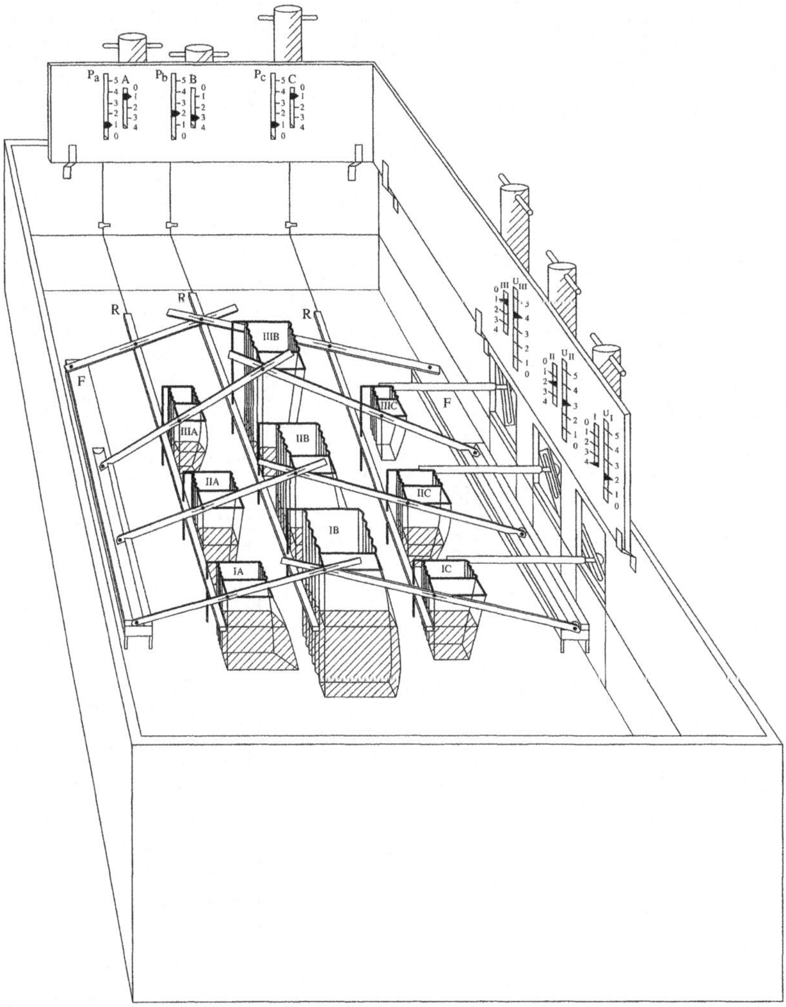

turn are connected by vertical pins with the rear walls of the cisterns. A motion of one of those rods causes all of the back compartments to expand or shrink in unison. The pivots 3, 4, etc. are so situated on these rods that if the levers *F*34, etc. should assume a right-and-left position along the dotted line *FF*, the back compartment of every cistern would be completely closed. Hence *R3* equals the thickness of each back compartment in th *A* row, *R4* the corresponding thickness in the *B* row and so on.

By the similar triangles *FR3* and *F34* in Figure 10 [our Figure 6], it is clear that the lines *R3* and *R4*, and consequently the rear thickness in the *A* and *B* rows are proportional to the distances of the *A* and *B* rods *R* and *R* from the float *F*. But we have just seen that the ordinates of *IA* and *IB* are proportional to these same distances. Hence the thickness of the back

Figure 6

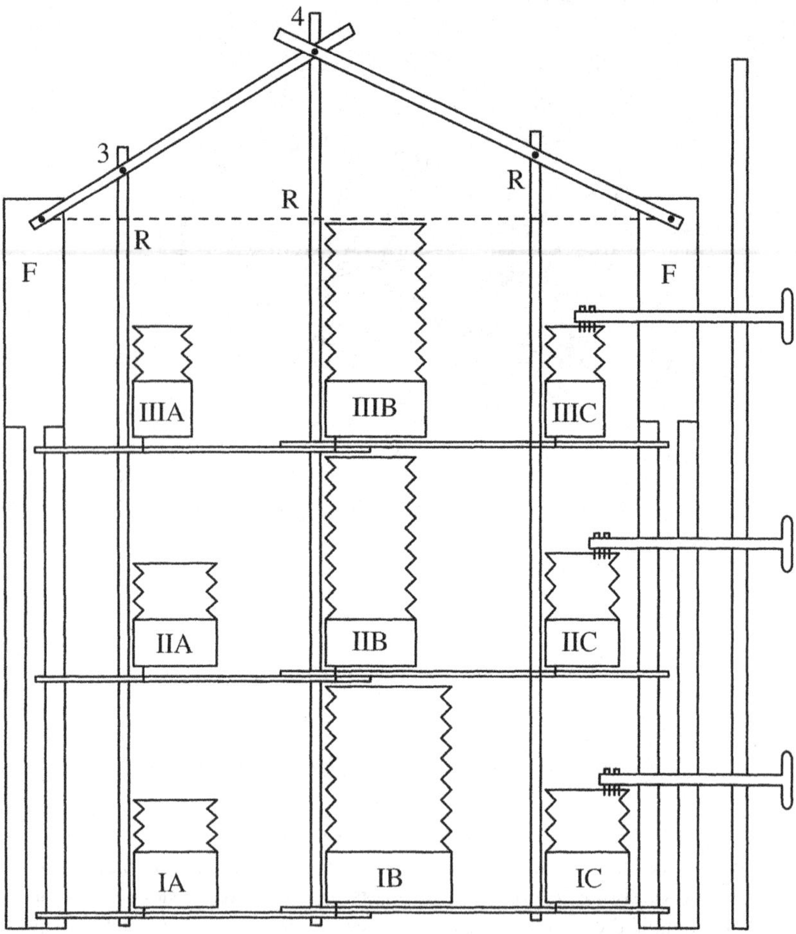

> compartments of the cisterns are proportional to the ordinates of those cisterns, that is to marginal utilities. Hence we are free to call the thickness of each back compartment, the money price of the commodity to which that cistern relates.
>
> It is to be observed that the cisterns are free to move only *vertically*, the rods and rear cistern walls only *forward* and *backward*, the wooden floats can shift sidewise *right and left* while the levers assume such positions as the mechanism compels.

This ends our direct quotation from Fisher's thesis, and his description of his machine. In the next section, we describe our computer simulation of his model.

The Digital Version of the Fisher Machine

Did Fisher's machine work? We knew it must have, at least after a fashion, because Fisher reports that for 25 years he used his first model in teaching. But we were curious to see it work, and could not help wondering whether the floats would come to rest against their stops rather than in a "market" equilibrium. After some romantic thoughts about replicating the machine, tub, water, and all, we settled on simulating the machine in Matlab. The physical features of the Fisher apparatus fall into two groups. The properties of the first group—the quantity and expenditure cisterns and the system of rods controlling the elevations of the cisterns and the price dimension of the expenditure cisterns—determine the equilibrium prices and allocation, and when the system is out of equilibrium they determine the forces and pressures that move the rods, cisterns, floats, and bellows themselves. The second group of features—the tubes connecting the quantity and expenditure cisterns, the mass and surface area of the floats, the viscosity of water—govern the speed of adjustment of the system when it is out of equilibrium.

Our mathematical description of the first group of features is straightforward and faithful to the hydraulic model, except for ignoring the actual model's "imperfections"—the nonzero mass of the rods and the thickness and mass of the walls of the cisterns. For any position of the consumer and price rods, we use Archimedes principle and the weight of water in each of the cisterns to calculate the vertical forces they exert; these forces are resolved into a rotational force on each consumer's rods, and a force inward or outward on the two floats. The inward or outward pressures on the price bellows of each consumer's expenditure boxes are calculated from the difference in the level of water inside and out of the expenditure cisterns. The resulting forces are transmitted to the price rods, and are also resolved into rotational forces and inward or outward forces on the floats.

The construction of the Fisher model guarantees that in equilibrium or out, the quantity of water summed over each individual's expenditure cisterns always equals that individual's money income, and the quantity of water, summed over an individual's quantity cisterns, always equals the social endowment for each commodity. Tubes allow these fixed quantities to flow among the expenditure cisterns for each individual, and among commodity cisterns across individuals for each commodity. This preservation of quantities is easy to mimic in the Matlab version. As explained in the previous section by Fisher, if the level of the water in each of the quantity and expenditure cisterns is the same as the level of water in the tub, each consumer will be maximizing utility subject to his or her budget constraint and the prices and allocations will correspond to a competitive equilibrium. This condition obviously implies that for each cistern, the Archimedes forces are exactly balanced by the weight of water in the cistern; in both the hydraulic and Matlab model, if the system is at rest in a competitive equilibrium, there are no net forces to disturb it. It is an intriguing question, whose answer we do not know, whether there are any rest points in which the level of water in the cisterns is different from the level in the tub.

In contrast to its accurate description of the features of the hydraulic model determining equilibrium, the Matlab model is an approximation of several features governing the dynamics of adjustment. Rather than the continuous, real-time, adjustments in the hydraulic machine, adjustments in the Matlab model are discrete, iteration by iteration. Three speeds of adjustment are crucial to the dynamics—the speed with which water flows among cisterns, the speed with which the cisterns move up or down in the tub and the price bellows expand or contract, and the speed with which the pivot floats move in or out. The diameter, length, and surface characteristics of the tubes used by Fisher to connect the cisterns are not known to us, nor are the mass, displacement, or surface area of the floats. If the dimensions of the tubes were known, textbook fluid mechanics could be used to calculate the flow as a function of pressure differentials, viscosity, surface frictions, etc.; those same textbooks suggest that as a practical matter, there is no substitute for estimating the flow experimentally. Similarly, while it might be theoretically possible to calculate how far in a moment of time a given force would move a cistern—up or down—in the tub, as a function of its mass, shape, and surface areas, it would have been a daunting task. In our simulations, what is important are the relative speeds of adjustment. Our intuition suggested that the vertical movements of the cisterns, the inward or outward movements of the floats, and the adjustment of the price bellows were likely to be much quicker than the adjustments of the fluid levels through the tubes. The results of a casual experiment, using a one-liter coke bottle as a proxy for a cistern and a one-foot length of 5/8″ hose for a tube, were consistent with that intuition; a bottle of water two/thirds full came to a displacement equilibrium in a tub much faster (by a factor of something like 10) than when the same bottle was emptied into the tub by the hose. This led us to choose the parameters in the model so that the adjustments of the consumer rods, bellows, and floats are much more rapid than the equalization of water levels in the commodity or expenditure cisterns.

Given these parameter choices, price and consumer rods adjust to almost completely eliminate the net forces on them, while significant differences in the level of water in the various cisterns remain. Starting from an arbitrary initial condition, there is typically a rapid adjustment of rods and floats, followed by a much longer period during which the water flows among the cisterns and the entire set of variables move slowly together. In our actual simulations it does not appear that the stability of the adjustment mechanism is much affected by the precise values of these parameters, so long as the step size, corresponding to an iteration, is kept small. As will be seen, the adjustment paths display this qualitative behavior; from an initial disequilibrium of both prices and quantities, prices adjust rapidly to levels that balance the forces on the rods, followed by much slower adjustment as the water flows between cisterns. The Matlab model also ignores two physical phenomena that could, in principle, be important to the dynamics of adjustment—the increase in drag that results from increases in velocity, and inertia. Inertia could, even with continuous time, result in overshooting, with damped oscillations of the system, around equilibrium values. The equations used in the MatLab program are found in the Appendix.

Fisher's Use of the Machine

Fisher regarded his model as "the physical analogue of the ideal economic market" (Mathematical investigations, p. 44), with the virtue that "[t]he elements which contribute to the determination of prices are represented each with its appropriate role and open to the scrutiny of the eye . . ." providing "a clear and analytical picture of the interdependence of the many elements in the causation of prices." Fisher also saw the machine as way of demonstrating comparative statics results "to employ the mechanism as an instrument of investigation and by it, study some complicated variations which could scarcely be successfully followed without its aid." We do not know how transparent the model was to Fisher's students, but it is easy to imagine the excitement they may have felt in watching the model at work, accompanied by enthusiastic commentary by Fisher.

In principle the Fisher model will find the competitive equilibrium for any three-commodity, three-person exchange economy with additively separable preferences, with the restriction that individuals' endowments are some fraction of the aggregate commodity endowment bundle—a restriction implicit in the assumption that individuals are endowed with fixed money incomes rather than arbitrary bundles of commodities. To find a particular equilibrium merely requires specifying the shapes of the 3×3 cisterns, and prescribing the aggregate supplies and individual endowments. As previously explained, for the Fisher machine to work, the preferences and quantity endowments must be assigned to rows so that in equilibrium the commodity in the middle row has the highest marginal utility. Given preferences and initial quantities, comparative static results can be obtained simply by altering the aggregate supplies or individual endowments as desired and observing the new equilibrium prices and allocation.

Although we do not know what experiments Fisher actually ran with his machine, he does describe eight comparative static exercises. Some of these illustrate basic features of the system, for example, that proportional increases in money incomes result in an equal proportional increase in each price, with no change in the allocation of goods. Another simple exercise discussed by Fisher examines whether proportional increases in the endowment of goods necessarily result in proportional decreases in prices, as was apparently, and incorrectly, believed by Mill. Some exercises illustrate less intuitive properties of exchange economies: increasing one individual's income may make some other individual better off and also the possibility of "immiserating growth," i.e., increasing an individual's endowment of a good may actually lower his or her welfare.

Although Fisher discusses the way in which changing an individual's preferences alters the equilibrium, it was expensive to change the cisterns in his model and it seems unlikely they were changed after some initial experimentation. The cisterns in Fisher's original 1893 model included a fairly rich variety of shapes; the cisterns in his 1925 model look like they may all have rectangular faces, corresponding to quadratic utility functions. While Fisher's construction made it difficult to vary preferences, his set up made it easy to change quantities; by simply moving a plunger for a commodity or individual's income he could force more water into the associated column or row of cisterns.

Dynamics of the Machine

We used our Matlab representation of the hydraulic machine to simulate the path of adjustment for a variety of preferences, endowments, and initial conditions. We do not have a basis for comparison with Fisher's actual model; Fisher does not analyze or describe the dynamic behavior of his machine.

It is easy to imagine that, as Fisher slowly depressed a quantity plunger to change the equilibrium, the flows of water between cisterns and the movements of lever arms were rapid enough to keep the system in the neighborhood of the shifting equilibrium; it is likely that in Fisher's experiments the initial conditions were never very far from equilibrium. In contrast, in our simulations we typically started the system with arbitrary allocations of the quantities to the cisterns (dividing the quantities equally across individuals and expenditures by individuals equally across commodities) and arbitrary prices. As a consequence our simulations show rapid movements of prices early in the adjustment process, with substantial discrepancies between the quantity of a commodity j being allocated to individual i, $q[i, j]$ and the quantity of that good that could be purchased by the allocation of expenditures on commodity j by individual i, $qe[i, j]$, given current prices. These characteristics are evident in three examples given in Figure 5, which display paths of prices, and these discrepancies for the first commodity ($q[i, 1] - qe[i, 1]$) during the adjustment process.

It is difficult to imagine an economic interpretation of Fisher's adjustment process. Throughout the adjustment process individuals' commodity allocations sum to the social endowment, and each individual's money income is exactly exhausted in that individual's expenditure cisterns. However, allocations are not on the contract curve (ratios of marginal utilities are not the same across individuals), individuals are not maximizing utility (the ratios of the marginal utilities of the quantities being consumed by an individual are not the same as the ratios of prices), and the value at current prices of a good allocated to an individual is typically not equal to the nominal income allocated to purchase that good by the individual (the water level in the front and back cisterns for a given commodity need not be equal).

An Example of Multiple Equilibria

The restrictive assumptions on preferences and endowments embodied in the Fisher machine are not sufficient to guarantee uniqueness. Indeed it is possible to have multiple equilibria even if the additively separable preferences are restricted to be quadratic. How would the machine behave if in fact there is more than one equilibrium? A combination of preferences and endowments that gives rise to multiple equilibria is specified in the following example.

Example

Each cistern is a rectangle.

Consumer 1 has income of 5 and cisterns of size:

46 × 3.6	3 × 12	13 × 26

Consumer 2 has income of 2.5 and cisterns:

6.5 × 26	1.5 × 12	23 × 3.6

Consumer 3 has income of 2.5 and cisterns:

6.5 × 26	1.5 × 12	23 × 3.6

The supplies of the three goods are:

400, 49.5, 400

This example has several special features that helped make it relatively easy to construct, for example, two of the individuals are identical. It was not difficult to find the three equilibria of this example by starting the simulations in appropriate places. The paths of adjustment for the three different initial conditions shown in Figure 7 display the characteristics expected of the Matlab model. Consistent with the relatively rapid adjustment of the lever arms and floats compared to fluid flows, prices adjust rapidly at the start and are almost coincident with the *y* axis, whereas elimination of discrepancies in the levels of water in the cisterns (not shown), and discrepancies between *q*[·] and *qe*[·] are much more gradual. It is interesting to note that for equilibrium 2 the process of adjustment seems to have been almost completed after 2,500 iterations, but, reminiscent of Lorentz's examples from meteorology, after another 1,000 iterations the system moves off and converges to equilibrium 1. This adjustment path is

Figure 7

Dynamics of adjustment.

Equilibrium 1

$$p^* = [0.6199\ \ 1.9600\ \ 1.6370]$$

$$(q-qe)^* = \begin{bmatrix} 0.03E_1 & 0.44E_2 & -0.04E_3 \\ 0.005E_1 & 0.22E_2 & -0.07E_3 \\ 0.005E_1 & 0.22E_2 & -0.07E_3 \end{bmatrix} \times 10^{-2}$$

Equilibrium 2

$$p^* = [1.1054\ \ 2.4060\ \ 1.0964]$$

$$(q-qe)^* = \begin{bmatrix} -0.14E_1 & -0.10E_2 & -0.05E_3 \\ -0.005E_1 & -0.44E_2 & -0.04E_3 \\ -0.005E_1 & -0.04E_2 & -0.04E_3 \end{bmatrix} \times 10^{-2}$$

Equilibrium 3

$$p^* = [1.6560\ \ 1.9310\ \ 0.6082]$$

$$(q-qe)^* = \begin{bmatrix} -0.07E_1 & 0.13E_2 & -0.00E_3 \\ -0.00E_1 & 0.08E_2 & 0.02E_3 \\ -0.00E_1 & 0.08E_2 & 0.02E_3 \end{bmatrix} \times 10^{-2}$$

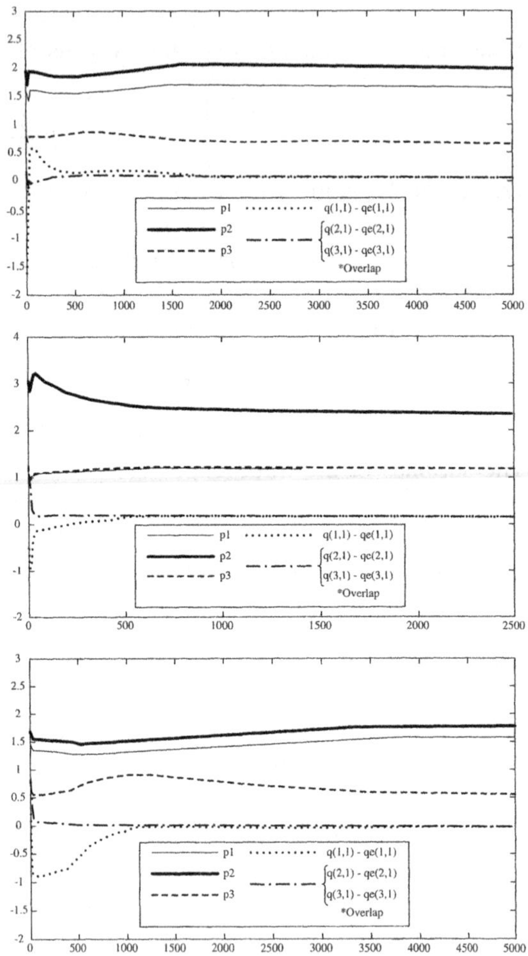

*At last iteration

shown in Figure 8. Since we do not have an economic interpretation of the dynamics of adjustment in the hydraulic model, we cannot make use of the usual economic propositions about the equilibria, for example, the role of the assumption of gross substitutability in guaranteeing uniqueness of the competitive equilibrium and stability of the Walrasian price adjustment mechanism.

Appendix

The equations used in the digital version of the Fisher machine are given in Figure 9. The state of the system is given by the values of 24 state variables—the nine commodity and nine expenditure allocations (x_{ij}, y_{ij}), two float locations (a, c), three consumer rod angles

Figure 8

Equilibrium 2 (12,000 iterations)

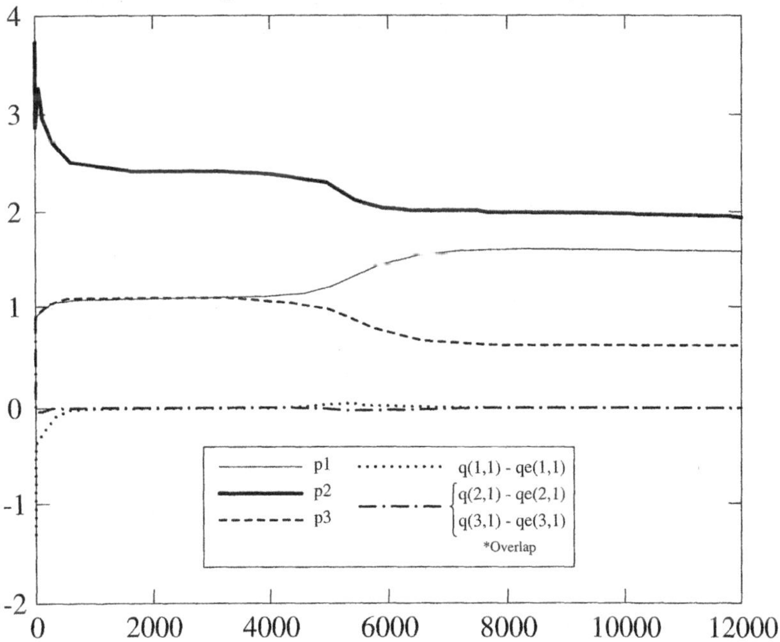

Figure 9

Fisher Machine

				Equations	Variables (New)
(1)	Market clearing	$\Sigma_i x_{ij} = E_j$	$j = 1,3$	3	9
(2)	Expenditure constraints	$\Sigma_i y_{ij} = Y_i$	$i = 1,3$	3	9
(3)	Heights (h_{ij}) of cisterns above surface level where α_i = angle of consumer i's float A rod to surface	$h_{i1} = \ell a_1 \tan(\alpha_i)$; $h_{i2} = \ell a_2 \tan(\alpha_i)$; $h_{i3} = \ell a_3 \tan(\alpha_i)$	$i = 1,3$	9	15
(3′)	ℓa_i, ℓc_i = lever arm of cisterns relative to floats A, C_i where floats A and C at locations $-(1 + a)$ and $(1 + c)$	$\ell a_1 = a$, $\ell a_2 = (1 + a)$, $\ell a_3 = (1 + a)c/(1 + c)$		3	2
		$\ell c_1 = c$, $\ell c_2 = (1 + c)$, $\ell c_3 = (1 + c)a/(1 + a)$		3	3
(3″)	Angle (γ_i) of consumer i's float C rod	$\gamma_i = \tan^{-1}((1 + a)\tan(\alpha_i)/(1 + c))$		3	3
(4)	Prices (p_j) as function of price rod's angle β to perpendicular to axis of float A	$p_1 = \ell a_1 \tan(\beta) = \ell c_3 \tan(\delta)$ $p_2 = \ell a_2 \tan(\beta) = \ell c_2 \tan(\delta)$ $p_3 = \ell a_3 \tan(\beta) = \ell c_1 \tan(\delta)$		3	4
(4′)	Angle (δ) of float C price rod	$\delta = \tan^{-1}((1 + a)\tan(\beta)/(1 + c))$		1	1

(5)	Marginal utilities of commodity allocation	$(D_{ij} - \xi_{ij}) = u'_{ij}(x_{ij})$		9	9
(6)	Marginal utilities of expenditure allocation where ξ_{ij}, ψ_{ij} = depth of water in commodity, expenditure cistern; D_{ij} = maximum depth of cistern	$(D_{ij} - \psi_{ij}) = u'_{ij}(y_{ij}/p_j)$		9	9
(7)	Change in angles of consumers' rods (a function of weight of undisplaced water in cistern) where s_α = speed of adjustment	$\Delta\alpha_i = S_\alpha/((1 + \tan(\alpha_i)^2)\Sigma_j \ell a_j^2) \times \Sigma_j \ell a_j [x_{ij} - u_{ij}^{i-1}(h_{ij}) + y_{ij} - p_j u_{ij}^{i-1}(h_{ij})]$	i = 1,3	3	–
(8)	change in price rod angle (function of pressures on price bellows) where s_β = speed of adjustment	$\Delta\beta = S_\beta/((1 + \tan(\beta)^2)\Sigma_j \ell a_j^2) \times \Sigma_j\Sigma_i[\ell a_j pr_{ij}(\psi_{ij}, h_{ij})]$		1	–
(8′)	$pr_{ij}(\psi_{ij}, h_{ij})$ = pressure on price bellows ij where $f(t)$ = width of cistern at depth t	$pr_{ij}(\psi_{ij}, h_{ij}) = \int_0^{\psi_{ij}-(D_{ij}-h_{ij})} t f(t)\,dt$			

Figure 9 *Continued*

				Equa- tions	Variables (New)
(9)	Change in float locations (change in relative prices)	$\Delta a = -S_a/(1 + a)\Sigma_i\{\tan(\alpha_i)(x_{i1} - u_{i1}^{i-1}(h_{i1})$ $+ y_{i1} - p_1 u_{i1}^{i-1}(h_{i1}))$ $- \tan(\beta)p_{ri1}(\psi_{i1}, h_{i1})\}$ $\Delta c = -S_c/(1 + c)\Sigma_i\{\tan(\gamma_i)(x_{i3} - u_{i3}^{i-1}(h_{i3})$ $+ y_{i3} - p_3 u_{i3}^{i-1}(h_{i3}))$ $- \tan(\delta)pr_{i3}\ (\psi_{i3}, h_{i3})\}$		2	–
(10)	Quantity adjustments (S_x = flow as function of pressure differential)	$\Delta x_{1j} = S_x(\xi_{2j} - \xi_{1i}) + S_x(\xi_{3j} - \xi_{1j})$ $\Delta x_{2j} = S_x(\xi_{1j} - \xi_{2i}) + S_x(\xi_{3j} - \xi_{2j})$ $\Delta x_{3j} = S_x(\xi_{1j} - \xi_{3i}) + S_x(\xi_{2j} - \xi_{3j})$	j =1,3	6	–
(11)	Expenditure adjustments	$\Delta y_{1j} = S_x(\psi_{2j} - \psi_{1i}) + S_x(\psi_{3j} - \psi_{1j})$ $\Delta y_{2j} = S_x(\psi_{1j} - \psi_{2i}) + S_x(\psi_{3j} - \psi_{2j})$ $\Delta y_{3j} = S_x(\psi 1j - \psi_{3i}) + S_x(\psi_{2j} - \psi_{3j})$	j = 1,3	6	–
			64	64	

(a_i), and a single price rod angle (b). Together these 24 variables determine 40 other variables used in the solution of the model. The sets of equations in (1) through (6) give the constraints and relationships among these variables. The condition that the commodity and expenditure allocations add up to the exogenous commodities and incomes (E_j, Y_i) are given by six equations in (1) and (2). Not counting these equations there are 18 independent equations and variables. The equations in (3) give the heights of the cisterns above the surface of the water (h_{ij}) as determined by the lever arms laj, lcj implied by the float locations and consumer rod angles (a_i). Equations in (4) give prices as a function of the same lever arms and the price rod angle (b). Equations (5) and (6) give the depth of water in the commodity and expenditure cisterns (x_{ij}, Y_{ij}) implied by the commodity and expenditure allocations.

In equilibrium the heights for the cisterns above the surface of the water in the tub (h_{ij}), the marginal utilities implied by the commodity allocations ($u'_{ij}(x_{ij})$) and the marginal utilities implied by the expenditure allocations ($u'_{ij}(y_{ij}/p_j)$) are all equal and proportional to the prices.

Equations (7) through (11) give the adjustment of the 24 state variables iteration by iteration as a function of the forces on the rods and floats when the system is out of equilibrium. (For economy of presentation and computation the adjustments of a and c assume that the moments of the consumer rods are zero, equivalently that the (a_i) and (b) are changing so slowly that the motion of the cisterns through the water induces neglible resistance.)

Comment on William C. Brainard and Herbert E. Scarf's "How to Compute Equilibrium Prices in 1891"

By DONALD BROWN and FELIX KUBLER*

ABSTRACT. A comment on Brainard and Scarf's article in this volume.

Bill and Herb have provided an illuminating and interesting presentation of Irving Fisher's Ph.D. dissertation *Mathematical Investigations in the Theory of Value and Prices.* They correctly emphasize that Fisher's fundamental contribution to the early theory of general equilibrium was the construction of a machine to compute the equilibrium quantities in a Walrasian model of competitive markets. As Fisher notes, Walras deserves priority for deriving a system of equations that characterize equilibrium in competitive markets. Even in this area, however, Fisher makes a subtle and interesting contribution in his system of equilibrium equations, discussed later.

The first modern treatment of computing equilibrium prices in Walrasian economies is due to Herb, as everyone in this audience knows. His seminal paper, "On the Computation of Equilibrium Prices," appears, most appropriately, in *Ten Essays in Honor of Irving Fisher.* The modern treatment of the existence question in the general equilibrium model, due to Arrow and Debreu, converts the equilibrium conditions into a fixed point of a continuous map, say from the price simplex into itself. It follows from Brouwer's fixed point theorem that this map will have a fixed point. The Scarf algorithm computes approximate fixed points of any continuous map of the simplex into itself. Hence the Scarf algorithm can be used to compute equilibrium quantities.

Subsequent to Scarf's research, a more direct method of solving nonlinear systems of equilibrium equations was suggested by Eaves. The so-called homotopy method deforms a set of equations whose solution we know into the equilibrium equations, tracing out a path

*Donald Brown is a professor of economics at Yale University. Felix Kubler is a professor of economics at the University of Mannheim.

The American Journal of Economics and Sociology, Vol. 64, No. 1 (January, 2005).

of solutions terminating in a solution for the equilibrium equations. Unfortunately, there is no price-adjustment interpretation of the disequilibrium prices along the homotopy path. In this way they are similar to the prices generated by the Fisher machine out of equilibrium.

Below we give a system of equations characterizing equilibrium in an exchange economy with two agents and three goods. Agents are assumed to be endowed with money income and additive separable utility functions, which are monotone, strictly concave, and smooth. The unknowns in our equations are the state variables of Fisher's machine, in other words, prices, individual consumptions, expenditures, marginal utilities of income, and marginal utilities of the consumptions implied by expenditures and prices. Equilibrium values are computed using the homotopy method.

Fisher's Equations: A System of Equilibrium Conditions for Fisher's Machine

LET $u_i(\cdot)$ BE THE UTILITY FUNCTION of agent i and assume that she is endowed with income I_i. The social endowment will be denoted as ω.

The equilibrium conditions for Fisher's machine can be expressed as a system of 24 nonlinear equations in 24 unknowns.

The unknowns are: E_{ij}, the expenditure of the ith agent on the jth good; λ_i, the marginal utility of agent i, $p = (p_1, p_2, p_3)$; and the market prices, where $i = 1,2$ and $j = 1,2,3$.

The equations are

$$\text{(A)} \quad \begin{cases} Du_1(x_1) = \lambda_1 p \\ Du_2(x_2) = \lambda_2 p \\ Du_3(x_3) = \lambda_3 p \end{cases}$$

$$\text{(B)} \quad x_1 + x_2 + x_3 = \omega$$

$$\text{(C)} \quad \begin{cases} Du_1(E_{11}/p_1, E_{12}/p_2, E_{13}/p_3) = Du_1(x_1) \\ Du_2(E_{21}/p_1, E_{22}/p_2, E_{23}/p_3) = Du_2(x_2) \\ Du_3(E_{31}/p_1, E_{32}/p_2, E_{33}/p_3) = Du_3(x_3) \end{cases}$$

$$\text{(D)} \quad \begin{cases} E_{11} + E_{12} + E_{13} = I_1 \\ E_{21} + E_{22} + E_{23} = I_2 \\ E_{31} + E_{32} + E_{33} = I_3. \end{cases}$$

The equations in (A) and (B) characterize Pareto optimal allocations. The equations in (C) and (D) imply the budget constraint for each agent in equilibrium, given additive separable utility functions.

In order to solve the system of equations (A)–(B), we set up a linear homotopy. While this homotopy might not be the best way to solve the system, it allows for an intuitive interpretation.

Given the arbitrary starting point $(\bar{x}, \bar{p}, \bar{E})$ that satisfied Equalities (B) and (D), the equations that define the homotopy path $H(t; E, c, p) = 0$ and that correspond to Equations (A) and (C) are defined below:

$$t\left(\partial_{x_j} U^h(x) - \lambda^h p_j\right) + (1-t)\left(\bar{x}_j^h - x_j^h\right) = 0 \quad \text{for} \quad h \neq j$$
$$t\left(\partial_{x_j} U^h(x) - \lambda^h p_j\right) + (1-t)\left(\bar{\lambda}^h - \lambda^h\right) = 0 \quad \text{for} \quad h = j$$

for Equations (A) and

$$t\left(\partial^h, U^h\left(E_{h1}/p_1, E_{h2}/p_2, E_{h3}/p_3\right) - \partial_{x_j}, U^h\left(x^h\right)\right) + (1-t)\left(E_{hj} - \bar{E}^{hj}\right) = 0$$
for $h \neq j$
$$t\left(\partial_{x_j}, U^h\left(E_{h1}/p_1, E_{h2}/p_2, E_{h3}/p_3\right) - \partial_{x_j}, U^h\left(x^h\right)\right) + (1-t)\left(p_j - \bar{p}_j\right) = 0$$
for $h = j$

for Equation (C).

In Fisher's machine, Equations (B) and (D) always hold, hence we require Equations (B) and (D) to always hold along the homotopy path, while Equations (A) and (C) will hold for $t = 1$. For all smaller t the system is not in equilibrium and 18 different variables have to be adjusted to reach a solution.

The intuition behind the adjustment process is that Equations (A) determine all Lagrange multipliers λ^h as well as all consumptions x_j^h for $j \neq h$ (all x_h^h are determined by Equation (B)) and that Equations (C) determine all prices p_j as well as all E_{hj} for $j \neq h$ (all E_{hh}) are determined by Equation (D)).

We use this homotopy to recomputed equilibrium 1 of the example computed by the digital Fisher machine in the paper. Figure 1a shows how the prices change along the homotopy. It is quite striking that the dynamics of this linear homotopy have no resemblance to the dynamics of the digital Fisher machine. Figure 1b shows how the differences and consumption times prices and expenditures converge to zero. Here the qualitative features of the paths are more similar.

Comment on William C. Brainard and Herbert E. Scarf's "How to Compute Equilibrium Prices in 1891"

By K. R. Sreenivasan*

Abstract. In commenting on Brainard and Scarf's essay, the engineer and physicist K. R. Sreenivasan considers why Fisher resorted to hydraulic machines in the first place.

A reading of Irving Fisher's thesis shows that mathematical economics was in its infancy at the time, and that skepticism about its value was the norm. Fisher did not seem to have received expert advice on the subject, so it is remarkable that he went as far as he did; equally impressive is his attempt to compute equilibrium prices *quantitatively* by seeking analogy to hydraulics and building an appropriate apparatus to do so. Brainard and Scarf present a highly readable account of how the apparatus may have worked, and I have little of substance to add. I myself was curious to discover why Fisher resorted to hydraulic machines in the first place, and will make a few remarks in that context. I am afraid that these remarks have not been researched as thoroughly as I would wish.

*K. R. Sreenivasan taught at Yale for twenty-two years, where he was the Harold W. Cheel Professor of Mechanical Engineering, holding concurrent appointments in the Departments of Physics, Applied Physics, and Mathematics. He moved to the University of Maryland in 2002, where he was appointed Distinguished University Professor, Glenn L. Martin Professor of Engineering and Professor of Physics, and served as the Director of the Institute of Physical Science and Technology for a year and a half. He then took up his current position as Director of the International Centre for Theoretical Physics in Trieste, Italy, where he holds the Abdus Salam Honorary Professorship. One of his Centre's missions is to support research careers of young and promising physicists and mathematicians in developing nations. His research interests are in fluid dynamics, but they have touched on a few other areas of physics. Professor Sreenivasan has received various honors for his work, including membership of the National Academy of Engineering and the Otto Laporte Award of the American Physical Society.
He is grateful to Bill Brainard, Don Brown, John Geanakoplos, and Herb Scarf for their generous encouragement to commit these random thoughts to paper.

The American Journal of Economics and Sociology, Vol. 64, No. 1 (January, 2005).

Having written down the equations for equilibrium, why didn't Fisher attempt to find their fixed points, at least in some special instances, and examine their stability in mathematical terms? After all, he was a competent mathematician, and later, for awhile, held an appointment in the mathematics department at Yale. It was because few of the tools available in 1891 were adequate for the purpose. People had known—in fact for a long time by then—how to solve a great many initial and boundary value problems, but possessed little knowledge of the qualitative theory of differential equations (despite some impressive works by the likes of Johan Adams of the Neptune discovery). Henri Poincare's celebrated essay on the restricted three-body problem, which pioneered these methods, appeared in 1899 (although an incorrect version had appeared a few years earlier). Aleksandr Lyapunov's thesis, the first work to consider nonlinear stability systematically and provide clean definitions and rigorous results, was completed in 1892 and translated into French in 1907. So, providing a mathematical treatment was not in the cards.

Computational tools available were meager. Tables of logarithms, trigonometric functions, squares, square roots, and so on were available, as were primitive computing machines (Thomas de Colmar's "Arithometer," ca. 1850, Leon Bollee's "Multiplier," ca. 1889, perhaps Otto Steiger's "Millionaire," ca. 1890, and various special-purpose machines employed by big business and the census office). Yet, that was the age of levers and pulleys, and machines based on mechanical principles were being used as analog computers in many different ways. For instance, Lord Kelvin had built a machine to predict tides, and William Jevons (on whose shoulders Fisher stood with regard to mathematical economics) had devised a logic machine based on mechanics and Boolean logic. Thus it seems natural that Fisher turned to mechanical analogies, in particular to hydraulics.

Before assessing the value of Fisher's invention, let us ask what inspiration he may have derived locally. His own advisor does not seem to have been of direct help, nor was there an expert hydrodynamicist at Yale. Fisher acknowledged having received advice from Josiah Willard Gibbs and Hubert Anson Newton. The latter was a professor of mathematics and astronomy, but there is no record of his having evinced any interest in hydrodynamics. Gibbs, on the other hand, had a lively interest in the subject: he himself was working on a hydraulic device called the "center-vent" turbine (although it does not seem to have been completed). There was in New Haven at the time a nephew of Eli Whitney, by the name of Eli Whitney Blake, who had a strong interest in hydrodynamics; Fisher may have known about Blake's work. But the inspiration seems to have been essentially internal, and Fisher appears to have been drawn to the analogy by the ubiquitous use in economics of words of mechanics origin—*equilibrium, stability, elasticity, force, expansion, pressure, resistance, reaction, levels*, and so forth. He must have thought that a systematic representation of economic equilibria in terms of these mechanical metaphors was worthwhile. He was a gadget lover in any case, and later designed and built several other machines, including a calibrated triangular pan for mechanically adjusting and evaluating a balanced diet.

Why didn't the Fisher machines become popular in later economics work? For an analogy to be truly deep—by which I mean that the qualitative and quantitative understanding of one problem is enhanced by the workings of a second—one needs to know that the dynamical equations of one system, when suitably transformed, are the same as those of the second. This is true of the analogies between high-speed flight and shallow water waves, flow on soap films and elasticity of solids, and of a number of other problems between electricity and magnetism on the one hand and hydrodynamics on the other. Analogies without this shared feature may be suggestive of something fundamental, yet should be discarded in the face of contrary physical evidence. Witness, for instance, Rene Descartes's vortex analogy for the distribution of matter in the universe, its resurrection in another form by Lord Kelvin for modeling atomic structure—the flow of ether through the universe—all of which later fell by the wayside when our understanding became more rigorous. While it is true that equilibrium systems near a critical point behave in universal ways that transcend details of dynamical equations, the behavior of nonequilibrium systems is much more diverse. For all these reasons, it is unclear if Fisher's analogy has any inevitability to it.

Fisher himself seems to have put the machines to some pedagogical use in teaching. If a student wants to develop some intuition about fluid dynamics, it is natural for him to build a device, watch the flow, or measure its properties; after some time, he might develop an intuition that cannot be acquired by any other means. It is interesting to speculate whether a student of economics could similarly develop some intuition for prices and their fluctuations by working with Fisher's apparatus. Somehow I doubt it.

Can one learn anything more from the Fisher machines now than was learnt by the originator himself? This brings us to the simulations of Brainard and Scarf, whose most interesting conclusion concerns the *dynamical* performance of the machines. Fisher himself seems not to have worried about dynamics, and, in this respect, the simulations go beyond his original aspirations. As Brainard and Scarf point out, the dynamical behaviors of the machines depend on a large number of parameters such as the mass and surface areas of the floats, the sizes of the tubes, and water temperature. Their simulation of the machines' dynamics makes many approximations and assumptions; while they are eminently reasonable, their effects are hard to assess. It is thus unclear if the simulations have replicated the behavior of the machines truthfully. I am therefore not convinced, for instance, that the multiple equilibria unearthed by the simulations are characteristic of the machines themselves (especially when operated close to equilibrium, as Fisher seems to have done). A reliable answer must await the reconstruction of the hardware—a long-standing, even if a low-key, intention of ours!

In an accompanying Comment, Brown and Kubler have pointed out that the modern methods of computing equilibria, while based on Fisher's equations, are quite different in nature and scope. Herb Scarf's own pioneering contributions in this regard need not be repeated here.

Altogether, in this era, Fisher's machines seem to have only historical significance. But this does not detract one bit from his ingenuity and innovation: he sought the most sophisticated answers possible for his times!

Controlling the Price Level

By Robert E. Hall

Abstract. Governments determine the size of the unit of value just as they determine the length and weight of physical units of measure. What are the different ways that a government can control the size of the unit of value, that is, control the price level? In general, the government designates a resource—gold, paper currency, another country's currency—and defines its unit of value as a particular amount of that resource. An interesting variant, proposed by Irving Fisher in 1913 and implemented more recently in Chile, is to alter the resource content of the unit to stabilize the price level. Another idea is to alter the interest rate paid on reserves in a way that stabilizes the price level. This essay originally appeared as "Controlling the Price Level," *Contributions to Macroeconomics* 2(1), Article 5. See http://www.bepress.com/bejm/contributions/vol2/iss1/art5. Reprinted with kind permission of the Berkeley Electronic Press.

*Robert E. Hall is the Robert and Carole McNeil Joint Professor of Economics and Hoover Senior Fellow at Stanford University. He is an applied economist with interests in productivity, employment, competition, and economic policy. Hall is co author of the college textbooks *Macroeconomics: Theory, Performance and Policy* and *Economics: Principles and Applications*, and has written numerous articles in the *American Economic Review*, the *Journal of Political Economy*, and other academic journals. Hall has advised a number of government agencies on national economic policy and served on the National Presidential Advisory Committee on Productivity. He is director of the research program on economic fluctuations and growth of the National Bureau of Economic Research, and chairs the Bureau's committee that maintains the semiofficial chronology of the U.S. business cycle. The holder of a Ph.D. in economics from MIT, he is a fellow of the American Academy of Arts and Sciences and of the Econometric Society.

This paper was prepared for the Irving Fisher Conference at Yale University, May 1998. This research was supported by the National Science Foundation under grant SOC SBR-9730341 and is part of the research program on Economic Fluctuations and Growth of the NBER. I am grateful to Robert Shiller and Christopher Sims for helpful comments.

The American Journal of Economics and Sociology, Vol. 64, No. 1 (January, 2005).

I

Introduction

MODERN ECONOMISTS GENERALLY THINK about the price level within the framework of the monetary institutions of the United States and other advanced economies. The central bank controls the quantity of money. The price level—in the longer run—equates the demand for money to the supply. But what about economies without central banks? What determines their price levels? Can an economy use different principles to control its price level besides the tried-and-true central bank paradigm?

In modern economies, the government is responsible for determining standards for weight, volume, distance, and value. It is helpful to think about the determination of the price level as an exercise of the government's standard-setting power. The government establishes the national unit of length by a reference unit. In the United States for many years, a metal bar stored in Washington determined the length of the yard (now the reference unit is a multiple of the wavelength of cesium). The government can set a national standard for the length of the yard without producing and selling yardsticks itself. The ultimate function of the government in this and other standards is rooted in contract law: when a contract calls for the delivery of a specified number of yards of wire, the legal standard to determine if the seller has complied with the contract is whether the length of wire is the agreed amount in terms of the government's reference standard.

The determination of the unit of value operates in precisely the same way. Article I of the U.S. Constitution grants Congress the power to determine the monetary unit in the same sentence as it grants the government the power to determine units of weight and measure. The government develops a monetary unit as an abstraction. Just as the yard is a certain number of wavelengths of cesium, the dollar, as originally defined by Congress, was 0.04838 of an ounce of gold. We teach today in the context of modern monetary institutions that the dollar is both a unit of value and a store of value. But the functions can be separated. The government need not produce dollars in order to define the dollar, any more than it has to produce yardsticks in order to define the yard.

Once the government has established a monetary unit, the rest of the economy typically adopts the unit for many different purposes. One central application is that merchants place prices on goods, stated in terms of the monetary unit. A second is that accounts are kept in the unit. And a third is that the unit denominates securities that are used to carry out transactions and to store wealth. In all modern economies, the government provides some of those securities itself. In particular, governments monopolize the supply of currency denominated in the national monetary unit. Because all modern governments issue currency denominated in their own monetary units, monetary economics has blurred the distinction between the monetary unit as an abstract unit, like the yard, and the store of value, analogous to the yardstick.

History provides one way to see the distinction. The U.S. government did not issue any currency until the Civil War. For the first 70 years of the country's history, the government defined the dollar and controlled the price level without supplying currency or any other security that had a role in transactions. There is considerable confusion in many accounts of how the government controlled the price level in that regime. The confusion arises from trying to answer the question within the framework of modern institutions, where control of the quantity of money is central to controlling the price level.

II

A General Framework

TO DEFINE THE UNIT of value, the government makes a definition of the following generic form:

The unit of value is x_t units of resource y.

Here are some examples:

Provenance	Name of Unit of Value	Resource	Rule for Number of Units of Resource
U.S. before the Civil War	Dollar	Gold	0.04838 oz.
Modern U.S.	Dollar	Paper dollar: bearer security issued by the Federal Reserve	1
Proposal by Irving Fisher (1913)	Dollar	Gold	Amount needed to buy the cost-of-living bundle
Modern Chile	Unidad de Fomento	Paper peso: bearer security issued by Bank of Chile	Number required to buy the cost-of-living bundle
Argentina, Burma	Peso, FEC	U.S. dollar	1

Let r_t be the value of one unit of the resource relative to the cost-of-living bundle. Then the purchasing power of the unit of value is

$$v_t = x_t r_t$$

and the price level is

$$p_t = \frac{1}{v_t} = \frac{1}{x_t r_t}.$$

Note that these relationships are purely definitional. They do not tell us whether a change in the resource content of the monetary unit, x_t, changes the purchasing power of the resource, r_t, or the purchasing power of the monetary unit, v_t. They also do not describe how an intervention in the resource market affects either r_t or other variables in the economy. In particular, nothing in these definitional equations takes a stand on issues of monetary nonneutrality.

Monetary policies for controlling the price level fall into three categories:

1. Passive policies that let a market determine r_t without government intervention and keep x_t at a constant level. The gold standard is a leading example: the government sets the gold content of the monetary unit once and for all, and does not intervene in the gold market. Argentina's policy as of 1998 of defining its monetary unit as one U.S. dollar is another example.
2. Active policies that let a market determine r_t without government intervention and alter x_t in order to keep the price level close to constant. An example is the compensated dollar advocated by Irving Fisher (1913).
3. Active policies that keep x_t at one and intervene in the market for the resource so as to stabilize its purchasing power r_t. Most modern governments use this type of policy, where the resource is a security issued by the government (currency and reserves) and the intervention alters the supply of the security.

III

Passive Policies for Controlling the Price Level

THE GOLD STANDARD as practiced by the United States before the Civil War is a good example of a completely passive policy. The government did not issue any transactional securities other than a small volume of gold coins that had full gold value. The government did not intervene in the gold market. Private securities, including bank notes, were denominated in dollars, which meant that each dollar obligation was, ultimately, an obligation to deliver 0.04838 of an ounce of gold.[1]

What controls the price level under the gold standard? A common answer is the specie flow mechanism. Should the U.S. price level rise above its equilibrium level, the reasoning goes, the purchasing power of gold would be lower in here than in, say, Britain. Gold would flow to Britain. With less gold in the United States, banks would issue less money and the price level would fall back to equilibrium. Under a gold standard, would the price level be indeterminate in a completely closed economy, where specie could not flow? The answer is "no"—the question reveals that the specie flow theory is incomplete.

Specie flow is just one of many mechanisms involved in the determination of the equilibrium purchasing power of gold. In addition, with low purchasing power of gold, more gold would be used for jewelry and less would be mined in the first place. Standard principles of economics apply to the complicated question of the equilibrium value of gold in terms of other goods and services.

One additional complication deserves mention. The involvement of gold in the monetary system is itself a determinant of the demand for gold and thus of its purchasing power. The demand for gold arising from its monetary role can change over time—in particular, it may rise during financial panics, when the public seeks to exchange its financial instruments denominated in gold for gold itself. Hence it would not be appropriate to look at the behavior of the purchasing power of gold during a period when the gold standard was not in effect as a guide to the likely behavior of the purchasing power of gold (and thus the price level) under the hypothetical alternative of a gold standard.

IV

Policies for Controlling the Price Level Based on Varying the Resource Content of the Monetary Unit

IRVING FISHER (1913) developed a detailed proposal for price stability based on systematic variation in the gold content of the dollar. His basic idea was to define the dollar as enough gold to buy the cost-of-living bundle. If this definition could be in effect from day to day, the purchasing power of the dollar would be exactly constant. Fisher thought carefully about how to apply this idea to achieve a stable dollar in practice.[2]

To stabilize the price level at a level p_0, the rule, in terms of the notation introduced above, is

$$x_t = \frac{1}{p_0 r_t}.$$

Fisher drew up detailed rules setting forth the mechanics of stabilized money based on this rule. The steps are as follows. First, measure the cost of living according to the prices quoted by merchants under the most recent definition of the monetary unit. Second, adjust the resource content of the monetary unit, x_t, by the same proportion that the measured price level misses the target, p_0. Fisher presumed the use of gold as the resource, so his rule was to adjust the gold content of the dollar as needed to keep the purchasing power of the dollar constant. Fisher pioneered measurement techniques for the cost of living in order to make this idea practical.

To my knowledge, Fisher's idea has never been used with a precious metal as the resource underlying the monetary unit. Most probably the neglect has been to society's benefit. Fluctuations in the purchasing power of gold have been sufficiently large that substantial changes in the gold content of the monetary unit would have been needed to stabilize prices. Moreover, the nature of the forces that change the dollar price of gold may be such that anticipatory, discretionary monetary policy would be less disruptive to economic activity than the mechanical application of Fisher's scheme.

Any credible method for price stabilization, including Fisher's, will prevent monetary panics precipitated by fears of coming inflation, when the prices of gold and other commodities rise sharply. Consequently, the wide swings in the purchasing power of gold seen during periods when the credibility of price stability was in doubt, such as 1980, cannot be used to measure the magnitude of the changes in the purchasing power of gold that Fisher's formula would be called upon to offset. Nonetheless, it appears that other sources of volatility in the purchasing power of gold would stand in the way of Fisher's scheme based on gold as the resource. One such source is financial panics, where the public loses faith in banks and seeks to hold more wealth in gold and other commodities. In the face of a panic, the necessary decline in the gold content of the monetary unit could be achieved under Fisher's scheme only by waiting for actual deflation to trigger the appropriate adjustment. Portfolio shifts originating in other countries also put stress on Fisher's formula—for example, the revolution in Iran coincided with a large increase in the purchasing power of gold that would have required months or years of grinding application of the formula before it found the right decrease in the gold content of the dollar.

In place of Fisher's mechanical formula, it appears in retrospect that it would be better to define the gold content of the dollar, x_t, as an instrument of discretionary monetary policy. Alan Greenspan could probably considerably outperform Fisher's formula, because he could use all available information about the current and likely future purchasing power of gold and adjust the gold content of the dollar before deflation or inflation actually occurred.

Fisher was aware of the practical problems that would attend variations in the gold content of the dollar. Anticipated and significant changes of the content would induce large movements between demand instruments denominated in dollars and the gold that these instruments entitle the holder to obtain on demand. He proposed a fee on these transactions to limit their magnitude. The administration of the compensated dollar is similar to the operation of a crawling peg in foreign exchange markets. Chile has successfully overcome the same problems in more than 30 years of operation of the Unidad de Fomento, to be discussed shortly.

Fisher's discussion of the compensated dollar is marred by his dedication to monetary institutions as they existed in the United States at the time he wrote. During the Civil War, the federal government imposed a monopoly on currency that it has retained to the present. Fisher presumed the continuation of the monopoly, so that his discussion deals simultaneously with the definitional role of the government—setting the gold content of the dollar, x_t, at each moment—and with the role of the government as the sole issuer of currency denominated in that unit. His discussion deals extensively with the question of the credibility of the government's promise to redeem gold certificates with the designated weight of gold. This is a problem of government finance that is logically separate from the definition of the monetary unit. Had Fisher placed his discussion in the context of the monetary institutions existing before the Civil War, his explanation of the idea would have been vastly simpler. In those institutions, private organizations would issue securities, including currency, denominated in the dollar. The market value of the instruments would reflect public knowledge of the creditworthiness of the issuers, just as for all private securities at all times. The successful issuers of currency would be the organizations with reputations strong enough to maintain the market values of their securities at exact par. These topics are no different under a monetary unit defined as a time-varying amount of a resource than under a unit defined as a fixed amount of the resource.

The better application of Fisher's program for defining a self-stabilizing monetary unit is to use a resource with more stable purchasing power. The best idea in theory would be to define the unit of value directly in terms of the cost-of-living bundle, but this approach is completely impractical. The resource underlying the definition must be one in which actual transactions can occur. In practice, this principle limits the resource to standardized metals and other commodities, or to securities. Earlier research of mine in Fisher's framework demonstrated to my satisfaction that no bundle of commodities would work (Hall 1982). This leaves securities. Actual experience, not just armchair research, has demonstrated beyond doubt that defining the monetary unit as x_t units of a standardized security is a foolproof way to create a self-stabilized monetary unit.

Though Fisher was regarded during his lifetime and long after as a crackpot visionary, his idea for self-stabilized money has been a complete success in actual practice. Since 1967, Chile has had a monetary unit, the Unidad de Fomento, operating according to Fisher's principles. The resource underlying the UF is a bearer security of the Bank of Chile. The number x_t is published every day in every newspaper. An elaborate but successful formula changes the peso content of the UF each day so as to track the best estimate of that day's cost of living; the formula is driven by monthly data from the cost-of-living index. Soon after the introduction of the UF, essentially all forward contracts in Chile came to be written in UFs—the country achieved universal cost-of-living indexation painlessly. Every apartment lease, mortgage, savings account, and pension is stated in UFs. The idea is also in practice in Colombia, Ecuador, Mexico, and Uruguay, but its use is less widespread in those countries.

Interestingly, the success of the UF has remained unknown, or at least unremarked upon, among economists in every country of the world outside Latin America. A notable exception is the recent work of Robert Shiller (1998a, 1998b).

As I noted earlier, fluctuations in the purchasing power of the resource underlying the definition of the monetary unit are an inconvenience in Fisher's scheme. Could we design a security whose purchasing power is constant? If we could, it would be unnecessary to distinguish between the security and the monetary unit. Chile would not need to have a peso and a UF if the terms of the peso could be altered so that its purchasing power was constant. It turns out to be straightforward to create such a security. I will discuss it in the second part of the next section. Shiller (1998a) discusses an interesting alternative, in which a secondary monetary unit along the lines of the UF becomes the standard way to quote prices and denominate securities and the primary monetary unit lurks in the background to provide a reference level of value.

V

Policies for Controlling the Price Level Based on Intervening in the Resource Market

INTERVENTION IN A RESOURCE MARKET can take the form of altering the supply of the resource or the return that it pays. The first is the basis of price-level control in all modern economies and the second is an alternative with certain potential advantages.

A. Controlling the Supply of the Resource

When the resource is a physical substance, such as gold, the government can influence its purchasing power by altering the supply of the resource in the hands of the public. The government raises the purchasing power of gold (and lowers the price level under a passive gold standard) by purchasing gold and retiring it to an inactive stockpile. If a stockpile has been built up in the past, the government lowers the purchasing power of gold and raises the price level by selling from the stockpile.

Stabilizing the price level by buying and selling gold or another physical resource that defines the monetary unit has all the problems of any commodity price stabilization scheme. In order to guard against deflation, the government must hold an expensive stockpile of the resource. At all times, there will be political pressure from producers to purchase more of the resource, and opposition to sales when the policy rule calls for sales. Further, because gold and other resources typically trade in world markets, the government must act on a scale large enough to influence the world purchasing power of the resource. Among the governments that define their monetary units in a particular resource, no more than one can stabilize the purchasing power of its monetary unit by intervening in the resource market.

The use of a financial security as the resource—and stabilization of the price level through variations in the quantity supplied—forms the basis of the monetary systems of all large modern economies. The security is non–interest-bearing reserves together with currency. Because the government invariably stands ready to exchange currency notes of different denominations and reserves at fixed ratios, the various securities form a Hicksian composite good. I will refer to the composite as *reserves*, but currency is actually the larger component by far.

The purchasing power of a unit of reserves is determined by the standard considerations of traditional monetary economics. There is a demand for reserves arising from their usefulness in carrying out transactions. The demand is greater if there are reserve requirements, but demand is positive even without reserve requirements.[3] The issue can be framed as: In an economy with a given number of pieces of paper with $1 written on them, useful for carrying out transactions, what will be the value of those pieces of paper relative to goods and services in general? The analysis determines the level of the variable r_t in the notation introduced earlier. Since the resource content of the monetary unit, x_t, is held at one in every country except those using the UF, the price level is simply the reciprocal of the purchasing power of a unit of reserves: $p_t = \frac{1}{r_t}$.

Notice that the analysis is exclusively real. It balances the physical volume of currency and reserves against other goods and services and finds the relative price that achieves equilibrium. Building a detailed model of the demand for reserves involves the contentious issues of standard monetary economics: Does money belong in the utility function? In the production function? Whatever the resolution of these issues, it remains the case that there will be an equilibrium relative price between reserves and other goods and services.

Control over the price level is achieved, in this type of system, by adjustment of the supply of reserves. The demand for reserves fluctuates predictably and unpredictably over time. Stability of prices requires that supply be adjusted to match every movement of demand. Moreover, there is an important low-frequency random element to money demand as payment institutions evolve. Because of the instability of demand, a satisfactory price-stabilization policy does not try to prescribe the supply of reserves, but rather uses a feedback mechanism to respond automatically to shifts of the demand function.

Central bankers in all advanced countries have mastered the design of effective feedback mechanisms through a combination of automatic and human components. In the short run, the central bank adjusts reserves as needed to keep a short-term interest rate at a target level. This part is essentially automatic. It accommodates all of the predictable and random shifts in the demand for reserves. In the longer run, human decision making adjusts the interest-rate target to keep inflation at a low level. The central banks of all advanced countries and many lower-income countries have achieved stable prices over the past 15 years through this type of policy making.

B. Controlling the Return on the Resource

With the achievement of effective price stability, attention has turned to second-order objectives of policy design with respect to the control of the price level. First is the familiar deadweight burden from the lack of interest on currency and reserves. Second, and less well known, is the churning of the central bank's portfolio associated with responding to shifts in money demand by adjusting the stock of reserves.

The deadweight burden from the failure to pay interest on reserves is approximately proportional to the squared value of the short-term nominal interest rate. With respect to reserves but not currency, paying interest easily eliminates the deadweight burden. I will not enter the more complicated issue of the technical practicality and economic desirability of paying interest on currency.

The central bank's use of the quantity of reserves as the tool for controlling the price level inevitably results in a huge volume of trades of reserves for interest-bearing debt and vice versa. The accommodation of weekly, seasonal, and weather-related fluctuations in the demand for reserves calls for ceaseless buying and selling of government securities (generally in the form of repurchase agreements).

I have considered this issue earlier in Hall (1983). Suppose that the central bank maintained a large fixed volume of reserves and responded to shifts in demand for reserves by altering the interest rate paid on those reserves. Specifically, the central bank would pay interest on reserves at a rate that was a specified differential below the rate on, say, the shortest-term treasury bills. The differential would be the daily instrument of monetary policy, replacing open-market operations. The central bank would use its short-term instrument to peg a short-term interest rate. The operation of monetary policy in the medium term would remain the same as today—the central bank would adjust the target value for the short-term interest rate as needed to keep inflation on target.

Each day, if the short-term interest rate threatened to rise above target, the central bank would expand as needed to push the rate back down to the target level. To expand, the central bank would lower the demand for reserves (instead of raising the supply, as central banks do today). To lower demand, the bank would increase the interest-rate differential between reserves and treasury bills. Holders of reserves would attempt to trade lower-yielding reserves for higher-yielding short-term securities and would lower the yield on those securities in the process.

By choosing the normal level of the differential to be small (by creating a large volume of reserves that would be held widely because they paid interest close to the treasury bill rate), the central bank could hold the deadweight burden to a low level. Because the policy eliminates any alteration in the size of the supply of reserves, churning of the central bank's portfolio would be replaced by alterations in the interest rate paid on reserves. It is an open question whether this replacement would result in savings.

In the monetary policy regime I have sketched, based on the use of the reserves differential as the daily instrument, the bigger picture of policy would remain the same. Human beings would determine the interest-rate target and adjust it as needed to stabilize the price level. There is no reason to expect that the performance of monetary policy would be different from that achieved in the recent past using conventional policy.

Could monetary policy be put on autopilot through the adoption of a formula for paying interest on reserves? The answer is yes, and the explanation reveals an interesting connection between paying interest on reserves and the nature of the resource underlying the monetary unit. What follows is drawn from Hall (1997).

Let $p(t)$ be the price level, and let $n(t)$ be the short-term nominal interest rate for treasury bills. The autopilot formula for the reserve differential is

$$d(t) = -[p(t) - 1]n(t) + \dot{p}(t).$$

The target value for the price level is 1. If the price level rises above 1, the formula says to lower the differential and contract the economy. In addition, the formula says to accommodate actual inflation by raising the differential by the amount of current inflation.

To determine the price level under this policy, I proceed as discussed earlier in this chapter. From the formula for the differential, one can see that reserves earn the floating rate

$$n(t) - d(t) = p(t)\left[n(t) - \frac{\dot{p}(t)}{p(t)}\right].$$

A simple model would hold that the purchasing power of the monetary unit in terms of goods and services, r_t, is the nominal present discounted value of future interest earnings divided by the current price level:

$$r(t) = \frac{1}{p(t)} \int_t^{\infty} e^{-\int_t^{t+\tau} n(s)ds} p(t+\tau)\left[n(t+\tau) - \frac{\dot{p}(t+\tau)}{p(t+\tau)}\right] d\tau. \tag{1}$$

Let

$$z(t+\tau) = e^{-\int_t^{t+\tau} n(s)ds} p(t+\tau). \tag{2}$$

Then the nominal value can be written as

$$\int_0^{p(t)} dz, \tag{3}$$

which is just $p(t)$. So the nominal value of a unit of reserves is equal to the price level. Its real value, $r(t)$, is 1.

The final step is to calculate the price level from the relationship:

$$p_t = \frac{1}{x_t r_t} = \frac{1}{1 \times 1} = 1. \tag{4}$$

According to this analysis, the price level resulting from this policy is always 1.

The analysis rests on only a single behavioral assumption, the present value relation of Equation (1). There are two reasons to doubt that the relation would hold at all closely. First, and of lesser importance, the interest earnings of reserves have different financial risk from treasury bills, so the present value should use a rate with a suitable risk premium or discount. Second, because reserves provide monetary services to their holders—even in an economy close to monetary saturation as proposed here—the valuation should consider these services. The equilibrium price level would actually be less than 1, so that the differential would be wide enough to accommodate the service value of reserves.

I would not advocate the use of the monetary autopilot. Any feedback rule for monetary policy has to consider seriously the performance in an economy with monetary nonneutrality. A policy that tries to lock the price level to a predetermined target invites serious disturbances to real activity whenever there is an inflationary shock from import prices, wages, or other sources. A realistic rule would have to consider unemployment as well as the price level, as proposed by Taylor (1993), for example. And advocates of such rules generally propose them as guidelines rather than autopilots.

VI

Controlling the Price Level After the Transition to Cybermoney

PAYMENT SYSTEMS ARE EVOLVING to lessen the public's dependence on currency and on deposits subject to reserve requirements. Will the central bank lose control over the price level as this process continues?[4]

The general framework of this paper suggests that there will remain a wide variety of methods for effective control of the price level even if private, electronic payment methods displace the use of the obligations of the central bank. The most appropriate method, in my view, would be to pay interest on reserves. The differential between the reserve rate and the market rate on treasury bills could decline to make up for the declining demand for reserves derived from the demand for checking accounts. Eventually, when the last checking account and the last dollar bill disappeared from use, reserves would be valued almost entirely from their interest earnings and just a little from the fact that the resource underlying the monetary unit enjoys a service value from that role.

In any case, there is little evidence of disappearance of checking accounts and currency from modern life in any country. Americans in particular cling to the use of checks despite the widespread availability of electronic alternatives that seem to be more convenient. And all central banks, especially the Federal Reserve, enjoy huge markets for their currency because of its anonymity.

VII

The Fiscal Theory of the Price Level

SARGENT AND WALLACE (1981) began a modern line of thought that examines the relation between the government budget and the price level. This line of thought presumes a modern set of monetary institutions in which the monetary unit and the resource underlying it are the same, namely, government-issued currency (including reserves). The issuance of currency is a source of revenue to the government. Sims (1994) and Woodford (1994, 1995) are other important contributions in this area. This fiscal theory of the price level presents a view of price determination seemingly quite different from the one described earlier in this chapter. Cochrane (1998) gives a simplified presentation of the fiscal theory.

The fiscal theory of the price level rests on the proposition that, because the government issues nominal instruments, the present value of its excess demands depends on the path of the price level. Equilibrium can occur only when the price level follows a path that results in the government satisfying its intertemporal budget constraint. The equilibrium would be indeterminate but for the government's sensitivity to the price level.

The logic of Sargent and Wallace and the resulting fiscal theory of the price level surely helps explain why Russia and Ukraine cannot have stable price levels today. These countries have government deficits that cannot be funded, apparently, by any method other than the printing of currency.

There are other, simpler ways to make the price level determinate. In the fiscal theory model, the public has to look into the indefinite future to see that the government will eventually go broke unless the price level follows the right path. But consider the following alternative. If the price level is not at the prescribed level, the government pays the purchasers of odd-numbered treasury bills enough at redemption so that their owners earn 5% more than they would from even-numbered, normal treasury bills. The market for odd-numbered bills cannot clear if the price level departs from the prescribed level. The only possible price level in general equilibrium is the target price level. We do not have to picture the actors in the economy as gazing into the indefinite future to understand the forces that make the price level determinate.

This example shows the connection between the method for controlling the price level advocated earlier in this chapter and the fiscal theory. A policy for paying interest on reserves and linking the interest rate adroitly to the price level seems to be just a variant of standard monetary policy, in which changes in the demand for reserves substitute for changes in the quantity of reserves. But another way to see the same arrangement is that the government creates a fiscal anomaly—paying the wrong interest rate on an important part of the national debt—unless the price level is on target.

VIII

Concluding Remarks

A GOVERNMENT HAS a wide choice of methods for defining the national monetary unit. The unit can be a specified weight of metal or amount of some other physical resource, it can be a security issued by another government, or a security issued by itself. With the definition in place, the government also has a wide choice of methods for controlling the price level. The resource content of the unit can be adjusted systematically over time, as proposed by Irving Fisher and implemented by Chile. The government can adjust the supply of the resource to stabilize its purchasing power, as all advanced economies have done so successfully in the past decade. Or, the government can adjust the demand for the resource and achieve the same control without incurring the costs of churning its portfolio.

My discussion has only hinted at the tough issues of monetary policy, which are common across all the methods for controlling the price level considered here. It appears that strict price stabilization may result in unstable output and employment. It is probably desirable to permit movements of the price level in the face of some types of macroeconomic shocks and then to reverse these movements gradually afterward. The reasons lie in the imperfectly understood realm of monetary nonneutrality, which may be defined broadly as sensitivity of real activity to any instrument of monetary policy whose theoretical effect is only to change the price level. As James Tobin has written:

> The tail wags the dog. By gently touching a tiny tail, Alan Greenspan wags the mammoth dog, the great American economy. Isn't that remarkable? The federal funds rate is the shortest of all interest rates, remote from the rates on assets and debts by which businesses and households finance real investment and consumption expenditures counted in GDP. Why does monetary policy [have real effects]? How? It's a mystery, fully understood by neither central bankers nor economists.[5]

Notes

1. The definition of the dollar was actually a little more complicated, because it involved the alternative of silver as well. But little is lost by my simplification.

2. At all times, the discussion of Fisher's idea has been confused by being embedded in a framework where the quantity of money was an important variable, in part because Fisher's own thinking prior to making the proposal emphasized the quantity of money. See Patinkin (1993) for a thorough discussion.

3. The study of the demand for currency or reserves is not fundamental to the determination of the price level in alternative monetary regimes, but is central when the resource defining the monetary unit is currency.

4. Jordan and Stevens (1997) discuss this issue. They foresee large reductions in the demand for reserves and currency and are concerned whether central banks can continue to maintain price stability in that setting. Their discussion is entirely limited to current institutions.

5. Tobin (1998: 7). Tobin wrote: "Why does monetary policy work?" rather than "Why does monetary policy have real effects?" but I believe my interpretation is consistent with his intent.

References

Cochrane, John. (1998). *A Frictionless View of U.S. Inflation.* NBER Working Paper 6646, July. (Forthcoming in the *NBER Macroeconomics Annual.*)

Fisher, Irving. (1913). "A Compensated Dollar." *Quarterly Journal of Economics* 27: 213–235.

Hall, Robert E. (1982). "Explorations in the Gold Standard and Related Policies for Stabilizing the Dollar." In *Inflation*. Ed. Robert E. Hall. Chicago: University of Chicago Press for the NBER.

——. (1983). "Optimal Fiduciary Monetary Systems." *Journal of Monetary Economics* 12(1): 33–50.

——. (1997)."Irving Fisher's Self-Stabilizing Money." *American Economic Review Papers and Proceedings* 107: 436–438.

Jordan, Jerry L., and Edward J. Stevens. (1997). "Money in the 21st Century." In *The Future of Money in the Information Age.* Ed. James A. Dorn. Washington, DC: Cato Institute.

Leeper, Eric. (1991). "Equilibrium Under 'Active' and 'Passive' Monetary Policies." *Journal of Monetary Economics* 27: 129–147.

Patinkin, Don. (1993). "Irving Fisher and His Compensated Dollar Plan." *Federal Reserve Bank of Richmond Economic Quarterly* 79: 1–33.

Sargent, Thomas J., and Neil Wallace. (1981). "Some Unpleasant Monetarist

Arithmetic." *Federal Reserve Bank of Minneapolis Quarterly Review* Fall.

Shiller, Robert J. (1998a). *Indexed Units of Account: Theory and Assessment of Historical Experience.* NBER Working Paper 6356, January.

——. (1998b). *Designing Indexed Units of Account.* Cowles Foundation Discussion Paper 1179, May.

Sims, Christopher. (1994). "A Simple Model for the Determination of the Price Level and the Interaction of Monetary and Fiscal Policy." *Economic Theory* 4: 381–399.

——. (1997). "Fiscal Foundations of Price Stability in Open Economies." Yale University.

Taylor, John B. (1993). "Discretion Versus Policy Rules in Practice." *Carnegie-Rochester Conference Series on Public Policy* 39: 195–214.

Tobin, James. (1998). *Monetary Policy: Recent Theory and Practice.* Cowles Foundation Discussion Paper 1187, July.

Woodford, Michael. (1994). "Monetary Policy and Price Level Determinacy in a Cash-in-Advance Economy." *Economic Theory* 4: 345–389.

——. (1995). "Price-Level Determinacy Without Control of a Monetary Aggregate." *Carnegie-Rochester Conference Series on Public Policy* 43: 1–46.

Comment on Robert Hall's "Controlling the Price Level"

By James Tobin*

Abstract. James Tobin discusses Fisher's compensated dollar plan and Robert Hall's proposal for controlling the price level.

Fisher's idea was quite simple. It applies to a commodity, or "representative," currency as distinguished from fiat money. In Fisher's day, paper money and token coin were the predominant means of payment. The public exchanged them for real commodities, in other words, for goods and services for consumption or for the making of consumption goods. The value of currency in goods, v, was free to move in markets from day to day. The currency was at the same time redeemable by the government for one or more particular real goods, at an administratively set rates, x units of currency for one unit of a standard good. At these rates the government promised either to buy or sell. Both the United States and Britain set prices of their currencies in two standards, silver and gold, through most of the 19th

*James Tobin (1918–2002), former Sterling Professor of Economics at Yale University, was on the Yale faculty from 1950, retiring from his teaching position in 1988. He graduated from Harvard College *summa cum laude* in economics in 1939. He then received a Ph.D. in economics from Harvard in 1947 and was a Junior Fellow of the Society of Fellows for three years, 1947–1950, the last of which he spent at the Department of Applied Economics at the University of Cambridge, England. In 1961–1962, on leave from Yale, he was a member of President Kennedy's Council of Economic Advisers in Washington. He was President of the Econometric Society (1958), of the American Economic Association (1971), and of the Eastern Economics Association (1977). In 1955 the American Economic Association awarded him the John Bates Clark Medal, given to one economist under age 40. He became a member of the National Academy of Sciences in 1972. In 1981 he received in Stockholm the Prize in Economic Science, established by the Bank of Sweden in Memory of Alfred Nobel. He was author or editor of 16 books and more than 400 articles. His main professional subjects were macroeconomics, monetary theory and policy, fiscal policy and public finance, consumption and saving, unemployment and inflation, portfolio theory and asset markets, and econometrics. He wrote both for professional readers and for the general public.

The American Journal of Economics and Sociology, Vol. 64, No. 1 (January, 2005).

century. But at the time Fisher was advocating the proposal Bob Hall is reviving today, silver had lost its status as a standard.

Fisher was concerned, therefore, with the value of gold in goods and services implied by gold's price at the mint, and the market value of gold in goods and services in production and trade as a commodity. Micro economic conditions determined this latter value. Let this value be g. Thus a consumer with currency could obtain a general real good, say the Consumer Price Index bundle, either by parting with $1/v$ units of currency in the currency-goods market, or by changing currency at the mint into enough gold to buy it, namely $1/g$ ounces. To obtain $1/g$ ounces of gold would cost the individual $1/gx$ in currency. In normal circumstances, with no advantage, no arbitrage incentive, to either route over the other, $gx = v$. However, Fisher thought the currency-goods market could and often would make v different from gx. Moreover, g itself could vary, leading to fluctuations in v, which Fisher wanted to stabilize, say at $v = 1$. So Fisher's proposal is periodically to set $x - v/g$, believing that the arbitrage between the two currency-to-goods channels are strong enough to set a new v equal to 1.

Although Fisher's proposal was not adopted as a routine of monetary stabilization, something like it has been do done on occasion, by altering the administered mint valuation of the currency relative to its commodity (gold) standard, usually by devaluations. In 1933 Fisher strongly advocated devaluation, increasing the dollar price of gold, long stuck at $20.67 per ounce, in other words, lowering the arbitrary setting of x. Fisher bombarded President Roosevelt with letters advocating this devaluation (he called it "revaluation"). Roosevelt was more strongly influenced by two Cornell agricultural economists, who assured FDR that ordinary farm prices would rise the same as the official increase in the price of gold, almost immediately. In 1933–34, the official dollars-to-gold price of gold at which the U.S. Treasury would make transactions was raised by 69.3%. Farm prices rose from 1933–35 53.2%, lending support to the claims of Warren and Pearson. However, as a more general macroeconomic proposition, closer to Fisher's objective, the result was less striking. Economy-wide prices rose only 9.2%. That was in fact fortunate, because it meant that the devaluation was a much-needed stimulus to economic activity, employment, and output, a more desirable outcome in Depression times than boosting prices. Indeed Fisher himself was thinking of price revaluation as a mechanism for quantitative recovery, which it could not have been if it completely absorbed the monetary stimulus to aggregate demand.

A favorite metaphor of Bob Hall is the idea that the government's designation of the unit of its currency in a standard commodity is an arbitrary definition, like the designation of weights and measures. These definitions are indeed prerogatives of the central government, and they are arbitrary, but there the resemblance stops. Fisher's proposal concerned a commodity standard currency in market economies in which standard money could be obtained either by offering currency to the government or by purchasing the standard commodity in ordinary trade in nongovernmental markets. There is nothing like that in the Bureau of Standards' definition of a yard in terms of particles.

Hall's paper diverges from Fisher when he tries to apply the Fisher model to fiat money. Certainly the government can say what paper and coin represent in fiat dollars, but that doesn't do anything to stabilize v, the commodity value of the fiat money. In the past, as Hall himself reminds us, he looked for a substitute for gold—a feasible collection of a few tradable durable commodities, whose value in representative goods and services, like the Consumer Price Index basket, would be reasonably stable. Then this could take the place of gold in the Fisher setup. But Bob couldn't find such a new standard. It turned out that Hall's proposed bundle was not a good mimic of the market's overall real bundle. He seems not to recognize that the Fisher proposal would not apply unless currency were exchangeable for the standard both at the mint and in ordinary markets. It's not enough to define a dollar as so much plywood unless private individuals are free to deal in plywood markets and are expected to deliver plywood if they have promised to deliver dollars. There would have to be more to the alchemy of plywood than definition alone, anyway.

Now, it seems to me, Hall has shifted the subject away from the Fisher stabilization proposal and away from the definition of currency. He has shifted it to the provision of a derivative asset of stable real value, a stable CPI. There's no doubt that such assets can be designed, offered by governments, and traded. This has been done by several governments—with Brazil's "monetary corrections" and the indexed obligations offered by the governments of the United Kingdom, United States, and other countries.

It is one thing to contrive a currency of constant purchasing power in representative goods and services. When this is not literally possible, it still may be that the corrections, for example in x, make the real value of the currency approximately constant, always "catching up." This is what Fisher was after. It is another thing to contrive new marketable assets, for example, derivatives of CPI-indexed bills and bonds, that would in principle enable an individual to avoid all risk of loss of real value of her holdings of fiat money.

The objective of stabilizing the real values of currency may be overrated. Its popularity stems from eras when currency was the dominant store of value for most citizens. This is no longer true. Citizens need a convenient safe store of value that offers them security against avoidable losses of real wealth from any source or provides them efficient risk/return choices. It need to be associated with monetary media of exchange. Inflation-indexed savings certificates fulfill this function admirably. It may not be practical to guarantee the real value of currency at every point in time, but is not necessary anyway.

Irving Fisher believed that monetary disturbances were the main source of real disturbances, and he sought ways of stabilizing real incomes by making money behave. Over his career he had several ideas about the sources and remedies of monetary shocks, and he elevated each one into a crusade. For example, he abandoned the idea of changing the value of money in terms of a commodity standard and turned to 100 percent reserves with equal enthusiasm and self-confidence. At the end of the century, monetary and economic stability does not seem to be as daunting a challenge as it appeared to Fisher. Fisher himself deserves considerable credit for this happy result.

Stable Prices, Money, and the Cost of Living

By Martin Shubik*

Abstract. An analysis of indexed units of account such as that proposed by Robert Hall.

I

The Macroeconomic Design of Indexed Units of Account

The question of the desirability of stable prices belongs to the realms of political economy. Political economy in its old-fashioned sense covered both theory and practice and involved or at least was openly qualified by political, administrative, sociological, and psychological considerations.

Currently, as the social sciences have developed, economics and political science are more or less separate disciplines and micro- and macroeconomic theory and practice are often far apart.

From the viewpoint of applied macroeconomics and in the belief of most economists, the proposition that the economy would benefit from a more or less stable price system is well accepted. Commonsense wisdom also coincides, in this instance, with the beliefs of most economists. The implications of wage stickiness and the possibility of a money illusion have been discussed at least since Keynes (1936).

*Dr. Martin Shubik is currently the Seymour H. Knox Professor of Mathematical Institutional Economics at Yale University. The title indicates an interest in the underlying abstractions of mathematical economics combined with a stress on understanding actual institutions and processes. He received his B.A. and M.S. degrees in Mathematics and Political Economy from the University of Toronto, Ontario, Canada in 1947 and 1949, respectively. He received his A.M. and Ph.D. degrees in Economics from Princeton University in 1951 and 1953, respectively. His main academic concerns are with the theory of money and financial institutions (how and why they are created and destroyed, and their social purpose); the theory of games and its relationship to strategic behavior; a third and somewhat different interest is in the management and economics of cultural institutions. He is the author of approximately 20 books and over 200 articles and specializes primarily in strategic analysis.

The American Journal of Economics and Sociology, Vol. 64, No. 1 (January, 2005).

The discussions of Robert Hall (1997) and Robert Shiller (1998) deal with the problem of how to construct an indexed unit of account via a new financial instrument. In both instances they note the successful utilization of the *unidad de fomento* in Chile as an example of where a small country has designed a bearer security linked to the peso, whose peso content changes daily, tracking the cost of living as closely as possible. Shiller in particular outlines various policy choices concerning the linkage of such an instrument to a consumer price index or to a per capita income index.

It is well known in medicine that one may stumble across a practical means to treat a disease without knowing why it works. I suggest that much of macroeconomic engineering falls in the same category. A further complicating feature in economics is that often we do not know how fatal is the disease. It can be argued that "a little inflation" is a good thing; but "too much inflation" is bad for the economy. My intuitive feeling is that an inflation rate of 1 or 2% may be a salutary "little inflation." Much above that level I suspect that in some broad sense inflation is not desirable, although if it were constant and cleanly predicable then larger rates might be acceptable.

In much of microeconomic theorizing Pareto optimality is discussed and attempts are often made to devise criteria for fair division, usually in a static model. In political reality neither optimality nor fairness are easy to define in a dynamic context. Billions of dollars are at stake, and large political constituencies influence and are influenced by choices of indices such as a cost-of-living index.

I believe that there are an array of new instruments of the variety indicated by Hall and Shiller that can be designed now. I am less sure how badly they are needed.

Recognizing that practical policy issues must be dealt with here and now on an ad hoc basis by the macroeconomists, the possible value-added contribution of the microeconomic theorist might be in raising some questions concerning what is being controlled and why?

II

What Are the Questions and Are There Microeconomic Answers to Them?

1. Do WE KNOW that a fixed high inflation (say 10% per annum) is necessarily bad for the economy? It is not clear to me that we do.

I suspect that the problem is in the variation and unpredictability of the inflation rate, not the size of the rate. If it were feasible to control the variation, the mean inflation might not be too important, although changing prices might be a nuisance.

2. Is the exercise in the design of an indexed unit of account essentially an ad hoc local fix we deem to be worth doing under the criteria of political feasibility and local, topical economic optimality, or can it be justified in terms of global properties?

I suspect that the problem is primarily political and administrative. The solution suggested is ad hoc, and the problem of controlling inflation could be treated better by the control of the money supply and the near money substitutes. My guess is that in much of South America the political and bureaucratic structure is such that a partial indexing serves to make it easier to write long-term contracts without having to worry as much about the politicians and bureaucrats.

3. Do we have a theory of economic dynamics that we believe in that at least enables us to say how important indexing is? Do we believe that what is at stake is of the order of 0.1% or 1% or 5% of GNP, or do we have some measure of efficiency?

We do not have a universally accepted dynamics, and I am not aware of a consensus on indexing and on its relative efficiency over other forms of monetary policy.

4. Is there any need whatsoever to engage in indexing? Could it be that the solution lies in money and credit control? Ricardo's reason for supporting the utilization of a gold or gold-backed currency was not that he regarded gold as a necessity, but that he regarded it as a better alternative than utilizing paper, which would be subject to manipulation by those who issued it.

This argument is central to political economy. It raises the basic questions concerning implementation. What are the administratively feasible political economic alternatives, and what do they imply in terms of who benefits in the society?

5. What is the model of the individual or individuals that lies behind the interest in indexing?

The model appears to be of individuals who are creatures of habit and not overly interested in too much data processing. Hence there may be sticky wages and slowly changing bankruptcy and fraud laws. In short, individuals are more or less viewed as, at best, local optimizers embedded in a bureaucratic structure.

I believe in this "limited rationality" view of the individual, but the policy implications of this observation are not clear. They involve deciding who acts as "big brother" for whom.

6. How important are smoothly varying prices for informational efficiency?

To the layman trying to buy an airline ticket, sticky but low enough prices and not having to shop for several days appears to be desirable. To the airline executive, the flexible adjustment of prices helps fill planes. The evaluation of the informational and search costs aspects of variable prices seems to vary from industry to industry.

My guess is that individual consumers are limited data processors and there is an important but hard to calculate middle level of price flexibility that is, in some sense, optimal.

7. In the construction of the cost-of-living index can we estimate how important are the influences of (a) innovation in organization and new products; (b) changes in quality; (c) the supply of public goods (and bads); (d) changes in population structure; (e) incomplete markets; (f) changes in velocity of payments; (g) the size of the barter or nonmonetized sector?

My guess is that these "imperfections" do not matter more than a percent or two. But this is a guess, not a clear specification of the problem followed with a measurement.

8. Can microeconomic theory provide an ideal definition of no inflation in a competitive economy with incomplete markets?

9. Can a microeconomic approach to money and financial institutions say anything useful about the control of inflation by central bank policy other than indexing?

A sketch of the answers to these two questions is noted below.

III

A Microeconomic Examination of Money, Efficiency, and Inflation

THE GENERAL EQUILIBRIUM STRUCTURE is precise, clear, and unrealistic from many points of view. It derives relative prices at equilibrium and makes no use of a monetary unit and is not a process model. Optimality is well defined and prices are homogeneous of order zero (h(0)).

One may introduce gold as a required means of payment, and if there is enough gold and it is well distributed the competitive price system is attained in equilibrium with a fixed price level in terms of gold. If the economy grows in an appropriately linear manner (population and production technology), then prices are not influenced. Without a linear structure there is no fully satisfactory one-dimensional measure of inflation.

If one considers a paper money as the means of payment, it is necessary to specify how its value is supported. Is it by fiat, by expectations, or is it intrinsic to the local dynamics? Is the money redeemable at the central bank? If so, in what is it redeemed? In order to well define this model the unit must be specified, issue conditions must be specified, and if loans are permitted then default conditions must be specified. The price level will be bounded but not necessarily fully determined.

If a multistage model of the economy is considered with or without overlapping generations, but with incomplete markets, even without production, considerable difficulties appear in being precise concerning inflation. In several models Karatzas, Shubik, and Sudderth (1995, 1997) and Geanakoplos, Karatzas, Shubik, and Sudderth (1998) have looked at highly simplified infinite horizon stochastic strategic game process models of an exchange economy utilizing fiat money that may be issued by a central bank. Even in these highly simplified models the control of the money supply is not simple. A noninflationary equilibrium can be defined precisely in these simple models as follows.

If the system in time $T + \tau$ is in precisely the same physical state as it was in time T, then the prices are identical in both periods. In an economy in which the overall macro variable of real income is fixed or cyclical but individual shares are stochastic, a noninflationary equilibrium exists.

In current ongoing work Karatzas, Shubik, and Sudderth have been able to show that if the overall income is stochastic with a passive central bank, in general no equilibrium with stationary prices may exist even though a stationary distribution of real resources exists.

If the overall income in the economy is stochastic and individual shares have a stochastic component, then although an optimum policy for each agent may still be defined, both the wealth distribution and the price levels may be determined by the complete history of the system.

The answer to Question 8 above is that microeconomic analysis can provide basic insight into the definition of inflation. Without a fully linear structure to the economy, at best an inflation index is an approximation. Even if we accept an approximation it is still an open question as to how much strategic activity is required from a central bank to control the inflationary process that may depend on the complete historical time path of the economy.[1]

Question 9 deals with the strategic input of the central bank. The ideal would be for a central bank to be more or less passive after it had set a basic interest rate. This is not sufficient to control inflation, even in a highly simplified model. Thus the open question is how much power in monetary policy and possibly also fiscal policy is required to control inflation and what the weapons are. This includes indexing as a possibility. It also raises questions concerning how perceptively a central bank can spot what is going on in an economy and how quickly it can act to prevent a happening or react to what has occurred.

IV

So What?

MUCH OF MICROECONOMIC THEORY deals with highly oversimplified "toy models." Rigorous theorem proving calls for considerable simplification in order to leave tractable problems. Even with the new interest in simulation and local optimization, the models of mass local optimizers are considerably simplified (see, for example, Arthur et al. 1997; Miller and Shubik 1995).

But the virtue of these simplifications is to see when basic phenomena or difficulties appear. If one finds difficulty in well defining phenomena such as the money supply, near money, expectations, or inflation in a highly oversimplified model, adding complications usually distracts from understanding. Current microeconomic theory is not developed enough to offer good macroeconomic policy advice, but it is valuable in trying to understand the basic structure of what is at stake.

On occasion the appropriate questions may help in finding reasonable answers. For example, in this conference Herbert Scarf is discussing computational methods for obtaining prices in a general equilibrium system. In spite of the elegance and deep mathematical content of his algorithms, a basic puzzle remains. If we ask most reasonably professional economists, "Do you believe that, at least as a crude approximation, correcting for indivisibilities, oligopoly, nonsymmetric information, etc. that the competitive price system has anything of value to say about the real economy?" the answer, in general, (including mine) will be, "Yes." Yet in spite of the fact that we know that in general no simple local hill-climbing algorithm will bring about the appropriate price system, it seems to have come about through locally optimizing behavior and some central bank and fiscal control.

The basic question is: How could this be?

Returning to the specific observations on indexing, I note that it is among the more interesting ideas in current applied macroeconomics for an anti-inflationary policy. The economic understanding of options and other new financial instruments has certainly reached the level at which the design of such instruments is feasible. Whether this is the optimal policy to pursue is neither supported nor denied by current economic theory, especially basic monetary theory. At this time any operational decision must be based on operational debating briefs. The mere fact that theory can offer only questions and qualifications suggests that more interaction between microeconomic and macroeconomic theory is needed in the development of both and that basic scientific understanding should not be confused with policy debate.

Note

1. It appears that in an economy with incomplete markets and a natural discount β the rate of interest ρ required to control the interest is related to the level of randomness in the economy. The higher the randomness, the lower the needed rate of interest, and in general the noninflation level of interest is such that $1 + \rho < 1/\beta$. A full discussion of this observation cannot be presented here, but the phenomenon is noted to indicate that even the elementary question of the appropriate rate of interest required to control inflation in a simple exchange economy with incomplete markets is relatively subtle.

References

Geanakoplos, J., I. Karatzas, M. Shubik, and W. D. Sudderth. (1998). "A Strategic Market Game with Active Bankruptcy." CFDP #1183.

Hall, R. E. (1997). "Irving Fisher's Self-Stabilizing Money." *American Economic Review Papers and Proceedings* 436–438.

Karatzas, I., M. Shubik, and W. D. Sudderth. (1994a). "Construction of Stationary Markov Equilibria on a Strategic Market Game." *Mathematics of Operations Research* 19(4).

——. (1994b). "A Strategic Market Game with Secured Lending." *Journal of Mathematical Economics* 28(2): 207–247.

Keynes, J. M. ([1936] 1957). *The General Theory of Employment, Interest and Money.* London: Macmillan.

Miller, J., and M. Shubik. (1994). "Some Dynamics of a Strategic Market Game with a Large Number of Agents." *Journal of Economics* 60(1): 1–28.

Shiller, R. J. (1998). *Indexed Units of Account: Theory and Assessment of Historical Experience.* Working Paper 6356, National Bureau of Economic Research.

Econometric Analysis of Fisher's Equation

By PETER C. B. PHILLIPS*

ABSTRACT. Fisher's equation for the determination of the real rate of interest is studied from a fresh econometric perspective. Some new methods of data description for nonstationary time series are introduced. The methods provide a nonparametric mechanism for modelling the spatial densities of a time series that displays random wandering characteristics, like interest rates and inflation. Hazard rate functionals are also constructed, an asymptotic theory is given, and the techniques are illustrated in some empirical applications to real interest rates for the United States. The paper ends by calculating semiparametric estimates of long-range dependence in U.S. real interest rates, using a new estimation procedure called modified log periodogram regression and new asymptotics that covers the nonstationary case. The empirical results indicate that the real rate of interest in the United States is (fractionally) nonstationary over 1934–1997 and over the more recent subperiods 1961–1985 and 1961–1997. Unit root nonstationarity and short memory stationarity are both strongly rejected for all these periods.

I

Introduction

SINCE IRVING FISHER (1896, 1930) formalized[1] the notion of a real rate of interest, the concept has played a significant role in the formulation of a wide range of economic models. These include individual agent decision making regarding investment, savings, and portfolio allocations, options pricing models in finance, and the modern theory of inflation targeting in macroeconomics, to name but a few. Naturally enough, in light of the role that the real rate plays in economic theory models, a good deal of attention has been devoted in the literature, especially in macroeconomics, to the measurement of the real

*Peter C. B. Phillips is a professor of economics and statistics at Yale University and the editor of *Econometric Theory*.

The American Journal of Economics and Sociology, Vol. 64, No. 1 (January, 2005).

rate and to the characterization of its temporal dependence properties. *Prima facie*, this task seems like a simple exercise in time series econometrics. However, the empirical analysis is complicated by two factors: (1) the apparent nonstationary behavior of the series involved, particularly interest rates but also sometimes inflation; and (2) the fact that the *ex ante* real rate of interest depends on inflation expectations and is therefore not directly measured. Perhaps because of these complicating factors, no consensus seems to have emerged about the time series properties of the real rate of interest, in spite of intensive empirical study. In particular, while economic theory models routinely assume that the real rate of interest is a constant, or fluctuates in a stationary way about a constant mean, the empirical work indicates that this is not so or at best holds only over short regimes.

Figure 1 shows monthly data for the *ex post* real interest rate in the United States over the period 1961:1–1985:12. The series is calculated by taking the U.S. 90-day treasury bill rate for the nominal interest rate and by using the U.S. monthly CPI (all commodities, with no adjustment for housing costs) to compute three-month inflation rates. The figure also shows subgroup means calculated over the subperiods 1961:1–1973:1, 1973:2–1982:1, and 1982:2–1985:12. The data cover the same period as that studied recently by Garcia and Perron (1994), who used regime shift methods to estimate the *ex ante* real rate over approximately these subperiods. These authors concluded that the *ex ante* real rate of interest was effectively constant but subject to occasional mean shifts over 1961–1985. They found two mean shifts over this time period and gave results very similar to those obtained by subgroup means that are displayed in Figure 1. For these data, at least, the conclusion does not seem unreasonable.

Figures 2 and 3 graph the *ex post* real interest rate series calculated in the same way over the longer periods 1961–1997 and 1934–1997. Over the 1961–1997 period the graphs shows subsample means for the additional two subperiods 1990–1993 and 1994–1997. Apparently, there is a need to allow for continuing regime shifts in the mean level if this approach to modeling the real rate of interest is to give acceptable results. For the longer period, an even larger number of mean shifts is needed to accommodate this approach, and the results seem

Figure 1

Ex post real interest rate: 1961–1985.

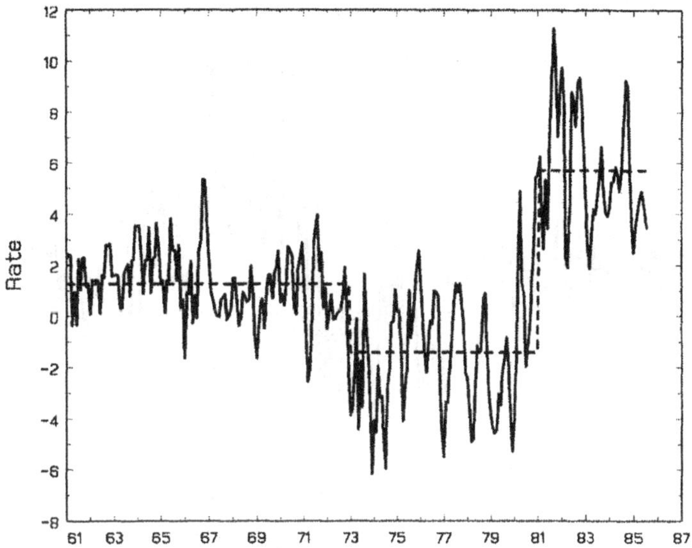

much less satisfying—we merely illustrate what is involved in Figure 3. It is hard to conclude that one is doing any more than simply curve fitting in such exercises and then possibly providing *ex post* rationalizations for the mean shifts. Note, however, that the data in Figure 3 clearly do support the conclusion reached in Fama's (1975) influential study that the real rate has a constant mean over the period 1953–1971. Notwithstanding the apparent constancy over 1953–1971, so many mean shifts are needed to model the data this way that the Garcia-Perron conclusion that the *ex ante* real rate of interest fluctuates about a constant mean, subject to occasional mean shifts, seems much less reasonable over the longer period 1934–1997 than it does for 1961–1986. Indeed, over longer periods such as this, most formal tests (e.g., Rose 1988; Walsh 1987) support a conclusion that is the opposite of stationarity and favor unit root nonstationary. One of the goals of the present paper is to determine whether there are other hypotheses that are more reasonable than these two alternatives.

Figure 2

Ex post real interest rate: 1961–1997.

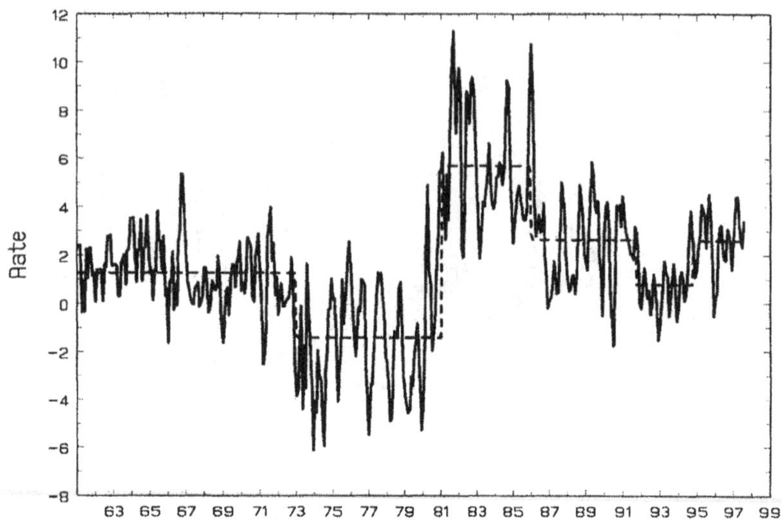

Figure 3

Ex post real interest rate: 1934–1997.

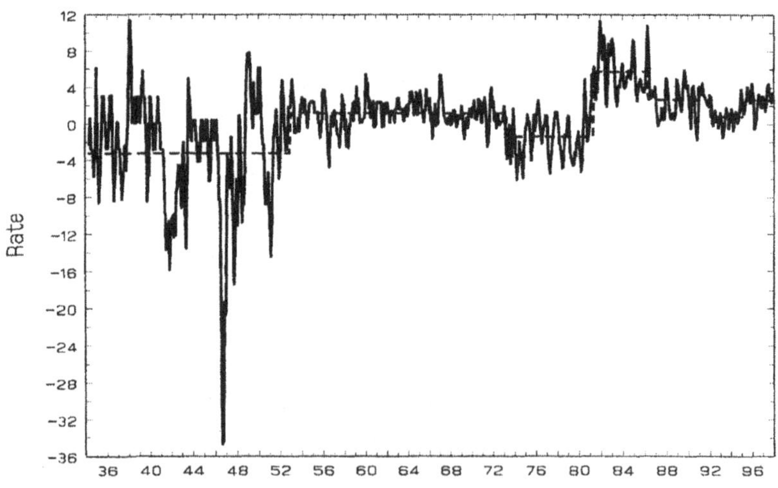

Another goal of the paper is to contribute some new methods to assist in the econometric analysis of data of this type. The methods given here furnish a new way of describing and characterizing data like interest rates and inflation that appear to have nonstationary elements. More specifically, the paper proposes a nonparametric spatial density estimate as a new descriptive tool for nonstationary time series. Many series like the interest rates shown in Figures 1–3 behave as if they have no fixed mean. The random wandering characteristic of these series is hard to describe quantitatively. What a spatial density does is provide useful quantitative information about the spatial location characteristics of a time series, in just the same way as a probability density can be used to characterize stationary time series. As will be shown, in contrast to a probability density, the spatial density is a random process. However, it turns out that we can still obtain consistent estimates of spatial densities using nonparametric techniques, like those of kernel methods, which have proved useful in studying iid and strictly stationary time series. We outline these new procedures here and provide an asymptotic theory that characterizes their large sample properties and facilitates inference.

Once nonparametric spatial density estimates have been obtained, we can use them in similar ways to that of a probability density—to study and quantify the locational characteristics of the time series. We illustrate these ideas by looking at nonparametric estimates of the spatial location of the *ex post* real rate of interest in the United States. This exercise provides some nonparametric evidence on recent empirical findings about real interest rates and the Fisher effect. In addition, we show how to construct a new type of hazard function for nonstationary time series. Hazard rates are particularly helpful in studying financial series, as they can be used to quantify the hazards of certain interest rate and inflation rate levels, for example. The methods can also be used to study how empirical hazard rates evolve over time. Again, we illustrate the techniques in some empirical applications to the *ex post* real rate of interest series for the U.S. economy shown in Figures 1–3.

Finally, we attempt to model the real rate of interest directly as a potentially nonstationary long memory process. This involves the econometric estimation of the long memory parameter (d), without making any delimiting assumptions about the short memory components in the data generating process. The procedure we use is a new semiparametric estimator developed by the author (1999a) in recent work on fractional processes. This new estimator is called modified log periodogram (LP) regression. Kim and Phillips (1999a) have shown that, in contrast to log periodogram regression, this method has good asymptotic properties for values of d over the full region $0 < d < 2$, so that it is well suited for use with time series, like interest rates, whose memory parameters may extend into the nonstationary region where

$$d \geq \frac{1}{2}.$$

We will briefly describe the new approach in Section VI and use the method to estimate d and to provide confidence intervals, thereby enabling us to answer the question of whether the preferred model for data on the real rate of interest is stationary or nonstationary.

The paper is organized as follows. The Fisher effect and associated regression equations are discussed in Section II. The econometric ideas that underlie the spatial modeling apparatus that we introduce are laid out in Sections III and IV. Section V provides an empirical application of the methods to U.S. data over the period 1934–1997. Section VI reports our new asymptotics and empirical estimates of the long memory parameter. Section VII concludes the paper and discusses some related issues. Proofs are collected together in Section VIII with some of the new asymptotic theory that is introduced in the paper.

II

The Fisher Effect

IRVING FISHER FORMULATED THE CONCEPT of the (*ex ante*) real rate of interest (r_t^e) to provide a rate of interest that accounted for the value of loan repayments in real dollar terms. That is, a nominal interest rate of i_t will assure a real rate of r_t^e when the anticipated price change is π_t^e provided $i_t = r_t^e + \pi_t^e + r_t^e\pi_t^e$, thereby adjusting the compensation to the lender for the anticipated losses in purchasing power in the principal and the interest. The term $r_t^e\pi_t^e$ is usually ignored because it is of smaller order, so that the Fisher equation is commonly written as

$$i_t = r_t^e + \pi_t^e. \tag{1}$$

Equation (1) is sometimes made more specific by indexing the interest rate by the time period (m) of the bond to maturity and by using m-period ahead inflation expectations, leading to the alternate formulation

$$i_t^m = r_t^{e,m} + \pi_t^{e,m}. \tag{2}$$

The empirical literature surrounding Equation (1) is vast and we will not attempt to provide a review here. Fisher himself began the empirical work and considered the problems surrounding the relationship between prices and interest rates to be "of such vital importance that I have gone to much trouble and expense to have such data as could be found compiled, compared, and analyzed" (1930: p.399).

The main object of Fisher's work was "to ascertain to what extent, if at all, a change in the general price level actually affects the market rates of interest" (1930: p.399). He conducted correlational studies between inflation and interest rates with annual data primarily for the United States and the United Kingdom, concluding as follows:

> Our first correlations seemed to indicate that the relationship between P' (inflation) and i (interest rate) is either very slight or obscured by other factors. But when we make the much more reasonable supposition that price changes do not exhaust their effects in a single year but manifest their influence with diminishing intensity over long periods which vary in length with the conditions, we find a very significant relationship, especially in the period which includes the World War, when prices were subject to violent fluctuations. (1930: 423)

Since this initial work by Fisher, a substantial amount of empirical work has been conducted with data from many countries, covering different periods of time and maturities. However, little consensus seems to have emerged from these studies about the nature of the Fisher effect. In particular, there seems to be little agreement about the statistical properties of the real rate r_t^e.

Two recent studies that make significant methodological departures in studying this problem are by Mishkin (1992) and the already cited paper by Garcia and Perron (1994). These papers bring some modern nonstationary time series and regime shift methods to bear in analyzing the Fisher equation. Using residual-based co-integration tests, Mishkin finds support in the data for a "long-run" Fisher effect in which inflation and interest rates share a common stochastic trend. Observe that if π_t^m is the *m*-period inflation rate, then Equation (2) gives the following relation between the *ex post* real rate of interest ($r_t^m = i_t^m - \pi_t^m$) and the *ex ante* rate of interest $r_t^{e,m}$:

$$r_t^m = r_t^{e,m} + (\pi_t^{e,m} - \pi_t^m) = r_t^{e,m} + \varepsilon_t. \tag{3}$$

Under rational expectations, where agents or the market use all information efficiently in forecasting inflation, the forecast error $\varepsilon_t = \pi_t^{e,m} - \pi_t^m$ will be a martingale difference and can be assumed to be stationary, or integrated of order zero ($I(0)$). Under this hypothesis, the *ex post* and *ex ante* real rates differ by a stationary component and therefore have the same long-run time series properties. Thus, following Mishkin (1992), the *ex post* real rate can only be $I(1)$ if $r_t^{e,m}$ is $I(1)$. Hence, a test for a unit root in r_t^m against stationary alternatives can be interpreted as a test for a unit root in $r_t^{e,m}$ against a stationary *ex ante* real rate. Put another way, co-integration between i_t^m and π_t^m is the alternative hypothesis in a test for a unit root in the *ex post* real rate of interest. The Fisher effect then corresponds to the hypothesis that the *ex ante* real rate of interest is stationary, so that, under rational expectations and stationary forecast errors for inflation, the Fisher effect implies a stationary *ex post* real rate of interest.

In spite of their apparent simplicity, Equations (1) and (3) present a host of econometric difficulties arising from the fact that the variables r_t^e and π_t^e are unmeasured latent variables, and from the time series difficulties in modeling apparently nonstationary series like interest rates and inflation.

While Fisher (1930) analyzed the relationship between interest rates and inflation using correlational techniques, modern approaches rely on regression methods—sometimes, as in Summers (1983), in the frequency domain where low frequencies can be used to emphasize long-run properties. Depending on the properties of the real rate r_t^e, Equation (3) suggests a regression link between i_t and π_t^e. In particular, the Fisher effect asserts that the coefficient *b* should be unity in a regression of the form

$$i_t = c + b\pi_t^e + u_t$$

and the residuals u_t should be stationary. Under this hypothesis, we can write the *ex post* real rate of interest as

$$r_t = i_t - \pi_t = c + b(\pi_t^e - \pi_t) + u_t = c + w_t, \tag{4}$$

which implies stationary fluctuations about a constant level c.

In a celebrated study mentioned earlier, Fama (1975) found empirical evidence of a constant real rate of interest over the period 1953–1971. Mishkin (1981) subsequently rejected constancy in the real rate in a more extensive study covering the longer periods 1953–1979 and 1931–1952. Later investigations by Rose (1988) and Walsh (1987) found evidence in support of unit root nonstationarity in *ex post* real rates. Most recently, Garcia and Perron (1996) reanalyzed data over the period 1961–1986 using regime shift techniques and found support for a constant real rate of interest, subject to infrequent changes in the constant c. In short, the empirical evidence gives a mixed picture about the statistical properties of the real rate of interest, and it is probably fair to say that the generating mechanism for the real rate is very imperfectly understood. Although the bulk of the econometric evidence now points against the hypothesis of a pure Fisher effect in which the real rate is stationary about a constant mean, this does not rule out modified Fisher effects such as those supported in the Garcia Perron study.

We now propose to take a very different approach to studying these data. The essence of the new approach is descriptive, but the asymptotic theory that we have developed for the quantities involved enables us to use them in an inferential framework as well. This helps us to corroborate and assess earlier empirical findings.

III

Spatial Densities for Nonstationary Series

Our proposal is to study the spatial characteristics of a time series rather than focus on their temporal dependence properties, as one would normally do in a stationary time series analysis. The starting point is to assume that, when appropriately normalized and transformed into a random function on the interval [0, 1], the time series trajectories converge weakly to those of a continuous stochastic process on the same interval. Such an assumption applies under a very wide variety of possible conditions, and it seems a very weak requirement if one is to make any headway in the development of asymptotic methods. Accordingly, we may suppose that the limit process, $M(r)$, say, of the normalized series is a continuous semi-martingale (see, e.g., Protter 1990). This requirement would then include the huge class of time series for which functional central limit theorems are known to apply, leading, for example, to Brownian motions and diffusion processes as special cases (see, e.g., Phillips and Solo 1992). While this class of time series is substantial, one case that is excluded by the semi-martingale requirement is time series that upon normalization tend to fractional processes like fractional Brownian motion (e.g., Mandlebrot and van Ness 1968; Taqqu 1975). This case does seem to be important in applications of our ideas to non-stationary series, because there is increasing evidence that economic time series are well modeled by long memory processes with fractional Brownian motion limits; for some recent macroeconomic time series evidence, see Gil-Alana and Robinson (1997) and Kim and Phillips (1999a). Fortunately, it seems that it will be possible to include fractional processes within our theory and, although this is not done here, some discussion and references are provided later (see the paragraph following Equation (12)).

For a semi-martingale $M(r)$ it is known that there exists an increasing stochastic process[2] (increasing in the argument r, that is) called the local time of M at s and denoted $L_M(r, s)$ that represents the amount of time that the limit process spends in the spatial vicinity of the point s. The local time process is defined as

$$L_M(r, s) = \lim_{\varepsilon \to 0} \frac{1}{2\varepsilon} \int_0^r 1(|M(t) - s| < \varepsilon) d[M]_t, \tag{5}$$

where $[M]_t$ is the quadratic variation process of M. Notice that this definition of "time spent in the vicinity of s" is expressed in units of variation, as measured by $d[M]_t$. In effect, $L_M(r, s)$ measures the contribution to the quadratic variation $[M]_r$ over the interval $[0, r]$ that comes from variation in $M(t)$ around the level s.

It turns out that we can also write down an inverse relation of the form

$$[M]_t = \int_{-\infty}^{\infty} L_M(t, s)ds, \tag{6}$$

which gives a decomposition of the quadratic variation into contributions to the conditional variance that come from fluctuations in the process that occur in the neighborhood of different spatial points $s \in [-\infty, \infty]$. In a sense, we can think of Equation (6) as the spatial equivalent for a continuous nonstationary random process of the decomposition of the variation of a stationary time series into contributions from different frequencies, that is,

$$\sigma^2 = \int_{-\pi}^{\pi} f_{xx}(\lambda)d\lambda,$$

where $f_x(\lambda)$ is the spectral density of X_t and $\sigma^2 = \text{var } X_t$. In this formula, λ is a continuous variable representing the frequency of the oscillations into which the time series variation is being decomposed. However, in Equation (6), the variable s represents spatial points in the real line, where the process spends some time. Fluctuations in the process around the point s, which can occur at various times in the time interval $[0, t]$, then contribute to the density $L_M(t, s)$ of the process at this spatial point.

Equation (6) is particularly interesting in the special case where $M(r)$ is the Brownian motion $B(r)$ with variance ω^2. Here, the parameter ω^2 arises as the long-run variance of the shocks which drive the unit root process that converges weakly to $B(r)$. In this case, we have

$$\omega^2 = \int_{-\infty}^{\infty} L_B(1, s)ds,$$

giving a decomposition of the long-run variance ω^2 into components that reflect the density of the fluctuations in the process around all spatial points $s \in (-\infty, \infty)$.

The local time process $L_M(r, s)$ is known to satisfy the following equation

$$|M(r) - s| = |M(0) - s| + \int_0^r \text{sgn}(M(t) - s)dM(t) + L_M(r, s), \tag{7}$$

where sgn(x) = 1, −1 for $x > 0$, $x \leq 0$. In fact, the process $L_M(r, s)$ is sometimes defined in this manner; for example, see Revuz and Yor (1994). Equation (7), gives a development of the function $|M(r) - s|$ is about its value at $r = 0$ and thereby provides a mechanism of generalizing the Ito stochastic calculus of functions that are continuously differentiable to the second order ($\mathbb{C}_2$ functions) to functions that are not everywhere differentiable and smooth, and, in particular, to convex functions, which we will show below. These extensions look to be particularly valuable in theoretical models where convex functions play a big role, but have not to my knowledge been used yet in economic analysis.

As is well known (e.g., Protter 1990: 74), if $f \in \mathbb{C}_2$ we have the Ito formula for continuous semi-martingales given by

$$f(M(r)) = f(M(0)) + \int_0^r f'(M(t))dM(t) + \frac{1}{2}\int_0^r f''(M(t))d[M]_t. \quad (8)$$

On the other hand, when f is convex we have, based on Equation (7),

$$f(M(r)) = f(M(0)) + \int_0^r f'_-(M(t))dM(t) + \frac{1}{2}\int_{-\infty}^{\infty} f''_g(p)L_M(r, p)dp, \quad (9)$$

where f'_- is the left derivative of f and f''_g is the second derivative of f in the generalized function sense. When $f \in \mathbb{C}_2$ we have $f'_-(M(t)) = f'(M(t))$, and $f''_g(p) = f''(p)$, the second derivative in the usual sense, and the occupation time formula (e.g., Revuz and Yor 1991: 209) gives

$$\frac{1}{2}\int_{-\infty}^{\infty} f''(p)L_M(r, p)dp = \frac{1}{2}\int_0^r f''(M(t))d[M]_t, \quad (10)$$

so that Equation (9) reduces to Equation (8) in this special case.

Observe that Equation (10) shows the sense in which $L_M(r, p)$ is a spatial density for the process $M(r)$, recording the amount of time (measured in units of the quadratic variation $[M]_t$) that the process has spent in the immediate vicinity of p over the time interval $t \in [0, r]$.

We now propose to use these concepts in studying the spatial properties of time series like interest rates and inflation. Our first task is to estimate the local time process $L_M(r, p)$ for a particular time series. Just as the spectral density of a stationary time series is estimated by nonparametric methods, the local time $L_M(r, p)$ can be estimated in a nonparametric manner as follows. Let X_t be a time series that satisfies a functional law of the form

$$\frac{1}{n^{\alpha}} X_{[nr]} \Rightarrow M(r), \tag{11}$$

where $M(r)$ is a continuous semi-martingale for $r \in [0, 1]$. For instance, when X_t is an integrated process of order 1, standard functional central limit theorems (e.g., Phillips and Solo 1992) lead to Equation (11) with

$$\alpha = \frac{1}{2} \text{ and } M(r) = B(r),$$

a Brownian motion with variance

$$\omega^2 = 2\pi f_{\Delta x}(0).$$

When X_t is near integrated, so that the quasi differences

$$\Delta_c X_t = X_t - \left(1 + \frac{c}{n}\right) X_{t-1}$$

are stationary with positive spectral density at the origin, then

$$\alpha = \frac{1}{2} \text{ and } M(r) = J_c(r),$$

a linear diffusion process (e.g., Phillips 1987). On the other hand, when X_t is a fractionally integrated process whose memory parameter

$$d \in \left(\frac{1}{2}, 1\right],$$

whose initialization is at $t = 0$, and for which the differenced process $(1 - L)^d X_t = u_t$ is stationary with positive spectrum $\omega^2 > 0$ at the origin, then we have the following functional law (cf. Akonom and Gourieroux 1987)

$$\frac{1}{n^{d-\frac{1}{2}}} X_{[nr]} \Rightarrow B_{d-1}(r) = \frac{\omega}{\Gamma(d)} \int_0^r (r-s)^{d-1} dW(s),$$

where $B_{d-1}(r)$ is a fractional Brownian motion. In this case, the limit process $M(r) = B_{d-1}(r)$ is not a semi-martingale and, indeed, the process B_{d-1} actually has infinite quadratic variation. Hence, in place of Equation (5), where quadratic variation is being distributed spatially, it is more helpful to define local time according to

$$\bar{L}_M(r, s) = \lim_{\varepsilon \to 0} \frac{1}{2\varepsilon} \int_0^r 1(|M(t) - s| < \varepsilon) dt, \tag{12}$$

which measures the amount of time in chronological units that M_t spends in the vicinity of s over the interval $[0, r]$. Accordingly, $\bar{L}_M(r, s)$ is called the chronological local time of M at s over $[0, r]$ (cf Phillips and Park 1998). Local time for the fractional process B_{d-1} can be defined using Equation (12), and Tyurin and Phillips (1999) give a development of the theory of local time using this approach and discuss its empirical estimation.

These examples seem to cover most cases of empirical interest that arise in the present literature on nonstationary economic time series. In the development that follows we will assume we are working with an integrated process X_t for which

$$n^{-\frac{1}{2}} X_{[nr]} \Rightarrow B(r).$$

Or, if we want to allow for distant initial conditions (at time $-[n\kappa]$ for some $\kappa \geq 0$) in the origination of X_t then we can use the limit

$$n^{-\frac{1}{2}} X_{[nr]} \Rightarrow B(r) + B_0(\kappa),$$

where B and B_0 are independent Brownian motions, with the process B_0 extending in a reverse (negative) direction reflecting the effect of distant initial conditions at some fraction κ of the sample size n. This will cover a wide class of interesting practical cases. Extensions of the theory to the more general case of Equation (11) are also possible but are more difficult and will call upon strong approximation versions of Equation (11) that, at least to the author's present knowledge, do not seem to be available in the probability literature as yet for a general class of processes (although a strong approximation for diffusion processes is given in Phillips 1998). A complete development of the asymptotic theory in our case to cover situations as general as Equation (11) is beyond the scope of the present paper. Extensions to the important fractional Brownian motion case are considered by Tyurin and Phillips (1999).

A natural candidate for estimating the local time of the limit process of

$$n^{-\frac{1}{2}} X_{[nr]}$$

at s is the scaled kernel estimate

$$\frac{\hat{\omega}^2}{nh_n}\sum_{t=1}^{n}K\left(\frac{s-X_t}{h_n}\right)=\frac{\hat{\omega}^2}{nh_n}\sum_{t=1}^{n}K\left(c_n\left\{\frac{s}{\sqrt{n}}-\frac{X_t}{\sqrt{n}}\right\}\right),\quad c_n=\frac{\sqrt{n}}{h_n},\qquad (13)$$

where h_n is a bandwidth parameter, $K(\cdot)$ is a symmetric kernel function, and $\hat{\omega}^2$ is a consistent estimate of $\omega^2 = 2\pi f_{\Delta x}(0)$. Upon restandardization of this estimate we have the following extension of a result obtained recently in Phillips and Park (1998).

A. Theorem

Suppose $\hat{\omega}^2 \to_p \omega^2 = 2\pi f_{\Delta x}(0)$. *If* $s = s_0 + \sqrt{n}\,a$, *with* s_0 *and* a *fixed, and if assumptions VIII.A–VIII.D in the Appendix hold, then as* $n \to \infty$

$$\hat{L}_B\left(r,\frac{s}{\sqrt{n}}\right)=\frac{\hat{\omega}^2}{\sqrt{n}h_n}\sum_{t=1}^{[nr]}K\left(\frac{s-X_t}{h_n}\right)\to_p L_B(r,a-B_0(\kappa)).\qquad (14)$$

The definition of

$$\hat{L}_B\left(r,n^{-\frac{1}{2}}s\right)$$

involves scaling the conventional kernel estimator given in Equation (13) by $\sqrt{n}$. The reason for this restandardization is that in the nonstationary case the process X_t wanders away from the location s at the rate $\sqrt{n}$ and, for such departures from s, $K(h_n^{-1}(s - X_t))$ is negligibly small. In effect, the stochastic trend property of X_t reduces the order of magnitude of the kernel estimate compared with the stationary case.

Note that the estimate

$$\hat{L}_B\left(r,n^{-\frac{1}{2}}s\right)$$

evaluates the local time at a spatial point

$$n^{-\frac{1}{2}}s$$

that is affected by the rate of convergence of

$$n^{-\frac{1}{2}}X_{[nr]}$$

to its Brownian motion limit process. Hence, if s is fixed and initial conditions are $O_p(1)$, i.e., $\kappa = 0$ as $n \to \infty$, then the estimate

$$\hat{L}_B\left(r,n^{-\frac{1}{2}}s\right)$$

is consistent for the local time of the limit process at the origin, that is, $L_B(r, 0)$. When $\kappa > 0$, the random initialization shifts the spatial point of evaluation of the local time estimate so that it is centered around $B_0(\kappa)$. So, initial conditions generally play a role in the spatial density of the process, as we might well expect for a nonstationary series.

Our next step is to construct confidence regions for the density estimate

$$\hat{L}_B\left(r, n^{-\frac{1}{2}}s\right).$$

This can be done using the limiting distribution theory for

$$\hat{L}_B\left(r, n^{-\frac{1}{2}}s\right)$$

given in Theorem III.B below. The limit distribution turns out to be mixed normal (denoted *MN* in what follows) with a mixing variate that is proportional to the spatial density itself. This limit theory justifies the construction of confidence intervals in the usual manner.

B. Theorem

If $s = s_0 + \sqrt{n}a$, *with* s_0 *and* a *fixed, if assumptions VIII.A–VIII.D in the Appendix hold, and if* $\sqrt{c_n}(\hat{\omega}^2 - \omega^2) = o_p(1)$ *where* $c_n = h_n^{-1}\sqrt{n}$, *then as* $n \to \infty$

$$\sqrt{c_n}\left[\hat{L}_B\left(r, n^{-\frac{1}{2}}s\right) - L_B(r, a - B_0(\kappa))\right]$$

$$\Rightarrow 2\int_{-\infty}^{\infty} K(p)Q(L_B(r, a - B_0(\kappa)), p)dp$$

$$\equiv MN(0, 8K_2L_B(r, a - B_0(\kappa))),$$

where $Q(a, b)$ *is a standard Brownian sheet,* $W(p)$ *is a standard Brownian motion, and*

$$K_2 = \int_0^{\infty}\int_0^{\infty} K(p)(p \wedge t)K(t)dpdt.$$

This result enables us to construct confidence intervals for $L_B(r, a - B_0(\kappa))$ for each spatial point. Thus,

$$\hat{L}_B\left(r, n^{-\frac{1}{2}}s\right) \pm 1.96\left(\frac{8K_2\hat{L}_B\left(r, n^{-\frac{1}{2}}s\right)}{c_n}\right)^{\frac{1}{2}}$$

is a 95% confidence interval for $L_B(r, a - B_0(\kappa))$. When $K(\cdot)$ is a normal kernel, some calculations show that K_2 takes the value

$$K_2 = \pi^{-\frac{1}{2}}\left(2^{\frac{1}{2}} - 1\right).$$

Note that we are measuring spatial departures from the origin in units of $\sqrt{n}$ in the limit. So, if we want a confidence interval for the spatial density of the process at a point like $\sqrt{n}\,a^0$, we set $s = \sqrt{n}\,a^0 + X_0$ and compute

$$\hat{L}_B\left(r, a^0 + n^{-\frac{1}{2}}X_0\right) \pm 1.96\left(\frac{8K_2\hat{L}_B\left(r, a^0 + n^{-\frac{1}{2}}X_0\right)}{c_n}\right)^{\frac{1}{2}}. \tag{15}$$

It is interesting to compare local time confidence intervals like Equation (15) above with the confidence intervals for a probability density from kernel estimates of a probability density. By traditional theory here (e.g., Silverman 1986) we have the following 95% confidence interval for a density $f(x)$,

$$\hat{f}(x) \pm 1.96\left(\frac{k_2\hat{f}(x)}{nh}\right)^{\frac{1}{2}} \tag{16}$$

where

$$k_2 = \int_{-\infty}^{\infty} K(r)^2 dr. \tag{17}$$

The differences between Equations (15) and (16) involve: (1) the scale factors k_2 and $8K_2$, where the difference is due to the temporal dependence in the trajectory of X_t (so that the covariance kernel enters the definition of K_2) and definitional differences between local time and a probability density; and (2) the rate of convergence $-\sqrt{c_n}$ in the case of the spatial density, compared with $\sqrt{nh}$ in the case of the probability density. In other respects, Equation (15) simply extends our existing theory of nonparametric density estimation to spatial density estimation for stochastic processes.

IV

Hazard Rates for Nonstationary Time Series

ONE ADVANTAGE OF A NONPARAMETRIC TREATMENT of spatial density is that we can define interesting functionals derived from the density that help us to shed light on the nature of variation in the data. While there are many obvious notions that arise in this way, one that we will pay attention to here is the idea of a spatial hazard function. We define the spatial hazard function $H_M(t, a)$ associated with a given spatial density $L_M(t, s)$ as follows:

$$H_M(t, a) = \frac{L_M(t, a)}{\int_a^{\infty} L_M(t, s)ds}. \tag{18}$$

The form of Equation (18) is analogous to that of the hazard rate $\theta(x)$ associated with a probability density $f(x)$ as

$$\theta(x) = \frac{f(x)}{\int_x^{\infty} f(s)ds} = \frac{f(x)}{1 - F(x)} = \frac{f(x)}{\bar{F}(x)},$$

where $F(x)$ is the *cdf* of the distribution and $\bar{F}(x) = 1 - F(x)$ is the survivor function. Such conventional hazard rates are now extensively used in empirical econometric work to help model and understand phenomena like unemployment duration and quits in the labor market and have widespread use in other fields, such as the statistical analysis of medical phenomena relating to the contraction of diseases.

How do we interpret such hazard rates in the case of nonstationary time series? Suppose the time series under study X_t is inflation and $M(r)$ is the weak limit process of $n^{-\alpha}X_{[nr]}$, with local time $L_M(r, s)$. The spatial hazard

$$H_M\left(t, a = \frac{s}{n^{\alpha}}\right)$$

measures the conditional risk over the period $[0, t]$ (which is expressed in standardized units of fractions of the overall sample) of an inflation rate of s, given that inflation is at least as great as s. We can then study the form of this hazard as a function of the inflation rate s, just as we might look at unemployment duration in the conventional hazard analysis of independent data. Thus, we can see whether the hazard declines, increases, or stays constant as we increase s. We can also look at the hazard as a function of the length of the time interval t and examine what happens to the hazard rate as the time period evolves and new data are introduced. So, we can see whether the hazard rate of a certain rate of inflation rises or falls over time. Of course, we might ultimately contemplate modeling such hazard rates through the use of covariates or policy interventions. These possibilities exploit the dual-argument property of the spatial density $L_M(r, s)$ and hazard $H_M(t, a)$ so that it becomes possible to analyze time series effects on hazard rates. Like $L_M(r, s)$, the function $H_M(t, a)$ is a random process in its two arguments, but unlike conventional hazard rates which depend on the unknown but estimable probability distribution of the data, the hazard $H_M(t, a)$ is an unknown but estimable path dependent stochastic process.

Now take the case where $M(r)$ is Brownian motion $B(r)$. The spatial hazard function $H_B(t, a)$ is empirically estimable using the nonparametric spatial density estimate

$$\hat{L}_B\left(t, \frac{s}{\sqrt{n}}\right)$$

discussed in the last section of the paper. For $s = s_0 + \sqrt{n}\dot{a}$, we construct the estimator

$$\hat{H}_B(t, a) = \frac{\hat{L}_B(t, a)}{\int_a^\infty \hat{L}_B\left(t, \frac{p}{\sqrt{n}}\right)\frac{dp}{\sqrt{n}}}.$$

This estimator is consistent for $H_M(t, a)$ as the following theorem shows, where the result is given in the case of $\sqrt{n}$ convergence to a Brownian motion limit process.

A. Theorem

Suppose $\hat{\omega}^2 \to_p \omega^2 = 2\pi f_{\Delta x}(0)$. If $s = s_0 + \sqrt{n}a$, with s_0 and a fixed, and if Assumptions VIII.A–VIII.D in the Appendix hold, then as $n \to \infty$

$$\hat{H}_B\left(t, \frac{s}{\sqrt{n}}\right) = \frac{\hat{L}_B\left(t, \frac{s}{\sqrt{n}}\right)}{\int_{\frac{s}{\sqrt{n}}}^\infty \hat{L}_B\left(t, \frac{p}{\sqrt{n}}\right)\frac{dp}{\sqrt{n}}} \to_p H_B(t, a - B_0(\kappa))$$

where

$$\hat{L}_B\left(r, \frac{s}{\sqrt{n}}\right) = \frac{\hat{\omega}^2}{\sqrt{n}h_n} \sum_{t=1}^{[nr]} K\left(\frac{s - X_t}{h_n}\right).$$

As in the case of the spatial density, when the limit process is reached at a $\sqrt{n}$ rate of convergence, we measure spatial departures from the origin in units of $\sqrt{n}$. So, if we want to estimate the hazard of the process at a point like a^0, we set $s = \sqrt{n}a^0 + X_0$ and compute

$$\hat{H}_B\left(t, a^0 + \frac{X_0}{\sqrt{n}}\right).$$

The function $F_M(t, a) = \int_a^{\infty} L_M(t, s)ds$ can be called the survivor function corresponding to $L_M(t, s)$, and is analogous to the survivor function $\bar{F}(a) = \int_a^{\infty} f(s)ds$ of a probability density f. Since we are using kernel estimates of $L_M(t, s)$ we can estimate $F_M(t, a)$ using

$$\begin{aligned}\hat{F}_M\left(t, \frac{s}{\sqrt{n}}\right) &= \int_{\frac{s}{\sqrt{n}}}^{\infty} \hat{L}_M\left(t, \frac{p}{\sqrt{n}}\right)\frac{dp}{\sqrt{n}} \\ &= \frac{\hat{\omega}^2}{\sqrt{n}} \sum_{t=1}^{[nr]} \overline{\mathbb{K}}\left(\frac{s - X_t}{h_n}\right)\end{aligned}$$

where

$$\mathbb{K}(b) = \int_{-\infty}^{b} \mathbb{K}(x)dx, \quad \overline{\mathbb{K}}(b) = 1 - \mathbb{K}(b).$$

For most kernels, although not the Gaussian, $\overline{\mathbb{K}}(b)$ is available in closed form, simplifying calculations for the hazard and survivor functions. For example, if K is the Epanechnikov kernel, we have

$$K(s) = \begin{cases} \dfrac{3}{4\sqrt{5}}\left(1 - \dfrac{s^2}{\sqrt{5}}\right) & -\sqrt{5} \le s \le \sqrt{5} \\ 0 & \text{otherwise} \end{cases},$$

and

$$\mathbb{K}(s) = \begin{cases} 0 & s < -\sqrt{5} \\ \dfrac{3}{4\sqrt{5}}(s + \sqrt{5}) - \dfrac{1}{45^{\frac{3}{2}}}\left(s^3 + 5^{\frac{3}{2}}\right) & -\sqrt{5} \le s \le \sqrt{5}. \\ 1 & s > \sqrt{5} \end{cases}$$

An asymptotic theory for the estimated hazard function

$$\hat{H}_B\left(t, \frac{s}{\sqrt{n}}\right)$$

is given in the following theorem.

B. Theorem

If $s = s_0 + \sqrt{n}\,a$, with s_0 and a fixed, if Assumptions VIII.A–VIII.D in the Appendix hold with $h_n \to 0$, and if $\sqrt{c_n}(\hat{\omega}^2 - \omega^2) = o_p(1)$ where $c_n = h_n^{-1}\sqrt{n}$, then as $n \to \infty$

$$\sqrt{c_n}\left[\hat{H}_B\left(r, n^{-\frac{1}{2}}s\right) - H_B(r, a - B_0(\kappa))\right]$$

$$\Rightarrow 2\int_{-\infty}^{\infty} K(p)Q\left(\frac{L_B(r, a - B_0(\kappa))}{\left(\int_{a-B_0(\kappa)}^{\infty} L_M(r, s)ds\right)^2}, p\right)dp$$

$$\equiv MN\left(0, 8K_2\frac{H_B(r, a - B_0(\kappa))^2}{L_B(r, a - B_0(\kappa))}\right),$$

where $Q(a, b)$ is a standard Brownian sheet.

This result delivers an asymptotic standard error for the hazard

$$\hat{H}_B\left(r, n^{-\frac{1}{2}}s\right),$$

viz.

$$\left(\frac{8K_2\hat{H}_B\left(r, n^{-\frac{1}{2}}s\right)^2}{c_n\hat{L}_B\left(r, n^{-\frac{1}{2}}s\right)}\right)^{\frac{1}{2}},$$

which can be used to assess significance of the hazard estimates in practical applications. Interestingly, this formula is analogous to that obtained in traditional hazard analysis for a probability density, which takes the well-known form (cf. Silverman 1986: 148)

$$\left(\frac{k_2\theta(x)^2}{nhf(s)}\right)^{\frac{1}{2}}.$$

The differences arise only from differences in the rate of convergence to the spatial density and the probability density and the scale constants $8K_2$ and k_2.

V

The Empirical Density of Real Interest Rates

We now illustrate the use of these concepts in analyzing the empirical spatial density of the real rate of interest. Hopefully, this will help to shed some new light on the nature of the Fisher effect and provide corroborative evidence for other studies that use conventional econometric methods.

We start with the period 1961–1985 studied by Garcia and Perron (1994). Figure 4 gives the spatial density estimate[3] for the *ex post* real rate of interest shown in Figure 1. The estimated spatial density shows a dominant mode around the level 1.5% and evidence for four minor modes around −4%, −2%, 4%, and 9%. Only the modes at 1.5% and 9% appear to be statistically significant. These results provide partial

Figure 4

Spatial density of *ex post* real rate: 1961–1985.

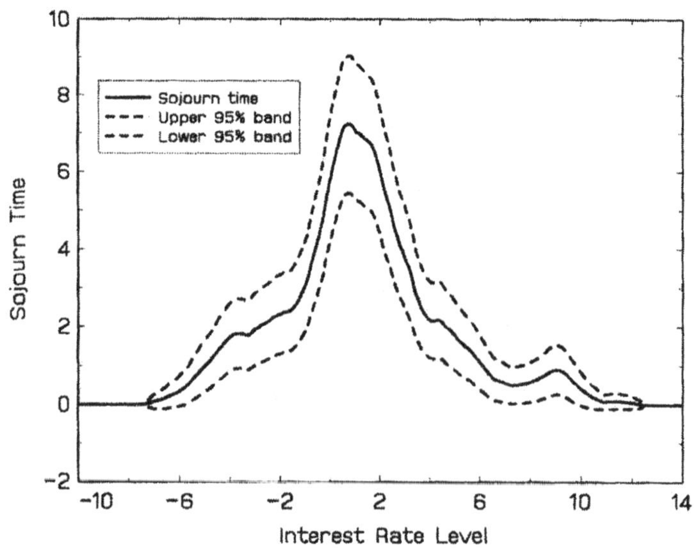

support for Garcia and Perron's conclusion in favor of the hypothesis that the real rate of interest over 1961–1985 fluctuated about three constant levels around −2%, 1.5%, and 4%. However, our nonparametric analysis indicates that there are also secondary modes around −4% and 9% and that these modes, especially the latter, appear to be more significant than those around −2% and 4%, which were the only secondary levels identified in the Garcia-Perron switching regimes approach. The significant mode around 9% seems to have been missed by Garcia and Perron.

The estimated hazard rates for the same period of data are shown in Figure 5. The graph shows that there are two peak levels of hazard for the real rate—levels around 1.5% to 3% and 4.5% to 6%—and a further peak around 9%. The sharply rising hazard at higher levels is not significant and can be ignored. Roughly speaking, these results tell us that, if we are to have high real rates of interest, the risk rises with the real rate to a plateau when rates are around 1.5% to 3%, tapers off, and then rises again to a plateau in the 4.5% to 6% region before falling off again and rising to a further peak around 9%. Note

Figure 5

Hazard function for *ex post* real rate: 1961–1985.

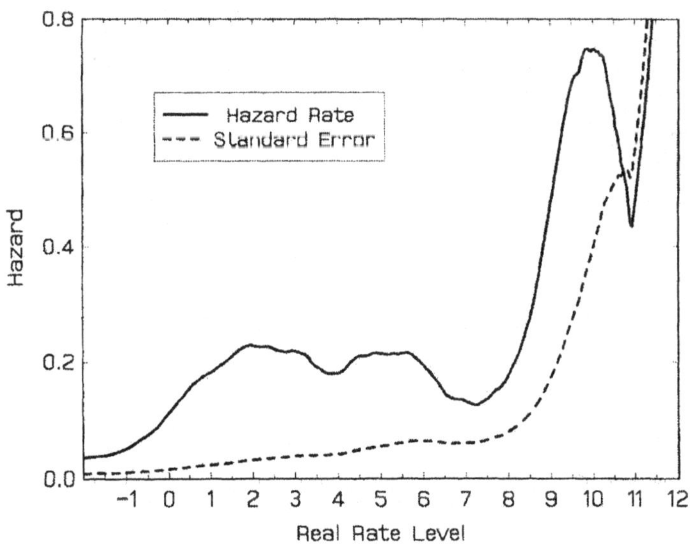

that the very high peak at 9% is not significant, as the standard error is rising quickly at this point. Moreover, the peak at 9% indicates that if the real rate is to be as high as this, then it is very likely that it will be in the region of 9%, given the observed data over the period 1961–1985.

The spatial density of the real rate changes as we add data for the period through to 1997 and back to 1934. First, consider the effect of the data through to 1997. As is apparent in Figure 6, there are now only three modes: around –4%, 1.5%, and 9% in the spatial density. Only the modes around 1.5% and 9% appear significant, as before. The data over 1985–1997 has smoothed out the spatial density in the region between 2% to 6% and there is no evidence of modes around 4% and –2%, at least for the bandwidth choice

$$h_n = n^{-\frac{1}{5}}$$

that we are using here. Next, as we add data for the period back to 1934, we see from Figure 8 that modes around –5% and –2% have

Figure 6

Spatial density of *ex post* real rate: 1961–1997.

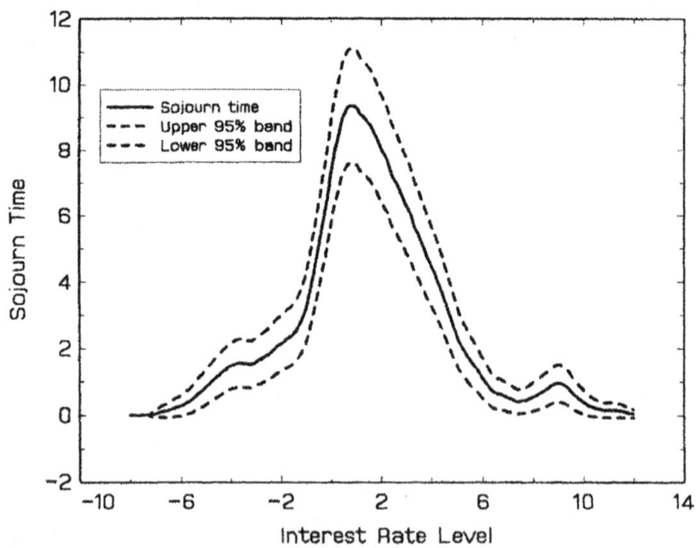

Figure 7

Hazard function for *ex post* real rate: 1961–1997.

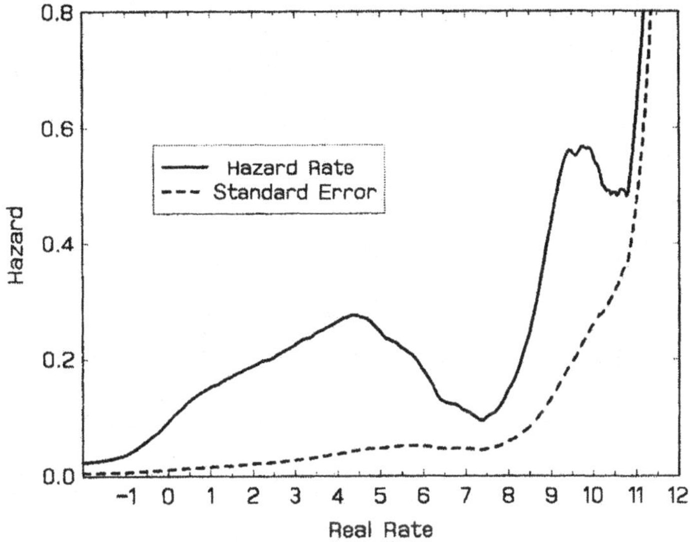

reappeared, although there is no evidence of a mode around 4%. At least for this data set, the spatial density computed over the full period 1934–1997 indicates that the real interest rate has regions of sojourn time around –5%, –2%, and 9% and the dominant mode is around 1.5%.

Hazard rates over the period 1961–1997 are shown in Figure 7 and in Figure 9 for 1934–1997. In both cases, there are now only two peaks in the hazard function, around 3% to 4% and 9%. Both of these appear to be more significant than they are for the shorter data set. Looking at Figure 9, it seems clear that the substantial region of hazard for positive real rates is in the 1% to 6% zone, and for high rates, a zone around 9%.

VI

Is the Real Rate Nonstationary?

TESTS FOR NONSTATIONARITY in the real rate of interest have in the past focused on comparing unit root nonstationarity with stationary

Figure 8

Spatial density of real rate: 1934–1997.

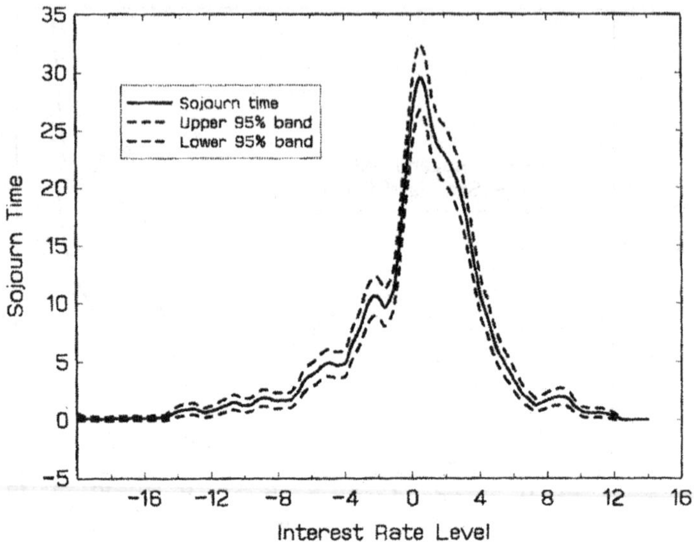

alternatives. We now consider a broader range of alternatives accommodated by allowing for fractional integration.

Our approach is semi-parametric, so that we can retain as much generality as possible regarding the generating mechanism for the real rate of interest r_t. In particular, we consider a model for the *ex post* real rate of the form

$$(1 - L)^d r_t = u_t, \tag{19}$$

where u_t is a zero mean stationary process with spectral density $f_{uu}(\lambda)$ and is assumed to satisfy Assumption VIII.A in the Appendix. By virtue of Equation (19), the spectrum of r_t has the following asymptotic form in the vicinity of the origin

$$f_{rr}(\lambda) \sim \frac{f_{uu}(0)}{\lambda^{2d}}, \lambda \sim 0. \tag{20}$$

Several semi-parametric estimation procedures for d are available, and a brief review of some of the procedures is given in Robinson

Figure 9

Hazard function for real rate: 1934–1997.

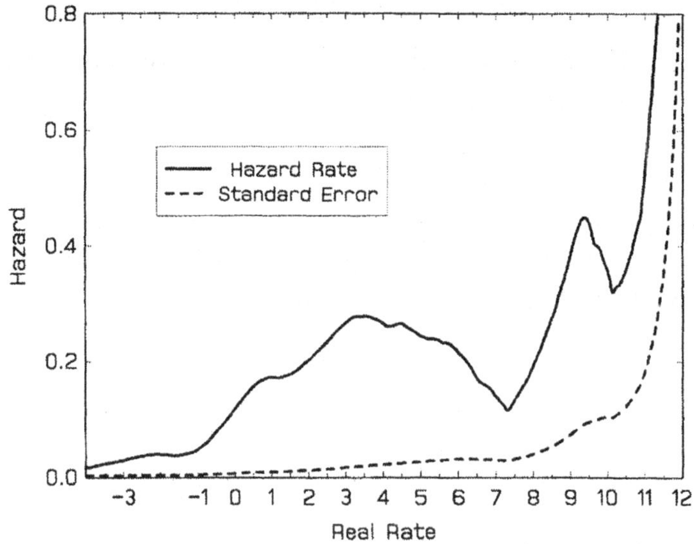

(1995). We propose to use the modified log periodogram estimator suggested recently in Phillips (1999a). This estimator is, like log periodogram regression, simple to use, as it employs only least squares techniques. Kim and Phillips (1999a) have shown that the estimator has good asymptotic properties that make it suitable for inference in possibly nonstationary regions of d and have validated the construction of confidence intervals that extend into the nonstationary region. It therefore seems well suited to the study of interest-rate data.

Log periodogram (LP) regression involves the least squares regression (over $s = 1, \ldots, m$ for some $m < n$ with

$$\frac{1}{m} + \frac{m}{n} \to 0$$

as $n \to \infty$)

$$\ln(I_r(\lambda_s)) = c^* - d^* \ln|1 - e^{i\lambda_s}|^2 + \text{error},$$

where $I_r(\lambda_s) = |w_r(\lambda_s)|^2$ is the periodogram and $w_r(\lambda_s)$ is the discrete Fourier transform of r_t, both evaluated at the fundamental frequencies

$$\lambda_s = \frac{2\pi s}{n} \text{ for } s = 1, \ldots, m.$$

Modified LP regression involves the similar linear regression

$$\ln(I_v(\lambda_s)) = \hat{c} - \hat{d}\ln|1 - e^{i\lambda_s}|^2 + \text{error}, \tag{21}$$

in which the periodogram ordinates, $I_r(\lambda_s)$, are replaced by the modified periodogram ordinates $I_v(\lambda_s) = |v_x(\lambda_s)|^2$, where

$$v_x(\lambda_s) = w_r(\lambda_s) + \frac{e^{i\lambda_s}}{1 - e^{i\lambda_s}} \frac{r_n}{\sqrt{2\pi n}}. \tag{22}$$

This procedure was suggested in Phillips (1999a), and Kim and Phillips (1999a) show that the modified LP estimator $\hat{d}$ is consistent for all $d \in (0, 2)$ and has the following limit theory

$$\sqrt{m}\left(\hat{d} - d\right) \xrightarrow{d} N\left(0, \frac{\pi^2}{24}\right) \tag{23}$$

for

$$d \in \left(\frac{1}{2}, 2\right).$$

Thus, the limit theory for $\hat{d}$ is the same as that of the conventional LP estimator d^* in the stationary case (Robinson 1995 and Hurvich; Deo, and Brodsky 1998). By contrast, the usual log periodogram estimator d^* has a mixed normal limit theory when $d = 1$, as shown in Phillips (1999b) and is inconsistent when $d > 1$ (Kim and Phillips 1999b). Thus, the modified regression in Equation (21) is especially useful in the nonstationary case when

$$d > \frac{1}{2}$$

and the limit theory makes possible statistical testing and the construction of confidence intervals for d that extend into the nonstationary case.

With this methodology and using

$$m = n^{\frac{3}{4}}$$

frequency ordinates, we found semi-parametric estimates of d in Equation (19) for the *ex post* real rate for the three time periods 1961–1985, 1961–1997, and 1934–1997. The results are given in Table 1.

For each period the estimates of d are greater than 0.5 and indi-

Table 1

Empirical Estimates of *d*: *Ex Post* Real Rate

Period	$\hat{d}$	$s_{\hat{d}}$	95% Confidence Interval
1961–1985	0.6353	0.0761	[0.486,0.784]
1961–1997	0.5538	0.0654	[0.426,0.682]
1934–1997	0.5159	0.0532	[0.412,0.620]

cate that the *ex post* real rate of interest is nonstationary. Moreover, the estimates of *d* are all quite close, which is interesting and perhaps surprising given that the sample path of r_t varies substantially over the full time period and that other approaches require multiple regime shifts to model this data even over shorter periods. The confidence intervals show that unit root nonstationarity and short memory are both clearly rejected. However, in every case the confidence intervals for *d* include some long memory stationary alternatives with *d* less than 0.5 but greater than 0.4.

Thus, our estimates of *d* provide empirical evidence that supports the conclusion of Rose (1988) and Walsh (1987) that the real rate is nonstationary. But we reject unit root nonstationarity and the estimates of *d* are in every case not significantly greater than 0.5, so there is also some support from our estimates for the hypothesis that the real rate is marginally stationary but with very long memory.

Figures 10–12 show the effect of *d*-differencing the real rate of interest using the relevant estimates $\hat{d}$ for each of the subperiods. The figures also display the mean value of the residual series $\hat{u}_t = (1 - L)^{\hat{d}} r_t$ for each period. As is apparent from the figures, in each case $\hat{u}_t$ appears to be stationary with short memory.

Finally, Figure 13 gives spatial density estimates for the differenced series $\hat{u}_t = (1 - L)^{\hat{d}} r_t$ calculated for each subperiod. The densities are calculated here by normalizing the spatial densities in the same way for each subperiod—that is, by

$$\frac{1}{nh}$$

in place of

$$\frac{\hat{\omega}^2}{\sqrt{n}h}$$

Figure 10

$(1 - L)^{\hat{d}} r_t$ for 1934–1997.

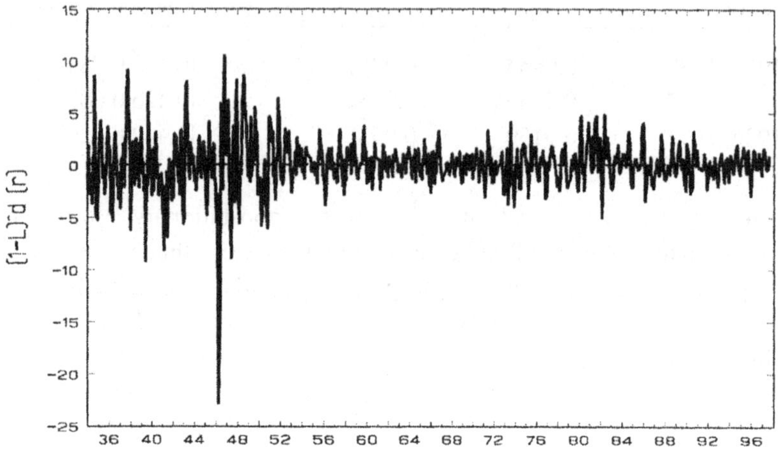

Figure 11

$(1 - L)^{\hat{d}} r_t$ for 1961–1985.

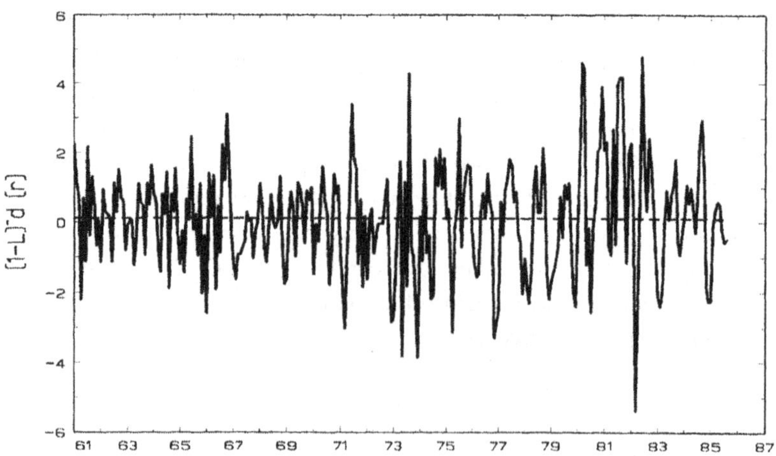

Figure 12

$(1 - L)^{\hat{d}} r_t$ for 1961–1997.

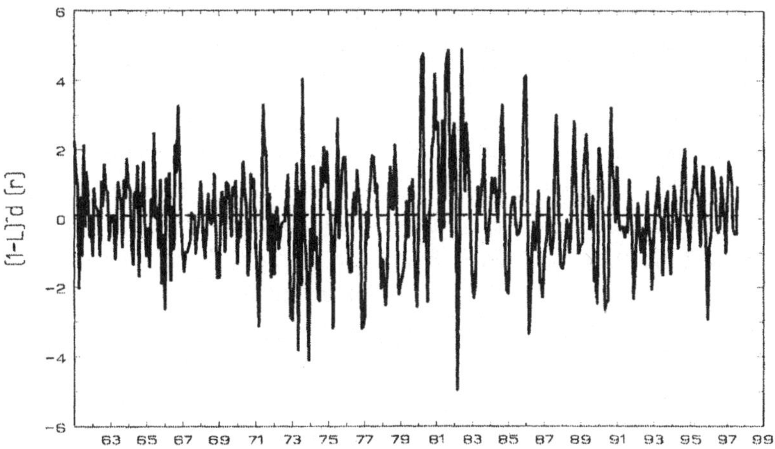

Figure 13

Densities of $(1 - L)^{\hat{d}} r_t$.

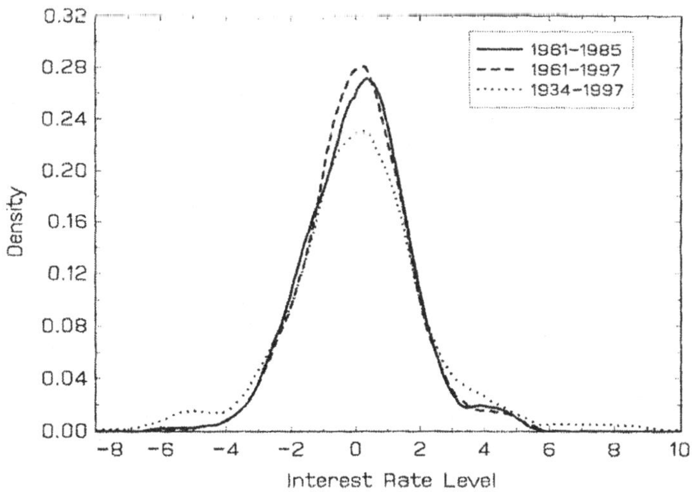

in Equation (14)—so that they are directly comparable and correspond to conventional kernel estimates for a stationary density. As is apparent from the figure, the fitted densities are symmetric and quite close, although there is apparently greater dispersion in the case of the longer data set 1934–1997.

In a similar way, we found semi-parametric estimates of d for the nominal rate and inflation over the three time periods 1961–1985, 1961–1997, and 1934–1997. The results are given in Tables 2 and 3. The results in Table 2 corroborate many earlier findings that the nominal rate of interest is nonstationary. Unit root nonstationarity is included in the confidence band for d over the longer periods 1961–1997 and 1934–1997. The point estimates of d increase from 0.82 to 0.96 as the time period lengthens.

The estimates reported in Table 3 show that inflation appears to be nonstationary over 1961–1985, but long memory stationary dependence in inflation is not rejected for the longer periods 1961–1997 and 1934–1997. For all time periods, unit root nonstationarity and short

Table 2

Empirical Estimates of d: Nominal Rate

Period	$\hat{d}$	$s_{\hat{d}}$	95% Confidence Interval
1961–1985	0.823	0.076	[0.673,0.971]
1961–1997	0.968	0.065	[0.840,1.096]
1934–1997	0.967	0.053	[0.863,1.071]

Table 3

Empirical Estimates of d: Inflation

Period	$\hat{d}$	$s_{\hat{d}}$	95% Confidence Interval
1961–1985	0.775	0.076	[0.626,0.924]
1961–1997	0.663	0.065	[0.535,0.792]
1934–1997	0.538	0.053	[0.434,0.643]

memory dependence are rejected. These estimates therefore do not support results like those in Miskin (1992), where inflation is treated as an $I(1)$ variable. The point estimates of d decrease as the time period lengthens, although in each case these exceed 0.5.

Comparing the results in Table 1 with those in Tables 2–3, the point estimates of d appear to be more stable over the three subperiods for the real rate than for either the nominal rate or inflation. Also, there is some incompatibility between the three sets of estimates. In a model with three fractionally integrated variables $y_t \equiv I(d_y)$, $x_t \equiv I(d_x)$, $z_t \equiv I(d_z)$, satisfying the simple linear relation $y_t = x_t - z_t$, the behaviour of y_t is necessarily dominated by the dominant component of x_t and z_t. Thus, if $d_x > d_z$, then $d_y = d_x$. In the present case, this suggests that the fractional integration of the nominal rate should dominate the real rate. However, the separate empirical estimates indicate that the fractional integration of the real rate is significantly less than that of the nominal rate. There are several possible explanations for this type of empirical incompatibility, including model misspecification and scale differences between the variables. It seems likely in the present case that the greater volatility of inflation over the nominal rate of interest is a contributing factor in these differences. Similar phenomena have been found to arise in the context of exchange-rate data, where there are major differences in scale between spot returns and the forward premium (see Maynard and Phillips 1998). The data are graphed in Figures 14–15 and seem to support this explanation.

VII

Conclusion

THIS PAPER INTRODUCES SOME NEW statistical procedures for describing and analyzing nonstationary data and applies these techniques to the study of Fisher's equation for the real rate of interest. Under weak conditions that assure some form of functional limit theorem for standardized forms of the data, we construct asymptotically valid spatial density and hazard function measures for the series, both of which take the form of random processes rather than nonrandom functions as in the case of stationary time series. Consistent techniques for

Figure 14

Nominal 90-day TB rate.

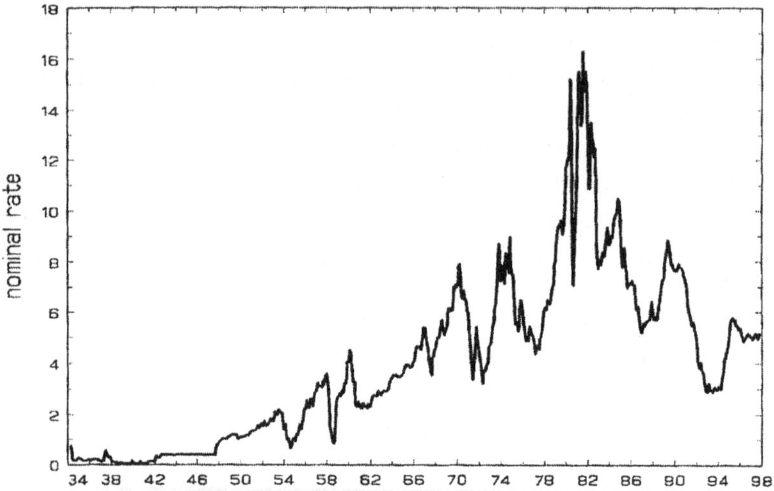

Figure 15

CPI three-month inflation rate.

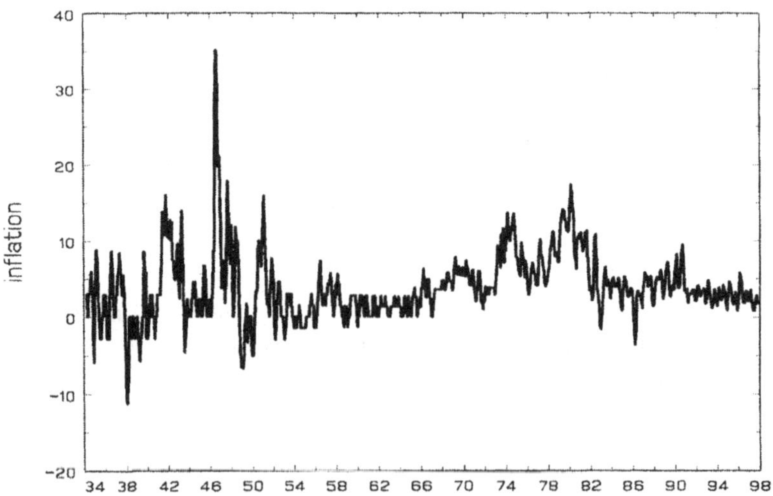

estimating these quantities are given, together with a limit theory that enables the measures to be used in inference.

Using these spatial density techniques, we analyze the *ex post* real rate of interest in the United States over the period 1934–1997. Results over the subperiod 1961–1985 provide some corroborating evidence to support the conclusion of a recent study by Garcia and Perron (1994) that the real rate fluctuates about constant levels that change over regimes. However, over the longer period 1934–1997, the regime change approach requires many change points, seems artificial, and lacks parsimony.

An alternative semiparametric model is considered that allows for fractional integration in the real rate, including unit root nonstationary and stationary long-range dependence as special cases, to account for various types of long-run behavior and that retains generality with respect to the modeling of the short-run component of the series. Through the fractional integration parameter in this model the extent of nonstationarity in the real rate can be directly measured. A new modified log periodogram estimation of the fractional integration parameter is performed using recently obtained asymptotic results by Kim and Phillips (1999a) that apply in the nonstationary case. Empirical estimates of the fractional differencing parameter are computed for the *ex post* rate over 1934–1997 and two shorter subperiods. The results confirm evidence of nonstationarity in the real rate for all time periods, and therefore generally support the conclusion reached by Rose (1988). Our estimates also confirm Mishkin's (1992) rejection of unit root nonstationarity in the real rate of interest. However, although unit root nonstationarity and short memory can be rejected and point estimates indicate nonstationarity, confidence intervals for the fractional differencing parameter are in the region [0.4, 0.6] and therefore do not completely rule out the possibility of a stationary real rate of interest with very long-range dependence.

The fractional integration model for the real rate of interest seems to be successful in transforming the data to stationarity over all three periods 1934–1997, 1961–1985, and 1961–1997, all with a very similar fractional integration parameter. In this respect, the model is at once more parsimonious and more generally applicable than a model with many regime shifts.

VIII

Technical Appendix and Proofs

OUR APPROACH TO AN ASYMPTOTIC THEORY for spatial density and hazard rate estimation relies on recent work in Phillips and Park (1998), hereafter P^2, for kernel density estimation and regression for nonstationary time series. We only sketch the derivations we need here.

Suppose X_t is a unit root time series with differences $\Delta X_t = u_t$ and initialization X_0 that satisfy Conditions VIII.A and VIII.B below. Distant initial conditions are permitted in VIII.B and play a role in the spatial density asymptotics. Conditions VIII.C and VIII.D relate to the kernel function and restrictions on the bandwidth h, and they are used in P^2. Note the important difference between VIII.D and conventional assumptions about bandwidth in kernel density estimation; here, the bandwidth can be of the form

$$h_n = cn^k,\ k \in \left[-\frac{1}{4}+\delta, \frac{1}{12}-\delta\right],$$

so that bandwidths that increase with n are permissible. The bandwidth cannot decrease too fast or increase too fast, as $n \to \infty$. Condition VIII.A allows for differences u_t that follow a linear process and are standard (Phillips and Solo 1992). The higher moment condition in VIII.A is useful in assuring the validity of a strong approximation to partial sums of u_t.

A. Assumption

(a) *u_t is a linear process $u_t = C(L)\varepsilon_t = \Sigma_{j=0}^{\infty} c_j \varepsilon_{t-j}$ with $C(1) \neq 0$ and*

$$\sum_{j=0}^{\infty} j^{\frac{1}{2}}|c_j| < \infty.$$

(b) *ε_t is iid $(0, \sigma^2)$ with $E(|\varepsilon_j|^q) < \infty$ for some $q > 2p > 4$.*

B. Assumption

The initial conditions of X_t are set at $t = 0$, and X_0 has the following general form allowing for effects in the distant past

$$X_0 = u + \sum_{j=0}^{[n\kappa]} u_{-j}, \text{ for some } \kappa \geq 0,$$

where u is an $O_{a.s.}(1)$ *random variable with* $E(|u|^p)$ *for some* $p > 2$.

C. Assumption

The kernel $K(\cdot)$ *is a symmetric and nonnegative density with integrable characteristic function* φ_K *and satisfies the following conditions for some* $r > 2$:

$$\int_{-\infty}^{\infty} K(s) = 1, \int_{-\infty}^{\infty} s^{2r} K(s)ds < \infty, \quad \sup_s K(s) < \infty.$$

D. Assumption

$n^{1-\delta} h_n^4 \to \infty$, *and* $h_n / n^{(1 \ \delta)/12} \to 0$ *for some* $\delta > 0$.

E. Proof of Theorem 3.1

The proof follows the same lines as that of Theorem 3.1 of P^2. As in that theorem, we need to augment the probability space so that a strong approximation to the limit Brownian motion $B(r)$ of

$$n^{-\frac{1}{2}} X_{[nr]}$$

can be used. The only changes in the proof are:

(i) Since u_t is a linear process, we need to rely on extended versions of the preliminary Lemmas 5.5 and 5.7 in P^2 that apply for linear processes instead of iid random variables. These extensions follow in precisely the same way but make use of Lemma D of Phillips (1999b), which provides a strong approximation result for linear processes.

(ii) We use the consistent scale estimate $\hat{\omega}^2$ of the long-run variance $\omega^2 = 2\pi f_{\Delta x}(0)$ in the definition of the spatial density estimate. This is not needed in Theorem 3.1 of P^2 because chronological local time $\bar{L}_B(r, a) = \omega^{-2} L_B(r, a)$ is used in P^2 in place of local time.

(iii) Since $\hat{\omega}^2 \to_p \omega^2$, the resulting limit holds in probability rather than almost surely.

F. Proof of Theorem 3.2

From Lemma 2.9(d) of P^2 we have

$$2^{-1}\lambda^{1/2}\left\{L_B\left(t, r+\frac{s}{\lambda}\right) - L_B(t,r)\right\} \xrightarrow{d} Q(L_B(t,r), s),$$

where $Q(a, b)$ is a standard Brownian sheet. Then, using Theorem III.A of P[2], we have

$$\begin{aligned}
&\sqrt{c_n}\left[\hat{L}_B\left(r, n^{-\frac{1}{2}}s\right) - L_B(r, a - B_0(\kappa))\right] \\
&= \sqrt{c_n}\left[\frac{\hat{\omega}^2}{\sqrt{n}h_n}\sum_{t=1}^{[nr]} K\left(\frac{s - X_t}{h_n}\right) - L_B(r, a - B_0(\kappa))\right] \\
&= \sqrt{c_n}\left[c_n\omega^2\int_0^r K\left(c_n\left\{\frac{s - X_0}{\sqrt{n}} - B(g)\right\}\right)dg - L_B(r, a - B_0(\kappa))\right] + o_p(1) \\
&= \sqrt{c_n}\left[c_n\int_{-\infty}^{\infty} K\left(c_n\left\{\frac{s - X_0}{\sqrt{n}} - p\right\}\right)L_B(r, p)dp - L_B(r, a - B_0(\kappa))\right] + o_p(1) \\
&= \sqrt{c_n}\int_{-\infty}^{\infty} K(q)\left[L_B\left(r, \frac{s - X_0}{\sqrt{n}} - \frac{q}{c_n}\right) - L_B(r, a - B_0(\kappa))\right]dq + o_p(1) \\
&= \int_{-\infty}^{\infty} K(q)\sqrt{c_n}\left[L_B\left(r, \frac{s - X_0}{\sqrt{n}} - \frac{q}{c_n}\right) - L_B(r, a - B_0(\kappa))\right]dq + o_p(1) \\
&\to_d 2\int_{-\infty}^{\infty} K(q)Q(L_B(r, a - B_0(\kappa)), q)dq \\
&=_d 2L_B(r, a - B_0(\kappa))^{\frac{1}{2}}\int_{-\infty}^{\infty} K(q)Q(1, q)dq \\
&=_d 2L_B(r, a - B_0(\kappa))^{\frac{1}{2}}N(0, V),
\end{aligned}$$

where

$$V = \int_0^{\infty}\int_0^{\infty} K(q)(q \wedge p)K(p)dqdp + \int_0^{\infty}\int_0^{\infty} K(-q)(q \wedge p)K(-p)dqdp,$$

which gives the stated mixed normal distribution

$$MN\left(0, 8L_B(r, a - B_0(\kappa))\int_0^{\infty}\int_0^{\infty} K(q)(q \wedge p)K(p)dqdp\right).$$

G. Proof of Theorem 4.1

By virtue of Theorem III.A and since $s = s_0 + \sqrt{n}\,a$, we have

$$
\begin{aligned}
\hat{H}_B\left(t, \frac{s}{\sqrt{n}}\right) &= \frac{\hat{L}_B\left(t, \frac{s}{\sqrt{n}}\right)}{\int_{\frac{s}{\sqrt{n}}}^{\infty} \hat{L}_B\left(t, \frac{p}{\sqrt{n}}\right) \frac{dp}{\sqrt{n}}} \\
&\to_p \frac{L_B(t, a - B_0(\kappa))}{\int_a^{\infty} L_B(t, b - B_0(\kappa)) db} \\
&= \frac{L_B(t, a - B_0(\kappa))}{\int_{a - B_0(\kappa)}^{\infty} L_B(t, c) dc} = H_B(t, a - B_0(\kappa))
\end{aligned}
$$

giving the stated result.

H. *Proof of Theorem 4.2*

We have

$$
\begin{aligned}
&\sqrt{c_n}\left[\hat{H}_B\left(r, n^{-\frac{1}{2}} s\right) - H_B(r, a - B_0(\kappa))\right] \\
&= \sqrt{c_n}\left[\frac{\hat{L}_B\left(t, \frac{s}{\sqrt{n}}\right)}{\int_{\frac{s}{\sqrt{n}}}^{\infty} \hat{L}_B\left(t, \frac{p}{\sqrt{n}}\right) \frac{dp}{\sqrt{n}}} - \frac{L_B(t, a - B_0(\kappa))}{\int_{a - B_0(\kappa)}^{\infty} L_B(t, c) dc}\right].
\end{aligned} \tag{24}
$$

Observe that

$$
\begin{aligned}
\int_{\frac{s}{\sqrt{n}}}^{\infty} \hat{L}_B\left(t, \frac{p}{\sqrt{n}}\right) \frac{dp}{\sqrt{n}} &= \frac{\hat{\omega}^2}{\sqrt{n} h_n} \sum_{t=1}^{[nr]} \int_{\frac{s}{\sqrt{n}}}^{\infty} K\left(\frac{p - X_t}{h_n}\right) \frac{dp}{\sqrt{n}} \\
&= \frac{\hat{\omega}^2}{\sqrt{n} h_n} \sum_{t=1}^{[nr]} \int_{\frac{s}{\sqrt{n}}}^{\infty} K\left(c_n\left[\frac{p - X_t}{\sqrt{n}}\right]\right) \frac{dp}{\sqrt{n}} \\
&= \frac{\hat{\omega}^2}{\sqrt{n} h_n} \sum_{t=1}^{[nr]} \int_a^{\infty} K\left(c_n\left\{b - \frac{X_t}{\sqrt{n}}\right\}\right) db \\
&= \frac{\hat{\omega}^2}{\sqrt{n} h_n} \sum_{t=1}^{[nr]} \frac{1}{c_n} \overline{\mathbb{K}}\left(c_n\left\{a - \frac{X_t}{\sqrt{n}}\right\}\right) \\
&= \frac{\hat{\omega}^2}{\sqrt{n} h_n} \sum_{t=1}^{[nr]} \overline{\mathbb{K}}\left(c_n\left\{a - \frac{X_t}{\sqrt{n}}\right\}\right).
\end{aligned} \tag{25}
$$

Now, under the assumption that $\sqrt{c_n}(\hat{\omega}^2 - \omega^2) = o_p(1)$, using the strong approximation

$$\frac{X_{[nr]}}{\sqrt{n}} = B_0(\kappa) + B(r) + o_{a.s.}\left(n^{-\frac{1}{2}+\frac{1}{P}}\right)$$

as in P[2] and proceeding as in the proof of Theorem 3.1 of P[2], we get

$$\begin{aligned}\frac{\hat{\omega}^2}{n}\sum_{t=1}^{[nr]}\overline{\mathbb{K}}\left(c_n\left\{a-\frac{X_t}{\sqrt{n}}\right\}\right) &= \omega^2\int_0^r \overline{\mathbb{K}}(c_n\{a - B_0(\kappa) - B(s)\})ds + o_p\left(\frac{1}{\sqrt{c_n}}\right)\\ &= \omega^2\int_{-\infty}^{\infty}\overline{\mathbb{K}}(c_n\{a - B_0(\kappa) - c\})L_B(r, c)dc + \\ &\quad o_p\left(\frac{1}{\sqrt{c_n}}\right)\\ &= \omega^2\int_{a-B_0(\kappa)}^{\infty} L_B(r, c)dc + o_p\left(\frac{1}{\sqrt{c_n}}\right) \qquad (26)\end{aligned}$$

since

$$\overline{\mathbb{K}}(c_n\{a - B_0(\kappa) - c\}) = \int_{c_n\{a-B_0(\kappa)-c\}}^{\infty} K(s)ds = \begin{cases} O\left(\frac{1}{c_n^{2r-1}}\right) & \text{for } c < a - B_0(\kappa)\\ 1 + O\left(\frac{1}{c_n^{2r-1}}\right) & \text{for } c > a - B_0(\kappa)\end{cases}$$

from the given tail behavior of the kernel $K(s)$ and where $r > 2$ (see Assumption VIII.C).

It follows from Equation (24)–(25) and Theorem 3.2 that

$$
\begin{aligned}
&\sqrt{c_n}\left[\hat{H}_B\left(r, n^{-\frac{1}{2}}s\right) - H_B(r, a - B_0(\kappa))\right] \\
&= \sqrt{c_n}\left[\frac{\hat{L}_B\left(t, \frac{p}{\sqrt{n}}\right)}{\int_{a-B_0(\kappa)}^{\infty} L_B(t,c)dc + o_p\left(\frac{1}{\sqrt{c_n}}\right)} - \frac{L_B(t, a - B_0(\kappa))}{\int_{a-B_0(\kappa)}^{\infty} L_B(t,c)dc}\right] \\
&= \frac{1}{\int_{a-B_0(\kappa)}^{\infty} L_B(t,c)dc}\sqrt{c_n}\left[\hat{L}_B\left(t, \frac{s}{\sqrt{n}}\right) - L_B(t, a - B_0(\kappa))\right] \\
&\Rightarrow \frac{2}{\int_{a-B_0(\kappa)}^{\infty} L_B(t,c)dc}\int_{-\infty}^{\infty} K(q)Q(L_B(r, a - B_0(\kappa)), q)dq \\
&\equiv MN\left(0, 8K_2\frac{L_B(r, a - B_0(\kappa))}{\left(\int_{a-B_0(\kappa)}^{\infty} L_B(r,s)ds\right)^2}\right),
\end{aligned}
$$

giving the required result.

I. Notation

$\rightarrow_{a.s.}$	almost sure convergence	$[\cdot]$	integer part of
$=_d$	distributional equivalence	$r \wedge s$	$\min(r, s)$
$:=$	definitional equality	$\equiv$	equivalence in distribution
$o_{a.s.}(1)$	tends to zero almost surely	$o_p(1)$	tends to zero in probability
$\rightarrow_p$	convergence in probability		
$(a)_k$	$(a)(a+1)\ldots(a+k-1)$		
$\Rightarrow$, $\rightarrow_d$	weak convergence		

J. Data Sources

(a) **Consumer Price Index**

Not seasonally adjusted

Area: U.S. city average (i.e., urban)

Items: All items

Base: 1982–1984 = 100

Source: Bureau of Labor Statistics, *Monthly Labor Review*

Code: CUUR0000SA0

(b) **Three-Month Treasury Bill Rate**

Secondary market

Average of daily closing bid

Annualized using a 360-day year for bank intèrest

Quoted on a discount basis

Source: Board of Governors of the Federal Reserve System, *Federal Reserve Bulletin*

Code: TB3MS

Notes

1. Fisher (1896) credited Marshall (1895) for making the distinction between real and nominal interest. It appears the idea that expected inflation affects interest rates can be traced to earlier political speeches and political economy pamphlets. Howitt (1992) and Laidler (1991) provide some further information about the history of the concept and the distinction between real and nominal rates. Fisher seems to have been the first to conduct a sustained study and to explore the matter in serious empirical research.

2. The reader is referred to Revuz and Yor (1994) for much of the underlying stochastic process theory used here. Good introductions are Chung and Williams (1990) and Karatzas and Shreve (1991).

3. In these and in our other calculations we used a bandwidth of

$$b_n = n^{-\frac{1}{5}}.$$

References

Akonom, J., and C. Gourieroux. (1987). *A Functional Limit Theorem for Fractional Processes.* Unpublished ms.

Chung, K. L., and R. J. Williams. (1990). *Introduction to Stochastic Integration.* 2nd ed. Boston: Birkhäuser.

Fama, E. F. (1975). "Short Term Interest Rates as Predictors of Inflation." *American Economic Review* 65: 269–282.

Fisher, I. (1896). "Appreciation and Interest." *AEA Publications* 3(11): 331–442.

——. (1930). *The Theory of Interest.* New York: Macmillan.

Garcia, R., and P. Perron. (1996). "An Analysis of the Real Rate of Interest Under Regime Shifts." *Review of Economics and Statistics* 111–125.

Gil-Alana, L. A., and P. M. Robinson. (1997). "Testing for a Unit Root and Other Nonstationary Hypotheses in Macroeconomic Time Series." *Journal of Econometrics* 80: 241–268.

Howitt, P. (1992). "Fisher Effect." In *New Palgrave Dictionary of Money and Finance.* London: Macmillan.

Hurvich, C. M., R. Deo, and J. Brodsky. (1998). "The Mean Squared Error of Geweke and Porter-Hudak's Estimator of the Memory Parameter of a Long-Memory Time Series." *Journal of Time Series Analysis* 19: 19–46.

Karatzas, I., and S. E. Shreve. (1988). *Brownian Motion and Stochastic Calculus.* New York: Springer-Verlag.

Kim, C. S., and P. C. B. Phillips. (1999a). *Modified Log Periodogram Regression.* Yale University, mimeo.

——. (1999b). *Log Periodogram Regression: The Nonstationary Case.* Yale University, mimeo.

Laidler, D. (1991). *The Golden Age of the Quantity Theory.* Hemel Hempstead: Philip Allan.

Mandlebrot, B., and J. van Ness. (1968). "Fractional Brownian Motion, Fractional Noises and Applications." *SIAM Review* 10: 422–437.

Marshall, A. (1895). *Principles of Economics.* 3rd ed. London: Macmillan.

Maynard, A., and P. C. B. Phillips. (1998). *Rethinking an Old Empirical Puzzle: Econometric Evidence on the Forward Discount Anomaly.* Yale University, mimeo.

Mishkin, F. S. (1981). "The Real Rate of Interest: An Empirical Investigation. The Cost and Consequences of Inflation." *Carnegie-Rochester Conference Series on Public Policy* 15: 151–200.

——. (1992). "Is the Fisher Effect for Real?" *Journal of Monetary Economics* 30: 195–215.

Phillips, P. C. B. (1987). "Towards a Unified Asymptotic Theory for Autoregression." *Biometrika* 74: 535–547.

——. (1999a). *Discrete Fourier Transforms of Fractional Processes.* Yale University, mimeo.

——. (1999b). *Unit Root Log Periodogram Regression.* Yale University, mimeo

Phillips, P. C. B., and J. Y. Park. (1998). *Nonstationary Density Estimation and Kernel Autoregression.* Yale University, mimeo.

Phillips, P. C. B., and V. Solo. (1992). "Asymptotics for Linear Processes." *Annals of Statistics* 20: 971–1001.

Protter, P. (1990). *Stochastic Integration and Differential Equations.* New York: Springer.

Revuz, D., and M. Yor. (1994). *Continuous Martingales and Brownian Motion.* 2nd ed. New York: Springer-Verlag.

Robinson, P. M. (1994). "Time Series with Strong Dependence." In A*dvances in Econometrics, Sixth World Congress, 1C.* Ed. A. Sims. Cambridge: Cambridge University Press.

——. (1995). "Gaussian Semiparametric Estimation of Long Range Dependence." *Annals of Statistics* 23: 1630–1661.

Rose, A. K. (1988). "Is the Real Interest Rate Stable?" *Journal of Finance* 43: 1095–1112.

Silverman, B. W. (1986). *Density Estimation for Statistics and Data Analysis.* London: Chapman and Hall.

Summers, L. H. (1983). "The Non-Adjustment of Nominal Interest Rates: A Study of the Fisher Effect." In *Macroeconomics, Prices, and Quantities: Essays in Memory of Arthur M. Okun*. Ed. James Tobin. Washington, DC: Brookings Institution.

Taqqu, M. S. (1975). "Weak Convergence to Fractional Brownian Motion and to the Rosenblatt Process." *Z. Wahrsch. Verw. Gebiete* 31: 287–302.

Tyurin, K., and P. C. B. Phillips. (1999). *The Occupation Density of Fractional Brownian Motion and Some of Its Applications*. Yale University, mimeo.

Walsh, C. E. (1987) "Three Questions Concerning Nominal and Real Interest Rates." *Economic Review* 4: 5–20.

Comments on "Econometric Analysis of Fisher's Equation" by Peter C. B. Phillips

By JOHN RUST*

ABSTRACT. A comment on the article by Peter C. B. Phillips in this volume.

I

Introductory Remarks

I AM HONORED to discuss Peter Phillips's fascinating contribution to this volume, although my remarks are tempered by the fact that this is not my area of expertise. Ostensibly this paper is an empirical analysis of the Fisher equation; however, I view its primary contribution as providing important new econometric tools for analyzing nonstationary time series. After summarizing its key theoretical contributions for the benefit of readers who are less familiar with continuous time stochastic processes, I offer my assessment of whether this elegant asymptotic approach yields new empirical insights into the Fisher equation. Overall, I think the paper leaves us with some important unresolved puzzles about the joint evolution of the nominal interest rate, the inflation rate, and the (*ex post*) real rate of interest. More heretically, I question whether the simple version of the Fisher

*John Rust is Professor of Economics at University of Maryland. He was previously a Professor of Economics at Yale University from 1996 to 2001 and a Professor of Economics at the University of Wisconsin from 1983 to 1995. Rust received his Ph.D. from MIT in 1983, specializing in applied econometrics. His research has focused on the development of computationally tractable methods for empirically modeling dynamic decision making under uncertainty. In a series of publications Rust has demonstrated that these discrete dynamic programming models provide accurate predictions of actual human decision making in a variety of contexts. The Econometric Society awarded him the Ragnar Frisch Medal in 1997 for his first empirical application of the method in the paper, "Optimal Replacement of GMC Bus Engines: An Empirical Model of Harold Zurcher."

The American Journal of Economics and Sociology, Vol. 64, No. 1 (January, 2005).

equation provides a useful framework for thinking about the behavior of nominal interest rates, especially since the simplest versions of this equation ignore the tremendous advances in finance in the years since Fisher's death.

II

Theoretical Contributions

THE NEW ECONOMETRIC CONTRIBUTIONS include derivation of asymptotic distributions for the "spatial density" and its associated hazard function, and the exponent d in "fractionally integrated" time series processes. The latter result is especially important, since for the first time we have a unified framework for conducting inference in a class of potentially nonstationary long memory univariate time series models that obviates the need for overly restrictive parametric assumptions (e.g., Gaussian error terms).

The spatial density is simply a rescaled version of the well-known nonparametric kernel density estimator for *IID* data, and the hazard function is constructed from the spatial density by the standard formula. The novel result of this paper is Theorem III.A, which shows that an appropriately rescaled version of the kernel density estimator still converges with probability 1 when applied to data-generating processes (DGPs) that have a unit root. However rather than converging to a deterministic limit (the true marginal or stationary density of the DGP in the *IID* or ergodic cases, respectively), Phillips shows that when the DGP has a unit root the kernel density estimator converges in probability to a random limiting object knows as a *local time*, a concept originally introduced by the probabilist Paul Lévy for the special case of Brownian motion back in the late 1930s. Lévy called the local time $L(r,s)$ *mesure du voisinage*, since it is (the density of) the measure of the time a Brownian path $B(t)$ spends in the vicinity of the point s over the time interval $[0,r]$. The most straightforward way to define $L(r,s)$ is in terms of the random *occupation time* that the Brownian path spends in the set A over the interval $[0,r]$:

$$\Gamma(r, A) \equiv \int_0^r I\{B(s) \in A\}ds. \tag{1}$$

The local time is just the density (Radon-Nikodym derivative) of the random measure $\Gamma(r, A)$:

$$\Gamma(r, A) = \int I\{x \in A\} L(r, x) dx. \tag{2}$$

The concept of local time can be generalized to the class of *semi-martingales* $M(t)$, that is, processes that can be represented as $M(t) = U(t) + V(t)$, where $U(t)$ is a (local) martingale and $V(t)$ is a finite variation process (the reader is referred to Karatzas and Shreve 1991 for more details). Unfortunately, the definition of local time given in this paper may be difficult for some readers to grasp since it depends on the additional concept of *quadratic variation* $[M]$ of the semi-martingale M defined, nonconstructively, as the unique increasing stochastic process obtained from the Doob-Meyer decomposition of the nonnegative (local) submartingale $U^2(t)$, where U is the local martingale component of the semi-martingale M. The Doob-Meyer decomposition establishes that any nonnegative submartingale $X(t)$ can be uniquely represented as the sum of a martingale $Y(t)$ plus an increasing stochastic process $Z(t)$. In the case of a Brownian motion, the quadratic variation turns out to be $[B]_t = t$ since the Doob-Myer decomposition of the nonnegative super-martingale $X(t) = B^2(t)$ is given by $B^2(t) = (B^2(t) - t) + t$, where $Y(t) = B^2(t) - t$ is a martingale, and $Z(t) = t$ is the increasing process. Thus, in the Brownian motion case the definition of the local time $L_M(r, s)$ reduces to

$$\begin{aligned} L_M(r, s) &= \lim_{\varepsilon \to 0} \frac{\Gamma(r, [0, s+\sigma]) - \Gamma(r, [0, s-\sigma])}{2\varepsilon} \\ &= \lim_{\sigma \to 0} \frac{1}{2\sigma} \int_0^r \{I|B(t) - s| \leq \sigma\} dt, \end{aligned} \tag{3}$$

where the right-hand side of Equation (3) is clearly the same as the right-hand side of the definition given in Equation (5) of Phillips's paper, since $dt = d[B]_t = d[M]_t$ in the case of a Brownian motion. Phillips provides some helpful intuition for local times via the inverse relation between local times and quadratic variation in Equation (6) of his paper, which he analogizes to the standard spectral density decomposition of long-run variance. This inverse relation of Equation (6) can be seen to be an immediate consequence of the original definition of local time as the density of occupation time in Equation (2) above since for the case $A = (-\infty, +\infty)$ we can see from Equation (1) that $\Gamma(t, A) = t$, so using the definition of local time in Equation (2) we have:

$$\Gamma(t, A) = t = \int_{-\infty}^{+\infty} L(t, x)dx - [B]_t. \qquad (4)$$

So it is clear from Equation (4) above that for a standard Brownian motion at $t = 1$, the local time $L_M(1,x)$ is a random probability density.

The beauty of Phillips's Theorem III.A is that is enables us to cut through all these definitions and see directly that the local time is a (rescaled) probability density function since it equals the limit of a sequence of kernel density estimates with probability 1. The interesting twist is that in the unit root case, the limiting density is random as a consequence of the fact that there are unavoidable path dependencies when we are dealing with nonstationary unit root data generating processes. I think this is a very interesting and deep asymptotic result that constitutes an important new contribution to the probability and statistics literature.

The other important theoretical contribution in this paper is a new result (the proof of which will actually appear in a subsequent paper) on the asymptotic distribution of the exponent d of a long memory or "fractionally integrated" representation of a univariate time series process $\{r_t\}$:

$$(I - L)^d r_t = u_t, \qquad (5)$$

where $\{u_t\}$ is a stationary error process, constructed as a moving average from an *IID* mean zero error process $\{\sigma_t\}$. Here L denotes the lag operator, $Lr_t = r_{t-1}$ and we can define the fractional difference operator $(I - L)^d$ by means of a binomial expansion,

$$(I - L)^d \equiv \sum_{i=0}^{\infty} a_i L^i, \qquad (6)$$

where

$$a_i = \prod_{0<k\leq i} \frac{k-1-d}{k}. \qquad (7)$$

Fractionally integrated processes are also known as "long memory processes" since their autocovariance functions decrease only arithmetically rather than geometrically fast:

$$\left(r_t, r_{t+k}\right) \simeq Ck^{2d-1}. \tag{8}$$

The reader should consult Chapter 13 of Brockwell and Davis (1991) for further details on fractionally integrated processes. Although Peter Robinson and others have derived asymptotic distributions for estimators in the stationary case ($d \in [-.5,.5]$), this paper derives asymptotic distribution for a Gaussian pseudo-maximum likelihood estimator $\hat{d}$ that covers the nonstationary case where the exponent d is allowed to range over the full interval $[-.5,1]$. This allows Phillips to conduct inference in a much richer class of time-series models that includes stationary MA processes ($d = 0$), nonstationary unit root processes ($d = 1$), and stationary and nonstationary fractionally integrated processes as special cases.

III

Empirical Contributions

Peter Phillips could have rested content after proving these difficult new asymptotic results, so I commend him for undertaking the additional work to illustrate how these results can be applied to make inferences about interest rates, inflation rates, and the Fisher equation. While the empirical work is primarily descriptive in nature, it does yield new insights and suggests that relatively parsimonious long memory models can capture key features of the data. At the same time it is hard to see any definitive conclusions emerging from this study, since it simultaneously corroborates and contradicts previous results that employed more conventional econometric methods. In particular, I don't think the rather sophisticated econometric apparatus employed here takes us appreciably closer to resolving some of the key outstanding puzzles surrounding the Fisher equation such as Mishkin's (1992) finding that the Fisher equation seems to hold in the "long run" but not in the "short run." Indeed, Professor Phillips's paper leaves us with a new puzzle: namely, the finding that the nominal interest-rate process is nonstationary but the real interest rate and the inflation-rate processes are (marginally) stationary. This finding is not only inconsistent with the validity of the Fisher equation, it also violates a basic identity that defines the *ex post* real rate of interest as the difference between the nominal rate of interest and the inflation rate. However, I do not want to be too critical since it is unrealistic to expect a brand new econometric methodology to resolve some long-standing empirical puzzles connected with the Fisher equation, especially since the question of "testing" the validity of the Fisher equation is somewhat ill posed for reasons I discuss in the next section. Before discussing this problem and presenting a more critical analysis of the empirical findings, it is useful to summarize Phillips's key empirical findings.

1. The spatial density estimates reveal a dominant mode in the distribution of *ex post* real interest rate of 1.5% with four minor modes around –4%, –2%, 4%, and 9%. This is roughly consistent with the various "regimes" identified in Garcia and Perron's (1994) analysis based on Hamilton's stationary Markov regime switching model.
2. The point estimates of the exponents d of fractionally integrated models of the *ex post* real interest rate, the inflation rate, and the *ex ante* nominal interest rate are all in the nonstationary range, i.e., $d > 0.5$. However, the point estimates for the former rates are close to the $d = 0.5$ boundary for stationarity, and considering the size of 95% confidence intervals for $\hat{d}$, Phillips concludes that the results "do not completely rule out the possibility of a stationary real rate of interest with very long-range dependence." However, the point estimate of d for the nominal interest rate is $\hat{d} = .95$, with a 95% confidence interval that does not intersect the stationary region of the parameter space. The results for the *ex post* real rate confirm Mishkin's (1992) rejection of unit root nonstationarity but cast doubt on his maintained hypothesis that the inflation-rate process has a unit root. Overall, the results are inconsistent with the validity of the Fisher equation, since it implies that if the nominal-rate process is nonstationary

then either the real rate or the inflation-rate process must be nonstationary as well.

3. The point estimates of d for the nominal interest rate, inflation rate, and *ex post* real rate processes are not only inconsistent with the validity of the Fisher equation, they violate a simple identity defining the *ex post* interest rate as the difference between the nominal rate and realized inflation rate:

$$r_t = i_t - \pi_t. \tag{9}$$

This implies that the degree of fractional integration in the $\{r_t\}$ process must be at least as large as the degree of fractional integration in the dominating component of the $\{i_t\}$ and $\{\pi_t\}$ processes. However, the empirical results reveal that the estimate of d for the left-hand side of Equation (9), $\hat{d} = .53$, is inexplicably smaller than the dominant estimate on the right-hand side of Equation (9), namely $\hat{d} = 0.95$ for the $\{i_t\}$ process.

IV

Is the Fisher Equation a Useful Concept for Understanding Nominal Interest Rates?

ALTHOUGH I DON'T want to be unnecessarily heretical at the anniversary of Fisher's death, my basic criticism of this paper is that I don't think the simple version of the Fisher equation provides an adequate framework for understanding the determination of nominal interest rates. Much of the previous literature that has been devoted to "testing" the validity of the Fisher equation strikes me as misplaced. This literature has employed increasingly sophisticated econometric methods to test an equation that even Fisher admitted had dubious validity. I can't be overly critical of Professor Phillips's efforts to relate his theoretical research to Fisher's work in an invited paper for this volume. Indeed, it seems that one of the most natural applications of Phillips's results is to interest and inflation rates and the Fisher equation. However the Fisher equation poses some very difficult challenges as a "proving ground" for the techniques introduced in this paper. The main problem is that the key ingredients of the Fisher equation, the *ex ante* inflation rate and real rate of interest, are latent variables. While it is possible to construct noisy proxies for these variables, depending on how we construct these proxies we obtain empirically testable versions of the Fisher equation that range from being obviously false to essentially tautological. In essence there is a serious identification problem in determining whether changes in the nominal rate are due to changes in the "real rate," the expected inflation rate, or other factors.

I am not questioning Fisher's important basic insight, namely, that nominal interest rates adjust to offset expected inflation. There is also undoubtedly an element of truth to the hypothesis that nominal rates are also affected by the underlying "real rate of interest" that equates the intertemporal marginal rate of transformation in investment to the marginal rate of substitution in consumption (Fisher's "market," "investment," and "impatience" principles). However, it seems almost obvious that the real interest rate and the expected inflation rate cannot be the only factors determining the nominal interest rate, unless we adopt the tautological approach of defining the real interest rate to be the nominal rate minus the expected inflation rate. It seems clear that there is significant "excess volatility" in nominal interest rates that cannot be explained by day-to-day fluctuations in expected inflation or in the real rate of return to capital (where the latter equals the real rate of interest in Fisher's framework).

Like stocks, bonds have uncertain payout streams and can be traded in secondary markets, so bondholders have the option of making capital gains (or losses) and are not necessarily committed to a "buy and hold" strategy. Thus, there is no reason why "asset bubbles" or any of the other explanations for the excess volatility of stock returns do not also apply to bond returns. Another important factor affecting nominal interest rates that is ignored in the simple Fisher equation is the impact of large players in the bond market such as the government and central banks. Even when these large players are not directly intervening in the Treasury Bill market, they can have huge impact on bond prices via simple "announcement effects" in an environment with market bubbles or when private traders have fickle expectations. Through various interventions the Federal Reserve can affect both the level and volatility of nominal interest rates.

The role of these additional factors as determinants of the nominal interest rate is evident from the plots of time series for the 90-day Treasury Bill rate and the three-month inflation rate in Figures 14 and 15 of Phillips's paper. For example, there is a suspiciously long period from 1942 to nearly 1948 where nominal interest rates remained virtually unchanged at a very low level of less than 1%. Of course, this was during World War II when the U.S. government and the Federal Reserve appealed to patriotism and moral suasion to "jawbone" investors into buying Treasury Bills at par for abnormally low nominal interest rates. For most of this period wartime price controls were also in effect (so inflation was essentially zero), but the simple Fisher equation would be hard-pressed to explain why real interest rates should have remained constant over this period as the wartime production effort was initially geared up and then wound down.

It seems clear that we need to account for these additional neglected factors to obtain an adequate statistical model of nominal interest rates. One way to do this is to include some sort of residual or additional factor in the Fisher equation. For example, we might account for the missing factors through a time varying "market risk premium," ρ_t, yielding a modified "three-factor" version of the Fisher equation:

$$i_t = r_t^e + \pi_t^e + \rho_t. \tag{10}$$

Fisher clearly recognized that risk premiums must be accounted for in a fuller account of the determination of nominal interest rates: "We see, then, that the element of risk introduces disturbances into those determining conditions which were expressed in previous chapters as explaining the rate of interest" ([1930] 1971. 222), "instead of a series of equalities which we found to hold true in the vacuum case, so to speak, where risk was absent, we have only a *tendency* toward equalities, interfered with by the limitations of the loan market, and which, therefore, result in series of inequalities. Rates of interest, rates of preference, and rates of return over cost are only ideally, not really, equal" ([1930] 1971: 226). However, once we acknowledge the presence of risk premiums, we essentially have a decomposition of nominal interest rates in terms of at least three latent variables. This compounds the identification problem, since with three factors it is even less clear whether any movement in nominal interest rates should be attributed to a change in the real rate of interest, expected inflation, or the risk premium ρ_t.

The situation in Russia in 1998 provides a good example of the sort of problems we encounter in a modified three-factor version of the Fisher equation. During this period short-term interest rates exceeded 150%. It is not clear whether the high rates reflected expectations of hyperinflation (or currency devaluation) or fear of government default. From a practical standpoint, it might not really matter whether the high rates are due to expectations of inflation or expectations of default. Hyperinflation is just another way a government can default on its debts. The important question from Russia's (and the IMF's) perspective is to identify the steps necessary to restore investor confidence; from an investor's perspective the most important questions are: What is the probability of default? For how long will the abnormally high interest rates persist?

It might be tempting to claim that in a stable country like the United States the risk of government default is negligible and therefore it is not a bad approximation to ignore the risk premium term in the Fisher equation. However it is evident from the time series of *ex post* real interest rates plotted in Figure 3 of Phillips's paper that even in the absence of default risk there is a huge amount of volatility in *ex post* returns due to unexpected variations in the price level that imposes a significant amount of risk on bondholders. For example, it is hard to ignore the –36% *ex post* real rate at the end of World War II. In 20/20 hindsight it seems like the bond market should have anticipated the huge increase in prices as pent-up demand was released and wartime prices controls were lifted. However, as James Tobin has pointed out, there was considerable concern *ex ante* that the U.S. economy would not be able to rapidly absorb the millions of returning GIs, causing the economy to go into a major recession. Another possible explanation for the failure of nominal rates to rise is the wartime moral suasion by the U.S. government described above.

It seems that the reason why the literature persists on focusing on the unrealistic "two-factor" version of the Fisher equation is that it can be "tested" using the realized inflation rate π_t and the *ex post* real interest rate $i_t - \pi_t$ as noisy proxies for the *ex ante* expected rate of inflation π_t^e and the real interest rate r_t^e. Under the rational expectations hypothesis, these *ex post* realized values should differ from the unobserved *ex ante* expected values by a white noise (or martingale difference) forecast error process, and simple regressions can be used to test the Fisher equation. For example, the Fisher equation implies that $\pi_t^e = i_t - r_t$. Under rational expectations we have $\pi_t = \pi_t^e + \sigma_t$, where σ_t is a forecast error uncorrelated with information available at time t. Combining these two equations, and assuming that at least over short periods the real interest rate is constant, we obtain the following regression equation that can be used to "test" the Fisher equation:

$$\pi_t = \alpha + \beta i_t + \sigma_t. \tag{11}$$

If the Fisher equation is valid, $\beta = 1$. Mishkin (1992) ran such regressions and found that, depending on the sample period, the estimated β coefficients ranged from $\beta = .09$ to $\beta = 1.24$, and during the relatively shorter sample periods where $\hat{\beta}$ is small, he could not reject the hypothesis that the true $\beta = 0$. These (and similar results for a version of Equation (11) estimated in first differences) are the basis of Mishkin's claim that there is no "short-run" Fisher effect. However, if we allow the possibility of a three-factor model with a time-varying risk premium ρ_t, then the error term in Equation (11) will not necessarily be orthogonal to the regressor i_t, and the resulting estimates of β could be inconsistent. Thus, Mishkin's claims of the absence of a short-run Fisher effect may be artifacts of the assumption of a two-factor version Fisher equation that abstracts from the existence of a time-varying risk premium ρ_t, and that ignores the possibility of short-run movements in the real interest rate r_t.

Although allowing for a risk premium ρ_t in a three-factor version of the Fisher equation creates difficult identification and estimation problems for studies that rely exclusively on nominal interest rates and *ex post* inflation rates, it is possible to gather additional data that can provide more powerful tests of the Fisher effect and possibly even enable us to infer the risk premium ρ_t. For example, the availability of indexed bonds provides a much more direct way to test the validity of the Fisher equation and the Fisher effect. If we assume that the rate of return on indexed bonds provides a direct measurement of the "real rate of interest," then if there is not too much dispersion in expert estimates of future inflation rates, we can directly check whether the Fisher equation holds by adding the consensus expected inflation rate to the current indexed bond rate and comparing how close this is to the unindexed nominal rate of interest. For example, in July 1998 the real rate of return guaranteed on 30-year CPI-indexed Treasury "I-Bonds" was 3.4%. The consensus inflation rate during that period was about 1.2%. Thus, the nominal rate of return predited by the Fisher equation was $i_t = 3.4 + 1.2 = 4.6\%$. Three- and six-month Treasury Bills were yielding 4.8%, so there is a 0.2% unexplained residual in the Fisher equation; this would constitute the risk premium ρ_t.[1]

V

Critique of Approach and Empirical Results

PROFESSOR PHILLIPS EMPHASIZES the role of nonstationarity and long memory in interest and inflation processes, devoting Section VI of his paper to the question, "Is the Real Rate Nonstationary?" However I am not sure that this question is well posed, since I am skeptical about whether it is possible to tell from a finite realization of data whether the underlying process in "really" nonstationary. As is well known (see, e.g., Brockwell and Davis 1991, Section 8.1), there is a fundamental identification problem in time series, namely, the Yule-Walker equations imply that as long as the autocorrelation matrix for a univariate stochastic process $\{X_t\}$ is nonsingular, then we can always construct a stationary $AR(p)$ process to match any given finite sequence of autocorrelations in the $\{X_t\}$ process. Thus, in principle there is no way to distinguish whether a process $\{X_t\}$ is stationary long memory, nonstationary long memory (including unit root), or a stationary AR process. Furthermore, a process may appear to be nonstationary when analyzed as a univariate stochastic process, even though it may actually be just the marginal of a stationary higher dimensional multivariate process. For these reasons, I don't think it is possible to provide a meaningful answer to questions such as "Is the Real Rate Nonstationary?"

On the one hand, nonstationarity seems quite plausible on an *a priori* basis when we think of the evolution of the economy and factors such as population growth and technological innovation. On the other hand, when thinking about univariate processes such as interest or inflation rates, nonstationarity seems implausible on *a priori* grounds to the extent that nonstationary processes like random walks imply steadily increasing variances and sample paths that approach plus or minus infinity with probability 1. Obviously, interest and inflation rates are controlled processes, under partial control of government policymakers. As inflation or interest rates get very high or low, counteracting government policies kick into effect in an attempt to move these rates back into acceptable ranges.

Nonstationarity has some potentially undesirable implications for how we interpret estimation results and do statistical reference. For example, when the underlying data-generating process has a unit root, the probability limits for the spatial density estimator are random, dependent on the particular realized sample paths for the observed time series. In such a case, it is difficult to attach much weight to conclusions about the typical levels (e.g., mean value) of interest rates since these can change dramatically depending on the sample period. If the DGP is really nonstationary this is a fact of life that we have to deal with. Although we do observe that estimation results are sensitive to sample period in many macroeconomic applications, it is not clear that the sample period sensitivity we observe might not be a result of high autocorrelation and relatively small sample sizes for an ergodic underlying DGP. It seems that we are on firmer ground for doing inference in the stationary, ergodic case since we are guaranteed that with sufficient data our inferences will not be artifacts of particular sample periods or historical outcomes.

Rather than risk entering a philosophical debate about nonstationarity, I think a more fruitful and practical approach is to regard the nonstationary processes presented in this paper as just an alternative way of modeling approximating economic time series. There are many models we can employ, including the stationary Markov switching model that Phillips criticizes. The type of model that is "best" depends on the specific application and the criteria we impose in judging these models. In many cases, parsimony and forecasting ability are two of the most important criteria. I believe the fractionally integrated models score high on the grounds of parsimony, but it is not clear how well they do in terms of forecasting ability. I think a subsequent study that shows that these more parsimonious models yield better inflation or interest-rate predictions than less parsimonious conventional econometric models (e.g., stationary multivariate VARs or "switching regime" models) would constitute a much more compelling argument for using fractionally integrated models.

However, if the goal of the analysis is to improve our "understanding" of the determinants of interest and inflation rates, I think that a lot of important information can be lost in univariate analyses such as this one. My comments in the previous section suggest that some understanding of the historical context is essential to an adequate understanding of the evolution of these series. For this reason I have some affinity to the stationary "regime switching" approach that Garcia and Perron (1996) used to analyze these time series. Regime shifts are a fact of life: wars, booms, recessions, Presidential administrations, energy price and technology shocks, and so forth are all concrete examples of regime shifts. Although the Hamilton procedure does not make explicit use of this contextual information, I find it easier to line up the results of this purely statistical "curve fitting" exercise with what I know about historical events than by attempting to eyeball the spatial densities, which squeeze out the time dimension of the data. While I acknowledge Phillips's criticism of the arbitrariness of the choice of number of regimes, I do not see any conceptual reason why a finite number of possible regimes could not be consistently estimated via appropriate model selection criteria such as the Akaike or Bayesian Information Criterion.

Although I am somewhat skeptical about whether interest and inflation processes are really nonstationary, I think there is good reason to believe that these processes exhibit long memory, if only because many economic agents have long memory and can be affected in long-lasting ways by economic shocks (an example is the effect of the Great Depression on risk aversion and savings habits of individuals who experienced it, or traders using more cautious investing strategies following a market crash). However, the data also display sudden "spikes" that do not appear to have long-lasting effects. An example is the large, rapid increase in inflation rates following World War II noted earlier. It is not clear whether the continuous-sample path limits of the long memory processes estimated in this paper are capable of exhibiting such sudden spikes. The large spike remaining in the plot of the fractionally differenced inflation rates in Figure 15 suggests that these models do have difficulty capturing this aspect of the data. The paper would be strengthened by including a battery of specification tests to determine whether the parsimonious models really do succeed in fitting the data. For example, it is not clear how well these fractionally differenced processes capture second-order properties such as persistent periods of volatility in inflation or interest rates.

My final comment concerns Phillips's conclusion that the nominal-rate process is nonstationary while the inflation process is borderline stationary. In previous work Mishkin (1992) found that the interest and inflation processes were co-integrated, which he interpreted as evidence of the existence of a "long-run Fisher effect." Even though Phillips finds that the *ex post* real rate is borderline stationary (which he interprets as supporting Mishkin's finding), as I have previously noted there is an unresolved puzzle of why Phillips obtains very different estimated d exponents for the inflation and nominal-interest rates processes. These diverging exponents are inconsistent with co-integration of $\{\pi_t\}$ and $\{i_t\}$ and can be interpreted as evidence contradicting Mishkin's claims for the existence of a long-run Fisher effect. Although I lack concrete suggestions for resolving this puzzle, I suspect that it could be an artifact of estimating these series in isolation. This suggests that there might be gains from a systems approach to estimation, perhaps in some fractionally differenced generalization of co-integration analysis. An alternative would be to estimate interest and inflation jointly as a VAR system to see if there is corroborating evidence of significant divergence in the dominant roots governing the evolution of these variables. However, I think it would be premature to conclude from Phillips's results that nominal interest rates fail to adjust to permanent changes in inflation expectations. In the final analysis I do think there are compelling reasons to believe in the Fisher effect, at least with respect to the adjustment of the nominal interest rate to changes in expected inflation over the long run.

Note

1. Interest on I-Bonds is free from state and local taxation and federal taxes on I-Bonds can be deferred until maturity (30 years). If the bonds are used to pay college tuition, they are completely tax exempt. This suggests that the relevant comparisons might be to tax-exempt municipal bonds.

References

Brockwell, R., and P. Davis. (1991). *Time Series Theory and Methods*. New York: Springer-Verlag.

Fisher, I. (1930). *The Theory of Interest*. New York: Macmillan. Rpt. in (1974) *Reprints in Economics Classics*. Clifton, NJ: Augustus M. Kelley.

Garcia, R., and P. Perron. (1996). "An Analysis of the Real Interest Rate Under Regime Shifts." *Review of Economics and Statistics* 111–125.

Karatzas, I., and S. Shreve. (1991). *Brownian Motion and Stochastic Calculus*. New York: Springer-Verlag.

Mishkin, F. (1992). "Is the Fisher Effect for Real?" *Journal of Monetary Economics* 30: 195–215.

Phillips, Peter C. B. (2005). "Econometric Analysis of Fisher's Equation." *American Journal of Economics and Sociology* 64(1): 125–168.

Fisher, Keynes, and the Corridor of Stability

By Robert W. Dimand*

Abstract. This chapter draws on the debt-deflation process of Fisher (1933) as well as on Keynes (1936, chapter 19) and Tobin (1975, 1980) to explore the concept of a corridor of stability, where an economy will be self-adjusting only for demand shocks small enough to leave it within that corridor.

"[I]t is an outstanding characteristic of the economic system in which we live that, whilst it is subject to severe fluctuations in respect of output and employment, it is not violently unstable," observed John Maynard Keynes (1936: 249). In contrast to the *Treatise on Money*'s parable of a thrift campaign in a banana plantation (in which cumulative contraction would continue until what Don Patinkin termed a "coroner solution" at zero ouput), Keynes's *General Theory* excluded such extreme instability. However, this particular insight of the *General Theory* has not been well captured in subsequent macroeconomic models. Many models, with a classical flavor at least in the long run, imply automatic restoration of full-employment equilibrium after any shock, no matter how large. Others, notably some in the post-Keynesian tradition, deny such an automatic readjustment mechanism but are unclear about a threshold of stability, with demand shocks smaller than the critical level being insufficiently large to cause a lasting disturbance. A promising way of analyzing such a threshold

*Robert W. Dimand is a Professor of Economics at Brock University, St. Catharines, Ontario, Canada, L2S 3A1, where he holds a Chancellor's Chair for Research Excellence. A graduate of McGill and Yale Universities, he writes on the history of macroeconomics, the early history of game theory, and the history of women in economics. He wrote *The Origins of the Keynesian Revolution* (Edward Elgar and Stanford University Press, 1988), edited *The Origins of Macroeconomics* (10 volumes, Routledge, 2002), and has published articles in the *American Economic Review: Papers and Proceedings, Economic Journal, British Journal for the History of Science, Journal of Economic Perspectives,* and *Journal of Money, Credit, and Banking.* He is grateful for helpful comments from Ronald Bodkin, T. K. Rymes, William Scarth, and participants in the Canadian Economics Association annual meeting at Brock University and the Fisher conference at Yale.

The American Journal of Economics and Sociology, Vol. 64, No. 1 (January, 2005).

of stability draws on the pathbreaking work of Irving Fisher (1932, 1933) when he sought to explain why there was a long-lasting, severe depression after 1929 in contrast to the rapid recovery from the sharp recession of 1920–1921.

The issue to be addressed is showing how a large demand shock, such as that associated with the stock market crash of October 1929, can cause years of mass unemployment without automatic movement back to market-clearing equilibrium, even when there exist stabilizing forces able to correct automatically for smaller demand shocks. Axel Leijonhufvud ([1973] 1981: 112n) has suggested "the notion of 'the corridor' within which market forces, as they were traditionally conceived, are strong enough to override the disorganizing tendencies arising from 'trading at false prices', etc." Such a "corridor of stability" (which, Leijonhufvud states, "is not in Keynes") can provide another way of looking at Keynes's insight that the economy is not violently unstable. Leijonhufvud ([1973] 1981: 129) offered the idea of a corridor of stability as a sketch of a theory, an agenda for and invitation to modeling. This could provide a response to the problem that "[m]athematical general equilibrium theorists have at their command an impressive array of proven techniques for modeling systems that 'always work well.' Keynesian economists have experience with modeling systems that 'never work.' But, as yet, no one has the recipe for modeling systems that function pretty well most of the time but sometimes work very badly to coordinate economic activities. And the analytical devices and routines of neo-Walrasian general equilibrium theory and Keynesian theory will not 'mix'" (Leijonhufvud [1976] 1981: 340).

It is argued in this paper that an approach based on work by James Tobin (1975, 1980), drawing on insights of Maynard Keynes and Irving Fisher, contains such a corridor of stability. Keynes (1931a, 1931b) mentioned such debt-deflation effects briefly, while Fisher placed them at the heart of his *Booms and Depressions* (1932) and his "Debt-Deflation Theory of Great Depressions" (1933), which appeared in the first volume of *Econometrica* in lieu of a presidential address to the Econometric Society. The paper also argues that more of such an analysis can be found in the *General Theory* than Leijonhufvud suggested. The key point is that the effect of a lower price level on real aggregate effective demand is not the same as the effect of a falling price level or expectations of a falling price level. This point was stressed in a debate over whether faster price adjustment can be destabilizing (De Long and Summers 1986, 1988; Driskill and Sheffrin 1986; Chadha 1989), but, except for Groth (1993), the emphasis of this literature has been on systems that, given certain parameter values, are either everywhere stable or unstable, rather than having a corridor of stability.

A. C. Pigou (1941, 1943, 1947) and Gottfried Haberler (1941)[1] advanced the real balance effect as an argument for why lower prices and wages would suffice to restore output to its full-employment level, even if an increase in the real money supply could not cause any further reduction in nominal interest rates. Such a liquidity trap, in which deflation has lowered nominal interest rates nearly to zero, was invoked by Fischer Black (1987), with the new name "currency trap," to explain the failure of the automatic adjustment mechanism in the early 1930s. The Pigou-Haberler real balance effect of a lower price level is an increase in the real value of assets with a fixed nominal value, with a consequent wealth effect on consumption (in terms of the Harrod-Hicks-Meade framework: shifting the IS/LM intersection the right by moving the IS curve, even if the relevant portion of the LM curve is horizontal at or near zero). Pigou carefully distanced himself from the advocacy of deflation as a remedy for unemployment implied by his analysis: the final sentence of Pigou (1947: 251) warned that "the puzzles we have been considering in the last section are academic exercises, of some slight use perhaps for clarifying thought, but with very little chance of ever being posed on the chequer board of actual life." This inconsistency of theory and policy was in keeping with Pigou's position in the early 1930s, when he joined Keynes in supporting fiscal expansion in response to the Depression even though his *Theory of Unemployment* (Pigou 1933) implied that in theory an excess supply of labor could be eliminated by money wage cuts.

As Presley (1986) has shown, the real balance effect was already understood by Keynes and Dennis Robertson in their discussions during the composition of Robertson's *Banking Policy and the Price Level* (1926) (cf. Laidler 1995). The real balance effect has sometimes been thought to settle the issue of whether price and wage flexibility is sufficient in theory to guarantee restoration of full-employment equilibrium after a demand shock. However, Michal Kalecki (1944) pointed out that the real balance effect of Pigou (1943) does not apply to inside money (bank deposits backed by loans rather than reserves), as an increase in the real wealth of depositors would be balanced by an increase in the real liabilities of debtors. In editorial correspondence about Kalecki's comment on Pigou, Kalecki and Keynes agreed that if the interest on government bonds is financed by taxation, the bonds are not net wealth either, so that the real balance effect acts only on the monetary base, a small fraction of the money supply and national debt (Dimand 1991; Patinkin 1982: 102–103).

The arguments of Kalecki and Keynes about the range of assets relevant for the real balance effect weakened, but did not eliminate, the inverse relation between the price level and real aggregate effective demand in a closed economy in the presence of a liquidity trap. Terms of trade effects of price-level changes were excluded from this debate, as they simply redistributed demand between countries, the world as a whole being a closed economy. Keynes (1931b; 1936: ch. 19) and Fisher (1932, 1933), on the other hand, provided grounds for a positive effect of the (expected) rate of change of the price level on the level of real aggregate effective demand.

Keynes argued in Chapter 19 of the *General Theory* that increased money wage flexibility (and consequently increased price flexibility) might not tend to be stabilizing. The expectation of falling money wages (and hence falling prices as lower money wages shifted the aggregate supply curve) would increase the expected real rate of return on holding real money balances, since currency and reserves have a fixed nominal return of zero. The real return on other assets would also increase (assuming a portfolio equilibrium in which positive amounts of both money and other assets are held as imperfect substitutes for each other): "the effect of an expectation that wages are going to sag by, say 2 percent in the coming year will be roughly equivalent to the effect of a rise of 2 percent in the amount of interest payable for the same period" (Keynes 1936: 265). Such an increase in real interest rates would reduce investment. The faster prices are expected to decline, the greater will be the depressing effect on investment. This effect does not depend on the economy being in a liquidity trap in which the nominal interest rate cannot fall further, but only on the fixed own-rate of interest on the monetary base and imperfect substitution between money and other assets. Keynes (1923: 23) had already made this point in his *Tract on Monetary Reform*: "When prices are falling 30 to 40 per cent between the average of one year and that of the next, as they were in Great Britain and in the United States during 1921, even a bank rate of 1 per cent would have been oppressive to business, since it would have corresponded to a very high rate of real interest. Anyone who could have foreseen the movement even partially would have done well for himself by selling out his assets and staying out of business."

The real balance effect will also be offset by what Tobin (1980: 9–11) terms the Fisher effect of a change in the real value of inside debt. An unanticipated decline in prices redistributes wealth to creditors from debtors, who presumably became debtors because of a higher marginal propensity to spend from wealth or other available resources. Since there is so much more inside debt than outside money, even a tiny difference between debtors and creditors in marginal propensities to spend could lead this Fisher effect to swamp the real balance effect. Fisher (1932, 1933) also argued that, given the level of outstanding nominal debt, the fear of costly bankruptcies, induced as falling prices increase the real value of debt, would cause a scramble for liquidity that would further reduce asset and commodity prices (cf. Dimand 1994). The individually rational scramble for liquidity by debtors would end up increasing their real burden of debt in aggregate: "By March, 1933, liquidation had reduced the debts by about 20 percent, but had increased the dollar by about 75 percent, so that the *real* debt, that is debt measured in terms of commodities, was increased about 40 percent" (Fisher 1933: 346). Fisher's attention was focused on the debt-deflation process by the asset price deflation that began in 1929 and that reduced by 11 million dollars Fisher's net worth of 10 million dollars. This analysis provided Fisher with an explanation of why the stock market crash of 1929 was followed by a lasting, major depression while the deflation of 1920–1921 was followed by a much briefer depression. The volume of inside debt denominated in money terms was substantially larger in 1929, so that deflation caused a larger increase in real inside debt than had occurred in 1920–1921. Such a debt-deflation theory of great depressions has recently been the subject of renewed interest (Bernanke 1995; Dimand 1994; Gertler 1994; King 1994; Minsky 1982b; Spotton 1996; Wolfson 1996).

This Fisher effect was independently noted, without reference to Fisher, by Don Patinkin in a 1951 addition to the reprint of an earlier article, as the first of "two reservations, neither one of which has been considered by Haberler or Pigou. First of all, we have tacitly been assuming that the depressing effect of a price decline on a debtor is roughly offset by its stimulating effect on a creditor; hence the private sector, being on balance a creditor with respect to the government, can ultimately be stimulated by a price decline. But allowance must be made for the possibility of a differential reaction of debtors and creditors. That is, if debtors are discouraged by a price decline more than creditors are encouraged, it may be possible that there exists no price decline which would have an encouraging effect on expenditures" (Patinkin 1951: 262–263).

Keynes did not refer to the debt-deflation process in the *General Theory* or in his 1937 contribution to a volume of essays in honor of Fisher. However, he twice made independent reference to it in 1931. In June 1931, Keynes gave three Harris Foundation lectures at the University of Chicago on "The Economic Analysis of Unemployment." In his concluding lecture, Keynes (1931a: 359–362) rejected a proposal by O. M. W. Sprague of Harvard, economic advisor to the Bank of England, to rely on deflation to restore equilibrium: "national debts, war debts, obligations between the creditor and debtor nations, farm mortgages, real estate mortgages—all this financial structure would be deranged by the adoption of Dr Sprague's proposal. A widespread bankruptcy, default, and repudiation of bonds would necessarily ensue. Banks would be in jeopardy. I need not continue the catalogue. And what would be the advantage of having caused so much ruin? I do not know. Dr Sprague did not tell us that" (1931a: 361).

In August 1931, Keynes wrote on "The Consequences to the Banks of the Collapse of Money Values" for his *Essays in Persuasion*. He warned that a sufficiently large decline in the money value of collateral for bank loans would disrupt the process of financial intermediation, depressing the economy as banks curtailed credit: "Modern capitalism is faced, in my belief, with the choice between finding some way to increase money values towards their former figure, or seeing widespread insolvencies and defaults with a collapse of a large part of the financial structure;—after which we should all start again, not nearly so much poorer as we should expect, and much more cheerful perhaps, but having suffered a period of waste and disturbance and social injustice, and a general re-arrangement of private fortunes and the ownership of wealth" (Keynes 1931b: 177; cf. King 1994: 429). He explained: "There was a large downward movement in the slump of 1921, but that was from an exceptionally high level of values which had ruled for only a few months or weeks, so that only a small proportion of the banks' loans had been based on such values and these values had not lasted long enough to be trusted. *Never* before has there been such a world-wide collapse over almost the whole field of the money values of real assets as we have experienced in the last two years" (Keynes 1931b: 171–172). Keynes's 1931 lecture and essay about the disruptive effect of rapid deflation on the system of financial intermediation lead to the later analyses of financial instability by Hyman Minsky (e.g., Minsky 1975). Like Fisher (1932, 1933), Keynes (1931a, 1931b) passed unmentioned in the *General Theory* (see Dimand 1995 on Fisher's displacement by Keynes in the attention of macroeconomists). Twentieth Century Fund studies by Evans Clark (1933) and Albert G. Hart (1938) considered the role of debt in deflation and as a barrier to recovery, but remained outside the mainstream of economic discussion.

Thus, while a lower price level implies a larger real aggregate effective demand, a falling price level on the contrary tends to reduce effective demand. In the WKP (Walras-Keynes-Phillips) model of Tobin (1975), one effect or the other will dominate. What made Tobin label this model Walrasian rather than Marshallian is that differences between desired expenditure (E) and output (Y) cause changes in output rather than in prices:

$$dY = A_y(E(p, x, y) - Y) \qquad (2.1.1)$$

$$dp/p = A_p(Y - Y^*) + x \tag{2.2.1}$$

$$dx = A_x(dp/p - x), \tag{2.3.1}$$

where x is the expected rate of change of the price level (p), and with the equations numbered as in Tobin (1975). Possible non-uniqueness of potential output (Y^*) is not considered in this model, which is used to illustrate the possibility that, even if there is only one level of Y^*, the economy may move further away from Y^* after a sufficiently large shock.

Substituting Equation (2.2.1) into Equation (2.3.1) yields

$$dx = A_x A_p(Y - Y^*). \tag{3.1}$$

Tobin (1975, 1980) protested: "By here assuming (2.2.1) I do not mean necessarily to associate myself—much less Keynes!—with the natural-rate hypothesis in all its power and glory." Tobin's WKP model is in fact closer to Fisher than to any of the economists for whom Tobin named it. Fisher believed in the long-run neutrality of money and, unlike Keynes, stressed money illusion as an explanation of short-run nonneutrality, so he would have accepted the natural rate hypothesis of Equation (2.2.1) that output varies from potential output Y^* only when expectations are mistaken. Fisher used monetary shocks and slowly adjusting price expectations to explain output, while Phillips had used unemployment to explain changes in money wage rates (cf. Dimand 1993, 1994). The adaptive expectations hypothesis of Equation (2.3.1) matches Fisher's practice, when decomposing the money interest rate into real interest and expected inflation, of representing expectations by a distributed lag of past price changes (see Dimand 1994).

The issue of stability is whether expenditure E increases when Y is less than Y^*. Since $E = E(p, x, Y)$,

$$dE = E_p dp + E_x dx + E_y dY. \tag{4}$$

Multiplying Equation (2.2.1) through by p, and substituting it and Equation (3.1) into Equation (4) yields

$$dE = E_p p A_p(Y - Y^*) + px + E_x A_x A_p(Y - Y^*) + E_y dY. \tag{5.1}$$

Collecting terms involving $(Y - Y^*)$ gives

$$dE = (pE_p + A_xE_x)A_p(Y - Y^*) + px + E_ydY \qquad (5.2)$$

with $E_p < 0, E_x > 0, A_x > 0, A_p > 0, 0 < E_y < 1.$

The critical necessary condition for stability (for E to increase when Y is less than Y^* and decrease when Y is less than Y^*) is $pE_p + A_xE_x < 0$, which is Tobin's Equation (3.4). When Equation (3.4) is satisfied, the partial derivative of dE with respect to $(Y - Y^*)$ is negative. The real balance effect would tend to make the first term negative, as a lower price level stimulates consumption by increasing net wealth, and the effect on investment of a larger real money supply due to lower prices would act in the same direction. On the other hand, the redistribution of wealth between debtors and creditors by an unanticipated price change would act in the same direction. The second term is positive, as higher inflation reduces the real return on holding the monetary base, hence lowering real interest rates and stimulating investment. "As would be expected," wrote Tobin (1975: 199–200), "a strong negative price-level effect on aggregate demand [E_p], a weak price-expectation effect [E_x], and a slow response of price expectations to experience [A_x] are conducive to stability." If expectations of inflation did not respond at all to experience ($A_x = 0$), the second term of Equation (3.4) would vanish, and, provided that $E_p < 0$ the necessary condition for stability of the system must be satisfied.

Tobin (1975: 201) noted the possibility that "[t]he system might be stable for small deviations from its equilibrium but unstable for large shocks." This is because the price-level effect on expenditure (E_p) is the sum of a "Keynes effect" of a larger real money supply lowering interest rates and stimulating investment (a lower price level shifting the LM curve outward along the IS curve) and a (Pigou-Haberler-Scitovsky) real balance effect on consumption, minus the Fisher effect reflecting the redistribution of wealth as the value of inside debt changes. "The weakening or vanishing of the 'Keynes effect' at low values of Y and p tends to reduce E_p in absolute value" (Tobin 1975: 200) with the result that the stability condition of Equation (3.4) might not be satisfied once a shock had displaced Y far below Y^*. Similarly, Scarth (1996: 74–80, following Groth 1993) suggests that a high interest-elasticity of money demand at very low levels of Y (causing fears of widespread bankruptcy and hence a scramble for liquidity) and of nominal interest rates can cause a stability condition (in their case, the convergence requirement of Cagan's model of hyperinflation) not to hold, so that a Keynesian corridor will exist (see also Flaschel and Franke 2000; Klausinger 2002).

Given that, by this argument, E_p depends on Y and p, the boundary of the corridor of stability is the level of Y given by

$$E_p(p, Y) = -A_x E_x / p. \tag{6}$$

This critical value of Y will be below Y^*. The system will be unstable for shocks that drive the system outside its corridor of stability by driving Y below this critical level. The width of the corridor would depend on the volume of outstanding nominal debt, which influences the force of the Fisher effect and thus the size (and perhaps even the sign) of E_p. Consequently, the width of the corridor of stability could narrow during a long boom, in keeping with Minsky's discussions of the changing stability of the economy as financial structure changes over the course of the cycle (Minsky 1982a, 1986). This was Fisher's explanation of why the sharp deflation of 1920–1921 did not result in a great depression: inside debt denominated in fixed nominal terms was significantly smaller relative to the size of the economy in 1920–1921 than in 1929 (Fisher 1932, 1933).

The way in which this analysis leads to a corridor of stability is the plausible assumption that prices will change more rapidly the further the system is from equilibrium (cf. Arrow 1959). A small displacement from full-employment equilibrium due to a negative demand shock would cause only a slow deflation. The economy would reach a lower price level (with a positive real balance effect on consumption) without any substantial increase in real interest rates that would reduce investment. An automatic adjustment back to full-employment equilibrium would result. A larger negative demand shock, however, could cause a sufficiently rapid deflation that real aggregate effective demand would be further decreased—which would then lead to even more rapid deflation, as output would be even further below its full-employment level. A cumulative deflation would occur, as in Keynes's *Treatise on Money*, until some offsetting demand shock happened (cf. Dimand 1986; 1988: ch. 2).

A corridor of stability could be incorporated in macroeconomic models by making appropriate demand depend negatively on the price level but positively on the rate of change of prices, while how rapidly prices change depends on how far the system is from full-employment equilibrium. In such a model, given some flexibility of prices and money wages, the self-adjusting mechanism would return the economy to full employment after a demand shock that was not too large. However, a large negative demand shock shifting the economy's output far below potential would induce a rapid deflation that would further reduce aggregate demand and move the economy even further away from its full-employment equilibrium.

The real balance effect does not suffice to ensure that, in the absence of nominal rigidities, an economy will automatically return to a full-employment equilibrium after a negative demand shock. The issue of whether an economy will return to full employment without government intervention is not settled by the comparative static argument that, if prices were not changing and if the price level had been correctly foreseen when all outstanding nominal debts were contracted, a lower price level would be associated with a higher level of real expenditure, *ceteris paribus.* While, as Leijonhufvud notes, Keynes did not derive or discuss the corridor of stability in the *General Theory*, his Chapter 19 examination of what happens when money wages are flexible, together with his Fisher-like 1931 remarks on debt and deflation, provide the building blocks for an approach in which the economy is self-adjusting only for shocks up to a certain size. Tobin (1975, 1980) points the road toward the class of macroeconomic models called for by Leijonhufvud, models of economies that usually coordinate activities well and that are self-adjusting in response to most shocks they encounter, but that suffer coordination and adjustment failures in the face of exceptionally large shocks.

Such models would be consistent with Keynes's view of the stability of the economy. He did not believe that the economy was violently unstable and did not advocate continual fine-tuning of aggregate demand by the fiscal and monetary authorities. Instead, he recognized and respected the automatic adjustment mechanism through which the market could handle most shocks. He felt that these authorities had a responsibility to stabilize the economy in the wake of major shocks too strong for the classical adjustment mechanism to cope with and to create an institutional framework conducive to stability (such as Keynes sought at Bretton Woods). In his last, posthumously published *Economic Journal* article, Keynes stated, "I find myself moved, not for the first time, to remind contemporary economists that the classical teaching embodied some permanent truths of great significance, which we are liable to-day to overlook because we associate them with doctrines which we cannot now accept without much qualification. There are in these matters deep undercurrents at work, natural forces, one can call them, or even the invisible hand, which are operating towards equilibrium. If it were not so, we could not have got on even so well as we have for many decades past" (quoted in Moggridge 1992: 823). As Keynes said, both in a House of Lords speech in December 1945 defending the Bretton Woods Agreements and in his final article, he stood for "an attempt to use what we have learned from modern experience and modern analysis, not to defeat, but to implement the wisdom of Adam Smith" (quoted in Moggridge 1992: 824). This was a point of view strongly and more consistently held by Irving Fisher who, notably in *The Purchasing Power of Money* (Fisher with Brown 1911), argued for the long-run classical neutrality of money, while devoting his life to the need for reform of the monetary system so that the economy would actually behave in short-run "transition periods" as though it were in the idealized long-run of the classical economists (see Dimand 1993, 1999 on Fisher's monetary macroeconomics). The debt-deflation process of Fisher (1932, 1933), which was also mentioned briefly by Keynes (1931a, 1931b), provides a way to introduce such a corridor of stability into macroeconomic models when combined with a recognition that some parameters (such as that representing the so-called Keynes effect) change value at low levels of output, prices, and nominal interest.

Note

1. Keynes is unlikely to have encountered the real balance effect in Haberler's third edition (1941: 491–503). The *Economic Journal* published Richard Kahn's review of the first edition, Haberler's reply, a note by Keynes denying Haberler's claim that Kahn had misinterpreted Keynes, and Keynes's short unsigned review of the second edition but no review of the third edition.

References

Arrow, K. J. (1959). "Toward a Theory of Price Adjustment." In *The Allocation of Economic Resources.* Eds. M. Abramovitz et al. Stanford, CA: Stanford University Press.

Bernanke, B. S. (1995). "Money, Credit, and Banking Lecture: The Macroeconomics of the Great Depression: A Comparative Approach." *Journal of Money, Credit and Banking* 27(1): 16–29.

Black, F. (1987). *Business Cycles and Equilibrium.* Oxford: Basil Blackwell.

Chadha, B. (1989). "Is Increased Price Inflexibility Stabilizing?" *Journal of Money, Credit and Banking* 21(4): 481–497.

Clark, E., assisted by G. B. Galloway, ed. (1933). *The Internal Debts of the United States.* New York: Macmillan for Twentieth Century Fund.

De Long, J. B., and L. H. Summers. (1986). "Is Increased Price Flexibility Stabilizing?" *American Economic Review* 76(5): 1031–1044.

——. (1988). "Is Increased Flexibility Stabilizing? Reply." *American Economic Review* 78(1): 273–276.

Dimand, R. W. (1986). "The Macroeconomics of the *Treatise on Money.*" *Eastern Economic Journal* 12(4): 431–441.

——. (1988). *The Origins of the Keynesian Revolution.* Upleadon, UK: Edward Elgar, and Stanford, CA: Stanford University Press.

——. (1991). "Keynes, Kalecki, Ricardian Equivalence and the Real Balance Effect." *Bulletin of Economic Research* 43(3): 289–292.

——. (1993). "The Dance of the Dollar: Irving Fisher's Monetary Theory of Economic Fluctuations." *History of Economics Review* 20: 161–172.

——. (1994). "Irving Fisher's Debt-Deflation Theory of Great Depressions." *Review of Social Economy* 52(1): 92–107. Rpt. in Hans-E. Loef and Hans G. Monissen, eds. (1999) *The Economics of Irving Fisher.* Cheltenham, UK, and Northampton, MA: Edward Elgar.

——. (1995). "Irving Fisher, J. M. Keynes, and the Transition to Modern Macroeconomics." In *New Perspectives on Keynes.* Eds. A. F. Cottrel and M. S. Lawlor. Annual Supplement to *History of Political Economy* 27: 247–266.

——. (1999). "Fisher's Monetary Macroeconomics." In *The Economics of Irving Fisher.* Eds. H. E. Loef and H. G. Monissen. Cheltenham, UK, and Northampton, MA: Edward Elgar.

Driskill, R. A., and S. M. Sheffrin. (1986). "Is Price Flexibility Destabilizing?" *American Economic Review* 76(4): 802–807.

Fisher, I. (1932). *Booms and Depressions.* New York: Adelphi. Rpt. in Fisher (1997) *The Works of Irving Fisher.* Vol. 10. Ed. William J. Barber. London: Pickering & Chatto.

——. (1933). "The Debt-Deflation Theory of Great Depressions." *Econometrica* 1(3): 337–357. Rpt. in Fisher (1997) *The Works of Irving Fisher.* Vol. 10. Ed. William J. Barber. London: Pickering & Chatto.

——. (1997). *The Works of Irving Fisher*, 14 vols. Ed. William J. Barber. London: Pickering & Chatto.

Fisher, I., assisted by H. G. Brown. (1911). *The Purchasing Power of Money*. New York: Macmillan. Rpt. in Fisher (1997) *The Works of Irving Fisher*. Vol. 4. Ed. William J. Barber. London: Pickering & Chatto.

Flaschel, P., and R. Franke. (2000). "An Old Keynesian Note on Destabilizing Price Stability." *Review of Political Economy* 12: 272–283.

Gertler, M. (1994). "Financial Conditions and Macroeconomic Behavior." *NBER Reporter* (Summer): 10–14.

Groth, C. (1993). "Some Unfamiliar Dynamics of a Familiar Macro Model: A Note." *Journal of Economics (Zeitschrift fuer Nationaloekonomie)* 58(3): 293–305.

Haberler, G. (1941). *Prosperity and Depression*. 3rd ed. Geneva: League of Nations.

Hart, A. G. (1938). *Debts and Recovery: A Study of Changes in the Internal Debt Structure from 1929 to 1937 and a Program for the Future: The Factual Findings by Albert Gailord Hart the Program by the Committee on Debt Adjustment*. New York: Twentieth Century Fund. Rpt in A. G. Hart and P. Merhling (1995) *Debt, Crisis, and Recovery: The 1930s and the 1990s*. Armonk, NY: M. E. Sharpe.

Kalecki, M. (1944). "Professor Pigou on 'The Classical Stationary State': A Comment." *Economic Journal* 54(2): 131–132.

Keynes, J. M. (1923). *A Tract on Money Reform*. London: Macmillan.

——. (1930). *A Treatise on Money*. 2 vols. London: Macmillan.

——. (1931a). "An Economic Analysis of Unemployment." In *Unemployment as a World Problem*. Ed. Q. Wright. Chicago: University of Chicago Press. Rpt. in Keynes (1973) *Collected Writings of John Maynard Keynes*. Vol. XIII. Ed. D. E. Moggridge. London: Macmillan, and New York: Cambridge University Press for the Royal Economic Society.

——. (1931b). "The Consequences to the Banks of the Collapse of Money Values."In *Essays in Persuasion*. London: Macmillan.

——. (1936). *The General Theory of Employment, Interest and Money*. London: Macmillan.

King, M. (1994). "Presidential Address: Debt Deflation: Theory and Evidence." *European Economic Review* 38: 419–445.

Klausinger, H. (2002). "A Note on the Stability of Full Employment." *Review of Political* Economy 14: 211–225.

Laidler, D. (1995). "Robertson in the 1920s." *European Journal of the History of Economic Thought* 2(1): 151–174.

Leijonhufvud, A. ([1973] 1981). "Effective Demand Failures." *Swedish Journal of Economics*. Rpt. in Leijonhufvud (1981) *Information and Coordination: Essays in Macroeconomic Theory*. New York: Oxford University Press.

——. ([1976] 1981). "Schools, 'Revolutions,' and Research Programmes in Economic Theory." In *Method and Appraisal in Economics.* Ed. Spiro Latsis. Cambridge: Cambridge University Press. Rpt. in Leijonhufvud (1981) *Information and Coordination: Essays in Macroeconomic Theory.* New York: Oxford University Press.

Minsky, H. P. (1975). *John Maynard Keynes.* New York: Columbia University Press.

——. (1982a). *Can "IT" Happen Again? Essays on Instability & Finance.* Armonk, NY: M. E. Sharpe.

——. (1982b). "Debt-Deflation Processes in Today's Institutional Environment." *Banca Nazionale del Lavoro Quarterly Review* 143.

——. (1986). *Stabilizing an Unstable Economy.* New Haven, CT: Yale University Press.

Moggridge, D. E. (1992). *Maynard Keynes: An Economist's Biography.* London and New York: Routledge.

Patinkin, D. (1951). "Price Flexibility and Full Employment." In *Readings in Monetary Theory.* Eds. F. A. Lutz and L. W. Mints. New York, Philadelphia, and Toronto: Blakiston.

——. (1982). *Anticipations of the General Theory? And Other Essays on Keynes.* Chicago: University of Chicago Press.

Pigou, A. C. (1933). *The Theory of Unemployment.* London: Macmillan.

——. (1941). *Employment and Equilibrium.* London: Macmillan.

——. (1943). "The Classical Stationary State." *Economic Journal* 53(4): 343–351.

——. (1947). "Economic Progress in a Stable Environment." *Economica* 14: 180–188. Rpt. in F. A. Lutz and L. W. Mints, eds. (1951) *Readings in Monetary Theory.* New York, Philadelphia and Toronto: Blakiston.

Presley, J. R. (1986). "J. M. Keynes and the Real Balance Effect." *Manchester School* 54 (1): 22–30.

Robertson, D. H. (1926). *Banking Policy and the Price Level.* London: P. S. King and Son. Rpt. (1949) New York: A. M. Kelley.

Scarth, W. M. (1996). *Macroeconomics: An Introduction to Advanced Methods.* 2nd ed. Toronto: Dryden.

Spotton, B. L. (1996). "Financial Instability: Some Stylized Facts." *Canadian Journal of Economics* 29(Special Issue Part 1): S202–S206.

Tobin, J. (1975). "Keynesian Models of Recession and Depression." *American Economic Review* 65(2): 195–202.

——. (1980). *Asset Accumulation and Economic Activity.* Chicago: University of Chicago Press.

Wolfson, M. H. (1996). "Irving Fisher's Debt-Deflation Theory: Its Relevance to Current Conditions." *Cambridge Journal of Economics* 20(3): 315–333.

Fisher's Introductory Text

By JAMES TOBIN*

ABSTRACT. In this essay, James Tobin discusses Fisher's *Elementary Principles of Economics* (1912). This essay was first published in the *American Economic Review: Papers and Proceedings*, 87 (May 1997): pp. 430–432. We are grateful to the American Economic Association for permission to republish this essay.

Irving Fisher was a dedicated teacher—in classrooms, in books, and in the personal contacts by which he sought to educate presidents of the United States and influential business and government leaders throughout the world.

At Yale, Fisher liked to prepare for his students his own written expositions. He even wrote a calculus text for fellow students he was tutoring. Not surprisingly, when he assumed responsibility for the economics introductory course in 1910 he was dissatisfied with existing texts and wrote his own. He and a half dozen other instructors taught from experimental editions for two years before he settled on the published version of *Elementary Principles of Economics* (1912). It was reprinted ten times, the last in 1932, but never substantively revised.

Elementary Principles was not very popular outside Yale. However, much of the material survived, incorporated in the more conventional textbook published first in 1926 and in its fifth and final version in 1948, by Fisher's Yale students and colleagues F. R. Fairchild, E. S. Furniss, and N. S. Buck. Their *Elementary Economics* was the market leader between the world wars.

Maybe Fisher's text was too good for the market. Anyway it is very different from other texts of his day and of ours. Fisher does not try to capture students' attention by covering contemporary events,

*Professor James Tobin (1918–2002) received the Nobel Prize in economics in 1981. He served as the Sterling Professor of Economics at Yale University and served on the Yale faculty from 1950 until his retirement from teaching in 1988. Additional biographical information about James Tobin can be found above on p. 113.

The American Journal of Economics and Sociology, Vol. 64, No. 1 (January, 2005).

controversies, and policies. He includes few statistics, none that have to be up-to-date to be useful. He does not tailor his expositions and illustrations too closely to the experiences and institution of one country. He does not try to cover the entire domain of economics with its many applied fields; he urges students to take applied courses or explore those fields on their own.

Fisher tries to equip readers to think like economists. He stresses the basic concepts, not algebraic models and formulas. He does not train students to do synthetic numerical problems.

Why should a Principles text have to be revised every three or five years? Presumably the basic concepts and methods of the discipline are more durable than that. Rather it is the economic journalism which most textbooks combine with theory that compels frequent revision—perhaps to the profit of authors and publishers. A book like Fisher's does not build in obsolescence and does not need revision until the profession rethinks principles.

Are there any modern elementary texts in the same spirit? I am aware of two, Donald Nichols and Clark Reynolds (1971) and Edmund S. Phelps (1985). I am afraid their market success was similar to Fisher's.

Fisher suspects that his student-readers are unconsciously confused about simple basic concepts. He would set them straight about the differences and connections between stocks and flows; capital and income; insolvency and illiquidity; wealth and saving; deficits and debts; price level and relative prices. He wants them to distinguish "money" as used colloquially to refer to wealth or income from money as an asset with the definite properties of currency. He reminds them that bygones are bygones.

The book is unorthodox in its selection of topics and in their order and weight. He starts with 143 pages on capital and income accounting, individual and social. Then come 114 pages of his monetary theory. Only after half the book does he get to standard micro, supply and demand (which he deprecates [Fisher, 1912 p. 145] as an overused "glib" phrase that substitutes for "real analyses"), and relative prices. After 96 pages he returns to economy-wide concerns, the theory of interest, and the distribution of income and wealth.

Fisher's textbook implements his conviction that he can make even his most esoteric results understandable to nonprofessional readers. The accounting chapters carry the message of *The Nature of Capital and Income* (1906); the monetary chapters expound the gist of *The Purchasing Power of Money* (1911); and the theories of interest and of distribution are based on *The Rate of Interest* (1907). Fisher's first great work, *Mathematical Investigations in the Theory of Value and Prices* (1892) is not represented in the textbook. This is surprising; one would expect Fisher to enjoy explaining to students how the economy can be regarded as a system of simultaneous equations; he had, after all, built an instructive mechanical-hydraulic model to depict general equilibrium.

As would be expected, this book is particularly strong in treatment of intertemporal choices and markets. According to Fisher, interest is "by far the most important sort of price with which economics has to deal" (Fisher, 1912 p. 354). But these chapters would have been better if written after Fisher's second book on interest theory, *The Theory of Interest* (1930). In the textbook, Fisher appears to subscribe to "impatience" as the sole determinant of the rate of interest, neglecting the other blade of the scissors, opportunities, clearly awarded a parallel role in the later book. Here he scornfully dismisses as vulgar fallacies the concepts of productivity as a source of interest and the idea that the rate of return on capital could be a determinant of the interest rate. Like Joan Robinson later, he objects that the latter argument is circular, because the value of capital is itself determined by the rate of interest used to capitalize future earnings on capital goods. He ignores the fact that from the earnings or rents on reproducible capital can be determined a "rate of return over cost"—Fisher's own term subsequently—independent of the interest rate.

In contrast to his rival John Bates Clark, Fisher does not regard interest as a return to a factor-of-production "capital" comparable to labor and land. Interest is an allowance for time delays between inputs of labor and land and their outputs. Capital goods are essentially like other intermediate goods, part of the time-consuming nexus of ultimate inputs and final outputs of consumer goods. Sometimes, indeed, he seems to be expounding a labor theory of value (e.g., Fisher, 1912 pp. 77, 306), but all he means is that the utilities (he calls them "desirabilities" for some reason) of consumption have to compensate for the disutilities of work. Only human beings, not machines and acres of land, have utilities and disutilities. (Fisher does play with the idea of human capital [p. 139], but he sees the prohibition of slavery as a drawback to the concept.)

The main messages to freshmen are those of classical economics, with exceptions. Money is neutral—except during monetary transitions, where interest rates lag price changes (pp. 359–62). This is the only mention of business cycles in the book. Markets generally work for the best—except that scale economies lead to cutthroat competition or collusion or monopoly and price discrimination. "Make work" is a fallacy. Free trade and labor-saving progress benefit society, but they do hurt some workers in the short run. Inequality of wealth is mainly due to differences in thriftiness, thus differential impatience (Fisher allows himself thus to explain the prosperity of Holland, Scotland, England, and France in contrast to the poverty of Ireland, China, India, and Java, and of Negroes, peasants, and American Indians everywhere.)

Nevertheless, there are some Fisherian heresies. What he calls "unequal foresight" (p. 362), anticipating asymmetrical information, can distort market interest rates. The efficiency of asset markets is impaired by those who would now be called "noise traders." Government regulation is essential to handle problems commodity markets do not solve: eugenics, alcoholism, unhealthful and unsafe hours and conditions of employment, and pollution, all subjects of Fisher crusades. Despite his theory of inequality, above, he sees a case for inheritance taxation and despises the very rich, whose irrational acquisitiveness he attributes to competitive spirals of "vanity."

Fisher is an ingenious architect of tables, balance sheets, diagrams, and figures. They all assist his verbal arguments, though some require considerable intellectual effort. In the textbook he is especially fond of pictures of reservoirs connected by flows that equalize their levels, or sometimes do not, and of scales balanced by weights representing, for example, supplies and demands. But there is less curve-shifting than in a typical modern textbook.

Matrix tables for flows of funds and asset stocks (columns for sectors and rows for asset groups) would greatly improve Fisher's accounting chapters. Likewise Leontief input-output matrices would clarify his discussion of intermediate durable and nondurable goods.

The textbook appears in Volume 5 of the forthcoming collection of Fisher's works, where the editor, William Barber, reviews comments on the book from prepublication readers (especially Edwin Kemmerer) and postpublication reviewers. These were quite negative: the book is too difficult for beginners, and too eccentric. It coverage is incomplete. Fisher was not impressed.

References

Fairchild, F. R., Furniss, E. S. and Buck, N. S. *Elementary economics*, 5th Ed. (2 Vols). New York: Macmillan, 1948.

Fisher, Irving. *Mathematical investigations in the theory of value and prices*, Transactions of the Connecticut Academy of Arts and Sciences No. 9. New Haven, CT: Connecticut Academy of Arts and Sciences, 1892; reprinted, New York: Augustus M. Kelley, 1961.

——. *The nature of capital and income.* New York: Macmillan, 1906.

——. *The rate of interest.* New York: Macmillan, 1907.

——. *The purchasing power of money.* New York: Macmillan, 1911.

——. *Elementary principles of economics.* New York: Macmillan, 1912.

——. *The theory of interest.* New York: Macmillan, 1930.

Nichols, Donald A. and Reynolds, Clark W. *Principles of economics.* New York: Holt, Rinehart and Winston, 1971.

Phelps, Edmunds S. *Political economy: An introductory text.* New York: Norton, 1985.

Fisher's *The Nature of Capital and Income**

By JAMES TOBIN

ABSTRACT. In this essay James Tobin reminds us of the importance of Irving Fisher's great book and how that book was favorably received by economists. Fisher presented fundamental definitions and supplied a path breaking exposition of the mathematics of interest rates and their relationship to the valuation of assets. This essay was originally published as the "Editorial Introduction to Volume 2 of *The Works of Irving Fisher*, 14 vols London: Pickering & Chatto, 1997; 2:1–6.

> "[The book] . . . , besides presenting the first modern theory of accounting, is (or should be) the basis of modern income analysis."
> Joseph A. Schumpeter

The Background

SCHUMPETER REGARDED *The Nature of Capital and Income* as one of the three of Fisher's contributions to general theory generally recognized, at the time Schumpeter was writing, as "of first-class importance and originality." The other two were Fisher's *Mathematical Investigations* (1892) and his statistical method for measuring the marginal utility of income (1927). Actually Schumpeter cites, as if still another, Fisher's theory of interest—presented in *The Rate of Interest* (1907) and *The Theory of Interest* (1930)—but it is not quite clear whether he gives it full rank.[1]

*A version of this essay has been published in German as the Introduction to the reissue of *The Nature of Capital and Income* in Germany by Verlag Wirtschaft and Finanz GmbH.

Professor James Tobin (1918–2002) received the Nobel Prize in economics in 1981. He served as the Sterling Professor of Economics at Yale University and served on the Yale faculty from 1950 until his retirement from teaching in 1988. Additional biographical information about James Tobin can be found above on p. 113.

The American Journal of Economics and Sociology, Vol. 64, No. 1 (January, 2005).

Nature is the bridge, both in sequence and in logic, between the other two great works, the timeless general equilibrium theory of the 1892 dissertation and the extension of that theory to intertemporal choices in production and consumption in the theory of interest.

Fisher himself confessed that he had not appreciated the element of time when he was writing his doctoral thesis (1892), and accordingly he had not understood the importance of distinguishing between capital and income. "Just 'as accountants distinguish sharply between capital accounts or balance sheets relating to a point of time and income accounts relating to a period of time,' he came to realize that the theory of capital and income should be built along similar lines. But . . . in 1895 economics and accountancy were almost total strangers' . . ."[2]

Fisher became a member of Yale University's faculty of political economy in 1895, and he began immediately to attack the problems of capital, income, and time in both accounting and economic theory. His work quickly bore fruit. He published three articles in the *Economic Journal* in 1896 and 1897 and what amounts to a book, *Appreciation and Interest* (1896), as an issue of the American Economic Association's series of *Publications.* (Theses contributions are reproduced in Volume 1 of *The Works of Irving Fisher.*)

His courageous victorious bout with tuberculosis left him with an intense lifelong personal and intellectual interest in hygiene. His experience was fresh in his mind when he wrote in *The Nature* (p. 176):

> "A large part of our *subjective* income is due to our condition of health or disease. A man with a good constitution has a more agreeable stream of consciousness than one without . . . . [A] healthy body is absolutely essential for receiving and enjoying the income from external wealth . . . . Economists, by fixing attention exclusively on physical phenomena leave out the most essential element of all, the vigor of human life. The true 'wealth of nations' is the health of its individuals."

With characteristic vigor Fisher picked up in 1904 where he had left off six years before. His exhaustive historical survey of economists' treatment of capital continued. He reviewed books regularly for the *Yale Review*, among them works on capital and interest by two predecessors he greatly admired, Böhm-Bawerk and John Rae.

The stage had been set. The enterprise Fisher had begun in 1895 culminated in the two classic books of 1906 and 1907.

The Nature of the Book

In writings he regarded as of practical importance, Fisher addressed lay readers as well as economists. He generally had a message to policy-makers in business, finance, and government: here is a way you can do things more rationally, with benefits to yourselves and to the world. In those cases, Fisher started from scratch and designed his exposition so that any intelligent and concerned reader could understand. The main points are made in successive approximations, from primer-style simplicity to refined analysis. Mathematical derivations and other difficult or detailed materials are often consigned to appendices.

The Nature is such a book. Its style can seem tedious and repetitious to a modern professional economist. It is easy to forget that concepts and distinctions which are second nature to economists today were matters of confusion in the early twentieth century. Seeking generality for his system of accounts, Fisher devotes many words to fine points and to tortured interpretations of definitions and concepts. As Thorstein Veblen complained in an irreverent review, "[It] is a work of taxonomy, of definition, and classification."[3] It is, after all, a treatise on the logic of accounting, but Fisher's approach creates new economic theory at the same time.

The Nature was received in the profession as an important book. It was widely reviewed, generally admired, but not always agreed with. The controversies that Fisher's earlier articles had inspired were rekindled. Fisher was busy defending his views. A lively discussion on "Are Savings Income?" took place at 1907 meeting of the American Economic Association. (Fisher's replies to critics on this occasion are reproduced in *The Works of Irving Fisher.*)

A significant achievement of *The Nature* is its clarity in insisting on the distinction between stocks and flows and on careful attention to the dimensionalities of the concepts used in economic discourse. One of Fisher's complaints about Adam Smith and his followers was their confusion on these points. According to Fisher, writers before Smith made more sense. (See Chapter IV of the text.)

Is "wealth" in Smith's title a stock or a flow? Maybe both, maybe neither. Maybe it just means material things of value. Although "stock" in Smith appears to refer to a stock of business capital, Smith confuses the reader by saying that a part of "stock" is invested to yield profits, while another part pays wages or other current expenditures. This muddle is frequently repeated in connection with classical economists' distinction between fixed and circulating (or working) capital, not that the distinction is itself faulty. Even John Stuart Mill, Fisher notes, says that wages are determined by dividing the wages fund by the number of workers, without informing the reader how long the fund has to last, how soon it will be replenished (p. 59).

Likewise Fisher cleared up many misunderstandings about interest rates and their relations to asset valuations. His exposition of the mathematics involved could hardly be improved upon. He treats compounding, both discrete and continuous. He shows how to compute present values, even when the future incomes being valued fluctuate and even jump and the discount rates themselves vary. He discusses interest rates in different standards – money, wheat, gold, silver, bundles of goods – and the relationships among them. Many of these topics had appeared in *Appreciation and Interest* ten years earlier, but *The Nature* is the complete and definitive exposition. (See Chapters VII–XV, XVII of the text and their appendices.)

The Nature contains quite a modern discussion of relation of asset values and interest rates to uncertainties and risks (Chapter XVI). Fisher took the view that the world is deterministic, that it is only our ignorance of nature's laws that makes events unpredictable. He recognizes the role of risk aversion and speaks of "coefficients of caution." In the appendix to the chapter he suggests the standard deviation as a measure of risk. He perceives that willingness to assume risks will differ among individuals, and that these differences will affect markets' allocations of risk among them. Yet, for all his insights, it cannot be said that he succeeds in integrating risk into his theory of valuation or in explaining the risk premiums in market interest rates and asset yields.

The Concept of Capital

Fisher's basic concept of capital is simple and comprehensive. Capital embraces all stocks of material objects that yield services that human beings like. Thus Fisher would include: land and other natural resources as well as reproducible goods; objects owned by households and governments as well as by businesses; houses and other consumer durable goods as well as producers' durables; objects whose yields are always in kind, like houses occupied by their owners, as well as those whose yields are marketed for cash; the bodies of human beings—perhaps their minds too—as well as nonhuman objects. Contemporaries schooled in the classical trilogy of "land, labor, capital" found Fisher's comprehensive view hard to take.

Services are ultimately psychic, subjective satisfactions in "the stream of consciousness" of a human being. Fisher goes so far as to count a loaf of bread as capital. Consumption occurs only as and when the body eats the bread and generates sensations the consumer feels. The difference between the bread and a house or a factory, he says, is a matter not of kind but of degree, the length of time over which the object yields services (Chapter X).

Fisher recognized disservices and negative psychic sensations too, from working, for example. (Yet he himself got only pleasure from his work) at times he came quite close to washing out net social product from labor inputs, by treating them like intermediate goods and counting all wages as compensation for disutility of work. Although Fisher pushed the logic of his arguments to extremes, he was quite prepared to sacrifice purity to practicality in applications.

Fisher explained at length that many of the ultimate capital assets of a society, those that bring sensations of satisfaction to its members, are owned by its members indirectly, by complicated networks of financial and business institutions and intermediary claims and debts. Double-entry bookkeeping, he showed, makes it clear how intermediary claims and obligations wash out – his "method of couples." What is left is the value of the social capital, whose yield is society's income. This is necessarily equal to the sum of the net worths of all individual members, obtained by his "method of balances" (Chapter VI).

The Concept of Income

Fisher's "nature of capital" was controversial at the time, but it is much less so now. His "nature of income" was even more controversial then, and it remains controversial to this day. Fisher defined income as consumption. The implication that a wealthy household or society has a low "income" in periods when it chooses to live frugally and accumulate capital, and a high "income" in periods when it is depleting capital, is difficult to swallow. Some concept of *sustainable* consumption seems preferable. That is why what came to be known as the Haig-Marshall concept of income, namely that rate of consumption consistent with maintaining capital intact, gained wider acceptance than Fisher's proposed definition.

Fisher was well aware of the problem, and in *The Nature* he called the hypothetical intact-capital rate of consumption "standard income" (p.110). In his 1946 memoir, he confesses some regret that he lost some acceptance of his idea by insisting too strongly on identifying income with actual consumption. At that time, he agreed that actual consumption plus capital accumulation, positive or negative, was a useful definition (See the Appendix to Volume 2 of *The Works of Irving Fisher.*)

However, Fisher had a strong point in favor of his original position. His larger vision, brought to fruition in *The Rate of Interest* (1907), was that capital assets throw off streams of services of value in consumption, and that the *values* of those assets are the discounted values of those future services. Asset values are oriented to the future, not to historical cost. This clearly must be so in the case of land, and the principle applies generally. The rates of discount are determined jointly by intertemporal consumption preferences and production opportunities. It is not in principle possible to know what Haig-Marshall income would be, and to know how much saving and accumulation are taking place, without knowing what valuations of capital would prevail if capital actually were being held intact and its valuations were not changing. But capital valuations themselves depend on interest rates, which would be different in a steady state from what they are when consumption is irregular. For one thing, the provision for capital depreciation that must be made to maintain capital intact is not independent of interest rates – consider how to write off a machine that yields constant services for a finite time and then collapses. If Haig-Marshall income is well defined only when it is steadily equal to Fisher income, i.e. to consumption, then it is not so clearly a preferable concept.

Considerations of this kind led J.R. Hicks to say that in economic dynamics income and saving "are bad tools, which break in our hands."[4] In Paul Samuelson's famous 1961 article on the subjects Fisher tackled in 1906, he showed hat neither the Haig-Marshall nor the Fisher income definitions can be relied upon for reliable and sensible comparisons of welfare over time or between economies. For example, would you rather live in economy J or economy U, when U is currently producing and consuming more but J is building more capital facilities and is growing faster? Samuelson's conclusion is in the spirit of Fisher and of Hicks. Do not compare current incomes on any definition. Instead, measure welfare as the discounted value of the expected consumption stream of an individual or an economy.[5]

One of Fisher's often stated arguments was that the inclusion of saving in income is double counting. A dollar of income is counted when it is received, and its future yields, which presumably equal a dollar in present value, are counted in future incomes. Fisher fought a lifelong crusade, publishing a tract as late as 1942, against double taxation of saving. (See Volume XII in *The Works of Irving Fisher* (1997)) He was essentially advocating a consumption tax to replace the conventional income tax. This is one of several Fisher causes that have picked up adherents in the profession in recent years.

The Rate of Interest, published the following year, deserves Samuelson's judgment as the greater of the two books.[6] It is profound and seminal economic theory, while *The Nature* is a sophisticated treatise on accounting. Yet the first book was the indispensable prelude of the second. In *The Rate* there are no less than thirty-seven references to *The Nature*. Most important is the idea that the value of an asset is the capitalization of the stream of future services expected to be thrown off by the asset. That insight is central to both books. In the first, it is the central principle of individual and social accounting. In the second, it becomes the equilibrium condition for determining interest rates.

Notes

1. Schumpeter, *History of Economic Analysis*, New York: Oxford University Press, 1954, 871–2. The reason for Schumpeter's hesitation on Fisher's theory of interest, which most theorists would regard as Fisher's crowning contribution to pure theory, appears to be Fisher's generous, probably too generous, acknowledgement of the priority of John Rae and Eugen von Böhm-Bawerk.

2. Irving Norton Fisher, quoting from his father's unfinished and unpublished memoir of 1946 in *My Father Irving Fisher*, New York: Comet Press, 1956, 123.

3. Thorstein Veblen, "Fisher's Capital and Income," *Political Science Quarterly* 23, March 1908, 112–28.

4. John R. Hicks, *Value and Capital*, Oxford University Press, 1939, 177.

5. Paul A. Samuelson, "The Evaluation of the 'Social Income': Capital Formation and Wealth," Chapter 3 in F.A. Lutz and D.C. Hague, eds., *The Theory of Capital*, London: Macmillan, 1961, 32–57. Also in his *Collected Papers*, I, Chapter 27, 299–324,

6. Samuelson, "Irving Fisher and the Theory of Capital," Chapter 2 in William Fellner et al., *Ten Studies in the Tradition of Irving Fisher*, New York: John Wiley and Son, 1967, 17–37.

Irving Fisher's Spendings (Consumption) Tax in Retrospect

By JOHN B. SHOVEN and JOHN WHALLEY*

ABSTRACT. Irving Fisher wrote a significant number of papers towards the end of his career on the design of the U.S. tax system. These writings culminated in a book that he wrote with his brother Herbert in 1942. Fisher thought that the double taxation of saving under an income tax was extremely harmful to the economy and he therefore proposed a "spendings" tax or what he referred to as a "real income" tax. Even though he disliked the terminology, he advocated what today would be referred to as a progressive consumption tax. Fisher's analysis was both theoretical and practical. His 1942 book contained a proposed tax return that implemented his ideas. His analysis is surprisingly modern and relevant today. This paper presents the Fisher proposal and examines the current U.S. tax system in light of his tax views. We argue that Fisher would find that the U.S. tax system lacks intellectual coherence, is economically inefficient, and unnecessarily complex.

I

Introduction

IRVING FISHER'S REMARKABLE CAREER, and even more remarkable writings, left their indelible marks everywhere across what has emerged as the discipline of economics. From mathematical formalization to intertemporal optimization, general equilibrium, monetary theory, and public finance, the imprint remains sharp and strong. What is striking is that

*Professor John B. Shoven is the Wallace R. Hawley Director of the Stanford Institute for Economic Policy Research and the Charles R. Schwab Professor of Economics at Stanford University, Stanford, California 94305. His recent books include *Private Pensions and Public Policies*, Brookings Institution Press, 2004. Professor John Whalley teaches at the University of Warwick and the University of Western Ontario in Canada and holds a research position at the National Bureau of Economic Research in Boston, Massachusetts.

The American Journal of Economics and Sociology, Vol. 64, No. 1 (January, 2005).

the deepest conceptual contributions repeatedly are driven by the most practical of concerns and presented in language that is aimed at persuasion for implementation of practical proposals, logically following from his conceptual or theoretical economic analysis.

In 1942, when he was an Emeritus Professor at Yale, Irving Fisher, together with his brother Herbert, published a 277-page book entitled *Constructive Income Taxation* that was subtitled "A Proposal for Reform." In it the brothers Fisher set out a proposal for what we call today a consumption tax, a progressive tax on income less savings, rather than a progressive tax on income alone. This was not a new idea for Fisher; rather, it built on his work on capital theory going back to 1896 and reflected what he saw as the logical implications for public policy of his long-standing notion that the term *income* had no economic meaning as an accounting term reflecting calculations of flows of cash. Income, in Fisher's view, could only be meaningfully thought of as "yields" or "cash flows." Yields were what led to benefits, and benefits came from spending (i.e., consumption). Fisher vigorously opposed using the term *consumption* (which he equated with destructive acts). Rather, he argued that *spendings*, not income as measured by accountants, should be the base of any progressive tax used for revenue-raising purposes. Fisher equated the term *spendings* with the term *real income*, which he based on economic welfare.

Fisher went to great lengths to show how taxing conventionally measured income resulted in the double taxation of saving, arguing that this was extremely socially destructive. Fisher wrote papers in *Econometrica* (1937) and the *American Economic Review* (1939) showing analytically how this double taxation, well known today, comes about. In his 1942 volume, he shows how with a corporate tax there is triple taxation, and even argued that there can be quadruple taxation by taking into account estate taxes and taxes on capital gains.

The Fishers also set out in great detail how their proposal would work. They provide a sample tax return, they discuss what would happen to the corporate tax and the capital gains tax under their proposal, how interest should be treated, how timing issues are to be addressed, how to treat bequests and inheritances, and other issues.

Sections of their book are decades ahead of their time, discussing such matters as human capital, though the term is not used. They discuss the constitutionality of their proposal, all the while copiously documenting and citing the works of previous authors. While the book is written to be persuasive, it is extraordinarily closely argued and clear in its logic.

If there is one thing that is even more remarkable than the book itself, it has to be its fate since its publication. The consumption tax, as it has since been labeled, has had a series of academic advocates, but it has not been implemented in its full Fisherian form anywhere in the world to our knowledge. Even worse, it has come to be labeled by the term to which Fisher objected. In the decades that followed the publication of *Constructive Income Taxation*, the intellectual high ground of public finance tax reformers was occupied by the Haig-Simons concept of income as consumption plus the change in net worth, despite the timid and even confused efforts of public finance economists to refute Fisher's notions. Fisher's proposal was, and remains, easy (and even easier today) to implement simply by removing the caps on qualified savings accounts such as individual retirement accounts. Needless to say, there would be a large number of important transition issues to be resolved. The income concept to which Fisher objected so strongly still drives tax reform debates in legislatures, debates on how equal or unequal conditions have become, and seems unshakable from public discourse.

Our paper reviews Fisher's proposal more than 60 years after its publication, asking why it failed to be influential. At an intellectual level, we identify as key the inability of the public finance economists of Fisher's generation to fully understand and appreciate his ideas and their instinct to discuss them on seemingly weak grounds. These economists, specialists in their area, through successive generations of students perpetuated an attachment to income taxation that still persists despite Fisher's arguments. The true significance of Fisher's work was not incorporated into the public finance mainstream for at least 30 years after the publication of his work. At a policy level, Fisher's income concept of "yields" (or, today, consumption) comes across as alien and counterintuitive to policymakers: consumption is not income; income is the yardstick for evaluating fairness; and income is where you begin with the income tax. At an analytical level, we identify the more recent ambiguity (not recognized by Fisher) that with a labor-leisure choice a consumption tax (with one major distortion between labor and leisure) need not dominate an income tax (with its two distortions: labor-leisure and consumption-saving); and finally, we note the evolution of the income tax in practice to a hybrid income-consumption tax, with the consumption tax component growing sharply in the last two or three decades. The choice between the two forms of tax is now not the simple binary choice posed by Irving Fisher.

We conclude by arguing that, after a long lag and despite the slowness of public finance economists to pick them up, the spread of Fisher's ideas in this area grows more each year, as seen by recent publications of a number of macroeconomists. In the policy arena, the current hybrid U.S. income-consumption tax seems to move ever closer to a consumption tax. Like Fisher's ideas in other areas, his views on taxation seem to become more rather than less powerful over time.

II

Fisher's Proposal

THE DEEPER ORIGINS OF THE FISHERS' BOOK in 1942 and their proposal to change the-then income tax into a spendings (or consumption) tax lie in Irving Fisher's long-standing advocacy of a concept of income that he called "real income." The immediate catalyst for the book's completion and publication was the onset of World War II and the sharp increase in tax rates that accompanied the war effort. In the Fishers' preface they argue that "now that income taxes have, of necessity, been revised to unheard of heights, the evils which come from both the taxation of saving and from the exemption of dissaving have brought about a very critical situation—one threatening the very existence of the American economic system as we have known it."

The Fishers essentially posed the central problem with the income tax as: "What is income?" Their proposal was simply to make taxable income approximate the Fisherian concept of "real income" or "spendings," or what we now refer to as "consumption." The Fishers saw their plan as "the simplest income tax proposal ever made." In their words, "it would require no appraisals, and it would levy the tax only where there is the wherewithal to pay it"; and in characteristic fashion, the Fishers claimed no originality for the proposal, noting that "the central argument is so simple that it is substantially contained in a single paragraph of John Stuart Mill."[1] The paragraph that Fisher refers to is the following:

> If, indeed, reliance could be placed on the conscience of the contributors, or sufficient security taken for the correctness of their statements by collateral precautions, the proper mode of assessing an income-tax would be to tax only the part of income devoted to expenditure, exempting that which is saved. For when saved and invested (and all savings, speaking generally, are invested) it thenceforth pays income-tax on the interest or profit which it brings, notwithstanding that it has already been taxed on the principal. Unless, therefore, savings are exempted from income-tax, the contributors are twice taxed on what they save, and only once on what they spend. To tax the sum invested, and afterward tax also the proceeds of the investment, is to tax the same portion of the contributor's means twice over.[2]

Fisher noted that "the proposal and the argument for it have been contested by many writers without . . . adequate study . . . ; were it not for existing controversies this book could end with Chapter 1."

The proposal is set out in some detail in the early parts of the book. The tax base is to be income received less income saved. This base, Fisher noted, had been "praised as 'ideal'" by John Stuart Mill, Alfred Marshall, Arthur C. Pigou, Liugi Einaudi, and others; but most of these authorities had regarded this ideal as unattainable because (so they thought) "spendings" can be measured only by means of records that might be "incomplete or incorrect." They thought that measuring spending or consumption necessarily meant totaling all the receipts over the accounting period. Fisher pointed out that only two pieces of information were needed to correctly measure the amount spent over a period of time: the amount available to spend (initial cash balances plus cash flow income) and the amount not spent (ending cash balance). Fisher then emphasized that his simple procedure for taxing consumption was "the only novelty in the present proposal." He also argued that the data needed for such calculations were "considerably more trustworthy than those used in our present income taxes, which often depend on debatable estimates."

Having set out the base, Fisher then noted that a progressive rate schedule could be applied to this base, and an exemption could be used (converting the whole levy to what he termed a "luxury-spendings tax"). Concomitant with the introduction of such a tax, the corporate and capital gains taxes would be abolished, as they would no longer have any rationale on the grounds of offsetting deferral advantages relative to the conventional income tax. The Fishers included inheritances in the tax base of the recipients of intergenerational transfers (although they would only be taxable when spent), and at one point they also indicated that lifetime averaging à la Vickery (1939) could be adopted.

Table 1 reproduces Fisher's proposed tax return for his spendings tax as set out in the first few pages of his book with his brother. Fisher arrived at the gross tax base (or "Total Net Cash Yield") by summing the totals from three schedules in the return. The first schedule simply reports total labor income, while the second reports net cash inflows involving capital (to include interest, dividends, financial asset sales or purchases, and gifts and bequests received); finally, the third schedule reports net change in cash balances. From total net cash yield various allowable expenditures would be deducted (medical, life insurance, minimum exemptions) to yield taxable spendings.

Fisher discussed a wide range of implementation issues with his proposal, and on many of these he was ahead of his time. He understood the investment nature of consumer durables (including housing) and described what we know today as the prepayment method. That is, he realized that there were two equivalent ways to tax capital assets, equivalent at least in their intertemporal neutrality. Either you allow the purchase of capital to be expensed or deducted and tax the returns from the investment, or you require that the initial purchase be made from after-tax dollars and allow the returns to be distributed without taxation. The latter method has come to be known as the "prepayment method" and applies to consumer durables and owner-occupied housing.

Table 1

Fisher's Proposed Spendings Tax Return

THE TAX RETURN

To Be Filled Out by Taxpayer for a Given Taxable Year (Under a Net Cash Yield System)

Reporting all Cash Yields (from (A) Work; (B) "Investments, Etc."; and (C) Cash Balance)

A. Work

1. Net cash receipts from Salaries, Wages, Fees, Commissions

B. Investments, Etc.

2. Net cash receipts from Private Business, Partnerships, Syndicates, Pools
3. Dividends
4. Rents and Royalties
5. Interest Received less interest paid (the difference may be either plus or minus)
6. (As to principal of loans *to* others) repayments received on such loans less any lendings made in the taxable year (may be plus or minus)
7. (As to principal of loans *from* others) any borrowings less repayments* (either plus or minus)
8. All cash received from sales of investments, less all cash paid out in purchase of investments and less all brokerage and other expenses incidental to said transactions (plus or minus)
9. Cash from windfalls, gifts, bonuses, insurance, bequests, etc.
10. Net cash from any other sources (specify)
11. Total Net Cash Yield from "investments, etc." (Sum of lines 2–10)

C. Cash Balance

12. Cash on hand at beginning of year
13. Cash on hand at end of year
14. Net cash yield from Cash Balance (line 12 less line 13) (plus or minus)

Table 1 *Continued*

SUMMARY

15. (A) From work (line 1 repeated)
16. (B) From "Investments, etc." (line 11 repeated)
17. (C) Drawn (net) from cash balance (line 14 repeated)
18. Gross Taxable Income = Total Net Cash Yield from all sources (sum of lines 15, 16, &17)

DEDUCTIONS (OF OUTGO) TO BE SPECIFICALLY AUTHORIZED BY LAW

19. Payments, made within taxable year, of *all* taxes
20. Payments of insurance premiums for business purposes and all life insurance premiums
21. Costs of medical, nursing, surgical, and dental care, subject to specific legal limitations
22. Funeral expenses; birth expenses; both subject to specific legal limitations
23. Fines, forfeitures, penalties, and payments for damages
24. Gifts and contributions made by the taxpayer, subject to specific legal limitations
25. Minimum exemptions of taxpayer and dependents
26. Any other deductions authorized by law
27. Total deductions (sum of lines 19–26)

FINAL RESULT

28. Net Taxable Income = Taxable Spendings (line 18 less line 27)

*But when these repayments to others consist of paying off a mortgage on a dwelling or other consumer good, the repayment may be treated as spendings.

Fisher clearly understood how investment in human capital operated and the tax consequences for his proposal. He proposed that the corporate income tax and the capital gains tax be abolished when the spendings tax was introduced. He discussed the treatment of interest, showing that the appropriate treatment was to include interest as a receipt and have interest paid on borrowings deducted as an expense. He also clearly understood that by including the change in bank and other cash balances, his tax base was in effect a cash flow tax and so also referred to his tax with the alternative name of a "cash yields" tax. Fisher seems to have been less than clear on only one point, although even that is implicit in much of his discussion. The point that could have been made more clearly involves the information requirements of his system. Not only is the information requirement modest (as the Fishers point out), but its administration can be further simplified by using one single consolidated account for all transactions covered by the tax. This is the qualifying account approach set out in the U.S. Treasury publication *Blueprints for Basic Tax Reform* of January 1977 (reprinted in Bradford et al. 1984). *Blueprints* develops a tax system remarkably similar to the Fishers' constructive income tax, although there is no reference at all to Fisher's contributions.

The response to Fisher's tax proposal (described in his articles in the late 1930s as well as in the 1942 book) can only be termed strange. Henry Simons (1938) devotes a six-page supplementary note to Fisher's proposal, rejecting it on the grounds that Fisher wished to "abandon the best part of an established revenue system and to start anew with an untried form of personal tax." Simons argued that Fisher's tax calculation would "depart widely from established business practices of income accounting, . . . [and] the tax would probably be unenforceable." Simons cited Pigou's (1928) comment that "if saving were exempted, dishonest citizens might save in one year, thus escaping taxation, and secretly sell out and spend their savings in the next year." Simons suggested difficulties of treating income in kind, problems in dealing with inheritances, and argued that Fisher's advocacy simply affected political interests seeking "larger loopholes for avoidance." From our reading, none of Simon's objections have merit, and nowhere does he argue the case against the assertion that an income tax involves the double taxation of saving.

Musgrave (1939), in a curious *American Economic Review* comment on Fisher's (1939) paper, attempted to argue that under an income tax there is no double tax of saving as Fisher had long claimed. Fisher (1942a) responded vigorously with typically lengthy, copious, and clear numerical examples, explaining his argument. Vickery (1939) pointed to a long list of adjustments that would be needed to be made to Fisher's tax base, including adjustments for interpersonal transfers, borrowings, lendings, bank account positions, life insurance payments and premiums, and various forms of investment and disinvestment. In fact, not only were most of these already accounted for in Fisher's proposal (such as insurance, bank accounts, and borrowing/lending), but with the use of qualifying accounts they pose no particular problem. Slitor (1973) offers an even longer list of claimed administrative complexities with Fisher's scheme, including transitional problems of anticipatory buying, hoarding cash, international movement of persons, consumer durables, interpersonal loans, and others. Again, not only are many of these accommodated by the use of qualified accounts, most of them are explicitly discussed by Fisher (as in Fisher's discussion of transitional problems on pages 16–17), but not subsequently acknowledged.

As Miller (1967) notes, Fisher supervised only six Ph.D. students during his time at Yale. Further, his policy-oriented work on taxes occurred after he had retired. Most of his energy went into his writing, his promotion of various causes, and his (only sometimes successful) pursuit of personal business interests. Of Fisher's 25 publications on tax issues cited in his 1942 book, none are co-authored. Fisher left no immediate collegial inheritance of students and co-authors, no immediate intellectual heir either at Yale or elsewhere, and certainly no inheritor of Fisher's thinking among public finance economists. In contrast, the intellectual linkage between Haig and Seligman at Columbia and Simons at Chicago to the next generation within public finance is quite strong. Implementing the Haig-Simons concept of income and broadening tax bases and lowering rates became the battle cry of the next generation of tax reformers (notably, Goode, Pechman, and Musgrave). Fisher's ideas were essentially forgotten. They had some immediate impact in that the U.S. Treasury did produce a proposal for a progressive spendings tax as their war finance option in 1942, but the proposal was soon dropped[3] and not seriously revived for 35 years until the publication of *Blueprints*.

As late as 1955, Kaldor in his book *An Expenditure Tax* again noted the list of luminaries opposed to such a system. Keynes had described the tax as "perhaps theoretically sound, [but] . . . practically impossible."[4] Marshall (1917) had described a consumption tax as a "Utopian goal." Fisher's original paper, noted Kaldor, "published in 1937, attracted little notice," and (writing in 1955) "Fisher's work attracted no notice whatsoever, and as far as I [Kaldor] know, his book has never been reviewed by any of the English periodicals." In Bradford et al. (1984), the consumption tax proposal is credited to Kaldor and to Hobbes (in *Leviathan* and quoted by Kaldor), not to Fisher.

But as with Vivaldi, whose music was not heard for 250 years, Fisher's contribution has endured and continues to resurface in various guises. Much of the work in public finance on taxation and saving in the 1980s concerned Fisher's consumption tax, even though he was usually not cited. The more recent interest of real-side macro modelers in tax issues often focuses on the impact of consumption taxes, and tax measures to stimulate saving and capital formation have been a constant of recent tax reform debate. Fisher's proposal, with its alleged administrative simplicity, seemingly will not go away.

III

What Would Irving Fisher Think of Today's U.S. Tax Code?

IRVING FISHER THOUGHT AND WROTE about intertemporal consumption, the determination of interest rates, the definition of income, and the optimal design of an income tax system for at least the 50 years between his 1892 dissertation and the 1942 publication of *Constructive Income Taxation* with his brother. Of course, the U.S. tax system has changed enormously since 1942 in ways that Fisher could not have anticipated. In this section we survey some of the important changes, speculate on how Fisher would have reacted to them, and further speculate on how he would assess contemporary proposals for fundamental tax reform.

Perhaps the most dramatic change is the scale of the tax system itself. Figure 1 plots the receipts of the federal personal income tax, the corporation income tax, and the Social Security payroll tax (all as a percentage of GDP) from the publication of *Constructive Income Taxation* through 1997. When Fisher was writing the book, most households earned less than the exempt amount and were therefore not paying income taxes at all. Most of the households that did pay taxes faced a marginal income tax rate of 4%. Even though the highest

Figure 1

Federal tax receipts as a percent of GDP.

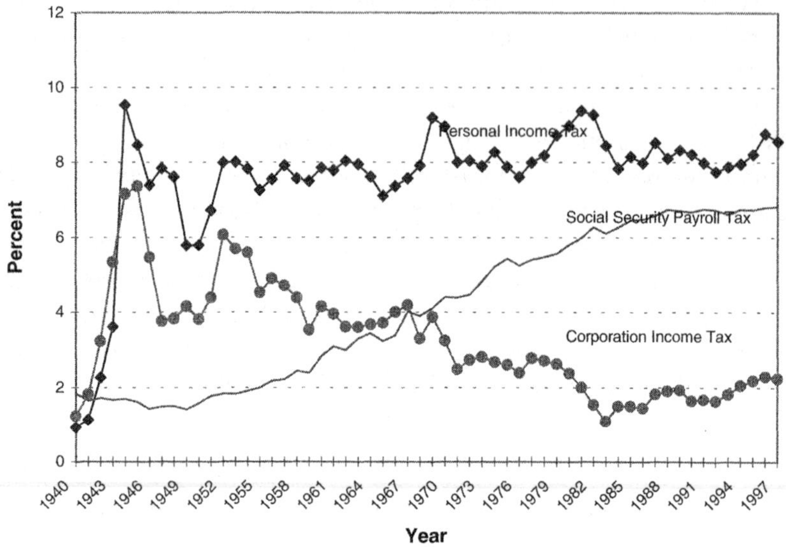

marginal income tax rate was 81%, it applied only to taxable incomes over \$5 million (roughly \$58 million in 1998 dollars). The total revenue of the personal income tax in 1940 was just under 1% of GDP. As can be seen in the figure, the personal income tax receipts rose dramatically during World War II to 8–9% of GDP and have roughly stayed at that level ever since. The revenue produced by the corporation income tax was slightly greater than personal income tax receipts in 1940 and rose during the war, but fell steadily as a fraction of the economy from 1952 to 1982. By the late 1990s the corporation income tax raised only about one-fourth as much revenue as the personal income tax. Finally, the payroll tax financing Social Security (and later Medicare) steadily rose relative to GDP from less than 2% to almost 7%.

It seems safe to say that Irving Fisher would be extremely concerned with the nature of the tax system today with its much higher average rates (and, for the vast majority of the population, higher marginal rates) than he witnessed in the 1930s and early 1940s. He would probably not be surprised by the extraordinary complexity of the income tax system but would be dismayed by its failure to adopt a consistent definition of income. Of course, he opposed taxing income altogether, at least what most people define as "income."

Fisher's biggest concern about taxing income (or *accretion*, as he referred to it) was the double taxation of saving and the distortions that this caused in the intertemporal allocation of resources by households. In this regard, he would give the current U.S. tax system a mixed but decidedly negative review. From Fisher's point of view, the good news would be that a very significant part of saving takes place through the pension system, where the tax system loosely follows the cash-flow principles that he advocated. When a household saves for retirement in a tax-qualified pension plan (employer-provided defined benefit or defined contribution plan or an IRA or Keogh plan), the contributions (i.e., saving) are deductible from the tax base. The dividends, interest, and rent earned on the assets inside the plan are free from tax; withdrawals in retirement are subject to full ordinary tax rates. At this level of abstraction, Fisher would applaud these institutions and declare victory. However, upon examining the details of the tax treatment of the plans, he would be less enthusiastic. Recall that Fisher's primary goal was to come up with a tax system that did not distort the intertemporal choices of households. In order to do that, the tax system must let savers earn the full gross rate of return on their investments. The pension system does that, but it has a number of important limitations that mean that the rate of marginal transformation between present and future consumption is often not the full gross rate of return $(1 + r)$. There are limits on how much individuals can contribute to these accounts, which depend on the exact offering of one's employer. Only half of all jobs offer any kind of pension; without such, people are limited to the $2,000 contribution in either a traditional or Roth IRA. Those whose employer offers a 401(k) plan can put roughly $10,000 into these accounts. The self-employed and some defined contribution plans have limits as high as $30,000 per year. It seems safe to say that Irving Fisher would oppose the limits altogether and be perplexed as to why they are so variable across households. Of course, there are other tax regulations attached to these accounts that Fisher would oppose. Withdrawals before age 59 and a half are subject to a penalty tax; minimum withdrawals are required of most households beginning at age 70 and a half. Fisher would find this all arbitrary and unnecessary and argue that all contributions should be deductible and all withdrawals taxable regardless of age or amount. Still, he might find some satisfaction in the large fraction of saving that escapes what he would term the triple taxation of a Haig-Simons income tax system (although he would certainly rail against the corporate income tax as still representing double taxation, even for assets held in pension accounts).

For most households, the largest assets owned are human capital, owner-occupied housing, and the value of future claims on Social Security. As we have already stated, Fisher completely understood the concept of human capital. Its current taxation, whereby some of the costs of acquiring higher education are free from tax (the foregone earnings of the employment alternative to college) and others are not (tuition and books, etc.), is not consistent with either income tax or cash-flow tax principles. The treatment that would be consistent with Fisher's framework of income and taxation would make tuition and educational supplies deductible (but not room and board). The return to human capital investments (wages and salary) would be taxed unless they were used to finance other investments via saving. Fisher understood the equivalence of taxing the purchase price of consumer durables (including housing) and taxing the returns they generate. He recognized that it often is administratively easier to simply tax the initial purchase.

The current income taxation of Social Security is not consistent with Irving Fisher's tax framework. Half of workers' contributions are said to be paid for by employers and half by the employees themselves. Despite this, all of the checks are sent to the Treasury by the employer. Social Security benefits are untaxed for relatively low-income beneficiaries but 85% taxable for higher-income recipients. Almost certainly Fisher would have Social Security "assets" taxed like any other—he would have made all contributions deductible and all benefits taxable.

Perhaps the aspect of the current tax environment that would disappoint Irving Fisher the most is the incredibly uneven treatment of capital income, particularly that received outside of the pension system. Figure 2 illustrates the situation where the total nonhuman capital stock is divided into housing and business capital. To the extent that the capital stock is acquired outside of the pension system, it has to be purchased with after-tax money. Because of the payment of personal taxes before asset acquisition, the figure shows T_P in the top ellipse. For owner-occupied housing, that is the only time the personal income tax applies to the asset (other than what Fisher

Figure 2

The current taxation of tangible capital in the United States.

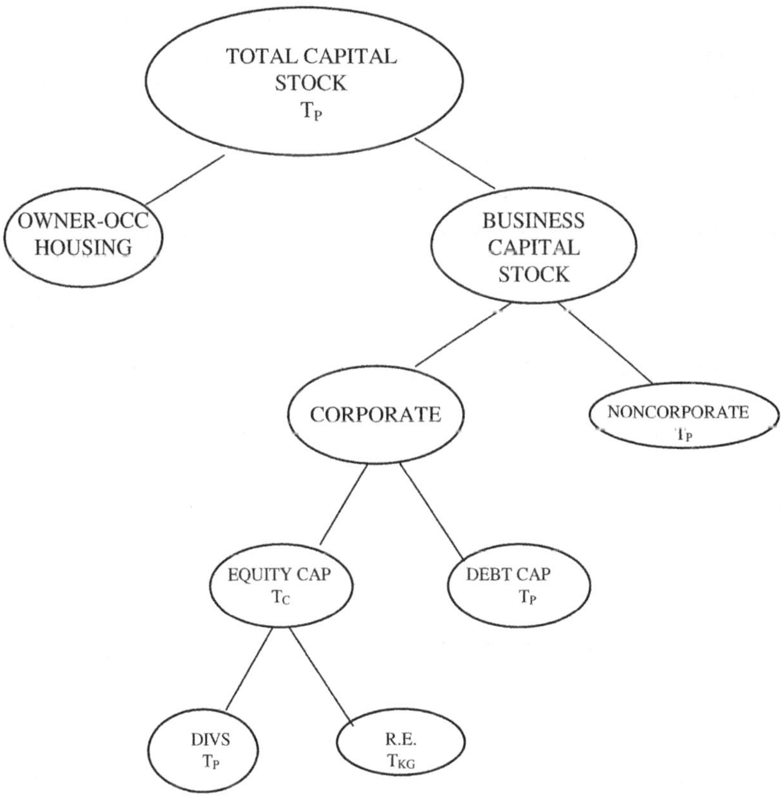

would see as the inappropriate mortgage interest deduction). For business capital, the figure shows what disturbed Fisher the most: the double and triple taxation of capital income.

Noncorporate business returns are taxed twice, once when the capital is acquired with after-tax money and once when the returns are realized. The returns to corporate capital are taxed twice for debt capital and three times for corporate equity capital. Fisher wanted to scrap this uneven maze of taxes by removing the tax at the top, removing the corporation income tax applying to the returns to equity capital in the corporate sector, and removing the separate capital gains taxation applying to realized capital gains. Instead, he would impose a tax on all net business cash flow. Interest income, dividend income, the income from noncorporate businesses, and the net proceeds from capital transactions would all be taxed unless the taxpayer could document that the money had been reinvested (i.e., not spent or consumed).

Fisher would have extended the "retained earnings" treatment of equity investments to all financial investments. That is, if a taxpayer receives cash flows from capital (from a mutual fund, for instance), he or she would have the ability to reinvest the money (i.e., retain the earnings) and therefore not trigger any taxation. Capital would face precisely one level of taxation, and that level would be when the resulting returns are spent or consumed. Even today's pension environment would not completely please Fisher. Contributions made to qualifying pension plans can be made with before-tax money, and he would approve of that. Withdrawals are taxable, and again that would be okay with Fisher. He would applaud that no tax is collected during the accumulation period of returns (dividends and capital gains) inside a pension. What he would find objectionable is that equity investments still face double taxation—once by the corporation income tax and once by individuals when the money is spent in retirement.

This uneven taxation of capital income depicted in Figure 2 and assailed by Irving Fisher has been the focus of a great deal of public finance research over the last 40 years. Harberger and many others (including the authors of this paper) have evaluated the efficiency costs of the separate corporate income tax. At least in terms of this figure, corporate tax integration amounts to corporate tax elimination with all corporate earnings facing taxation at the personal level. Fisher would look at this as a step in the right direction, lowering the number of times corporate equity capital is taxed from three to two. A particularly interesting form of corporate tax integration was evaluated by the Treasury Department under the first President Bush (U.S. Department of Treasury 1992). It termed its proposal the Comprehensive Business Income Tax (CBIT). It would have replaced the corporate income tax with a tax on the net return to capital for all businesses. In terms of Figure 2, the CBIT proposal would have eliminated the personal income tax on dividends, interest, and capital gains and would have eliminated the corporate income tax on the net equity income of corporations. In their place, it would have imposed a 31% tax on the return to all business capital (corporate or noncorporate), and it would have not allowed interest payments to be deductible from the tax base. The proposed taxation of capital income under CBIT is shown in Figure 3.

All business capital income would be taxed the same, whether the income takes the form of returns to partnerships or corporate dividends, interest, or realized capital gains. The achievement would be a tremendous improvement in economic neutrality with no sacrifice in revenue. Irving Fisher would almost certainly have politely applauded this proposal, thinking that it was a step in the right direction. His lack of enthusiasm would only reflect the fact that even with this proposal, business capital income faces double taxation. The one additional step that would bring about true enthusiasm from Fisher would involve replacing depreciation accounting with expensing for investments. With this one additional step, CBIT would be converted to a business cash-flow tax and Irving Fisher would be fully on board.

There are other proposals that would make the taxation of various forms of capital income more even. A simple one that Fisher would almost certainly support (although, again, he would only think it a step in the right direction) would be to establish tax-deferred dividend reinvestment plans. The way these would work is that investors who participate in the dividend reinvestment plans of companies or mutual funds would pay taxes on dividends and distributions only if they actually take the proceeds in cash. If they reinvest the proceeds,

Figure 3

Capital taxation under a proposed comprehensive business income tax.

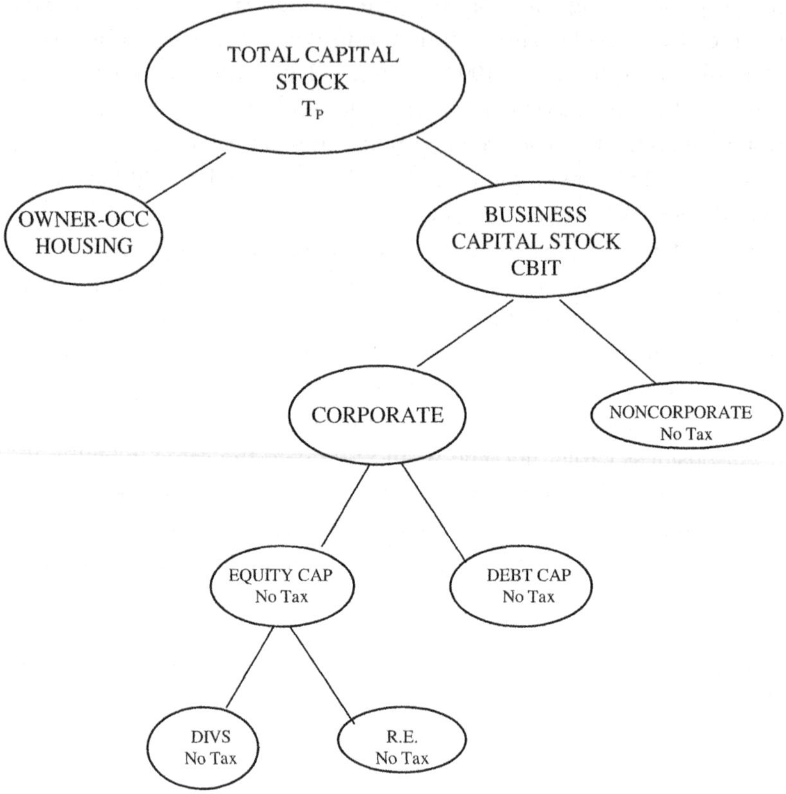

then they will have made an individual decision to "retain earnings" and they would not face current taxation. Tax-deferred dividend reinvestment plans (TD-DRIPs) would simplify the tax calculation when a participant liquidates his or her position (or a portion of the position) in the security. The cost basis would simply be the original purchase cost. If a fractional position is sold, then the basis would be the same fraction of original cost. There would be no need to keep track of the amount of intermediate purchases with reinvested distributions and the prices of those purchases. Fisher would view TD-DRIPs as only a partial solution, but would probably support them relative to not making any fundamental changes at all regarding capital taxation.

A more comprehensive proposal that is consistent with Irving Fisher's tax philosophy is the Hall-Rabushka flat-tax proposal (1995). They propose to tax business cash flow at the business level and labor income at the personal level at a flat marginal rate. As with Fisher's proposal, they would have significant minimum exemptions and thereby achieve a degree of progressivity. Essentially, the Hall-Rabushka plan amounts to a value-added tax, with a particular collection method that permits exemptions for those with low levels of consumption. Fisher anticipated using the corporation for withholding taxes à la Hall-Rabushka. He probably would have opposed their flat marginal rate—he explicitly discusses graduated marginal rates. Further, he supported a separate estate tax (over and above his constructive income tax), thereby increasing the taxes of the truly wealthy. Overall, however, the Hall-Rabushka plan captures much of what Fisher advocated. Like most modern tax designers, Hall and Rabushka fail to acknowledge Fisher's much earlier contribution.

IV

Conclusion

OUR OVERALL CONCLUSION IS THAT Irving Fisher was way ahead of his time with his proposal for a spendings or constructive income tax. He had thought through most of the problems raised by his critics and even anticipated more recent developments in economics (such as human capital theory and the so-called prepayment method of taxation). His proposal still sounds modern today, and his ideas keep cropping up in the proposals of people who think that they are at the cutting edge. It is our opinion that Irving Fisher not only identified very real problems with the American tax system, but that he also had innovative ideas to address these problems, ideas that are still appealing some 60 years after he began to publish them. Irving

Fisher is often thought of as an early mathematical economist and a monetary economist—but public finance should also claim him as a founding father.

Notes

1. Fisher also acknowledged an intellectual debt for his proposal to operationalize the tax to Ogden Mills, who as a congressman in 1921 had introduced a spendings tax bill, appeared at hearings, and wrote an article in its favor. Mills subsequently recanted his views on the grounds that (later in the Depression) saving should not be encouraged by tax measures. See the discussion in Fisher (1942b: 208).

2. Mill (1884: 543).

3. Fisher's claim of simplicity did not convince the members of Congress. Kaldor (1955: 16) reports on the congressional debate on the 1942 proposal and quotes one senator as describing it as "the most complicated monstrosity" he had ever seen. Another predicted that it would "lower the standard of living to a dead level."

4. Kaldor also reports attending a meeting of the Econometric Society in 1936 where Fisher first presented his spending tax paper. In the discussion Keynes criticized Fisher for wanting to use taxes to stimulate saving when there was already oversaving.

References

Bradford, D. F., et al. (1984). *Blueprints for Basic Tax Reform*. Arlington, VA: Tax Analysts.

Fisher, I. (1937). "Income in Theory and Income Taxation in Practice." *Econometrica* January: 1–55.

——. (1939). "The Double Taxation of Savings." *American Economic Review* March: 16–33.

——. (1942a). "A Rebuttal to W. L. Crum and R. A. Musgrave." *American Economic Review* March: 111–117.

——. (1942b). "Paradoxes in Taxing Saving." *Econometrica* April: 147–158.

Fisher, I., and H. W. Fisher. (1942). *Constructive Income Taxation: A Proposal for Reform*. New York: Harper and Brothers.

Goode, R. (1976). *The Individual Income Tax*. Washington, DC: Brookings Institution.

Hall, Robert E., and Alvin Rabushka. (1995). *The Flat Tax*, 2nd ed. Stanford, CA: Hoover Institution Press.

Kaldor, N. (1955). *An Expenditure Tax*. London: Allen and Unwin.

Marshall, A. (1917). *The Equitable Distribution of Taxation*. Rpt. in the memorials of Alfred Marshall: 351.

Mill, J. S. (1884). *Principles of Political Economy*. Ed. Laughlin. New York: Appleton & Co.

Miller, J. P. (1967). "Irving Fisher of Yale." In *Ten Economic Studies in the Tradition of Irving Fisher*. Ed. W. Fellner. New York: John Wiley.

Musgrave, Richard A. (1939). "A Further Note on the Double Taxation of Savings." *American Economic Review* September: 549–550.

Pigou, A. C. (1928). *A Study in Public Finance*. London: Macmillan & Co.

Simons, H. C. (1938). *Personal Income Taxation*. Chicago: University of Chicago Press.

Slitor, R. E. (1973). "Administrative Aspects of Expenditure Taxation." In *Broad-Based Taxes: New Options and Sources*. Ed. R. A. Musgrave. New York: Johns Hopkins University Press.

U.S. Department of Treasury. (1992). *Integration of the Individual and Corporate Tax Systems: Taxing Business Income Once*. Washington, DC: U.S. Government Printing Office.

Vickrey, W. (1939). "Averaging of Income for Income Tax Purposes." *Journal of Political Economy* June: 381.

Comments on John B. Shoven and John Whalley's, "Irving Fisher's Spendings (Consumption) Tax in Retrospect"

By ALAN J. AUERBACH*

ABSTRACT. A comment on the article by John Shoven and John Whalley in this volume.

It is useful to start my review of the Shoven-Whalley paper with a quote from Irving Fisher himself:

> All students of the problem are fully agreed on at least one point—namely, that existing income taxes must be radically reformed. But some of the reformers would include all capital-increases, while others would exclude them all. There are arguments on both sides, but both agree that either system would be an improvement over the present system or lack of system. (Fisher 1939)

This could well be the statement of a serious observer today, rather than of Irving Fisher six decades ago. Fisher favored a tax on "net paid income"—income distributed and consumed—because he thought it fairer and not subject to the income measurement problems of the other pure alternative, based on the Schanz-Haig-Simons accretion concept of income.

These are points that have continued to loom large in the more recent debate over consumption taxes. Indeed, issues of fairness and administration are probably receiving more attention from economists now than they did just a few years ago, when our most commonly studied economy consisted of a representative agent residing in a very

*Alan J. Auerbach is the Robert D. Burch Professor of Economics and Law, Director of the Burch Center for Tax Policy and Public Finance, and former Chair of the Economics Department at the University of California, Berkeley. He is also a Research Associate of the National Bureau of Economic Research in Cambridge, MA. Previously, he taught at Harvard University and the University of Pennsylvania and was Deputy Chief of Staff of the Joint Committee on Taxation of the U.S. Congress. Professor Auerbach has served as a member of the Executive Committee and as Vice President of the American Economic Association, and is a Fellow of the Econometric Society and of the American Academy of Arts and Sciences.

The American Journal of Economics and Sociology, Vol. 64, No. 1 (January, 2005).

simple world. It is useful to start with the developments in this world, largely related to economic efficiency, and then reconsider the various complications, some of which occurred to Fisher and others of which did not.

I

Efficiency

IN A WORLD WITH EVEN THREE GOODS, two of which are subject to excise taxes, Corlett and Hague (1953–1954) told us that we can't know for sure which good should be taxed more heavily. This result notwithstanding, a consensus seems to have arisen that a consumption tax—equivalent to equal tax rates on current and future consumption—is superior to an income tax, which implies a higher tax rate on future consumption (e.g., Feldstein 1978). There is some sense to this—why should future consumption be a much greater complement to leisure?—but there is no general theorem here.

On the other hand, adding more periods to life leads to a much stronger result: that capital income taxes should converge to zero, in other words, that consumption should face uniform tax rates in the long run (Chamley 1986). This result is often misunderstood, but the easiest intuition is to imagine the contrary, with a steady-state capital income tax bounded away from zero. This implies implicit taxes on future consumption that rise without bound as time goes on. Given that the welfare cost of a distortion rises in nonlinear fashion with respect to the size of the distortion, one can see that eventually this ever-increasing consumption distortion is likely to be suboptimal. If implicit taxes on consumption cease rising over time, this implies that capital income taxes cannot be positive in the long run. But a long-run tax rate of zero in an infinite horizon model doesn't translate into a low or zero tax rate in a finite horizon model, and most of us don't behave as if we expect to live forever.

A more serious problem with this result is that the economy doesn't consist of a single individual living for two periods or an infinite number of them. Tax systems don't change on a generation-specific basis, and the enactment of a consumption tax has different generational consequences than enactment of a wage tax, which, with constant returns to scale in production, would be equivalent in a single-agent model. This is not simply an issue of distribution, for the same differences in burden have efficiency consequences. Failing to tax existing assets by adopting a tax on wages instead of a tax on consumption not only shifts the burden from the old to the young, but also reduces the efficiency of the tax reform, a difference that Larry Kotlikoff and I found, in our simulation model, to be large enough to turn an efficiency gain into an efficiency loss (Auerbach and Kotlikoff 1987). My more recent simulations of realistic tax proposals find that we would lose essentially all the potential efficiency gains from adopting a consumption tax if we maintain the existing level of progressivity and protect asset values in transition (Auerbach 1996).

II

Distribution

THIS LAST FINDING brings out a key issue regarding the consumption tax—whether it is inherently less progressive than an income tax. The previous discussion reminds us that it is necessary to take a perspective greater than one year; one can't compare the old and young using current income as a measure of ability to pay. If we do use income, even measured over a period of several years, recent work has emphasized that we should look at risk-adjusted returns in measuring capital income, a point that goes back to Tobin's work on taxation and risk taking (Gentry and Hubbard 1997).

But others ask why we should use income, rather than consumption, as a measure of ability to pay. If we do use consumption, then clearly we can make the tax progressive simply by having a personal consumption tax with a progressive rate structure. In standard models, this is likely to be a better approach than that adopted under European value-added taxes, which achieve progressivity via tax rate variations on luxuries and necessities. Variations in indirect taxes offer limited scope for redistribution at the cost of considerable distortion of consumer choice. However, this result is less clear if we expand models to incorporate conspicuous consumption (Bagwell and Bernheim 1996).

Opponents of consumption taxes often argue that progressivity with respect to consumption alone is not enough because there is "something else" to wealth accumulation beyond the ability to consume. If this "something else" is simply the option to consume in the future, it is already taken care of by future consumption taxes. But it could be unmeasured consumption—the availability of a stay in the Lincoln Bedroom at the White House, for example. Critics' uneasiness may, on the other hand, stem from concern about the option value that tax deferral provides. The tax system may change, or people may figure out a way to avoid taxes, as in recent years when some renounced U.S. citizenship to avoid income taxes on large accrued capital gains (U.S. Joint Committee on Taxation 1995).

This concern about equity brings to mind the fact that Fisher favored a tax on estates or inheritances as the best way to augment the consumption tax for purposes of achieving progressivity. Given that, even now, some wealth is accumulated for precautionary purposes, it seems clear that such taxes may impose less of a distortion than taxes on capital income imposed during a person's life. Yet estate taxes seem very unpopular, for political reasons that are somewhat unclear.

In light of the recent tax reform debate, it is useful to remind ourselves that we don't need a progressive marginal tax rate structure to achieve progressivity. The Hall-Rabushka flat tax that Shoven and Whalley discuss accomplishes progressivity with a large exemption. Whether this is enough depends on where in the income distribution one measures progressivity. One could modify the flat tax to have more than one marginal rate bracket. However, simulations of two-bracket linear income taxes suggest, in the spirit of Mirrlees's (1971) optimal income tax results, that such flexibility would lead to us to want falling, rather than rising, marginal tax rates (Slemrod et al. 1994).

III

Saving

MANY FAVOR the consumption tax because it would increase national saving. It is not clear why this should be an end in itself, unless we believe there are spillovers from capital accumulation. Whatever our objective, it is worth pointing out that the saving impact from adoption of a consumption tax doesn't just come from the substitution effect but also from the shift in burden from savers to consumers (e.g., from rich to poor and from young to old). But it is important as well to note that these predictions hold for standard models of intertemporal choice.

More and more, saving is being done through means already tax-sheltered and through collective action, as in 401K plans and defined contribution pension plans. It may be that some households save only because of the existence of such plans. If we put all saving on an equal footing, will these forms of saving remain or wither? If they wither, will household saving necessarily increase? We can't know for sure.

IV

Other Issues

I HAVE GOTTEN almost completely through my comments without saying anything about administrative issues or "competitiveness." On this latter issue, not much needs to be said. If one compares a consumption tax with border adjustments that capture imports and release exports—a standard VAT, for example—to a consumption tax without border adjustments—the flat tax, for example—bases differ only by a cash-flow tax on net foreign investment, which is basically a lump-sum tax. This difference will have indirect efficiency effects—for a country that is a net debtor, the border adjustments lose revenue that must be made up using distortionary taxes—but no direct ones (Auerbach 1997).

Finally, one should say something about the deficit (or, for the moment, the surplus) or, more specifically, how arbitrary conventions can influence real policy decisions. A consumption tax collects revenue from individuals later in life than an income tax. A labor income tax collects revenue earlier in life than an income tax. Thus, leaving aside the capital levy that distinguishes the consumption tax from the tax on labor income, a consumption tax will appear to raise less money in the short run. It is this timing difference that led to the

1997 adoption of the "Roth" IRA, which exempts the income from saving (as under a labor income tax) in place of a traditional IRA, which provides a deduction for saving (as under a consumption tax). This difference could also lead to more general adoption of the yield-exemption approach instead of the deduction approach when considering how to reduce the tax burden on capital income. Unfortunately, the yield exemption approach could well be inferior, if the reported return to capital actually includes disguised labor income, as in the case of a closely held business and rents to fixed factors.

In summary, the interesting issues regarding the choice between income and consumption taxes are revealed in the details, rather than in efficiency calculations based on simple models. Ultimately, though, we must also feed all this through a model of the political process to know whether what appears to be a desirable alternative to the current system can be enacted in a form that will resemble its academic description, as begun by Irving Fisher.

References

Auerbach, Alan J. (1996). "Tax Reform, Capital Allocation, Efficiency and Growth." In *Economic Effects of Fundamental Tax Reform*. Eds. H. Aaron and W. Gale.

——. (1997). "The Future of Fundamental Tax Reform." *American Economic Review* 87: 1443–1446.

Auerbach, Alan J., and Laurence J. Kotlikoff. (1987). *Dynamic Fiscal Policy*. Cambridge: Cambridge University Press.

Bagwell, Laurie Simon, and B. Douglas Berhneim. (1996). "Veblen Effects in a Theory of Conspicuous Consumption." *American Economic Review* 86: 349–373.

Chamley, Christophe. (1986). "Optimal Taxation of Capital Income in General Equilibrium with Infinite Lives." *Econometrica* 54: 607–622.

Corlett, W. J., and D. C. Hague. (1953–1954). "Complementarity and the Excess Burden of Taxation." *Review of Economic Studies* 21: 21–30.

Feldstein, Martin. (1978). "The Welfare Cost of Capital Income Taxation." *Journal of Political Economy* 86: 29–51.

Fisher, Irving. (1939). "The Double Taxation of Savings." *American Economic Review* 29: 16–33.

Gentry, William M., and R. Glenn Hubbard. (1997). *Distributional Implica-*

tions of a Consumption Tax. Washington, DC: American Enterprise Institute.

Mirrlees, James. (1971). "An Exploration in the Theory of Optimum Income Taxation." *Review of Economic Studies* 38: 175–208.

Slemrod, Joel, Shlomo Yitzhaki, Joram Mayshar, and Michael Lundholm. (1994). "The Optimal Two-Bracket Linear Income Tax." *Journal of Public Economics* 53: 269–290.

U.S. Joint Committee on Taxation. (1995). *Issues Presented by Proposals to Modify the Tax Treatment of Expatriation.* JCS-17-95.

Comments on John B. Shoven and John Whalley, "Irving Fisher's Spendings (Consumption) Tax in Retrospect"

By MICHAEL J. GRAETZ*

ABSTRACT. A comment on the article by John Shoven and John Whalley in this volume.

John Shoven and John Whalley are certainly correct in their two basic observations concerning Irving Fisher's contribution to the tax policy debate nearly six decades ago. First, Fisher was far ahead of his time substantively. His detailed treatment in his 1942 book *Constructive Income Taxation* of what we now call a personalized progressive consumption tax could have served as the blueprint for the "USA" ("unlimited savings allowance") tax (a progressive consumption tax) introduced in 1995 by Senators Sam Nunn (D-GA) and Pete Domenici (R-NM). Indeed, that tax would have avoided much complexity and many pitfalls had it simply followed Irving Fisher's recommendations of how to treat borrowing (Ginsburg 1995; Warren 1995).

Second, Shoven and Whalley properly remind us that Irving Fisher's contribution in detailing how to implement a progressive tax on consumption has largely been lost. The intellectual history of this subject usually goes back only as far as Nicholas Kaldor's 1955 book *The Expenditure Tax*, even though, as Shoven and Whalley point out, Kaldor himself made extensive references to Fisher's work. In fact, neither William Andrews's influential work nor my own detailed article on implementing a progressive consumption tax refer to Fisher's contribution (Andrews 1974; Graetz 1979), although we all agree about the proper resolution of many of the issues Fisher discussed.

*Michael J. Graetz is a professor of law at Yale University.

The American Journal of Economics and Sociology, Vol. 64, No. 1 (January, 2005).

I

Taxing Consumption Rather Than Income

IN THE POLITICAL ARENA, Irving Fisher was not the only member of the Yale economics department to play a key role in advocating a tax on consumption. Thomas Sewall Adams apparently was responsible for Congressman Ogden Mills's proposal for a "spendings" tax in 1921. (Mills, then a congressman from New York, later served as Herbert Hoover's Secretary of the Treasury.) Unlike Fisher, Adams played a key role in the tax legislative process during the early decades of the income tax. Not surprisingly, one finds in Adams's writings considerably greater sensitivity to the political difficulties of writing a tax law, to the pushes and pulls of tax politics (e.g., Adams 1928).

During the 1921 debate, Chester Jordan, a public accountant from Portland, Maine, told the Senate Finance Committee that he could reduce the size of his accounting firm from eight to three members if Congress only would substitute a tax on "spendings" for the income tax[1,2] (Reams, Jr. 1979). After Congress refused to go along, the demand for Chester Jordan's services grew, he changed his name to Price Waterhouse, and the rest is history. (I made that last part up, of course, but it should have happened that way.)

So even in the 1920s, taxing consumption rather than income was not a new idea. As Fisher emphasized, John Stuart Mill had favored taxing consumption. Alexander Hamilton also had only praise for consumption taxes. Hamilton claimed that with consumption taxes people could choose how much to pay; as he put it, "the rich may be extravagant, the poor may be frugal."

In 1942, the same year that Fisher's book *Constructive Income Taxation* was published, Franklin Roosevelt's Treasury secretary Henry Morgenthou advanced a progressive-rate tax on spendings as the way to finance World War II, but Congress once again rejected a consumption tax.[3] Instead, the Revenue Act of 1942 began the conversion of the income tax, which had applied only to high-income people, into a tax on the masses. Had this episode turned out differently, the income tax might have remained narrowly targeted to high-income people, and a consumption tax might have become the federal government's mainstay revenue producer. Although Fisher's goal of taxing consumption rather than income has been kept alive in the economics and legal literature, only recently has the idea of substituting a tax on consumption for the income tax reentered the national political debate.

Shoven and Whalley make the important—and surely true—point that there is great opportunity for more neutral taxation of income from capital by moving either in the direction of a consumption tax, as Fisher urged, or by revising the income tax. Shoven and Whalley illustrate distortions in the taxation of capital income within the current income tax, emphasizing the disparity between the overtaxation of corporate investment and the undertaxation of housing.

The comprehensive business income tax (CBIT) proposal, described in Shoven-Whalley, was developed by the Treasury Department while I served as Deputy Assistant Secretary (Tax Policy). In my view, CBIT is feasible and would be an important move in the right direction. It would simplify individual taxes by moving much of the tax collection of capital income taxes to the business level, thereby replicating one of the main advantages of sales and value-added taxes. As Shoven and Whalley point out, adjusting depreciation allowances within CBIT, or allowing for expensing of capital income taxes, would turn this tax into a consumption tax, which would impose no burden on new capital investments. Indeed, if under CBIT an immediate deduction for purchases of capital assets were allowed, the tax would essentially become a subtraction-method VAT.

CBIT has two problems, however, that are worth noting. One is substantive: because CBIT would eliminate one level of corporate tax, it would upset longstanding international arrangements for income taxation. Both the foreign tax credit and the nation's tax treaties would require substantial restructuring. This makes CBIT difficult to enact without knowing how our trading partners would respond. The second problem is political. CBIT implies taxation of only wages at the individual level. In this regard, it is like the Hall-Rabushka flat tax. Because of the political power of demonstrating that the tax system is "unfair" by pointing to untaxed individuals with substantial investment income, taxing only wages at the individual level does not seem likely to remain stable over time. In 1969, for example, the fact that Mrs. Dodge earned $1 million of tax-exempt interest and paid no tax was a powerful force leading to the enactment of the minimum tax. In 1986, General Electric's status as a nontaxpayer served as a similar catalyst for the corporate minimum tax.

With regard to income from housing—the most important under-taxed category of capital income under the income tax—Shoven and Whalley remind us that Irving Fisher would have treated borrowing properly under his consumption tax by including borrowed amounts in receipts and allowing a deduction for interest. In sharp contrast, the 1995 Nunn-Domenici progressive consumption tax would not include borrowing in receipts but still would allow a deduction for home mortgage interest. This treatment demonstrates how entrenched politically is favorable tax treatment of owner-occupied housing. It also suggests that a zero tax rate on capital income is not a lower bound.

Shoven and Whalley discuss the sizeable amount of capital income earned by pension funds and other retirement savings vehicles now exempt from income tax. Generally, today's consumption tax advocates have not responded to concerns about the potential effect that shifting from an income tax to a consumption tax might have on such social insurance protections now being provided on an income-tax-favored basis. In addition to retirement income, the bulk of health insurance for the nation's elderly, nonpoor population is currently provided through tax-preferred employer-based coverage. When Irving Fisher was writing in 1942, income tax advantages to stimulate and fund social insurance had not yet taken hold, but today's consumption tax proponents must explain the potential effects of their proposals on these important protections and propose alternatives.[4]

II

The Lifetime Perspective of Consumption Taxation

THE NOW-STANDARD economic view of savings as simply a temporary postponement of consumption has, as Shoven and Whalley point out, led many public finance economists to argue in favor of using consumption or "lifetime income" as the index of people's relative well-being, as the measure of their ability to pay taxes (Stein 1996: A-18).

A lifetime view has also been defended as a better approach in advancing equality of opportunity over equality of income. However, high lifetime income may not reflect a high current ability to pay taxes, since capital markets often do not permit people to borrow against their future earnings. Moreover, short-term precautionary savings, which is an important component of total savings, typically serves to smooth people's consumption over several years rather than over a lifetime. In the political process, it is difficult to muster a majority for the view that two persons, each of whom consume the same amount, should be taxed the same when one has amassed large amounts of capital and receives substantial sums of capital income, while the other has only the fruits of his or her labor available to consume.

The philosopher Norman Daniels has argued that a lifetime perspective in public policy is fair because "*consistent* differential treatment by age will equalize over time" (Daniels 1988: 41). He argues that the young and the old may be treated differently at any moment in time but that over time people will be treated both ways. The validity of this claim, however, depends on consistent treatment of various age groups over a long period of time, something that no Congress can assure and that congressional behavior has proved false.

Our system of government, with elections of the full House of Representatives and one-third of the Senate every two years and of presidents every four years, does not give one Congress the power to prevent different legislation by a subsequent Congress. It is impossible, therefore, for any legislative body to make a viable binding political commitment to fair taxation over any person's lifetime, much less over several generations. Indeed, as we have recently witnessed, each new Congress finds it virtually irresistible to change the tax law, or at least to threaten substantial change. The fact that no current Congress can effectively constrain policies of future Congresses encourages self-interested people lobbying legislators to try always to maximize their *present* interests. This alone might well make it of special concern to legislators and their constituents to know who wins and who loses in terms of their present status.

Ultimately, a lifetime view is not likely to hold much sway with legislators. As one economist on the staff of the Joint Committee on Taxation has put it, politicians do not regard an individual who is making $200,000 in a current year as having the same current ability to pay taxes as an elderly individual currently earning $35,000, even if their lifetime incomes are identical (Barthold 1993). Herbert Stein, Chairman of the Council of Economic Advisors for both Nixon and Ford, put well the ultimate test of the fairness of a consumption tax.

The question is whether a person who has an income of, say, $200,000 and spends on consumption $40,000 should be taxed like a person who has an income of $40,000 and spends $40,000 on consumption or like a person who has an income of $200,000 and spends $200,000 on consumption.[5]

III

The Effect of Consumption Taxation on the Distribution of the Burden

MOST OPPONENTS OF consumption taxation emphasize that since lower-income people consume a greater portion of their income than higher-income people, consumption taxes are more advantageous to higher-income people than income taxes. There can be little debate that if the federal income tax were to be fully replaced with a flat-rate consumption tax, the tax burden on low- and middle-income individuals would increase relative to that of upper-income individuals.

There are several ways, such as by exemptions for food, clothing, and medical expenses, by new income or payroll tax credits, or by exemptions for a specified amount of wages, to reduce or even eliminate the regressivity of consumption taxes at the bottom end of the wealth or income distribution. But it is difficult without quite high top rates to achieve a level of progressive taxation at the upper levels of income or wealth comparable to that under the current income tax by taxing only consumption and not taxing either income or wealth.[6] (Irving Fisher would have taxed wealth once a generation by taxing inheritances or estates as a complement to his consumption tax, but most congressional proponents of a consumption tax want to replace not only the income tax but also the estate tax.)

Thirty years ago, Dan Throop Smith, a Harvard economist who had served as the Treasury Department's top tax advisor during the Eisenhower Administration, accepted the invitation of his daughter, a teacher, to visit her one-room school in Montana. To get a better handle on tax equity, Smith asked three children what would be a fair tax on a family with an income of $5,000 if a family with an income of $2,000 paid a tax of $200.

The first child said, "Five hundred dollars," thereby showing a predisposition for proportional burdens and perhaps a desire to make use of a newly acquired familiarity with percentages. A second child immediately disagreed, adding the comment that the payment should be more than $500 because "each dollar isn't so important" to the family with the larger income. A third child agreed, but with the reservation that the additional tax over $500 shouldn't be "too much more or they won't work so hard." Smith subsequently relayed this story in a scholarly article, adding: "Elaborate theoretical structures concerning diminishing utility and incentives and disincentives are all really refinements of the quasi-intuitive opinions of those children and may not lead to any greater certainty" (Smith 1968).

Shortly after my book *The Decline (and Fall?) of the Income Tax*, which retells Smith's story, was published, my daughter's fifth-grade teacher asked me to visit her classroom to talk about it. While there, I repeated Dan Throop Smith's experiment. I asked the identical question and, remarkably, the first three students to speak gave the identical answers in exactly the same order. The intuitions about progressive taxation of the children of the 1990s in a large New Haven, Connecticut school mirrored precisely those of the Montana children of the 1960s. After I told them that they had given exactly the same answers in exactly the same order as did children three decades earlier in a one-room Montana schoolhouse, a number of them wrote to me remarking how "cool," "neat," "amazing," and "weird" that was. One concluded, "I guess that must be fair, if both of the schools got the same answers."

These two experiments should serve as a caution to those who believe that the American public will view as fair replacing a progressive tax on income with a flat-rate tax on consumption. That sentiment will last only until the second child speaks.

IV

What Is an Income Tax?

IRVING FISHER WOULD PROBABLY FEEL right at home in the rhetoric of today's political debate. Fisher insisted that his tax was taxing income, as the title of his 1942 book, *Constructive Income Taxation*, demonstrates. Shoven and Whalley have translated Fisher's writings into today's commonplace academic vernacular, relabeling his tax a consumption tax. But today's politicians prefer Fisher's semantics.

Neither the political proponents of the flat tax nor the parents of the "USA" tax have called their proposals consumption taxes. Instead, they have attempted to disguise what they are taxing and have constructed their proposals to look more like an income tax than a sales tax. They also often insist on using an income tax label, referring to their proposals as consumed income taxes, savings-exempt income taxes, "USA" taxes, or simply flat taxes.

As Professors Hall and Rabushka of Stanford, the inventors of the Armey-Forbes flat tax, acknowledged in a *New York Times* editorial, there are many "economically equivalent ways to impose consumption taxes." Despite their economic similarities, however, all methods are not *politically* equivalent. Politicians want to avoid a sales or value-added tax label, as well as any separate statement to consumers of the amount of taxes included in the price of the goods and services they buy. Achieving close association with the income tax apparently is also desirable politically, notwithstanding the decline in the public's support for the income tax. Politicians must believe that both of these features—looking more like an income tax than a sales tax and invisibility to consumers—provide them cover. They may think a good disguise and a clever label will allow them to deny that any federal consumption tax is being suggested.

V

Looking Ahead

PROBABLY THE GREATEST SURPRISE in looking back at Irving Fisher's tax policy work is how remarkably resistant the federal government in the United States has been to taxing consumption. When one compares this nation's tax system to those of our trading partners, the greatest disparity is their greater reliance on consumption taxes. The OECD countries, other than Japan, Australia, and the United States, on average, collect consumption taxes equal to 5–7% of their GDP. In the United States, consumption taxes amount to just over 2% of GDP, and the federal government's share of that is quite small (Messere 1999). Less than 5% of federal revenues come from excise taxes, and the federal government has no broad-based tax on consumption.

Why has there been such reluctance to tax consumption in the United States? First, one should not underestimate the resistance of governors and mayors to the idea of the federal government entering what they regard as their exclusive domain of consumption taxation. Second, as I have discussed, there has long been widespread concern about the fairness of taxing consumption rather than income. Indeed, the public perception that fairness in taxation demands the taxation of both labor and capital income motivated the adoption of the 16th Amendment, which served to give Congress the same taxing power over investment income as it already possessed over labor income and business profits.

Historically, arguments by conservatives against moving to a broad-based federal value-added or retail sales tax have been grounded in fears about the revenue-raising capacity of such taxes—fears that putting into place such a tax at the federal level would allow the collection of enormous sums of revenue simply by increasing rates over time and therefore might facilitate the unbridled expansion of government spending. Coupled with liberals' concerns about the distribution of such taxes, political support is hard to find.

Finally, politicians have generally been fearful of political rebuke from supporting consumption taxation. Congressman Al Ullman (D-OR), who followed the legendary Wilbur Mills as Chairman of the House Ways and Means Committee, became the first Ways and Means chairman to lose a reelection contest shortly after he introduced value-added tax legislation in the Congress. This incident seems to have taken on mythical proportions. Analysis of Ullman's campaign, which attributes his defeat to losing touch with his constituents, not to his

VAT proposal, has done little or nothing to counteract the widespread view that supporting a VAT is political suicide. But, despite all the political obstacles, I do not believe that the United States will forever avoid a national consumption tax, even if no politician will utter the phrase "value-added tax."

Ironically, it would be a great step forward to return the income tax to the relatively limited status it had when Irving Fisher was writing his 1942 book. We should restore the income tax to its pre–World War II status—a relatively low-rate, simple tax on a thin slice of the wealthiest Americans. Enacting a value-added tax of 10% to 15% could finance an income tax exemption of up to $100,000 and would allow a vastly simpler income tax at a 20% to 25% rate to be applied to incomes over $100,000. A VAT would be much easier to administer and far more difficult to evade than a national sales tax because it would be collected at all levels of production. This change would eliminate more than 100 million of the 115 million income tax returns filed each year. Such a VAT would also allow us to whittle the corporate income tax rate down to 20% or 25% and could eliminate the complex rules for taxing corporate income earned abroad (Graetz 2002). Even without integration of the corporate and individual income taxes, the United States would be an extremely attractive place for corporate investment.

Skeptics may fear that we will end up with the worst of both taxes, but if a super-majority vote—say, 60% of both the House and Senate—were required to lower the $100,000 income tax exemption or to raise either the VAT or income tax rates, America could have a tax system it could live with for the next century. And, as Congressman Billy Tauzin (R-LA) is fond of saying, for the 100 million people from whom no income tax would be required, April 15 would be just another spring day.

Notes

1. Testimony of Chester A. Jordan, public accountant, of Portland, Maine: "Before the law came into effect I had three or four men in my employ. Since being obliged to undertake all of these problems for my clients I am obliged to employ seven or eight men and two and three women. Those men are college graduates and they are employed about six months of

the year on tax work. I believe that if the tax law were simplified as it should be I might not be obliged to employ more than half that number" (*Report of the Treasury* 1942: 484).

2. *Report of the Treasury* 1942: 92–95, 408–421.

3. See generally Graetz and Mashaw (1999).

4. There is considerable dispute in the literature as to how much of the disparity of wealth holdings is explained by life-cycle savings. See, e.g., Atkinson (1983: 76–77).

5. Senators Nunn and Domenici would allow both businesses and individuals to offset their consumption tax liability with the Social Security payroll taxes paid by people at different levels of income, even though amounts saved would be exempt from tax. The tax rates of their proposal are higher than those of other consumption tax proposals because of both their Social Security tax credit and their effort to limit the distributional shifts from their tax. Under the current income tax, a married couple with $25,000 of income is taxed at a rate of 15%, a 28% rate kicks in at about $40,000 of taxable income, and the top rate of nearly 40% is applicable only to income in excess of $250,000. In sharp contrast, under the Nunn-Domenici USA tax, a married couple with taxable consumption between $5,500 and $24,000 would pay tax at a rate of 27% and a top 40% rate would be applicable to all amounts over $24,000. With this rate schedule, the senators have not enjoyed a rush of co-sponsors.

6. For a detailed explanation of this proposal, see Graetz (2002).

References

Adams, Thomas Sewall. (1928). "Ideals and Idealism in Taxation." *American Economic Review* 18.

Andrews, William D. (1974). "A Consumption-Type or Cash-Flow Personal Income Tax." *Harvard Law Review* 87: 1113.

Atkinson, A. B. (1983). *The Economics of Inequality*. 2nd ed. Oxford; Clarendon Press.

Barthold, Thomas A. (1993). "How Should We Measure Distribution." *National Tax Journal* 46: 29.

Daniels, Norman. (1988). *Am I My Parents' Keeper?: An Essay on Justice Between the Young and Old*. New York: Oxford University Press.

Fisher, I., and H. W. Fisher. (1942). *Constructive Income Taxation: A Proposal for Reform*. New York: Harper and Brothers.

Ginsburg, Martin D. (1995). "Life Under a Personal Consumption Tax: Some Thoughts on Working, Saving and Consuming in Nunn-Domenici's Tax World." *National Tax Journal* 48: 585.

Graetz, Michael J. (1979). "Implementing a Progressive Consumption Tax." *Harvard Law Review* 92: 1575.

——. (1999). "Appendix." In *The U.S. Income Tax: What it Is, How it Got That Way, and Where We Go from Here*. New York: Norton.

——. (2002). "100 Million Unnecessary Returns: A Fresh Start for the U.S. Tax System." *Yale Law Journal* 112: 261.

Graetz, Michael J., and L. Mashaw, Jerry (1999). *True Security: Rethinking American Social Insurance*. New Haven: Yale University Press.

Kaldor, N. (1955). *An Expenditure Tax*. London: Allen and Unwin.

Messere, Ken (1999). "The Tax System in Industrialized Countries: An Overview." *Tax Notes International* February 25.

Reams, Jr., D. Bernard. Ed. (1979). "Internal Revenue Hearings Before the Committee on Finance of the U.S. Senate—The Proposed Revenue Act of 1921, 67th Cong., 1st Session, May 9–27 1921." In *United States Revenue Acts: 1909–1950, The Laws, Legislative Histories and Administrative Documents*, Vol. 1.

Smith, Dan Throop. (1968). "High Tax Rate: Inequity and Immorality?" *Florida Law Review* 20: 451, 452.

Stein, Herbert. (1996). "Regarding Henry . . ." *Wall Street Journal* 30 January: A-18, col. 3

Warren, Alvin C., Jr. (1995). "The Proposal for an Unlimited Savings Allowance." *Tax Notes* August 28: 1103.

The Ideal Inflation-Indexed Bond and Irving Fisher's Impatience Theory of Interest with Overlapping Generations*

By JOHN GEANAKOPLOS**

ABSTRACT. Irving Fisher long advocated inflation-indexed bonds. But with what index? I prove in the context of a multicommodity CAPM world that the best welfare-improving bond pays the minimum money needed to achieve the same utility, and not the minimum needed to buy an ideal commodity bundle.

Irving Fisher also developed and advocated the impatience theory of interest. But in OLG economics, the rate of interest is determined by population growth, not impatience. I reconcile this contradiction by proving that in stationary OLG economies with land, the interest rate at the unique steady state does depend on impatience. Indeed, the proposition that greater impatience creates higher interest rates holds more generally in OLG with land than in Fisher's two-period model, because then income effects and substitution effects naturally work in the same direction.

Irving Fisher viewed the real rate of interest as the most important price in the economy, since it gives the relative value of consumption today in terms of consumption in the future. He proposed a theory of impatience to explain what the rate of interest should be in a finite horizon economy. He lamented that many people did not directly trade off consumption today for consumption tomorrow but

*Presented on May 9, 1998 at the Conference in Celebration of Irving Fisher and the publication of *The Works of Irving Fisher*, sponsored by the Cowles Foundation for Research in Economics, Yale University.

**Professor John Geanakoplos is the James Tobin Professor of Economics (1994) at Yale University. He has served as the Director of the Cowles Foundation for Research in Economics since 1996. He was Co-Director of the Economics Program at the Santa Fe Institute from 1990–1991 and Director from 1999–2000. He was also Managing Director and Head of the Fixed Income Research department at Kidder, Peabody (1990–1995) and is a founding partner of Ellington Capital Management (1995).

The American Journal of Economics and Sociology, Vol. 64, No. 1 (January, 2005).

instead traded money today for money tomorrow, thus enabling unexpected inflation to garble the real rate of interest. In this paper I examine whether Fisher's impatience theory of interest holds in an infinite horizon world with overlapping generations, and I derive the optimal indexed bond in a two-period economy with uncertainty and quadratic utilities.

Irving Fisher was profoundly interested in the correct measurement of inflation and was a leading proponent of inflation-indexed bonds. He created an inflation index and meticulously published its values. He insisted his secretary sign an inflation-indexed contract linked to his index, and his company Rand Kardex issued an inflation-indexed bond on the same day it officially opened for business under its new name.[1] He evidently regarded the proper inflation-indexed bond as an important policy question with significant welfare implications. But he did not explain precisely what the welfare benefits are of choosing the right inflation-indexed bond.

The problem is that as prices evolve over time, no household will maintain exactly the same consumption or the same utility. Indeed, no household will even maintain the same ratio of consumption goods; it will substitute goods that become relatively cheaper for goods that become relatively more expensive. Neither a bond that promises the money required to purchase the same commodity bundle nor a bond that promises the money required to achieve the same utility will be sufficient by itself to provide for the needs of the holder. On what theoretical basis is there to choose one over the other?

Practically speaking, it is much simpler to measure inflation by the cost of buying a fixed commodity bundle. As Fisher pointed out, then one does not have to worry about inferring what utility is or how to deal with agents with heterogeneous utilities. And indeed, in actual practice in the United States and elsewhere, inflation-indexed bonds make payments that guarantee the purchase of the same commodity bundle.

But current practice should not necessarily be the last word on the subject. From a theoretical point of view, however, it is not obvious what the right indexed bond is or even what the criterion should be. (Fisher proposed 40 tests that an inflation index should satisfy.) Perhaps the best indexed bond should guarantee each agent the same marginal utility? Perhaps it should be tied to the growth of the economy? Fisher himself modified his view and suggested as an ideal inflation index the geometric average of the Laspeyre (1871) and Paasche (1874) indices of inflation. Since the Laspeyre index is greater than the Konüs (1939) index and the Paasche index is smaller, their geometric average is likely to be near the Konüs index. The Konüs index is meant to measure the increase in cost necessary to achieve the same utility as prices change. Thus, Fisher in the end advocated a practical index that could be used to create a bond that guarantees nearly the same utility. But that still leaves the theoretical question: What difference does it make?

Fisher's 40 criteria for the best index were mostly mechanical. For example, doubling all current prices ought to double the indexed price level. By contrast, I argue that the question of the correct indexed bond ought to become a portfolio welfare question: What additional asset will enable consumers operating in an economy with incomplete markets to best hedge the uncertainty caused by changes in relative prices and in future income? From this welfare point of view, I show that the ideal riskless bond should pay the Konüs index; that is, it should have a monetary payoff in each state equal to the minimum cost of achieving a given utility for the representative consumer. I show that the welfare consequences of adding this asset are dramatically superior to those of adding the so-called inflation-proof bonds we have in practice, even if every consumer's final equilibrium consumption necessarily gives a completely different utility in each state.

Irving Fisher was the inventor of the modern impatience theory of interest. Shortly after Fisher died, the great French economist Maurice Allais (1947), followed by the great American economist Paul Samuelson (1958), introduced the overlapping generations model, in which time goes on indefinitely into the infinite future. In that world there is always a steady state equilibrium in which the real rate of interest is equal to the rate of growth of the population and has nothing to do with impatience. This apparent contradiction has often troubled me, though it does not seem to have been much discussed. The resolution I propose is simple: if an infinitely lived asset like land, which yields a steady dividend forever, is added to the model, the old lessons of Fisher are restored, and the equilibrium interest rate does depend on the rate of impatience. Indeed, Fisher's lessons can be shown to hold under weaker conditions in the setting of OLG and land than they do in his original two-period setting.

In Section I, I describe an intertemporal model of stocks and bonds without uncertainty. I show, much like Fisher did in the appendix to his 1907 book on the rate of interest, that it can be reduced to a timeless Walrasian model. In that model it is easy to show that the real rate of interest increases with increased impatience, increases as the distribution of wealth shifts toward impatient people, increases as future endowments increase relative to current endowments, and increases as productivity improves, if aggregate demand for current consumption declines with the rate of interest and increases with wealth. However, the premise that aggregate demand declines in the real interest rate is not universally applicable; even if utilities are additively separable, it may not hold, since at least for one agent the substitution and income effect will go in opposite directions.

In Section II, I describe an intertemporal model with uncertainty. I begin by specializing to the famous capital asset pricing model (CAPM) pioneered by Markowitz (1952, 1958) and Tobin (1958), which has only one good per state. I show that in this model, as long as there is an asset (1, . . . , 1) that pays one unit of the good in every state, the equilibrium allocation is Pareto efficient, even if many assets are missing, and even if every agent's final consumption is very risky. (This result is due originally to Mossin 1977.) Without the (1, . . . , 1) asset, the final equilibrium would be dreadful. Then I review Tobin's famous mutual fund theorem (1958) that says that in this situation, everybody will hold the (1, . . . , 1) asset in his or her portfolio, together with only one other asset (the market). Thus the (1, . . . , 1) asset makes a dramatic difference to the welfare of the economy, and it is the unique asset that will do so. On this welfare basis, one could rigorously advocate introducing (1, . . . , 1) as the ideal riskless asset. But since there is only one good, the ideal riskless asset can be described equivalently as an asset that guarantees a constant consumption or a constant utility.

To distinguish these two I add many goods to the CAPM model, as I did in my paper with Martin Shubik (Geanakoplos and Shubik 1990). Now I find that there is still one asset that will bring the equilibrium to full efficiency (provided that every agent can sell shares in his or her future income). But it is not an asset that pays a fixed bundle in every state. Instead, it is a contingent bundle, calibrated to achieving the same utility at minimum cost, just as in the Konüs index. Once again it can be shown that all the agents will hold this in their portfolios, together with only one other asset.

Finally, in Section III, I consider the overlapping generations model of Allais and Samuelson. In the conventional presentation of that model, all goods are perishable, and there is always a steady-state equilibrium with rate of interest equal to the rate of population growth (and thus independent of impatience). I show that by adding land, or some other durable good that produces a fixed dividend in perpetuity, one gets only steady-state equilibria in which the rate of interest does depend in the usual way on impatience, on the distribution of wealth and endowments, and on productivity, provided only that agent utilities are additively separable and that all agents accumulate some savings for old age.

I

A Model of Bonds and Stocks in the Spirit of Fisher

The Yale economist Irving Fisher (1867–1947) was the first person to develop a rigorous model of interest rates and the stock market. In order to do so he had to include stock markets, bond markets, commodity markets, money, and production in an intertemporal model. He then reduced this model to a timeless model without assets, in which the rate of interest becomes simply a relative price between two goods. Though assets are missing from the model, their prices can nevertheless be deduced from the present value of their dividends. In this timeless model it is easy to do comparative statics, showing how the equilibrium interest rate is affected by changes in impatience, productivity, the growth of endowments, and the distribution of wealth between patient and impatient households. We give a modern version of Fisher's models, providing sufficient conditions to sign unambiguously the effects of these four factors on the real rate of interest.

I.A The Intertemporal Economy

I.A.1 Time

In order to explain interest rates one needs a model with several time periods. For ease of exposition we assume that there are two times

$s = 0,1$. In each period there is a set $\mathcal{L}$ of goods traded; we denote the price of good ℓ traded at time s by $p_{s\ell} \geq 0$, and the vector of all goods traded at time s by $p_s \in \mathbb{R}^{\mathcal{L}}_{+}$. We assume that there are H households $h \in \mathcal{H}$ that live for both time periods. The households have time-separable utility functions of the form

$$U^h(x) = u^h(x_0) + \delta_h u^h(x_1),$$

where $x_0 \in \mathbb{R}^{\mathcal{L}}_{+}$ and $x_1 \in \mathbb{R}^{\mathcal{L}}_{+}$ and u^h: $\mathbb{R}^{\mathcal{L}}_{+} \to \mathbb{R}$ is increasing concave and continuous.

I.A.2 Impatience

Following Fisher, we assume that households are impatient, in other words, that $\delta_h < 1$ for all $h \in \mathcal{H}$. Fisher tells long stories of why this is a realistic assumption and why the level of impatience differs among households.

It is surprising how few people have challenged Fisher's view that by introspection we know that we are all impatient. One of the most interesting critiques of impatience was given by Yale student George Loewenstein, who argued in his dissertation (1985) that utility stemmed from anticipation, not from consumption. If that were true, people would tend to postpone pleasant experiences, to increase the excitement of anticipating them, and get bad things over with as soon as possible, both of which are the opposite of what Fisher would predict.

I.A.3 Endowments

We suppose that each household h is endowed with goods when young and when old:

$$e^h = \left(e_0^h, e_1^h\right) \in \mathbb{R}^{\mathcal{L}}_{+} \times \mathbb{R}^{\mathcal{L}}_{+}.$$

The greater is the endowment of households in the latter part of their lives relative to the early part of their lives, the greater we say the rate of growth of endowments.

Fisher believed there is a correlation between the size of the endowments and the rate of impatience across people. In short, he felt that patient types of people accumulated wealth and passed both their wealth and their proclivity for patience on to their children.

I.A.4 Money

We suppose that the set of goods is $\mathcal{L} = \{0, 1, \ldots, L\}$. Good 0 represents money; it gives no utility to any agent, and is in zero supply: $e^h_{s0} = 0$ for all agents and time periods. A full-fledged model of money would require it to be in positive supply and to play a special role in transactions and so on. Fisher never developed such a model, and we shall not do so either in this paper. Nevertheless, even in our simple model, money takes on significance if assets promise payments in money.

I.A.5 Firms

We assume that there are F firms $f \in \mathcal{F}$ that are characterized by their production sets $Y^f \subset \mathbb{R}^L_- \times \mathbb{R}^L_+$. We write a production plan $y^f \in Y^f$ as $y^f = (y^f_0, y^f_1)$ and follow Debreu's convention that inputs are negative. Assuming that $Y^f \subset \mathbb{R}^L_- \times \mathbb{R}^L_+$ therefore implies that the firm has to invest in period 0 and produces in period 1; in other words, production takes time. The greater the outputs relative to the inputs, the more productive the economy is.

The firms are traded on a stock market and we denote by σ^h_f the amount of shares household h buys of firm f in period 0. This entitles the household to $\sigma^h_f y^f_1$ of the firm's output in period 1, and no dividend or obligation at time 0. This is in keeping with practice in American capital markets, where there is always an ex-dividend date. It is impossible that the instant a stock is purchased all the dividends can be redirected to the new owner. Instead, a reasonable amount of time must be left to transfer all the accounts, during which time the original owner maintains the responsibilities and benefits. Of course, the price the stock sells for will reflect this fact; if a new buyer realizes he has bought too late to receive the next dividend check, he will pay less for the stock.

We denote the price of the share by π_f. Households have initial ownerships in firms $\bar{\sigma}^h_f$, where $\Sigma_h \bar{\sigma}^h_f = 1$. We assume that the initial owners of firm f buy the inputs y^f_0 before the shares of the firm are traded on the stock market. We assume that each firm is controlled by only one household, which chooses the production plan y^f, and we write $\mathcal{F}(h)$ for the set of all firms controlled by household h.

The controller of a firm f is assumed to hold shares $\overline{\sigma}_f^h > 0$ that he is not allowed to sell. This maintains his incentive to choose a good production plan y^f. For simplicity we also prohibit the controller from buying more shares. Note that if some asset j promises the same payment, $A^j = y_1^f$, then the controller can effectively adjust his exposure to y^f by selling or buying A^j.

I.A.6 Bonds

A bond is a promise made at time $t = 0$ to deliver goods or money at time $t = 1$. We collect all bonds in a set $\mathfrak{J}$. We assume that bond 0 promises to pay \$1 in the second period and denote its price by π_0. All other bonds $j \in \mathfrak{J}$ are real bonds and promise to pay a bundle of goods $A^j \in \mathbb{R}_+^L$. Their prices are denoted by π_j. We assume that the first bond pays one unit of every good.

We denote the amount of bond j household h holds by θ_j^h. If $\theta_j^h > 0$, the household purchases the bond; if $\theta_j^h < 0$, the household sells the bond. Since there is no government in the model, the bonds must be in zero net supply and there can be trade in a bond j only when some household sells it short, that is, when $\theta_j^h < 0$ for some household h.

I.A.7 The Real Rate of Interest

With these definitions, the (gross) nominal interest rate $1 + \eta$ is just $1 + \eta = 1/\pi_0$. Under the simplifying assumption that there is only one good, $L = 1$, we have that the (gross) real interest rate $1 + r$, which measures how many of the good an investor gets in the second period by giving up one unit in the first period, is given by $1 + r = p_0/\pi_1$. Inflation is defined by $1 + i = p_1/p_0$. When there is more than one good, the definition of inflation and the real rate of interest requires a theory of the proper index. We come to this in Section II.

I.A.8 The Economy

The economy can now be described as a vector

$$E = \left(((e_0^h, e_1^h), U^h, \bar{\sigma}^h, \mathcal{F}(h))_{h \in \mathcal{H}}, (A^j)_{j \in J}, (Y^f)_{f \in \mathcal{F}} \right).$$

Prices are given by $(p_0, p_1, (\pi_j)_{j \in \mathfrak{J}}, (\pi_f)_{f \in \mathcal{F}})$, and each household h's choices are given by

$$\left(x_0^h, (\theta_j^h)_{j \in \mathfrak{J}}, (\sigma_f^h)_{f \notin \mathcal{F}(h)}, x_1^h, (y_0^f, y_1^f)_{f \in \mathcal{F}(h)} \right).$$

I.A.9 The Budget Set

Agent h's budget set is defined as

$$\begin{aligned}
&B^h\left(p, (\pi_f, y^f)_{f \notin \mathcal{F}(h)}\right) \\
&= \Big\{ \left(x_0, x_1, (\sigma_f)_{f \notin \mathcal{F}(h)}, (\theta_j)_{j \in \mathfrak{J}}, (y_0^f, y_1^f)_{f \in \mathcal{F}(h)} \right) \text{ s.t.} \\
&p_0 \cdot x_0 + \sum_{j \in \mathfrak{J}} \pi_j \theta_j + \sum_{f \notin \mathcal{F}(h)} \pi_f \sigma_f - \\
&p_0 \cdot \sum_{f \in \mathcal{F}(h)} y_0^f \bar{\sigma}_f^h \le p_0 \cdot e_0^h + \sum_{f \notin \mathcal{F}(h)} \pi_f \bar{\sigma}_f^h \\
&p_1 \cdot x_1 \le p_1 \cdot e_1 + \sum_{j \in \mathfrak{J}} \theta_j p_1 \cdot A^j + \\
&\sum_{f \notin \mathcal{F}(h)} p_1 \cdot y_1^f \sigma_f + \sum_{f \in \mathcal{F}(h)} p_1 \cdot y_1^f \bar{\sigma}_f^h \Big\}.
\end{aligned}$$

I.A.10 Equilibrium

A Fisher equilibrium is a collection of prices and choices $(p, \pi, (x^h, \theta^h, \sigma^h)_{h \in \mathcal{H}}, (y^f)_{f \in \mathcal{F}})$, with $\sigma_f^h = \bar{\sigma}_f^h$ if $f \in \mathcal{F}(h)$, such that

- Markets clear:
  Good markets:

$$\sum_{h \in \mathcal{H}} x_0^h = \sum_{h \in \mathcal{H}} e_0^h + \sum_{f \in \mathcal{F}} y_0^f$$

$$\sum_{h \in \mathcal{H}} x_1^h = \sum_{h \in \mathcal{H}} e_1^h + \sum_{f \in \mathcal{F}} y_1^f$$

  Bond markets:

$$\sum_{h \in \mathcal{H}} \theta^h = 0$$

Stock markets:

$$\sum_{h \in \mathcal{H}} \sigma^h = \sum_{h \in \mathcal{H}} \overline{\sigma}^h$$

- Agents maximize their utility functions subject to their budget sets.

I.A.11 Some Observations

Fisher made the following observations about the nature of intertemporal equilibrium.

1. Default: In the definition of equilibrium nobody is allowed to default. If a person buys an asset or the shares of a firm, he thinks for sure he will get the promised payoffs. Similarly, if he sells an asset, he never contemplates not paying what is owed, at least according to the budget constraint we have written. This is obviously unrealistic, and the analysis should be extended. Fisher never constructed a profound theory of default, but he did observe that the promised interest rate would be higher for assets that had a higher chance of default.

2. Fisher's equation: If there is only one real good, then in equilibrium it must be true that

$$1 + \eta = (1 + r)(1 + i) = r + i + ri. \tag{1}$$

This follows from what is called the absence of arbitrage. If Equation (1) did not hold we would have $1/\pi_0 \neq p_0/\pi_1 \cdot p_1/p_0$, or $\pi_1/\pi_0 \neq p_1/1$. However, in this case, households could buy the nominal bond and sell the real bond (or the other way around) and would make money today without having to pay anything on net tomorrow.

Note that in general one would expect $r \cdot i$ to be very small. In this case Equation (1) can be written as $\eta \equiv r + i$, which is what is usually called the Fisher equation.

3. Stock prices: By the same logic as above, the absence of arbitrage opportunities also implies that $\pi_f = \pi_0 p_1 \cdot y_1^f = \dfrac{1}{1+\eta} p_1 \cdot y_1^f$. Therefore, the price of a stock is nothing else than the discounted value of its dividends.

This holds incidentally for any bond as well. According to Fisher, the price of every asset is the discounted value of its dividends. Thus, even if there are many goods in the model, if we take the ratio of the value of any bond's payoffs to its price, we will always get the same number $1 + \eta$. The nominal rate of interest is thus well defined by the equilibrium. The real rate of interest is not well defined by itself with many goods because it depends on the rate of inflation, which also depends on an index. If potato inflation is much higher than apple inflation, then the potato cost today of one potato tomorrow will be higher than the apple cost today of one apple tomorrow.

4. Endogenous share prices: Since the price of a share depends on the firm's future output, it will change if the controller of the firm decides to change the production plan. This raises the question of whether there is an easy way to characterize the production plan that the controller of the firm chooses.

5. Separation principle: Inspecting the budget constraint reveals that every controller (who takes commodity prices as given) would like to see a production plan chosen that maximizes $p_0y_0 + \pi_0p_1y_1$. As long as the controller is at least a partial owner, $\bar{\sigma}_f^h > 0$, he will therefore optimize his utility by choosing y^f to maximize total discounted profits, or profit for short, and it is in fact irrelevant for the production choices who controls the firm. This is Fisher's so-called principle of separation (between production choices and consumption choices).

I.B A Simple Reformulation of the Fisher Model as a Walrasian Model

With the above insight that the owners of the firm will always choose production plans to maximize profits, we can simplify the model. Let us now define a Walrasian equilibrium for the economy:

$$E = \left(\left((e_0^h, e_1^h), U^h, \bar{\sigma}^h\right)_{h\in\mathcal{H}}, (Y^f)_{f\in\mathcal{F}}\right).$$

We denote by q_t the price at time 0 of goods consumed at time $t \geq 0$, but traded at time 0. We then have the following budget set for household $h \in \mathcal{H}$:

$$B^h(q)$$
$$= \left\{ x\colon q_0 \cdot x_0 + q_1 \cdot x_1 \le q_0 \cdot e_0^h + q_1 \cdot e_1^h + \sum_{f \in \mathcal{F}} \left(q_0 \cdot y_0^f + q_1 \cdot y_1^f \right) \bar{\sigma}_f^h \right\}.$$

An equilibrium $(q, (x^h)_{h\in\mathcal{H}}, (y^f)_{f\in\mathcal{F}})$ is then characterized by (1) goods-market clearing, by (2) households maximizing utilities subject to their budget sets, and by (3) firms maximizing profits:

$$\sum_{h\in\mathcal{H}} x^h = \sum_{h\in\mathcal{H}} e^h + \sum_{f\in\mathcal{F}} y^f$$
$$x^h \in \arg\max_{x\in B^h(q)} U^h(x)$$
$$y^f \in \arg\max_{y\in Y^f} q \cdot y.$$

Notice that the Walrasian budget set has only one constraint. Furthermore, the Walrasian model and its equilibrium make no explicit mention of time (treating goods x_1 exactly symmetrically with goods x_0), no mention of bonds, no mention of who controls the firm, and no mention of trading shares of stock. These omissions make the model much simpler. Notice finally that the Debreu notation, measuring inputs as negative and outputs as positive, makes it very easy to express the idea of profit as a simple dot product $q \cdot y$, which further simplifies the exposition of theWalrasian model.

The following theorem proves that essentially nothing real is lost in this simplification by showing that there is no difference between the production and consumption choices in the Fisher model and in the Walrasian model and, furthermore, that there is no difference in price ratios between contemporaneously traded objects in the two models. In particular, we can recover the bond and stock prices (relative to the price of some consumption good at time 0) from the Walrasian model, because stocks and time 0 goods are traded at the same time in the Fisher model. We cannot, however, recover the rate of inflation or the nominal rate of interest from the Walrasian model.

Theorem 1 *Consider any Fisher economy*

$$E = \left(\left((e_0^h, e_1^h), U^h, \bar{\sigma}^h, \mathcal{F}(h) \right)_{h\in\mathcal{H}}, (A^j)_{j\in\mathfrak{J}}, (Y^f)_{f\in\mathcal{F}} \right)$$

and the corresponding Walrasian economy

$$E = \left(\left((e_0^h, e_1^h), U^h, \bar{\sigma}^h\right)_{h\in\mathcal{H}}, (Y^f)_{f\in\mathcal{F}}\right).$$

Suppose the Fisher economy has at least one asset or stock with nonzero price. Then, given a Fisher equilibrium $(p, \pi, (x^h, \theta^h, \sigma^h)_{h\in\mathcal{H}}, (y^f)_{f\in\mathcal{F}})$ *there is a Walrasian equilibrium* $(q, (x^h)_{h\in\mathcal{H}}, (y^f)_{f\in\mathcal{F}})$ *that has the same equilibrium consumption and production choices and where* $q_0 = p_0$ *and* $q_1 = \pi_0 p_1$. *Conversely, given a Walrasian equilibrium* $(q, (x^h)_{h\in\mathcal{H}}, (y^f)_{f\in\mathcal{F}})$ *there is a Fisher equilibrium* $(p, \pi, (x^h, \theta^h, \sigma^h)_{h\in\mathcal{H}}, (y^f)_{f\in\mathcal{F}})$ *that has the same consumption and production choices and such that* $p_0 = q_0$ *and such that for all* $j \in \mathfrak{J}$ and $f \in \mathcal{F}$,

$$\pi_j = q_1 \cdot A^j$$
$$\pi_f = q_1 \cdot y_1^f$$
$$\frac{q_0}{q_1} = 1 + r \text{ (if } L = 1\text{)}.$$

The proof is left as an (easy) exercise.

Suppose there is no production. Then in this certainty model it makes no difference what the assets are, as long as there is at least one. We always get a reduction to the Walrasian model.

I.C Four Determinants of the Interest Rate

We now show how impatience, the distribution of wealth between patient and impatient agents, the distribution of endowments between the present and future, and the productivity of the firms affect the real rate of interest in a one-good economy. We start with an example and then generalize it to the case where excess demand for current consumption is normal and decreases as the rate of interest increases.

Production Example

Suppose we have two time periods, 0 and 1, one good per period, and two agents A and B with utilities:

$$U^A(x_0, x_1) = \log x_0 + \delta^A \log x_1$$
$$U^B(x_0, x_1) = \log x_0 + \delta^B \log x_1$$
$$0 \le \delta^B < \delta^A \le 1$$

and with endowments:

$$e^A(e_0^A, e_1^A) = (3/4, 1/4)$$
$$e^B(e_0^B, e_1^B) = (3/8, 1/8).$$

Suppose there is a firm, owned entirely by agent A with production function:

$$y_1 = C(-y_0)^\alpha$$
$$C \geq 0$$
$$0 < \alpha < 1.$$

Let the prices be given by $(q_1,q_2) = (1,q)$. Irving Fisher was the first one to recognize clearly that one could think of q as the discount rate,

$$q = \frac{1}{1+r},$$

where r is the real rate of interest.

For simplicity of notation, let us replace $-y_0$ with k. In equilibrium we must have that the firm maximizes profit:

$$\pi(q, k) = qf(k) - k,$$

where $f(k) = Ck^\alpha$, giving us the condition that marginal revenue product equals price:

$$q\alpha Ck^{\alpha-1} = 1.$$

This in turn gives:

$$k^{\alpha-1} = 1/q\alpha C$$
$$k^{1-\alpha} = q\alpha C$$
$$k(q) = q^{\frac{1}{1-\alpha}}(\alpha C)^{\frac{1}{1-\alpha}}$$

giving for maximum profit:

$$\Pi(q) = qC\left[q^{\frac{1}{1-\alpha}}(\alpha C)^{\frac{1}{1-\alpha}}\right]^\alpha - q^{\frac{1}{1-\alpha}}(\alpha C)^{\frac{1}{1-\alpha}}$$
$$= \alpha^{\frac{\alpha}{1-\alpha}} q^{\frac{1}{1-\alpha}} C^{\frac{1}{1-\alpha}} - q^{\frac{1}{1-\alpha}}(\alpha C)^{\frac{1}{1-\alpha}}$$
$$= \left(\alpha^{\frac{\alpha}{1-\alpha}} - \alpha^{\frac{1}{1-\alpha}}\right) q^{\frac{1}{1-\alpha}} C^{\frac{1}{1-\alpha}}.$$

The excess demand for the time 0 good is given by:

$$z_0(q) \equiv \frac{1}{1+\delta^A}\left[\frac{3}{4}+\frac{1}{4}q+\Pi(q)\right]+\frac{1}{1+\delta^B}\left[\frac{3}{8}+\frac{1}{8}q\right]+k(q)-\left(\frac{3}{4}+\frac{3}{8}\right).$$

When $C = 0$ and there is no production, one can easily see that $z_0(q)$ is monotonically increasing in q.[2] In general, the excess demand with two agents could be arbitrary (and thus nonmonotonic in q), as Debreu's decomposition theorem assures us.

When we add production, taking $C > 0$, we can confirm from our formulae that $z_0(q)$ is still increasing in q. Even without the formulae, it is evident that $\Pi(q)$ increases as q increases, giving the firm's owner more wealth. The firm's owner A spends more on good 0 when his wealth increases. And clearly the firm's demand for good 0, $k(q)$, is increasing in q, since the marginal revenue product increases in q.[3]

I.C.1 Some Comparative Statics

Suppose we have an economy with one good today and tomorrow, for which aggregate excess demand for current consumption, $z_0(q)$, is strictly increasing in $q = q_1/q_0$, that is, strictly decreasing in the real interest rate. Suppose also that all individual demands for current consumption are normal, so that increased wealth increases the demand if prices are held constant. These hypotheses will hold if all the consumers have Cobb-Douglas utilities, and if production is strictly concave, as we saw in our example. In this situation we can derive unambiguous comparative statics.

- When any agent, such as A in the example, becomes more impatient, the real rate of interest rises.

  At the old prices the excess demand for good 0 will become positive. Therefore, to clear the market, q must fall. Therefore, the real interest rate $1/q - 1$ must increase. Intuitively, we can describe this comparative statics result by saying that if people care less about the future, they will demand a higher interest in the bank in order to save. A shift in population attitudes toward more impatience (the Now Generation supposedly ushered in by Reagan) ought to raise real interest rates.

- If the distribution of wealth shifts from an impatient agent to a patient agent, such as from B to A in the example, that is, if e_0^B decreases but e_0^A increases by the same amount, then the real rate of interest goes down.

  The argument is as above, but in reverse. At the old equilibrium prices, there must now be less demand for good 0 because agent A will spend $1/(1 + \delta^A)$ of his new money on the good, but agent B will reduce his expenditure on the good by $1/(1 + \delta^B)$ of the money he lost. The only way to clear the market is to increase q. This lowers the real rate of interest. In words, we can say that if wealth in the economy shifts from people who are impatient to people who are patient, the interest rate the banks must give will go down. Fisher believed that the wealthy tended to be more patient, so during a period when the rich get richer, as has happened since 1980 in the United States, the real interest rate should go down, according to Fisher.
- If future endowments increase, all else equal, the real rate of interest will rise.

  At the old equilibrium prices, excess demand for good 0 must go up (since wealth has gone up and current consumption is a normal good). But to restore equilibrium, q must go down. Hence the interest rate goes up.
- If productivity and marginal productivity increase, the real rate of interest will rise. If the firm becomes more profitable at the old prices, income to its owners will rise and so demand for period 0 goods by its owners goes up (by agent A in the example). If marginal productivity goes up, then at the old prices the firm itself will also demand more input at the same prices. Together this creates excess demand for good 0 at the old prices. Hence q must go down.

It is worth mentioning that even if all utilities are of the form $U^h(x) = u^h(x_0) + \delta_h u^h(x_1)$, excess demands may not be monotonic in q, because price substitution effects and income effects may go in opposite directions (and definitely will go in opposite directions for at least one agent). Thus Fisher's comparative statics conclusions depend on additional restrictions on utilities, such as the Cobb-Douglas utilities of our example, where substitution effects always dominate.

II

Time and Uncertainty: The Ideal Inflation-Proof Bond

II.A The GEI Model

Now we add uncertainty to the model. To keep things simple, we stick with pure exchange. The analogue of the Walrasian model from last section is the Arrow-Debreu model, in which agents face only one budget constraint. The analogue of the Fisher temporal model is the GEI (general equilibrium with incomplete markets) model. The canonical GEI model $((U^h, e^h)_{h\in H}, A)$ has two time periods, period 0 and period 1, and S different states of the world ($s = 1, \ldots, S$) in period 1.

Agent utilities and endowments $(U^h, e^h)_{h\in H}$ are as in the Arrow-Debreu model. In case agents have von Neumann-Morgenstern preferences, we can write the utilities as

$$U^h(x) = u_0^h(x_0) + \sum_{s=1}^{S} \gamma_s^h u^h(x_s),$$

where γ_s^h is the subjective probability agent h attributes to the state s. A matrix of asset payoffs $A \in \mathbb{R}_+^{SLJ}$ is also given. The payoff $A_{s\ell j}$ represents the quantity of good ℓ promised for delivery in state s by asset j. As in the Fisher model, it will often be convenient to assume that agents are impatient, and to embody that with the hypothesis that $u^h(\cdot) = \delta^h u_0^h(\cdot)$, with the discount factor satisfying $0 < \delta^h < 1$.

The model preserves the same methodological premises of the Fisher intertemporal model and the Arrow-Debreu world: agent optimization, market clearing, rational expectations (in the sense that everybody anticipates what price will arise in the different states of the world), and perfect competition (in the sense that nobody can affect the prices by whatever he or she does). But it adds uncertainty, something Fisher never formally did in a state-space setting.

The GEI economy is analogous to the Fisher economy (without

production), but with many states of nature. It cannot be reduced to an Arrow-Debreu economy, however, because in the Arrow-Debreu model, agents can exchange commodities at time 0 for any one of the state contingent commodities in the future, whereas in the GEI model, agents are restricted to exchange commodities at time 0 for assets, and the assets are limited to payoffs specified by the matrix A. Of course, by buying and selling assets an agent can influence wealth in different states. But if there are only a very few assets, the agent can arrange very limited wealth transfers. For example, if there is only one asset, which pays one apple in all states at time 1, then by buying this asset an agent can effectively loan money (giving money today in exchange for a repayment tomorrow), while by selling the asset he can borrow money, getting money today but paying in the future. However, that single asset does not provide insurance, because it does not help to transfer wealth from, say, state 1 to state 5.

To keep our notation consistent with the standard GEI literature, we shall drop money from the set of explicitly named commodities, leaving us with $\mathcal{L} = \{1, \ldots, L\}$. The budget set for agent h is given by

$$\begin{aligned} B^h(p, \pi) &= B(p, \pi, e^h, A) \\ &= \Big\{ (x, \theta) \in \mathbb{R}_+^{L(S+1)} \times \mathbb{R}^J : p_0 \cdot (x_0 - e_0^h) + \pi \cdot \theta = 0 \\ &\qquad \text{and } \forall s = 1, \ldots, S,\ p_s \cdot (x_s - e_s^h) = p_s \cdot \sum_j A_s^j \theta_j \Big\}. \end{aligned}$$

Individuals choose among nonnegative consumption plans x, specifying the consumption of each commodity $\ell \in L$ in each state $s \in S^* = \{0, 1, \ldots, S\}$ at time 0 and in the future. A consumption plan can be chosen only if it can be financed by a portfolio of asset holdings, θ, which can be positive or negative. An agent who wants to consume beyond his endowment in state 0 can sell assets; this will require him to make deliveries in the future. We are still assuming that everybody keeps his or her promises so that default is not allowed. There are $S + 1$ budget constraints in the GEI model instead of just one budget constraint as in the Arrow-Debreu model.

Equilibrium is defined by:

$$\left(p, \pi, \left(x^h, \theta^h\right)_{h \in H}\right) \text{ is a GEI iff}$$

$$\sum_{h=1}^{H} (x^h - e^h) = 0 \tag{2.1}$$

$$\sum_{h=1}^{H} \theta^h = 0 \tag{2.2}$$

$$\left(x^h, \theta^h\right) \in B^h(p, \pi), h = 1, \ldots, H \tag{2.3}$$

$$(x, \theta) \in B^h(p, \pi) \Rightarrow U^h(x) \leq U^h(x^h), h = 1, \ldots, H. \tag{2.4}$$

As it is clear from Equations (2.1) (2.4), equilibrium is a price vector for commodities (at all date-event pairs), a price vector for the assets, and then plans for individuals that are optimal in their budget sets, such that supply equals demand for goods and assets.

Equations (2.1)–(2.2) translate aggregate feasibility, Equation (2.3) says that each agent chooses plans in his budget set, and Equation (2.4) adds that there is nothing in the budget set that is better than the selected plan.

II.A.1 Some Notation

Let us introduce a few pieces of notation. Given a vector $x \in \mathbb{R}^{S^*L}$, we take $\tilde{x}$ to be the (uncertain) period 1 components of x

$$p = (p_0, \underbrace{p_1, \ldots, p_S}_{\tilde{p} \in \mathbb{R}^{SL}}) = (p_0, \tilde{p})$$

$$y = (y_0, \underbrace{y_1, \ldots, y_S}_{\tilde{y} \in \mathbb{R}^{SL}}) = (y_0, \tilde{y}).$$

The box notation $\tilde{p} \boxdot \tilde{y}$ means the money value of the bundle y in every state (therefore, it is an S-dimensional vector).

$$\tilde{p} \boxdot \tilde{y} \equiv (p_1 \cdot y_1, \ldots, p_S \cdot y_S)' \in \mathbb{R}^S.$$

For the whole matrix $A \in (\mathbb{R}^{SL})^J$ we can take

$$\tilde{p} \boxdot A \equiv (\tilde{p} \boxdot A^1, \ldots, \tilde{p} \boxdot A^J) \in \mathbb{R}^{SJ},$$

where A^j is the jth column of A.

Each column j of $\tilde{p} \boxdot A$ corresponds to the money payoff in each state for asset j; each column j of $\tilde{p} \boxdot A$ collapses the SL dimensions of column j of A into S dimensions.

Let us introduce a piece of notation to designate an inner product that will be used in the sequel. If $\mu \in \mathbb{R}^S$ and $z \in \mathbb{R}^S$ and γ is a probability measure on S, then we write:

$$\mu \cdot_\gamma z \equiv \sum_{s=1}^{S} \gamma_s \mu_s z_s.$$

It goes without saying that all the usual projection theorems hold for this inner product. Given an arbitrary $S \times J$ matrix V, an arbitrary vector $b \in \mathbb{R}^J$, and an arbitrary strictly positive probability measure γ on S, there is a unique vector $\mu^* \in \text{span}[V] = \{V\theta : \theta \in \mathbb{R}^J\}$ such that $\mu^* \cdot_\gamma V^j = b_j$ for each column j of V. In particular, given an arbitrary vector $\mu \in \mathbb{R}^S$, the projection of μ onto span[V] is the unique vector $\mu^* \in \text{span}[V]$ such that $\mu^* \cdot_\gamma V^j = \mu \cdot_\gamma V^j$ for each column j of V.

II.A.2 Linear Pricing Lemma for GEI

The following lemma is fundamental in the theory of incomplete markets. For the sake of a briefer proof, we assume that some U^h is differentiable, even though the same conclusion holds without differentiability.

Unique Linear Pricing Lemma *Suppose* $(p, \pi, (x^h, \theta^h)_{h \in H})$ *is a* GEI *equilibrium for the* GEI *economy* $((U^h, e^h)_{h \in H}, A)$ *such that for some agent* $h \in H$, *the utility* U^h *is differentiable, and such that* $p_s \cdot x_s^h > 0$ *for all* $s \in S^*$. *Let* γ *be a strictly positive probability measure. Then there is a* unique *vector* $\mu^* \in \text{span}[\tilde{p} \boxdot A]$ *such that* $\pi_j = \mu^* \cdot_\gamma [\tilde{p} \boxdot A^j]$ *for all assets* j.

Proof We know that for each state $s \in S^*$, there is some commodity $\ell_s \in L$ such that $x_{s\ell_s} > 0$. Define

$$\mu_s^h = \frac{1}{\gamma_s} \frac{1}{p_{s\ell_s}} \frac{\partial U(x^h)}{\partial x_{s\ell_s}}$$

(where we take $\gamma_0 = 1$). From the first-order conditions of agent h's optimization, we must have

$$\pi_j = \frac{1}{\mu_0^h} \tilde{\mu}^h \cdot_\gamma [\tilde{p} \boxdot A^j] \quad \text{for all} \quad j \in J.$$

Define μ^* as the projection of $\frac{1}{\mu_0^h}\tilde{\mu}^h$ into span$[\tilde{p} \boxdot A]$. Then μ^* has the right inner product with each asset payoff, and it is the unique vector to do so, since any other vector in span$[\tilde{p} \boxdot A]$ would necessarily make a different inner product with at least one vector. Since the prices of the assets do not depend on the agent h, the projection μ^* also does not depend on the agent h.

II.A.3 Riskless Rate of Interest with Uncertainty

When there is uncertainty and more than one state of nature in the second period, how should we define the riskless rate of interest? The answer, of course, depends on how we define a riskless asset. The traditional answer, given by Fisher and others before him, is to look for an asset that always gives the same purchasing power. If there is only one good and agents have common priors and von Neumann-Morgenstern utilities, the answer seems straightforward. The riskless asset should simply pay off enough money in each state to enable the holder to buy one unit of the commodity in every state. Such an asset would always give the same purchasing power, by construction. It also gives the same utility in each state to an agent for whom it is the sole source of income.

Why is it important that it give the same utility in each state to any owner who holds no other asset, since no consumer will hold only that single asset? Typically, no consumer will end up with exactly the same utility in each state. Why shouldn't the ideal asset pay enough money to guarantee the same marginal utility in each state? Or why shouldn't the ideal asset pay a constant fraction of aggregate income (i.e., of GNP)?

Thus, even for the simple case of one consumption good, it is essential to make clear why it is important to have a riskless asset. This can be done in the capital asset pricing model, which we now review.

II.B CAPM with one commodity

We are going to show that when there is only one consumption good, the asset that pays off one unit of the good in every state does play a special role, at least under the conditions of the capital asset pricing model (CAPM). Let $\tilde{1} = (1, \ldots, 1) \in \mathbb{R}^S$. We shall show that:

(1) As long as every agent can sell off his future income today, the presence of the $(1, \ldots, 1)$ asset guarantees that interior equilibria are fully Pareto optimal.
(2) Everybody does indeed hold the $(1, \ldots, 1)$ asset in their portfolio, and in fact just one other asset, even though final consumption may be very risky.

We shall then show that even when there are multiple goods per state, there is still an asset that satisfies properties (1) and (2).

Capital Asset Pricing Model

Assumptions

$$L = 1 \tag{1}$$

$$U^h(x) = u_0^h(x_0) + \sum_{s=1}^{S} \gamma_s^h u^h(x_s) = u_0^h(x_0) + \sum_{s=1}^{S} \gamma_s^h \left(x_s - \frac{1}{2}\alpha^h x_s^2 \right) \tag{2}$$

$$\gamma_s^h = \gamma_s \quad \forall h, s \tag{3}$$

$$1 - \alpha^h e_s > 0 \quad \forall h, s \text{ where } e_s = \sum_{h \in H} e_s^h \tag{4}$$

$$\tilde{e}^h \in \text{span}[A] \quad \forall h \in H \tag{5}$$

$$\tilde{1} \in \text{span}[A] \tag{6}$$

Equation (1) says that there is only one good (we are also dropping money). In fact, it is only important that there is one good for each $s \in S$ in period 1. There could be many goods in period 0. Equation (2) says that people have von Neumann-Morgenstern quadratic utilities, and Assumption (3) says that agents have objective probabilities γ. Quadratic utilities guarantee that agents only care about the mean and variance of their consumption. That could also be achieved by assuming normality of endowments and asset payoffs. But in that context, the Pareto efficiency theorem below is not true.

Assumption (4) guarantees monotonicity. Since quadratic utility eventually declines with more consumption, we must suppose that the utilities are chosen such that agents still want to eat more even if they consume the whole endowment.

The fifth, crucial assumption is that agents' initial endowments are in the span of the assets (they are tradeable); this is a nongeneric assumption that is necessary to ensure Pareto optimality. This is perhaps not realistic, in view of real-life asymmetries of information and moral hazard issues that normally prevent people from selling their future income. We assume away all these problems.

Finally, Equation (6) says that the $(1, \ldots, 1)$ asset is tradeable in our economy. In this one-good model, the natural definition of a riskless asset is that of an asset that pays one unit of the good in every state of nature, and we shall see that the presence of $\tilde{1}$ in the economy is very important.

Let us state the following Pareto efficiency theorem. This was first proved by Mossin (1977), but we give the proof provided in Geanakoplos and Shubik (1990).

CAPM Efficiency Theorem *Let* $(p, \pi, (x^h, \theta^h)_{h\in H})$ *be an equilibrium with* $x^h >> 0\ \forall h \in H$ *at a* CAPM *economy satisfying Assumptions* (1)–(6), *including that* $(1, \ldots, 1) \in \text{span}[A]$. *Then* $(x^h)_{h\in H}$ *is Pareto optimal.*

This theorem says that even if the number of assets is much smaller than the number of the states (so that it is impossible to insure most risks), equilibrium allocations are fully Pareto optimal, if the $(1, \ldots, 1)$ asset is tradeable, and if every agent can sell shares in his future income. Without the $(1, \ldots, 1)$ asset, equilibrium allocations may be terrible. By adding the $(1, \ldots, 1)$ asset, equilibrium jumps to the Pareto frontier, even though there are many other missing asset markets that have not been added.

Proof Let the marginal utilities of consumption (unweighted by probabilities) be denoted, as in Lemma 1, by:

$$\left(\frac{\partial u^h(x_s)}{\partial x_s}\right)_{s\in S} = \tilde{\mu}^h = \tilde{1} - \alpha^h \tilde{x}^h.$$

Then from the first-order conditions of agent h, we know that:

$$\pi_j = \frac{1}{\mu_0^h} \tilde{\mu}^h \cdot_\gamma [\tilde{p} \boxdot A^j] \quad \text{for all} \quad j \in J.$$

But:

$$\begin{aligned} &\tilde{1} \in \text{span}[A] \\ &\tilde{x}^h = \tilde{e}^h + A\theta^h \in \text{span}[A] \\ \Rightarrow &\frac{1}{\mu_0^h} \tilde{\mu}^h \in \text{span}[A] \\ \Rightarrow &\frac{1}{\mu_0^h} \tilde{\mu}^h = \mu^* \quad \forall h \in H. \end{aligned}$$

The last implication follows from the unique linear pricing lemma proved in the last section. But now we know all individuals' marginal utilities of income across all states are equal, up to a proportionality coefficient. Hence the equilibrium is fully Pareto efficient.

The next theorem shows that the (1, . . . , 1) asset not only will be held by every consumer, but that in fact it is virtually the only thing that every consumer holds. This mutual fund theorem was first proved by Tobin (1958). The proof presented here follows Geanakoplos and Shubik (1990).

CAPM Mutual Fund Theorem *Let* $\tilde{x}^h >> 0 \ \forall h \in H$ *at a CAPM equilibrium arising from a GEI economy satisfying Assumptions (1)–(6). Then*

$$\tilde{x}^h \in \text{span}\left[\tilde{1}, \tilde{e}\right] \quad \forall h \in H$$

where

$$\tilde{e} = \sum_{h=1}^{H} \tilde{e}^h.$$

This theorem says that, at least in the CAPM model, even though all individual consumptions $\tilde{x}^h$ might turn out to be risky, every agent will hold a combination of the market portfolio and the (1, . . . , 1) asset. The (1, . . . , 1) asset is thus indispensable to agent optimization.

Proof From the last theorem, we know there is a scalar $\lambda^h = 1/\mu_0^h > 0$ such that

$$\lambda^h(\tilde{1} - \alpha^h \tilde{x}^h) = \mu^* \quad \forall h$$
$$\Rightarrow \tilde{x}^h = \frac{1}{\alpha^h}\tilde{1} - \frac{1}{\alpha^h \lambda^h}\mu^*.$$

So, everybody's final consumption is a combination of just two payoff vectors. Summing over all the agents we get:

$$\tilde{e} \equiv \sum_{h=1}^{H} \tilde{e}^h = \sum_{h=1}^{H} \tilde{x}^h = \sum_{h=1}^{H}\left[\frac{1}{\alpha^h}\tilde{1} - \frac{1}{\alpha^h\lambda^h}\mu^*\right] = \alpha\tilde{1} - \beta'\mu^*, \alpha > 0, \beta' > 0$$
$$\Rightarrow \mu^* = (1/\beta')(\alpha\tilde{1} - \tilde{e}) \in \text{span}\,[\tilde{1}, \tilde{e}]$$
$$\Rightarrow \tilde{x}^h \in \text{span}[\tilde{1}, \tilde{e}].$$

Before moving to the next section, we note in passing that we can give a more gripping interpretation of the GEI linear pricing theorem in the special case of CAPM. The following theorem is originally due to Sharpe (1964) and Lintner (1965).

CAPM Security Market Line *Let $\tilde{x}^h >> 0$ $\forall h$ at a CAPM GEI. Then $\exists r > -1$ and $\beta > 0$ such that $\forall j \in J$,*

$$\pi_j = \frac{E_\gamma A^j}{1+r} - \beta \text{Cov}_\gamma(\tilde{e}, A^h).$$

More generally, if $z \in$ span[A]

$$\pi(z) = \frac{E_\gamma z}{1+r} - \beta \text{Cov}_\gamma(\tilde{e}, z).$$

Proof Letting $\beta = 1/\beta' > 0$, and recalling from the last proof that $\alpha > 0$,

$$\begin{aligned}\pi_j &= \mu^* \cdot_\gamma A^j \\ &= \beta(\alpha\tilde{1} - \tilde{e}) \cdot {}_\gamma A^j, \alpha, \beta > 0 \\ &= \beta\alpha\tilde{1} \cdot_\gamma A^j - \beta\tilde{e} \cdot_\gamma A^j \\ &= \beta\alpha E_\gamma A^j - \beta\tilde{e} \cdot_\gamma A^j \\ &= \beta(\alpha - E_\gamma\tilde{e})E_\gamma A_j - \beta \text{Cov}_\gamma(\tilde{e}, A^j).\end{aligned}$$

Similarly,

$$\pi(z) = \beta(\alpha - E_\gamma\tilde{e})E_\gamma z - \beta\text{Cov}_\gamma(\tilde{e}, z).$$

Since $\pi(\tilde{e}) > 0$, $\alpha - E_\gamma\tilde{e} > 0$, hence letting $1/(1 + r) = \beta(\alpha - E_\gamma\tilde{e}) > 0$,

$$\pi(z) = \frac{E_\gamma z}{1+r} - \beta\text{Cov}_\gamma(\tilde{e}, z).$$

II.C Multicommodity CAPM

The main lesson of CAPM for us is that if we just add the asset (1, . . . 1), everybody is as well off as possible. The form this asset takes gives us a blueprint for what we should mean by a *riskless* asset. Not surprisingly, when there is only one good, the ideal riskless asset pays the same quantity of the real good in each state of nature. (This does rule out paying the same marginal utility in each state.) The surprise is that even when everybody ends up with risky consumption, everybody trades almost exclusively in the riskless asset, and social welfare is thus dramatically improved.

Once we go over to a multicommodity world, the form of the ideal riskless asset becomes much less obvious. Should it allow for the purchase of the same "ideal" consumption bundle in every state? Or should it allow each agent to achieve the same utility in every state? If every agent regarded consumption as twice as pleasurable in state 1 as in state 2, should the ideal riskless asset pay off the same bundle in both states, or twice as much in state 1, or half as much in state 1? We shall answer these questions by investigating whether in the multicommodity world, under some circumstances, there is again a special asset whose introduction guarantees the Pareto optimality of equilibrium. If there is, we shall take its form to define what we mean by the ideal riskless asset.

The practical world has already spoken on this issue. Inflation-proof bonds almost invariably take the form of guaranteeing the same consumption bundle in every state. Thus in the United States the so-called TIPs (Treasury inflation-protected bonds) are designed to enable holders to purchase the same CPI commodity bundle. But I shall demonstrate that an asset that guarantees the same utility is much more helpful. To see why, consider the following multicommodity CAPM model.

Multiple Commodity CAPM We now move to a world with many goods in each state, $L > 1$. If we allow for completely general utilities, it is hard to say anything concrete. So we specialize to a simple generalization of CAPM, keeping as many of the Assumptions (2)–(5) as possible. A crucial assumption will be made about utilities:

Assumption 2′: Let

$$U^h(x) \equiv u_0^h(x_0) + \sum_{s=1}^{S} \gamma_s^h \left(v_s(x_s) - \frac{1}{2}\alpha_h [v_s(x_s)]^2 \right),$$

where $v_s : \mathbb{R}^L \to \mathbb{R}$ is smooth, concave, homogeneous of degree 1 $\forall s \in S$, $\forall h \in H$ (v_s is the same across agents).

This utility is the composition of an (idiosyncratic) quadratic function with a (common) homogenous of degree 1 function. We will be relying very heavily on the hypothesis that there is a common v_s. This allows us to define one asset whose payoffs give each agent an equal utility across every state.

Because of the quadratic aspect, this utility also declines eventually with more and more consumption. So we need the natural counterpart of old Assumption (4) in this new setup:

Assumption 4′ $1 - \alpha^h v_s(e_s) > 0$.

Having made the previous assumption, we can formally prove the following theorem. This theorem was first stated in Geanakoplos and Shubik (1990). The proof here is new.

Multiple Commodity CAPM Efficiency Theorem *Consider a GEI satisfying Assumptions (2′), (3), (4′), and (5). Let* $(p, \pi, (x^h, \theta^h)_{h\in H})$ *be a GEI for which* $x^h \gg 0$ $\forall h \in H$. *Suppose there is an asset* $r \in \text{span}[A]$ *of the form*

$$r = \left(\frac{1}{v_1(e_1)} e_1, \ldots, \frac{1}{v_S(e_S)} e_S \right).$$

Then $(x^h)_{h \in H}$ *is Pareto optimal.*

Notice that by homogeneity of degree 1,

$$v_s\left(\frac{1}{v_s(e_s)} e_s \right) = \frac{v_s(e_s)}{v_s(e_s)} = 1$$

so that the "ideal" asset r yields the same utility of consumption $\left(1 - \frac{1}{2}\alpha_h\right)$ in every state to any agent h who consumes exclusively its payoff. But what is more important, it gives the cheapest possible bundle in each state achieving that utility, given the prices prevailing in that state. A fixed commodity bundle also gives the same utility in every state (assuming v_s does not depend on s), but it is not the cheapest bundle to achieve that utility, given changing prices. Thus the appropriate riskless asset does reflect what is available; in other words, it is not a fixed bundle. In general, no fixed commodity bundle would do as well.

Proof Let us begin by examining the given multicommodity CAPM equilibrium $(p, \pi, (x^h, \theta^h)_{h \in H})$. In equilibrium we know that in each state, prices will be proportional to each agent's marginal utilities:

$$\begin{aligned} p_{s\ell} &= \lambda_s^h \frac{\partial U^h(x)}{\partial x_{s\ell}} = \lambda_s^h \gamma_s \left[\frac{\partial v_s(x_s^h)}{\partial x_{s\ell}} - \alpha_h v(x_s^h) \frac{\partial v_s(x_s^h)}{\partial x_{s\ell}} \right] \\ &= \mu_s^h \frac{\partial v_s(x_s^h)}{\partial x_{s\ell}}, \end{aligned}$$

where $\mu_s^h = \lambda_s^h \gamma_s [1 - \alpha_h v_s(x_s)] > 0$.

Since v_s is homogeneous of degree 1 and common to all h, it follows from a standard theorem in aggregation that in equilibrium every x_s^h is proportional to e_s (see Deaton and Mullbauer 1980). Since the derivatives of v_s must be homogeneous of degree 0, $\partial v_s(x_s^h)/\partial x_{s\ell} = \partial v_s(e_s)/\partial x_{s\ell}$ does not depend on h. Furthermore, since scaling p_s up or down by itself does not affect equilibrium, we might as well assume $p_s = Dv_s(e_s)$.

Finally, by homogeneity, we conclude that $p_s \cdot e_s = v_s(e_s)$ and for any scalar multiple of e_s, such as any x_s^h, $p_s \cdot x_s^h = v_s(x_s^h)$. For any y_s with $p_s \cdot y_s = p_s \cdot x_s^h$, we know from the fact that x_s^h is equilibrium consumption that $v_s(y_s) \le v_s(x_s^h) = p_s \cdot x_s^h = p_s \cdot y_s$. By homogeneity, $v_s(y_s) \le p_s \cdot y_s \ \forall s \in S, \ \forall y_s \in \mathbb{R}_+^L$.

We shall now prove the theorem by reducing the economy to a one-commodity CAPM in which CAPM Assumptions (1)–(6) hold.

Now we define a related one-good CAPM economy $((\hat{U}^h, \hat{e}^h)_{h \in H}, \hat{A})$ where we maintain the same number of states and agents as in the multicommodity CAPM. Let

$$\hat{U}^h(\hat{y}_0, \hat{y}_1, \ldots, \hat{y}_s) = u_0^h(\hat{y}_0) + \sum_{s=1}^{S} \gamma_s \left[\hat{y}_s - \frac{1}{2} \alpha_h \hat{y}_s^2 \right] \quad \forall h \in H,$$

where the u_0^h and α_h parameters are the same as in the multicommodity CAPM utility. Define

$$\hat{e}^h = (e_0^h, p_1 \cdot e_1^h, \ldots, p_S \cdot e_S^h) \in \mathbb{R}_{++}^{L+S} \quad \forall h \in H,$$

where the p_s are taken from the multicommodity equilibrium. Define

$$\hat{A}_{sj} = p_s \cdot A_{sj}, \quad \forall s \in S, \quad j \in J.$$

Observe that since $r \in \text{span}[A]$, $(1, \ldots, 1) = \tilde{p} \,\square\, r \in \text{span}[\hat{A}]$. More generally, for any vector $y \in \mathbb{R}_+^{L(S+1)}$, define the vector $\hat{y} \in \mathbb{R}_+^{L+S}$ by $\hat{y}_0 = y_0$ and $\hat{y}_s = p_s \cdot y_s$, $\forall s \in S$. Conversely, for any vector $\hat{y} = (\hat{y}_0, \hat{y}_1, \ldots, \hat{y}_s) \in \mathbb{R}_+^{L+S}$, define the vector $\vec{y} \in \mathbb{R}_+^{L(1+S)}$ by

$$\vec{y}_0 = \hat{y}_0; \quad \vec{y}_s = \frac{\hat{y}_s}{p_s \cdot e_s} e_s \quad \text{for all} \quad s \in S.$$

Note that $v_s(\vec{y}_s) = \hat{y}_s v_s(e_s / p_s e_s) = \hat{y}_s$, and $p_s \cdot \vec{y}_s = \hat{y}_s$.

Define the price vector q in the CAPM economy by $q_0 = p_0$, and $q_s = 1$ for all $s \in S$. First let us see that $(q, \pi, (\hat{x}^h, \theta^h)_{h \in H})$ is an equilibrium for the economy $((\hat{U}^h, \hat{e}^h)_{h \in H}, \hat{A})_{h \in H}$, where the π and θ^h are as in the original multicommodity equilibrium. Since x_s^h is proportional to e_s for all h, $\hat{x}_s^h = p_s \cdot x_s^h = v_s(x_s^h)$. Thus $U^h(x^h) = \hat{U}^h(\hat{x}^h)$ for all $h \in H$.

Clearly, for all vectors (y^h, φ^h),

$$(y^h, \varphi^h) \in B^h(p, \pi, e^h, A) \Leftrightarrow (\hat{y}^h, \phi^h) \in B^h(q, \pi, \hat{e}^h, \hat{A})$$
$$\Leftrightarrow (\vec{y}^h, \phi^h) \in B^h(p, \pi, e^h, A).$$

Thus $(\hat{x}^h, \theta^h) \in B^h(q, \pi, \hat{e}^h, \hat{A})$. Moreover, if some $(\hat{x}, \hat{\theta}) \in B^h(q, \pi, \hat{e}, \hat{A})$, then $(\vec{x}, \hat{\theta}) \in B^h(p, \pi, e^h, A)$. By virtue of the fact that (x^h, θ^h) are equilibrium demands, $\hat{U}^h(\hat{x}^h) = U^h(x^h) \geq U^h(\vec{x}) = \hat{U}^h(\hat{x})$, so $(\hat{x}^h, \theta^h)$ are equilibrium demands in the one-good CAPM.

Our CAPM economy satisfies all Assumptions (1)–(6). Hence by our one-good Pareto efficiency theorem, $(\hat{x}^h)_{h\in H}$ is fully Pareto efficient in the one-good CAPM.

If $(y^h)_{h\in H}$ Pareto dominates $(x^h)_{h\in H}$ in the multicommodity CAPM, and if $\Sigma_{h\in H}y^h = \Sigma_{h\in H}e^h$, then $(\hat{y}^h)_{h\in H}$ must Pareto dominate $(\hat{x}^h)_{h\in H}$ and still be feasible in the one-good CAPM, a contradiction.

Multicommodity CAPM Mutual Fund Theorem *Under the assumptions of the last theorem, let* $\tilde{x}^h >> 0\ \forall h \in H$ *at a multicommodity CAPM GEI. Then*

$$\tilde{x}^h \in \text{span}[r, \tilde{e}] \quad \forall h \in H,$$

where r *is the appropriate ideal asset defined above.*

The proof is given by combining the one-commodity CAPM proof with the proof given above for the multicommodity CAPM efficiency theorem. Once again we are able to prove that there is a crucial asset that is necessary and sufficient for the economy to achieve full efficiency (assuming every agent can sell off his future endowment).

II.D The Ideal Inflation-Proof Bond

In the context of the multicommodity CAPM, we can positively describe the ideal inflation-proof bond. It does not pay the same amount of money in each state. It does not guarantee the same consumption in each state. It does not guarantee the same marginal utility in each state. On the contrary, *it guarantees the same utility in each state.* If agents feel twice as good about consumption in state 1 as in state 2, the ideal riskless asset will pay half as many goods in state 1.

II.D.1 What Would Fisher's Ideal Index Give?

The Konüs index measures inflation as the ratio of the cost of achieving the same utility between this period and a previous base period. Our ideal bond corresponds to a Konüs inflation-indexed bond. In

Fisher's proposal of 1925 for an indexed bond, he suggested using a fixed commodity bundle chosen in some previous base period. This corresponds to the Laspeyre index of inflation. As Fisher recognized clearly, using a fixed bundle to measure inflation tends to overestimate it (assuming the bundle chosen in the base year was utility maximizing) because, when the price of some commodities go up, agents substitute other cheaper commodities. His later recommendation for the ideal inflation index was more sophisticated than the Laspeyre index. He suggested taking the geometric average of the Laspeyre index and the Paasche index as an ideal index. The Paasche index is formed by taking the ratio of the cost of buying today's consumption bundle at today's prices to the cost of buying today's consumption bundle at yesterday's prices. Assuming that today's bundle was utility maximizing at today's prices, the Paasche index always underestimates the Konüs inflation. Averaging the two can give an index that is close to the Konüs index. It can be shown that if the functions v_s are all equal to Cobb-Douglas utilities with exponents $1/L$ for every commodity, then the Fisher index reduces precisely to the Konüs index (see Diewert 1976). The Fisher index would then provide for Pareto-efficient trade under the multicommodity CAPM assumptions of this section.

II.D.2 An Open Question

This result leaves open the question about what the ideal riskless bond should be in case there is more agent heterogeneity. For example, if v_s also depends on h, there may be no single asset that provides every agent with a state independent utility. Further analysis is required to see whether in this case it is helpful to have more than one inflation-proof bond, or whether there is indeed any particular advantage to introducing a bond linked to some consumer price index.

III

Overlapping Generations Economies (OLG)

IRVING FISHER ARGUED THAT the rate of interest depends on impatience, on productivity, on the distribution of endowments between today and tomorrow, and on the distribution of wealth between patient and impatient agents. In 1947, Maurice Allais of France introduced a model of overlapping generations in which he showed that neither impatience nor any of the other aforementioned factors has anything to do with the rate of interest, at least for some equilibria. He found that the rate of interest is equal to the rate of growth of population. In 1958, Paul Samuelson of MIT rediscovered the OLG model and added a new twist. He showed that there could be assets whose prices exceed the present discounted value of all their future dividends, thus contradicting another central tenet of Fisher. Samuelson concentrated on just one such asset, namely, green pieces of paper called fiat money, which provided no utility whatsoever and yet sold for a positive price. The situation in which an asset sells for more than its fundamental value is called a bubble.

OLG models have an infinite number of agents and an infinite number of goods. Each agent lives for two periods, when he is "young" and "old." In the simplest version of the model, which we shall concentrate on here, there is one good in each time period.

In Samuelson's original paper, he gave an endowment of 1 to the young and nothing to the old in each generation. He also assumed one agent per generation. See Figure 1.

Notice that at a given date, *t*, the old have nothing to offer the young, so according to Samuelson there could be no trading. Samuelson ascribed the inefficiencies we will see in this model to a lack of

Figure 1

OLG Endowments in Samuelson Economy.

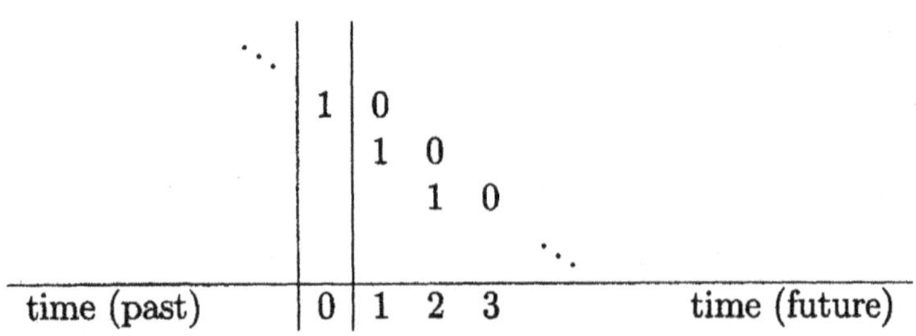

a double coincidence of wants. He suggested that one way to deal with this was to introduce money.

We will begin to analyze the OLG model as if it could be thought of as a Walrasian or Arrow-Debreu model with one budget constraint per agent, and infinity in a few places. That immediately rules out the lack of double coincidence of wants explanation for any of the OLG properties, since in Arrow-Debreu all goods and agents are directly linked. This is exactly analogous to the transformation of the temporal Fisher economy into the timeless Walrasian economy that we saw in Section I. We shall find that when agents have endowments for just a finite set of goods, there are typically two steady-state equilibria. One we call **F** after Fisher, since the rate of interest there depends on the impatience of the consumers, though the equilibrium real rate of interest is negative, and the equilibrium is inefficient. In the other steady state equilibrium, **S**, as Allais and Samuelson claimed, the rate of interest is equal to the growth rate of the population (namely, zero in our example), completely independent of the impatience of the consumers.

After examining the Allais-Samuelson case, we add land, which we interpret as an endowment of an infinite set of goods, and find that now there is only one steady-state equilibrium, which is efficient, and in which the rate of interest depends exactly as before on impatience and the other factors mentioned earlier in Fisher's two-period model.

III.A Description of the Basic OLG Model

The set of commodities and agents are now both infinite: $\mathcal{L} = \mathbb{Z} = \{\ldots, -1, 0, 1, \ldots\}$; $\mathcal{H} \equiv \{th : (t, h) \in \mathbb{Z} \times H\}$, where we think of one commodity per period and H agents per generation. Each period is regarded as the time of a generation (say 30 years). Each agent lives for two periods, and has an endowment $e^{th} = (\ldots, e_t^{th}, e_{t+1}^{th}, \ldots)$, where e_s^{th} is the endowment of an agent born at t in period s. Thus e_t^{th} is the endowment of agent th when young and e_{t+1}^{th} is the endowment of agent th when old. In the basic model without land, we assume there is no endowment other than these two. Payoffs depend only on consumption while alive $U^{th}(\ldots, x_t, x_{t+1}, \ldots) = U^{th}(x_t, x_{t+1})$. We shall assume that U^{th} is strictly concave and strictly increasing in goods corresponding to periods in which the agent is alive, and similarly that the endowments when young are positive, $e_t^{th} > 0$.

A *Walrasian OLG equilibrium* is a price vector $q = (\ldots, q_{-1}, q_0, q_1, \ldots)$ and an allocation $\{x^{th} = (\ldots, x_t^{th}, x_{t+1}^{th}, \ldots): th \in \mathcal{H}\}$ such that

(1) market clearing: $\Sigma_{th\in\mathcal{H}} x_s^{th} = \Sigma_{h\in H} x_s^{s-1,h} + \Sigma_{h\in H} x_s^{sh} = \Sigma_{th\in\mathcal{H}} e_s^{th}$, $\forall s$
(2) value of individual endowments are finite: $\Sigma_{-\infty}^{+\infty} q_s e_s^{th} < \infty$, $\forall th \in \mathcal{H}$
(3) $x^{th} \in B^{th}(q) = \{x : \Sigma_{-\infty}^{+\infty} q_s x_s \leq \Sigma_{-\infty}^{+\infty} q_s e_s^{th}\}$, $\forall th \in \mathcal{H}$
(4) $x \in B^{th}(q) \Rightarrow U^{th}(x) \leq U^{th}(x^{th})$, $\forall th \in \mathcal{H}$.

In case there is no land, $\Sigma_{th\in\mathcal{H}} e_s^{th} = \Sigma_{h\in H} e_s^{s-1,h} + \Sigma_{h\in H} e_s^{s,h}$, and $\Sigma_{-\infty}^{+\infty} q_s e_s^{th} = q_t e_t^{th} + q_{t+1} e_{t+1}^{th}$, so Condition (2) is trivial. Actually, Condition (2) follows from Conditions (1), (3), and (4) for economies in which agents are only interested in a finite number of goods, for if an agent had infinite wealth, he would still have money left over to spend after buying the whole of the aggregate endowment of the goods that he liked, and then he would want to buy still more, contradicting market clearing.

As in the two-period Walrasian equilibrium described earlier, the prices q_t represent the price that would be paid at time 0 to obtain one unit of consumption at time t.

In the following four examples we shall assume there is only one agent per generation, and drop the superscript h. In our theorems, however, we shall allow for multiple agents per generation.

Example 1 Let $U^t(\ldots, x_{t-1}, x_t, x_{t+1}, \ldots) = \log x_t + \log x_{t+1}$, and let $e_t^t = 3$, $e_{t+1}^t = 1$, and $e_s^t = 0$ otherwise, for all $t \in H$.

It can easily be seen that there are two stationary equilibria, where q_{t+1}/q_t is the same for all t. In one $q_t = 3^t$, $-\infty < t < \infty$, so $q_{t+1}/q_t = 3$. Each agent optimizes by consuming her endowment. Thus, $x_t^t = 3$, $x_{t+1}^t = 1$, for all $t \in \mathcal{H}$, and clearly the markets clear. We call this equilibrium **F**, after Fisher.

In the other stationary equilibrium, $q_t = 1$, $-\infty < t < \infty$. This clears all the markets because demand becomes $(x_t^t, x_{t+1}^t) = (2, 2)$ for all $t \in \mathcal{H}$. We call this the **S** equilibrium, after Samuelson.

Since the consumers' utility function is concave, consumers are better off smoothing consumption:

$$U^t(2, 2) > U^t(3, 1).$$

Thus Equilibrium **F** is *not* Pareto efficient.

In the **F** equilibrium $1 + r_t = q_t/q_{t+1} = 1/3 \Rightarrow r_t = -2/3$, while in the **S** equilibrium,

$$r_t = 0$$

equal to the rate of population growth.

Example 2 Consider again the utility functions in Example 1, $U^t(x_t, x_{t+1}) = \log x_t + \log x_{t+1}$, but now let the endowments for each generation t be $(e_t^t, e_{t+1}^t) = (6, 1)$. It is easy to find two steady-state equilibria as before. In Equilibrium 2**F**, we let $q = (\ldots, 1, 6, 36, \ldots)$ and $(x_t^t, x_{t+1}^t) = (6, 1) = (e_t^t, e_{t+1}^t)$. The interest rate is $1 + r = 1/6$, $r = -5/6$, so an increase in endowments when young decreases the rate of interest, just as Irving Fisher predicted. On the other hand, there is also an Equilibrium 2**S** in which $q = (\ldots, 1, 1, 1, \ldots)$ and $(x_t^t, x_{t+1}^t) = \left(3\frac{1}{2}, 3\frac{1}{2}\right)$ for all t. In this "Samuelson equilibrium," the interest rate is still 0 despite the change in endowments. The Samuelson equilibrium confirms the view of Allais that the distribution of endowments across the lifecycle will not change the interest rate.

Example 3 Suppose now that $U^t(x_t, x_{t+1}) = \log x_t + 0.5 \log x_{t+1}$, and that $(e_t^t, e_{t+1}^t) = (3, 1)$. Compared to Example 1, the agents have gotten more impatient. Again we can calculate that there are two stationary equilibria. In the Fisher equilibrium, $q = \left(\ldots, \frac{1}{2}, \frac{3}{2}, \frac{9}{4}, \ldots\right)$ and $(x_t^t, x_{t+1}^t) = (3, 1)$ for all t. The interest rate has risen to $1 + r_t = \frac{2}{3}$, $r_t = -\frac{1}{3}$. But in the other Samuelson equilibrium, $q = (\ldots, 1, 1, 1, \ldots)$ and $(x_t^t, x_{t+1}^t) = \left(\frac{8}{3}, \frac{4}{3}\right)$. Again the interest rate remains at 0 despite the increase in impatience of every agent.

In all three examples, the real interest rate in the Samuelson equilibrium was equal to the population growth rate, namely, zero.[4] Samuelson actually considered a variation of the economy we have been working with, in which time has a beginning at $t = 1$. He added a positive endowment of fiat money to the endowment of old agents at time $t = 1$. Then he showed that what we called the **S**-equilibrium could be realized as an equilibrium in his truncated model by giving money a positive value. Money is a durable good that yields no dividends and provides no utility, yet in the Samuelson model it has a positive value, contradicting another of Fisher's central tenets.

III.B Adding Land to the OLG Model

Land is meant to be an asset that yields a steady dividend forever. The owner of the land effectively owns all its dividends, and hence has an endowment stream that goes on forever, even though he will die after at most two periods. We start, as Samuelson suggested, at time 1, with the old agents from time 0 and the young agents born at time 1, but with no money and with all the land in the possession of agents born at time 0. The definition of Walrasian OLG equilibrium given above also applies with land, except that now we restrict to $t \geq 0$ and $s \geq 1$. The only other difference is that in the basic OLG economy, each agent owns goods in at most two periods, while with land, some agents $0h$ might own endowments of goods in every period. In fact, we shall always assume that in OLG with land, at least one agent's endowment includes a nonnegligible fraction of the aggregate endowment of *every* good.

Example 4 We assume individual endowments of fruit are (3, 1) when young and old, as in Examples 1 and 3.

Now we add an infinitely durable good to the OLG model that yields real dividends forever. In addition to the other endowments, we assume that the person born in time 0 owns a durable good called land or trees that yields one unit of the perishable consumption good per period, forever. We can write the effective endowments of the perishable goods as in Figure 3.

To solve for the Walrasian OLG equilibrium, we write the budget sets:

Figure 2

OLG Endowments in Examples 1 and 3.

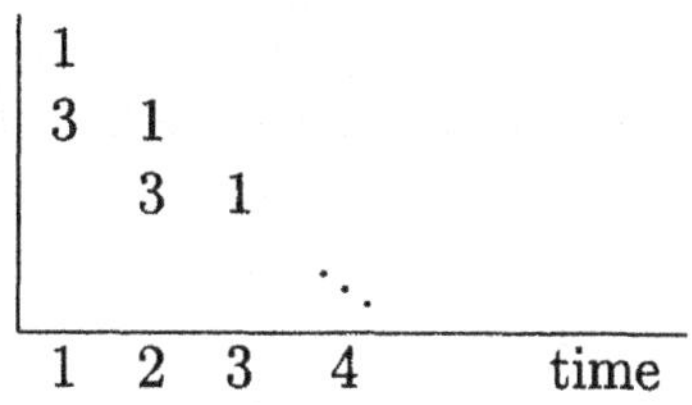

Figure 3

OLG Endowments with Land in Example 4.

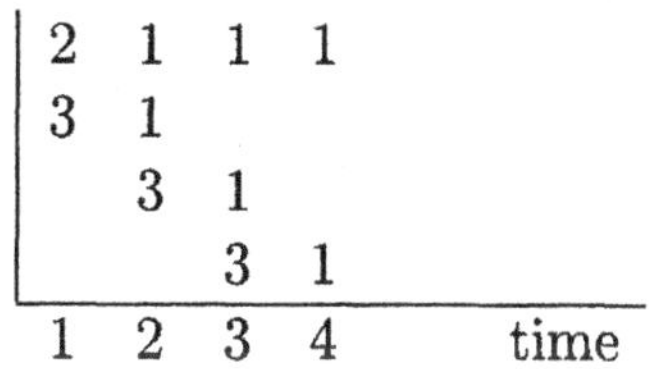

$$B^0(q) = \left\{ x_1^0 : q_1 x_1^0 \le q_1 + q_1 + \underbrace{\sum_{t=2}^{\infty} q_t}_{\text{value of the land}} \right\}$$

$$B^t(q) = \{(x_t^t, x_{t+1}^t) : q_t x_t^t + q_{t+1} x_{t+1}^t \le 3q_t + q_{t+1}\} \text{ for all } t \ge 1.$$

Market clearing now requires that $x_t^{t-1} + x_t^t = e_t^{t-1} + e_t^t + 1 = 1 + 3 + 1 = 5$, $t = 1, 2, \ldots$. We defer computing the stationary equilibrium until the next section.

Note that consumer 0 solves: max $\log x_1^0$ s.t. $x_1^0 \in B^0(p)$, so $x_1^0 = (q_1 + \Sigma_{t=1}^{\infty} q_t)/q_1$. We know that $x_1^0 \le 5$ (to satisfy market clearing), so

$$\sum_{t=1}^{\infty} q_t \le 4q_1 < \infty.$$

Thus in any equilibrium in Example 4, the value of the aggregate endowment $5\Sigma_{t=1}^{\infty} q_t$ must be finite. In Examples 1–3, it was infinite in every equilibrium.

III.B.1 Temporal OLG Equilibrium with Land

We have described the OLG model with land by adding the dividends of the land to the endowments of the time 0 generation, in accordance with how much land each of them owns to start. In the Walrasian (or Arrow-Debreu) equilibrium described in Section III.A, consumption goods in every period are traded simultaneously at some mythical place and time where the souls of the unborn and dead all meet. With durable goods like land, we can define a more realistic *temporal* OLG equilibrium by allowing trade to occur only between living agents. At any given time, two generations are living, and they can exchange fruit (consumption goods) and land, just as in the two-period temporal equilibrium described in Section I. And again we shall see that the temporal equilibrium is identical to the Walrasian equilibrium.

Define:

K_0^{0h} = acres of land owned initially by consumers $0h$.
K_s^{th} = acres of land purchased in year $s \geq 1$ by consumer th. We allow $K_s^{sh} < 0$, but require $K_s^{s-1,h} \geq 0$.
x_s^{th} = number of fruit consumed in year s by consumer th. We require $x_s^{th} \geq 0$.
p_t = price of a time t fruit *paid at time t.*
Π_t = price of a time t acre of land *paid at time t.*
f = output of fruit per acre of land in each period.
$\underline{f}$ = $f\Sigma_{h\in H}K_0^{0h}$ = total output of fruit from all land, in each period.

In the Walrasian setting, q_t was the price paid at time 0 for fruit at time t. That was the present value price, whereas p_t here is the current value price. Allowing $K_s^{sh} < 0$ is analogous to allowing short sales of assets in the two-period model. Insisting on $K_s^{s-1,h} \geq 0$ is necessary, since we do not allow for default, and the agent cannot pay back after he is dead.

Recalling that the owner of land at time t has the right to consume the fruit it bears at time $(t + 1)$, we define the temporal budget constraints for each agent $0h$ and th, $h \in H$, $t \geq 1$:

$$B^{0h}(p,\Pi)=\left\{(x_1^{0h},K_1^{0h}):\ p_1x_1^{0h}+\Pi_1K_1^{0h}\le \underbrace{p_1e_1^{0h}}_{\text{endowed fruit}}+\underbrace{p_1K_0^{0h}f}_{\text{fruit from endowed land}}+\underbrace{\Pi_1K_0^{0h}}_{\text{endowed land}}\right\}$$

$$B^{th}(p,\Pi)=\{(x_t^{th},K_t^{th},x_{t+1}^{th},K_{t+1}^{th}): p_tx_t^{th}+\Pi_tK_t^{th}\le p_1e_t^{th}\quad\text{and}$$
$$p_{t+1}x_{t+1}^{th}+\Pi_{t+1}K_{t+1}^{th}\le p_{t+1}e_{t+1}^{th}+p_{t+1}K_t^{th}f+\Pi_{t+1}K_t^{th}\}. \tag{2}$$

A consumer born in year $t \geq 1$ has two budget constraints. The first limits his purchase of fruit and land in year t. The second limits his purchase of fruit and land in year $(t+1)$. Increasing K_t^{th} has no direct effect on the consumer's utility, but allows him to increase x_{t+1}^{th}. Increasing K_{t+1}^{th} does not benefit the consumer in any way, so in equilibrium, $K_{t+1}^{th}=0$.

A temporal OLG equilibrium with land $((p_t, \Pi_t)_{t\geq 1}, (x^{th}, K^{th})_{th\in\mathcal{H}})$ satisfies

(1) market clearing in commodities:

$$\sum_{th\in\mathcal{H}} x_s^{th}=\sum_{h\in H} x_s^{s-1,h}+\sum_{h\in H} x_s^{sh}=\sum_{th\in\mathcal{H}} e_s^{th}+\bar{f},\quad \forall s\geq 1$$

(2) market clearing in land: $\Sigma_{th\in\mathcal{H}}K_s^{th}=\Sigma_{h\in H}K_0^{0h}, \forall s\geq 1$

(3) $(x^{th}, K^{th})\in B^{th}(p,\Pi), \forall th\in\mathcal{H}$

(4) $(x, K)\in B^{th}(p,\Pi)\Rightarrow U^{th}(x)\leq U^{th}(x^{th}), \forall th\in\mathcal{H}$.

In our next theorem we shall prove that temporal OLG is identical to Walrasian OLG. The idea is that the return on land in the temporal equilibrium implicitly defines the tradeoff between consumption at times t and $t+1$, and thus the rate of interest at time t:

$$1+r_t=\frac{p_{t+1}f+\Pi_{t+1}}{p_{t+1}}\Bigg/\frac{\Pi_t}{p_t}.$$

The denominator describes how much fruit can be acquired from the sale of one acre of land at time t, and the numerator describes how much fruit can be acquired at time $t+1$ from the dividends and sale of the land.

Walrasian-Temporal Equilibrium Equivalence Theorem for OLG with Land *Let* $E = ((U^{tb}, e^{tb})_{tb\in\mathcal{H}}, (K_0^{0b})_{b\in H}, f)$ *be an OLG economy with productive land* $\bar{f} = f\Sigma_{b\in H}K_0^{0b} > 0$. *Then there is a temporal OLG equilibrium* $((p_t, \Pi_t)_{t\geq 1}, (x^{tb}, K^{tb})_{tb\in\mathcal{H}})$ *for E if and only if there is a Walrasian OLG equilibrium* $(q_t, (x^{tb})_{tb\in\mathcal{H}})$ *for E, where for all* $t \geq 1$

$$\frac{q_t}{q_{t+1}} = \frac{p_{t+1}f + \Pi_{t+1}}{p_{t+1}} \bigg/ \frac{\Pi_t}{p_t}$$

$$\frac{\Pi_t}{p_t} = \frac{1}{q_t}\sum_{\tau=t+1}^{\infty} q_\tau f.$$

Proof We prove first that the two equations above are equivalent. Suppose first that $\Pi_t/p_t < \infty$ is defined for all $t \geq 1$ by the bottom equation. Then

$$\frac{p_{t+1}f + \Pi_{t+1}}{p_{t+1}} \bigg/ \frac{\Pi_t}{p_t} = \frac{f + \dfrac{1}{q_{t+1}}\sum_{\tau=t+2}^{\infty} q_\tau f}{\dfrac{1}{q_t}\sum_{\tau=t+1}^{\infty} q_\tau f}$$

$$= \frac{q_t}{q_{t+1}} \frac{q_{t+1}f + \sum_{\tau=t+2}^{\infty} q_\tau f}{\sum_{\tau=t+1}^{\infty} q_\tau f} = \frac{q_t}{q_{t+1}}.$$

Conversely, suppose the top equation holds for all $t = s \geq 1$. Rewriting it and iterating it back to $t < s$, we get

$$\frac{\Pi_s}{p_s} = \frac{q_{s+1}}{q_s}\left(f + \frac{\Pi_{s+1}}{p_{s+1}}\right)$$

$$\frac{\Pi_{s-1}}{p_{s-1}} = \frac{q_s}{q_{s-1}}\left(f + \frac{q_{s+1}}{q_s}\left(f + \frac{\Pi_{s+1}}{p_{s+1}}\right)\right) = \frac{1}{q_{s-1}}\left(q_s f + q_{s+1}f + q_{s+1}\frac{\Pi_{s+1}}{p_{s+1}}\right)$$

$$\frac{\Pi_t}{p_t} = \frac{1}{q_t}\left[\sum_{\tau=t+1}^{s+1} q_\tau f\right] + \frac{1}{q_t}\left[q_{s+1}\frac{\Pi_{s+1}}{p_{s+1}}\right].$$

Letting $s \to \infty$ shows that $\Sigma_{t=2}^{\infty} q_t < \infty$. Hence $q_{s+1}(\Pi_{s+1}/p_{s+1}) = \Sigma_{\tau=s+2}^{\infty} q_\tau f \to 0$, giving the bottom equation.

Next we show that given these two equations, the temporal and Walrasian budget sets contain exactly the same feasible consumption vectors for any individual. Observe that doubling both Π_t and p_t for any t does not affect any agent's budget set. Hence we can scale up

Π_t and p_t so that $\Pi_t = p_{t+1}f + \Pi_{t+1}$. Then from the top equation, $q_t/q_{t+1} = p_t/p_{t+1}$. And adding consumer th's budget constraints

$$p_t x_t^{th} + \Pi_t K_t^{th} \leq p_t e_t^{th}$$
$$p_{t+1} x_{t+1}^{th} + \Pi_{t+1} K_{t+1}^{th} \leq p_{t+1} e_{t+1}^{th} + p_{t+1} K_t^{th} f + \Pi_{t+1} K_t^{th}$$

gives

$$p_t x_t^{th} + p_{t+1} x_{t+1}^{th} \leq p_t e_t^{th} + p_{t+1} e_{t+1}^{th}.$$

This shows that if $(x, K) \in B^{th}(p, \Pi)$, then $x \in B^{th}(q)$ for every agent with $t \geq 1$. Conversely, if $x \in B^{th}(q)$, then $\frac{q_t}{q_{t+1}}(e_t^{ht} - x_t^{ht}) = (x_{t+1}^{ht} - e_{t+1}^{ht})$. Define

$$K_t = (e_t^{ht} - x_t^{ht}) \Big/ \frac{\Pi_t}{p_t}.$$

Using the first equation, the additional consumption this allows in period $t + 1$ is

$$\frac{p_{t+1}f + \Pi_{t+1}}{p_{t+1}} K_t = \frac{p_{t+1}f + \Pi_{t+1}}{p_{t+1}} (e_t^{ht} - x_t^{ht}) \Big/ \frac{\Pi_t}{p_t}$$
$$= \frac{q_t}{q_{t+1}} (e_t^{ht} - x_t^{ht}) = (x_{t+1}^{ht} - e_{t+1}^{ht}).$$

Hence $(x, K) \in B^{th}(p, \Pi)$. For agents $0h$, simply apply the bottom equation for Π_1/p_1.

Corollary *Let* $((p_t, \Pi_t)_{t\geq 1}, (x^{th}, K^{th})_{th\in \mathcal{H}})$ *be a temporal equilibrium for an OLG economy* $((U^{th}, e^{th})_{th\in\mathcal{H}}, (K_0^{0h})_{h\in H}, f)$ *with productive land,* $\bar{f} = f\Sigma_{h\in H}K_0^{0h} > 0$. *Then* $(x^{th})_{th\in\mathcal{H}}$ *is Pareto efficient, and land is always priced as the discounted value of its future dividends.*

Proof From the previous theorem, the temporal equilibrium is equivalent to a Walrasian equilibrium. From Condition (2) of Walrasian OLG equilibrium, when there is land, the requirement that the income of every individual agent be finite also guarantees that the total value of the *aggregate* endowment will be finite, since the latter is no more than a finite multiple of the former for some agent born at time 0. Hence the usual proof of the Pareto efficiency of competitive equilibrium goes through, as was pointed out by Wilson (1981).[5] By introducing a durable good whose payoff is a nonnegligible fraction of aggregate endowment, we have assured that there are no Pareto-inefficient competitive equilibria.[6] Furthermore, the proof of the last theorem also showed that the price of land must be equal to the present discounted value of its dividends.

In fact, it can easily be shown that if we add other durable goods, like paper money, to the OLG economy with land, then all of these will be priced at the present discounted value of their dividends.[7] This gives us a first indication that the OLG model with land will behave much more like the Fisher two-period model.

III.B.2 Stationary OLG Equilibrium with Land

If $U^{th}(x_t, x_{t+1}) = U^h(x_1, x_2)$ and $(e_t^{th}, e_{t+1}^{th}) = (e_1^h, e_2^h)$ do not depend on t, for $t \geq 1$, and if $\overline{f} > 0$, then we have a stationary OLG economy with (productive) land. A *stationary* OLG equilibrium is an OLG equilibrium where the one-period rate of interest remains constant over time, $q_1 = 1$, $q_2 = q$, $q_3 = q^2$. . . . We call $q = 1/(1 + r)$ the market discount rate and r the one-period rate of interest.

For each agent $h \in H$, let $(x_1^h(q), x_2^h(q)) \in \arg\max\{U^h(x_1, x_2): x_1 + qx_2 \leq e_t^h + qe_{t+1}^h, x_1, x_2 \geq 0\}$. Given our hypotheses on utilities, we must have that $(x_1^h(q), x_2^h(q))$ is a uniquely defined, continuous function, and $x_1^h(q) + x_2^h(q) \to \infty$ as $q \to 0$, for all $t \geq 1$.[8] Let $(z_1^h(q), z_2^h(q)) = ((x_1^h(q) - e_1^h), (x_2^h(q) - e_2^h))$ be the excess demand of agent h, and let $(z_1(q), z_2(q)) = (\Sigma_{h\in H}(z_1^h(q), z_2^h(q)))$ be the aggregate excess demand of each generation.

Stationary OLG Equilibrium Existence Theorem *Every stationary equilibrium for any OLG economy with productive land $\overline{f} > 0$ has a strictly positive interest rate, $0 < q \leq 1$. Moreover, every stationary OLG economy with productive land $\overline{f} > 0$ such that U^h is strictly concave and strictly monotonic, and such that $e_1^h > 0$, for all $h \in H$, has a stationary equilibrium.*

Proof From the last theorem we know that the value of land is finite, so $0 < \frac{1}{q}\Sigma_{\tau=2}^{\infty} q^{\tau} f < \infty$. Hence $0 < q < 1$.

In stationary equilibrium we must have that

$$z_1(q) + z_2(q) = \overline{f},$$

where $z_1(q)$ is the excess demand of one generation's young and $z_2(q)$ is the excess demand of the previous generation's old. For any q, each agent will spend all his money, and hence the budget set inequality will be an equality and $z_1(q) + qz_2(q) = 0$. Hence when $q = 1$, $z_1(q) + z_2(q) = 0 < \overline{f}$. But as $q \to 0$, $z_1(q) + z_2(q) \to \infty$. By continuity there is some $0 < q < 1$ with $z_1(q) + z_2(q) = \overline{f}$.

This clears all markets for time $t \geq 2$. What about $t = 1$? Luckily, we do not need to check anything more. Since the value of the aggregate endowment is finite, and since every agent spends all his money, total expenditures must equal the total value of endowments. But from the foregoing, for each good $t \geq 2$ total expenditures equal total value. Hence also for the one remaining good $t = 1$, we must have total expenditures equal total value. But since $q_1 = q^{1-1} = 1$, that means demand equals supply for time 1 goods as well.

Computing Stationary Equilibrium for Example 4 At each date $t \geq 2$, the young and the old must have demands that sum to all the goods in the economy, namely, their joint endowments plus the output of apples from the land. Consider the case $t = 2$. Then the present value (i.e., as of time 1) of income of the old (born at time 1) is $3 + q$, while for the young born at time 2 the present value of income (as of time 1 again) is $3q + q^2$. Recalling the formula for Cobb-Douglas demand, and recalling that the total supply of goods in every time period is $3 + 1 + 1 = 5$, we can solve

$$x_t^{t-1} + x_t^t = 5$$

$$\frac{\frac{1}{2}[3+1]}{q} + \frac{\frac{1}{2}[3q+q^2]}{q} = 5.$$

Solving the quadratic equation gives two solutions, only one of which has $0 < q < 1$: $\{q = 0.55, (x_t^t, x_{t+1}^t) = (1.78, 3.22)$, for all $t \geq 1\}$. It must therefore be the stationary equilibrium.

By stationarity the same solution clears the markets for all time $t \geq 2$. It also clears the market for $t = 1$, as can easily be verified by noting that $q/(1-q) = 1.22$. We must add the demand of the agent who is born at time 1 and the demand of the agent who is old at time 1:

$$x_1^1 = \frac{1}{2}(3+q) = \frac{3}{2} + \frac{1}{2}q$$

$$x_1^0 = 1 + 1 + \underbrace{[q + q^2 + q^3 + \cdots]}_{\text{value of land}} = 2 + \frac{q}{1-q} \text{ (assuming } q < 1)$$

$$q = 0.55$$

$$x_1^0 = 2 + \frac{q}{1-q} = 3.22$$

$$x_t^t = \frac{1}{2}(3+q) = 1.78$$

$$x_{t+1}^t = \frac{1}{2q}(3+q) = 3.22$$

$$r = 1/q - 1 = (1/0.55) - 1 = 82\%.$$

Taking advantage of the Fisher capital value equation that the land price must be equal to the present value of its dividends, we can immediately translate this Walrasian equilibrium into a temporal OLG equilibrium: $(p_t, \Pi_t) = (1, 1.22)$ for all $t \geq 1$.

III.B.3 Land Restores Many Two-Period Lessons

Adding land solves several problems. First, Pareto optimality is restored. Second, the value of every durable good is equal to the present value of its dividends. Third, we can imagine that trades take place between living agents, that is, we do not need a mythical market where all of the generations of consumers trade all of the goods simultaneously. Fourth, the interest rate is positive. And last, but not least, the rate of interest is determined by impatience and by the other factors mentioned earlier. (This last observation seems to be new.)

III.C What Determines the Rate of Interest

If in Example 4 we make each generation more impatient, the real rate of interest will go up. Taking $U^t(x_t, x_{t+1}) = \log x_t + 0.5 \log x_{t+1}$ we get $r = 139\%$. If we increase the productivity of the land, the rate of interest will go up. For example, if we take $\overline{f} = 2$, then $r = 154\%$. If we increase the endowment when young, the rate of interest will go down. For example, if we take $e_t^t = 6$, we get $r = 38\%$.

Thus the determinants of the rate of interest that we saw already in the two-period model affect the rate of interest in same way in OLG with land. We can prove this in a more general situation.

Before stating the next theorem, let us observe that in any stationary OLG equilibrium with productive land, the old agents at time 1 will consume their endowments of goods, plus all the dividends of land (since they own all the land), plus the goods obtained by selling off their land. From stationarity, it follows that in every period the old collectively will eat more than the sum of their old endowments.

III.C.1 Impatience Theorem in OLG with Land

Theorem *Consider any stationary OLG economy with productive land $\overline{f} > 0$ such that $U^{th}(x_t, x_{t+1}) = u^h(x_t) + \delta_h u^h(x_{t+1})$, where u^h is strictly concave, increasing, and twice differentiable, for all $th \in \mathcal{H}$. Suppose that in a stationary equilibrium every old agent consumes more than his old endowment, and every young agent consumes something positive. Then more impatience (decreasing any δ_h) implies a higher interest rate, as does higher productivity of land (greater $\overline{f}$), as does increasing any old endowment e_2^h, or lowering any young endowment e_1^h.*

Proof In stationary equilibrium, we must have that

$$z_1(q) + z_2(q) - \overline{f} = 0,$$

where the functions $(z_1(q), z_2(q))$ also implicitly depend on $(\delta_h, e_1^h, e_2^h)_{h \in H}$. Under the hypotheses of the theorem, we shall show that around the equilibrium, the left-hand side is differentiable in $(q, (\delta_h, e_1^h, e_2^h)_{h \in H})$ and decreasing in q. The implicit function theorem then tells us that any perturbation to the left-hand side of the above equation will move equilibrium q in the same direction and move equilibrium $r = 1/q - 1$ in the opposite direction.

From elementary consumer demand theory, we know that the individual excess demands ($z_1^b(q)$, $z_2^b(q)$) are differentiable in all the parameters at the equilibrium q (since they are positive there and since the utilities are twice differentiable). Let us define the Hicksian and Marshallian demands around the equilibrium price q. First we set $\bar{u}^b \equiv U^b(x_1^b(q), x_2^b(q))$, and $I^b = e_1^b + qe_2^b$. Then the Hicksian excess demands $z^{bH}(\hat{q}) = \arg\max_{(x_1,x_2)}\{x_1 + \hat{q}x_2 : U^b(x_1, x_2) \geq \bar{u}^b\} - (e_1^b, e_2^b)$ and the Marshallian excess demands $z^{bM}(\hat{q}, \hat{I}) = \arg\max_{(x_1,x_2)}\{U^b(x_1, x_2) : x_1 + \hat{q}x_2 \leq \hat{I}^b\} - (e_1^b, e_2^b)$ are differentiable at $\hat{q} = q$, $\hat{I}^b = I^b$. From Slutsky's equation, we know that we can decompose the derivative of any individual excess demand into a Hicksian term and an income-effect term

$$\frac{\partial z_1^b(q)}{\partial q} = \frac{\partial z_1^{bH}(q)}{\partial q} - \frac{\partial z_1^{bM}(q, I^b)}{\partial I} z_2^b(q)$$

$$\frac{\partial z_2^b(q)}{\partial q} = \frac{\partial z_2^{bH}(q)}{\partial q} - \frac{\partial z_2^{bM}(q, I^b)}{\partial I} z_2^b(q),$$

where the first term on the right-hand sides $\partial z_i^{bH}(q)/\partial q$ is the Hicksian or compensated demand of agent b, and $\partial z_i^{bM}(q, I^b)/\partial I$ is the income-effect term. We know that Hicksian own effects are negative, so $\partial z_2^{bH}(q)/\partial q < 0$. We also know that Hicksian demand keeps utility constant, so

$$\frac{\partial z_1^{bH}(q)}{\partial q} + q\frac{\partial z_2^{bH}(q)}{\partial q} = 0.$$

Since in stationary equilibrium $q < 1$, it follows that

$$\frac{\partial z_1^{bH}(q)}{\partial q} + \frac{\partial z_2^{bH}(q)}{\partial q} < 0.$$

From the fact that utility is additively separable, we know that demands are normal, $\partial z_i^{bM}(q, I^b)/\partial I > 0$, for $i = 1, 2$. By hypothesis, we have that the old consume more than their endowments, so $z_2^b(q) > 0$. Therefore

$$\frac{\partial z_1^b(q)}{\partial q} + \frac{\partial z_2^b(q)}{\partial q}$$
$$= \frac{\partial z_1^{bH}(q)}{\partial q} + \frac{\partial z_2^{bH}(q)}{\partial q} - \frac{\partial z_1^{bM}(q, I^b)}{\partial I} z_2^b(q) - \frac{\partial z_2^{bM}(q, I^b)}{\partial I} z_2^b(q) < 0$$

when evaluated at equilibrium q. Adding over all the agents in H, it follows that

$$\frac{\partial z_1(q)}{\partial q} + \frac{\partial z_2(q)}{\partial q} < 0.$$

It follows from the implicit function theorem that increasing $\bar{f}$ necessarily decreases $q = 1/(1 + r)$ and thus increases the interest rate. Increasing the impatience of some consumers makes them want to eat more today. But at the same prices, that means their total consumption over time must decrease, since the value of future consumption is less ($q < 1$). Hence to restore equilibrium, q must fall and interest rates must rise.

Finally, switching young endowment to old endowment reduces income at the old prices (since $q < 1$), thus reducing demand when young and old, but not affecting total supply (which is the sum of endowment when young and old). Hence to restore market clearing, q must again fall and interest rates rise. A similar argument can be given if endowments when young or old are changed separately.

The proof that more impatience raises the interest rate can be proved under weaker hypotheses in the case of OLG with land than it was in the two-period case. Far from contradicting Fisher's impatience theory of interest, OLG economies confirm it more emphatically.

Notes

1. See Dimand (1999).
2. Thus in equilibrium we would have an interest rate that lies between what would have prevailed with just agent A and the interest rate that would have prevailed had the economy consisted only of agent B, but closer to the former because A is richer.
3. Although it is not important for us, it is also true that demand for good 1 is decreasing in q. The excess demand for the second good is given by

$$z_1(q) \equiv \frac{\delta^A}{1+\delta^A}\left[\frac{3}{4}+\frac{1}{4}q+\Pi(q)\right]\Big)q+\frac{\delta^B}{1+\delta^B}\left[\frac{3}{8}+\frac{1}{8}q\right]\Big)q-$$
$$C\left[q^{\frac{1}{1-\alpha}}(\alpha C)^{\frac{1}{1-\alpha}}\right]^{\alpha}-\left(\frac{1}{4}+\frac{1}{8}\right).$$

Note that the extra term coming from production satisfies

$$\begin{aligned}\frac{\delta^A}{1+\delta^A}\Pi(q)\Big/q-f(k(q)) &= \frac{\delta^A}{1+\delta^A}[qf(k(q)-k(q)]/q-f(k(q))\\ &= \frac{-1}{1+\delta^A}f(k(q))-\frac{\delta^A}{1+\delta^A}k(q)\Big/q\\ &= \frac{-1}{1+\delta^A}f(k(q))-\frac{\delta^A}{1+\delta^A}q^{\frac{1}{1-\alpha}}(\alpha A)^{\frac{1}{1-\alpha}}\Big/q,\end{aligned}$$

which is clearly decreasing in q. Thus excess demand in our example satisfies gross substitutes. But for some other utility functions, $z_1(q)$ would not have been decreasing in q and gross substitutes would fail. However, with Cobb-Douglas utilities, no matter what concave, smooth production function we chose, we would find that $z_0(q)$ increases in q.

4. Another important point is that in all these economies the Fisher equilibrium was not Pareto efficient. Welfare is improved if every young person gives the contemporaneous old $\Delta > 0$ goods, much as happens in the U.S. pay-as-you-go Social Security system. Samuelson once regarded this as a powerful argument in favor of the U.S. Social Security system.

5. This proof works by arguing that if all agents could be made better off by an alternative allocation, this alternative allocation would cost more to each agent than his endowment; otherwise, he would have bought it. Adding over all agents, the cost of the aggregate consumption of the new allocation must be more than the aggegate value of endowments if both numbers are finite, contradicting the feasibility of the new allocation. When aggregate endowments have infinite value, this proof fails. (In the equilibria of Examples 1–3, the value of the aggregate endowment was infinite.)

6. Consequently, the rationale for Social Security must come from elsewhere.

7. Otherwise, the owners of the asset would spend more on consumption goods than the value of their endowments of consumption goods. Adding over all agents, we would get that total expenditure on consumption goods is greater than the total value of consumption goods, since the latter is finite, contradicting market clearing.

8. The latter is true because as the price of the second good goes to 0, holding fixed the price of the first good at 1, income is still bounded away from 0. Hence the monotonic agent will demand arbitrarily more of the second good, while the demand for the first good must remain nonnegative.

References

Allais, M. (1947). *Économie et Intérêt.* Paris: Imprimerie Nationale et Librairie des publications Officielles.

Deaton, A., and J. Muellbauer. (1980). *Economics and Consumer Behavior.* Cambridge: Cambridge University Press.

Diewert, W. E. (1976). "Exact and Superlative Index Numbers." *Journal of Econometrics* 4(2): 115–145.

Dimand, R. (1999). "Letter on Fisher and Indexed Bonds." *Journal of Economic Perspectives* 13(1): 224–225.

Fisher, I. (1907). *The Rate of Interest.* New York: MacMillan.

——. ([1918] 1997). *Stabilizing the Dollar.* In *The Works of Irving Fisher,* Vol. 6. Ed. W. J. Barber. London: Pickering & Chatto.

——. ([1925] [1928] 1997). "The Stabilized Bond—A New Idea in Finance." In *The Annalist,* as revised in *Economic Problems: A Book of Selected Readings.* Eds. Fred R. Fairchild and Ralph T. Compton. New York: Macmillan. Rpt. in *The Works of Irving Fisher,* Vol. 8. Ed. W. J. Barber. London: Pickering & Chatto.

——. (1930). *The Theory of Interest.* New York: MacMillan.

——. (1997). "The Making of Index Numbers." In *The Works of Irving Fisher,* Vol. 7. Ed. W. J. Barber. London: Pickering & Chatto.

Geanakoplos, J. D. (1987). "Overlapping Generations Model of General Equilibrium." In *The New Palgrave, A Dictionary of Economics,* Vol. 3. Eds. J. Eatwell, M. Milgate, and P. Newman. London and Basingstoke: Macmillan Press Limited.

——. (1990). "An Introduction to General Equilibrium with Incomplete Asset Markets." *Journal of Mathematical Economics* 19: 1–38.

Geanakoplos, J. D., and M. Shubik. (1990). "The Capital Asset Pricing Model as a General Equilibrium with Incomplete Markets." *Geneva Papers on Risk and Insurance Theory* 15(1): 55–71.

Konüs, A. A. (1939). "The Problem of the True Index of the Cost of Living." *Econometrica* 7: 10–29.

Lintner, J. (1965). "The Valuation of Risky Assets and the Selection of Risky Investments in Stock Portfolios and Capital Budget." *Review of Economics and Statistics* 47: 13–37.

Loewenstein, G. (1985). *Expectations and Intertemporal Choice.* Ph.D. diss. Yale University.

McCulloch, J. Huston. (1980). "The Ban on Indexed Bonds." *American Economic Review* 70(5): 1018–1021.

Mossin, J. (1977). *The Economic Efficiency of Financial Markets.* Lexington Books.

Samuelson, P. A. (1958). "An Exact Consumption Loan Model of Interest, With or Without the Social Contrivance of Money." *Journal of Political Economy* 66(5): 467–482.

Sharpe, W. (1964). "Capital Asset Prices: A Theory of Market Equilibrium Under Conditions of Risk." *Journal of Finance* 19: 425–442.

Tobin, J. (1958). "Liquidity Preference as Behavior Towards Risk." *Review of Economic Studies* 67: 65–86.

——. (1987). "Irving Fisher." In *The New Palgrave, A Dictionary of Economics*, Vol. 2. Eds. J. Eatwell, M. Milgate, and P. Newman. London and Basingstoke: Macmillan Press Limited.

Wilson, C. (1981). "Equilibrium in Dynamic Models of Pure Exchange." *Journal of Economic Theory* 24(1): 95–111.

Comments on John Geanakoplos's "The Ideal Inflation-Indexed Bond and Irving Fisher's Impatience Theory of Interest with Overlapping Generations"

By ROBERT J. SHILLER

ABSTRACT. A comment on the article by John Geanakoplos in this volume.

It is refreshing to hear an account of Irving Fisher's views on risk and indexation juxtaposed with an account of our modern concerns with the same issues. It is interesting for me to hear this, partly since it shows that many of the issues we worry about today were concerns 70 or more years ago, and thus perhaps that these issues are indeed as deep and fundamental as we now think they are. But I found this history-of-thought presentation most interesting because it clarifies, by starting with simple notions that were on Irving Fisher's mind and moving forward, some of the critical issues concerning the innovations of indexation and Social Security reform.

John's paper with Martin Shubik (1990), described here, is really a deep theory of indexation, a theory that I think Irving Fisher wanted to have but could not get with the theoretical apparatus of his day. As evidence that Fisher wanted this, I show a few quotes from his 1911 book, *The Purchasing Power of Money*.

Irving Fisher appreciated that index number theory is a central issue for economists because it will be applied to the specification of intertemporal contracts:

> Perhaps the most important purpose of index numbers is to serve as a basis of loan contracts. (1911: 208)

*Professor Robert J. Shiller is the Stanley B. Resor Professor of Economics at Yale University where he has served on the faculty since 1982. His book *Irrational Exuberance* (Princeton University Press, 2000) has received global recognition for its critical assessment of the stock market boom of the 1980s and 1990s. His most recent book is *The New Financial Order* (Princeton University Press, 2003).

The American Journal of Economics and Sociology, Vol. 64, No. 1 (January, 2005).

I would put this as saying that since index numbers have their most important application in long-term contracts, index number theory ought to be considered a topic in theoretical finance.

Fisher also appreciated that indexation of contracts is not something that should be thought of as an issue of "fairness" or "justice," even though much of the debate about it today tends to be put in these terms. Discussions of the importance of indexed bonds speak of the unfairness of a situation in which the real value of a debt has been eroded by inflation. Discussions today of Social Security reform and the indexation of benefits also often center on doing the fair or just policy toward Social Security beneficiaries. But instead, the issue should be how indexed contracts as part of a portfolio strategy, or social risk-sharing strategy, can be used to promote a broader purpose of real risk management for all parties. Fisher wrote:

> In the first place, it should be pointed out that though there is a gain or loss [on loan contracts due to unexpected price changes] there is not necessarily any "injustice" wrought because of a change in the level of prices. . . . Each party knew or should have known that the price level might change, and took the risk. (1911: 209)

Fisher, in his many researches on index numbers, was struggling with the central difficulty of defining an indexed contract that will be useful at large for contracts when there are many goods:

> Suppose, for example, that a lender receives back purchasing power over an amount of goods of the kinds he wished to use, equivalent to that he lent plus interest. Suppose also that, during the period of the loan, these goods appreciate relatively to others. Then the lender really gains, since he can now get more of other goods in exchange for those it was his original purpose to use. . . . To the borrower, however, the appreciation of the goods the basis of which repayment is made, relatively to the goods he is engaged in producing, might be regarded as causing him a loss. The *same purchasing* power over the goods, on the basis of which he is to make repayment, means in such a case, a *greater* purchasing power over the good he is engaged in producing.
>
> It is clear that no one kind of goods is a fair standard. An index number intended to serve as a standard for deferred payments must have a broad basis. (1922: 212–213)

> In this connection it may be well to call attention to another standard of purchasing power of money which has sometimes been suggested for

> adjusting contracts. This is the utility standard. According to this, each person would be expected to receive or pay back marginal utility equivalent to what he had lent or borrowed. But the marginal utility of the same goods is different for different persons at different periods of life. Hence, no such standard can be objectively applied. (1911: 220)

Fisher here shows clear awareness that defining optimal index numbers for use in intertemporal loan contracts is difficult, since people can have reasons for differing preferences about what goes into the index. He has an intuitive notion that somehow using a broad index is best overall but cannot articulate just what is the theory connecting the notion with a concrete index number formula.

John's paper with Martin Shubik (1990) has what I most admire: a theory that is both original and actionable. The theory is original in that it provides a rigorous justification of indexation in terms of that stellar economic concept, Pareto optimality. It is actionable in that it suggests how the price index for use in indexation could be defined. It shows a sense in which something like Fisher's "utility standard," or in more modern terms, a "superlative index," is indeed the right answer.

The Geanakoplos and Shubik story is based on the capital asset pricing model (CAPM). This model has formed the cornerstone of much thinking in finance for decades, and so the Geanakoplos and Shubik results gain some authority from this tradition. In some senses, though, this model is very restrictive. In the CAPM, everyone is the same except in one dimension, risk aversion. Notably, people are not stuck with individually different untradable endowments. Such differences in untradable endowments obviously exist in the world we know, and assuming them away in the CAPM to permit a theory that centers on something that may not exist, differences in risk aversions, has been a heroic step. Geanakoplos and Shubik's model relies on these individual differences in risk aversion as well, since there would be no role for their indexed bonds in their model if these differences did not exist.

I find it odd that a whole generation of CAPM theorists has seen fit to make these assumptions with virtually no empirical research on whether risk aversions differ importantly across people. A 1997 paper by Barsky, Juster, Kimball, and Shapiro is the first paper to study carefully whether people differ in risk aversion. They elicited measures of risk aversion based on answers individuals gave to hypothetical questions on the Health and Retirement Survey. They then showed that there were individual differences in risk aversions and that these differences helped explain some differences in their behaviors (such as whether they smoked or bought health insurance) even after other variables such as sex, religion, and race were taken into account.

The evidence on individual differences in risk aversion provided by Barsky et al. are also potentially very important for understanding the importance of indexation in the Social Security system. In the present U.S. system, benefits after retirement are indexed to the consumer price index (CPI). Thus, our society is providing completely riskless benefits to its retired people. Of course, riskless benefits do not come out of nowhere; they come only by transferring the risks these retired people would otherwise have borne onto other people, those who are not yet retired. One way of justifying such unequal bearing of risk could be that the elderly are just much more risk averse than the young. Barsky et al. did indeed find this.

We thus see in these empirical results some vindication of the notion that differences in risk aversions are important, and of the CAPM basis for the theory that John discusses. Whether the differences Barsky et al. found are really important is, however, a matter of judgment. By some interpretations (such as the R squared in their regressions explaining behavior), the differences in risk aversions they found were small.

References

Barsky, Robert F., Thomas Juster, Miles Kimball, and Matthew Shapiro. (1997). "Preference Parameters and Behavioral Heterogeneity: An Experimental Approach to the Health and Retirement Survey." *Quarterly Journal of Economics* 112(2): 537–579.

Fisher, Irving. (1911). *The Purchasing Power of Money*. New York: Macmillan.

Geanakoplos, John, and Martin Shubik. (1990). "The Capital Asset Pricing Model as a General Equilibrium with Incomplete Markets." *Geneva Papers on Risk and Insurance Theory* 15(1): 55–70.

Index Number Theory Using Differences Rather Than Ratios

By W. ERWIN DIEWERT

ABSTRACT. Traditional index number theory decomposes a value ratio into the product of a price index times a quantity index. The price (quantity) index is interpreted as an aggregate price (quantity) ratio. The present paper takes an alternative approach to index number theory, started by Bennet and Montgomery in the 1920s, which decomposes a value difference into the sum of a price difference plus a quantity difference. Axiomatic and economic approaches to this alternative branch of index theory are considered in the present paper. The analysis presented has some relevance to accounting theory in which revenue, cost, or profit changes need to be decomposed into price quantity components or where standard or budgeted performance is compared with actual performance (variance analysis). The methodology presented in the paper is also relevant for consumer surplus analysis.

I

Introduction

When, forty-two years ago, I wrote my doctor's thesis on certain mathematical investigations in the theory of value and prices, I was a student

*W. Erwin Diewert is a Professor of Economics at the University of British Columbia. He has published over 70 papers in journals and over 70 chapters in books. His main areas of research include duality theory, flexible functional forms, index number theory (including the concept of a superlative index number formula), the measurement of productivity, and the calculation of excess burdens of taxation. He has acted as a consultant on measurement and regulatory issues for the International Monetary Fund, the World Bank, the Bureau of Labor Statistics, the Bureau of Economic Analysis, the OECD, the New Zealand Treasury, the Business Roundtable in New Zealand, Bell Canada, B.C. Telephone, the American Association of Railways, the Victorian Treasury, and Industry Canada. The research for this paper was partially supported by a Strategic Grant to a team of researchers at the Universities of British Columbia and Alberta (the PEER Group). The author thanks Bert Balk and PEER Group members Alice Nakamura, Allan Russell, and Peter Lawrence for helpful comments.

The American Journal of Economics and Sociology, Vol. 64, No. 1 (January, 2005).

of mathematical physics and, with youthful enthusiasm, dreamed dreams of seeing economics, or one branch of it, grow into a true science by the same methods which had long since built up physics into a true and majestic science.

Irving Fisher (1933: 2)

Rather than review all of the many contributions of Irving Fisher to the index number literature, we will develop an alternative branch of index number theory that had its origins around the time that Fisher (1911, 1921, 1922) developed his test approach. This alternative branch of index number theory was started by T. L. Bennet (1920) and J. K. Montgomery (1929, 1937), but for various reasons, their approach never prospered and has been mostly forgotten by present-day index number theorists.[1]

In order to explain this alternative approach to index number theory, we first need to explain the traditional approach. Suppose we have collected price and quantity information on *N* commodities for a base period 0 and a current period 1. Denote the price and quantity of commodity *n* in period *t* as p_n^t and q_n^t, respectively, for $n = 1, 2, \ldots, N$ and $t = 0, 1$. Define the period *t* price and quantity vectors as $p_n^t \equiv (p_1^t, p_2^t, \ldots, p_N^t)$ and $q^t \equiv (q_1^t, q_2^t, \ldots, q_N^t)$ for $t = 0, 1$. Then the *value* of the N commodities in period *t* is

$$p^t \cdot q^t \equiv \sum_{n=1}^{N} p_n^t q_n^t \quad for \quad t = 0, 1. \tag{1}$$

Fisher (1911, 1922) framed the now-traditional test approach to index number theory as follows: find two functions of the 4N price and quantity variables that pertain to the two periods under consideration, say $P(p^0, p^1, q^0, q^1)$ and $Q(p^0, p^1, q^0, q^1)$, such that the value *ratio* for the two periods, $p^1 \cdot q^1/p^0 \cdot q^0$, is equal to the *product* of P and Q, that is,

$$p^1 \cdot q^1/p^0 \cdot q^0 = P(p^0, p^1, q^0, q^1)Q(p^0, p^1, q^0, q^1), \tag{2}$$

and the functions *P* and *Q* satisfy certain properties that allow us to identify $P(p^0, p^1, q^0, q^1)$ as an aggregate measure of relative price change and $Q(p^0, p^1, q^0, q^1)$ as an aggregate measure of relative quantity change. Fisher called these properties or axioms *tests.* The function $P(p^0, p^1, q^0, q^1)$ is called the *price index* and the function $Q(p^0, p^1, q^0, q^1)$ is called the *quantity index*. If the number of commodities is one (i.e., $N = 1$), then the price index P collapses down to the single price ratio p_1^1/p_1^0 and the quantity index Q collapses down to the single quantity ratio q_1^1/q_1^0. The index number problem (i.e., the problem of determining the functional forms for P and Q) is trivial in this $N = 1$ case. However, in the multiple commodity case where $N > 1$, the problem of finding functions P and Q that satisfy Equation (2) and satisfy appropriate tests is far from trivial.

Note that if we have somehow determined the appropriate functional form for P, then Equation (2) can be used to define the quantity index Q that will be consistent with it. Thus we can concentrate on finding a functional form for P that satisfies an appropriate set of tests. This is the traditional test approach to index number theory in a nutshell.

The alternative branch of index number theory that we wish to study is the one that uses a *difference* counterpart to the *ratio* Equation (2). Thus we look for two functions of 4N variables, $\Delta P(p^0, p^1, q^0, q^1)$ and $\Delta Q(p^0, p^1, q^0, q^1)$, which sum to the value *difference* between the two periods; in other words, we want ΔP and ΔQ to satisfy the following equation:

$$p^1 \cdot q^1 - p^0 \cdot q^0 = \Delta P(p^0, p^1, q^0, q^1) + \Delta Q(p^0, p^1, q^0, q^1) \qquad (3)$$

and the functions ΔP and ΔQ are to satisfy certain properties or tests that will allow us to identify ΔP as a *measure of aggregate price change* and ΔQ as a *measure of aggregate quantity or volume change* between the two periods.

As was the case with traditional index number theory where P and Q cannot be determined independently if Equation (2) is to hold, then if Equation (3) is to hold, ΔP and ΔQ cannot be determined independently. Thus in what follows, we will postulate axioms or tests for ΔP and once ΔP has been determined, we will define ΔQ using Equation (3).

As the notation ΔP and ΔQ is somewhat awkward, we will use the notation $I(p^0, p^1, q^0, q^1)$ (for *indicator* of price change) to replace $\Delta P(p^0, p^1, q^0, q^1)$ and we will use $V(p^0, p^1, q^0, q^1)$ (for indicator of *volume* change) to replace $\Delta Q(p^0, p^1, q^0, q^1)$. Using our new notation, Equation (3) can be rewritten as follows:

$$\sum_{n=1}^{N}[p_n^1 q_n^1 - p_n^0 q_n^1] = I(p^0, p^1, q^0, q^1) + V(p^0, p^1, q^0, q^1). \qquad (4)$$

In Sections III and IV below, we simplify the problem of finding a suitable *I* and *V* that satisfy Equation (4) by postulating that the overall indicators of price and volume change, *I* and *V*, decompose into a sum of *N* commodity-specific indicators of price and volume change, $\Sigma_{n=1}^{N} I_n(p_n^0, p_n^1, q_n^0, q_n^1)$ and $\Sigma_{n=1}^{N} V_n(p_n^0, p_n^1, q_n^0, q_n^1)$, where each of the functions I_n and V_n depend only on the two prices that pertain to commodity *n*, p_n^0 and p_n^1, and the corresponding commodity *n* quantities q_n^0 and q_n^1. Thus in this simplified *separable* approach, the value change for each commodity is postulated to have the following components of price change I_n and quantity change V_n:

$$p_n^1 q_n^1 - p_n^0 q_n^0 = I_n(p_n^0, p_n^1, q_n^0, q_n^1) + V_n(p_n^0, p_n^1, q_n^0, q_n^1); \quad n = 1, \ldots, N. \qquad (5)$$

Once the commodity-specific indicators of price change I_n have been determined, the overall indicator of price change *I* is defined as the sum of the specific indicators:

$$I(p^0, p^1, q^0, q^1) \equiv \sum_{n=1}^{N} I_n(p_n^0, q_n^0, p_n^1, q_n^1). \qquad (6)$$

Of course, once $I(p^0, p^1, q^0, q^1)$ has been defined, the corresponding aggregate volume change indicator $V(p^0, p^1, q^0, q^1)$ can be determined using Equation (4).

In comparing the value difference decomposition of Equation (3) or (4) with the value ratio decomposition of Equation (2), it is interesting to note that the value ratio decomposition is trivial in the one-commodity case ($N = 1$) but nontrivial in the general case ($N > 1$), while the value change decomposition of Equation (5) is nontrivial in the case of one commodity but once the one-commodity decompositions of the form in Equation (5) have been determined, the many-commodity case is a straightforward summation of the one-commodity effects; in other words, see Equation (6).

We summarize the above introductory material as follows: we are searching for "reasonable" candidates for the commodity-specific indicators of price change $I_n(p_n^0, p_n^1, q_n^0, q_n^1)$ to insert into the commodity-specific value difference Equation (5) or, more generally, we are looking for "reasonable" candidates for the overall indicator of price change $I(p^0, p^1, q^0, q^1)$ that we can insert into Equation (4) above. Once the "reasonable" $I(p^0, p^1, q^0, q^1)$ has been found, the corresponding indicator of volume change $V(p^0, p^1, q^0, q^1)$ can be determined by solving Equation (4) for V.

In Sections II and III below, we present the solutions of Bennet (1920) and Montgomery (1929, 1937) to this search for a "reasonable" indicator of price change. In Section IV, we follow the examples of Fisher (1911, 1922) and Montgomery (1929) and pursue axiomatic approaches to the determination of an indicator of price change. In Section VI, we show that many "reasonable" indicators of price change numerically approximate each other to the second order around equal price and quantity vectors. Section VII concludes. Proofs of various propositions may be found in Appendix 1. The remaining appendices pursue some more specialized topics.

At this point, it is useful to consider a couple of preliminary problems.

The first preliminary problem that needs to be addressed is concerned with the interpretation of the period t prices and quantities for commodity n, p_n^t, and q_n^t. In real-life applications of value decompositions into price and quantity parts, during any period t there will typically be many transactions in commodity n at a number of different prices. Hence, there is a need to provide a more precise definition for the "average" or "representative" price for commodity n in period t, p_n^t. Irving Fisher (1922: 318) addressed this preliminary aggregation problem as follows:

> Essentially the same problem enters, however, whenever, as is usually the case, the data for prices and quantities with which we start are averages instead of being the original market quotations. Throughout this book, "the price" of any commodity or "the quantity" of it for any year was assumed given. But what is such a price or such a quantity? . . . The quantities sold will, of course, vary widely. What is needed is their sum for the year. . . . Or, if it is worth while to put any finer point on it, we may take the weighted arithmetic average for the prices, the weights being the quantities sold.

Thus Fisher more or less advocated the use of the unit value (total value transacted divided by total quantity) as the appropriate price p_n^t for commodity n and the total quantity transacted during period *t* as the appropriate quantity q_n^t. As an aggregation formula at the first stage of aggregation, the unit value and total quantity transacted has been proposed by many economists and statisticians, perhaps starting with Walsh (1901: 96, 1921a: 88) and Davies (1924: 183, 1932: 59) and including many other more recent writers.[2] If we want q_n^t to equal the total quantity of commodity *n* transacted during period *t* and we also want the product of the price p_n^t times quantity q_n^t to equal the value of period *t* transactions in commodity *n*, then we are *forced* to define the aggregate period *t* price p_n^t to be the total value divided by the total quantity, or the unit value.

The second preliminary problem that needs to be addressed is also a fundamental one: For what purpose do we want to decompose a value change into price and quantity components? It is quite possible that a given decomposition with certain properties would be appropriate for one purpose but not another.[3]

There are at least five general areas in which it would be useful to be able to decompose a value change into price and quantity components. The first four areas of application pertain to business units, while the fifth pertains to households.

1. *Revenue Change Decompositions.* When a company reports its current period revenue and compares it to the revenue of the previous accounting period, it is useful to be able to decompose this revenue change into a part that is due to the change in prices that the firm faced in the two periods and a part that is due to increased (or decreased) production; in other words, a volume change. While this type of revenue decomposition is not widespread in financial accounting, oil producers frequently make this type of decomposition in their annual reports so that shareholders can determine the effects of changes in the world price for oil on the revenue change.

2. *Cost Change Decompositions.* Shareholders are not only interested in revenue decompositions, they are also interested in decomposing a company's change in costs into a change in prices part (an exogenous effect that is mostly beyond the control of the firm) and a change in quantities part (an endogenous effect that is presumably under the control of the firm). This type of decomposition is not yet common in annual reports, presumably due to the difficulties involved in decomposing cost values into identifiable price and quantity

components. However, as computerization of all transactions proceeds, in the future it should be possible to construct detailed unit values for cost components.

3. *Profit Change Decompositions.* As was the case with areas 1 and 2 above, shareholders will be very interested in the decomposition of profit change over two accounting periods into a price change component and a quantity or volume change component. Investor interest will focus on the volume change indicator because this is an indicator of firm efficiency improvement: the more positive is the volume change, the greater is the *ex post* efficiency gain for the firm. Note that profit change is equal to revenue change less cost change, so if revenue and cost decompositions have been calculated, then the profit change decomposition is simply equal to the revenue decomposition less the cost decomposition. Profit change decompositions can also be used by the firm for internal control and performance evaluation purposes.[4]

4. *Variance Analysis.* For this use of the value decomposition, the period 0 prices and quantities are interpreted as period 1 *budgeted* or *forecasted* or "*standard*" prices and quantities that are supposed to prevail in period 1. Then the value difference is the difference between the period 1 actual value, $p^1 \cdot q^1$, and budgeted performance, $p^0 \cdot q^0$. The indicator of price change, $I(p^0, p^1, q^0, q^1)$, is now interpreted as the contribution of price change (between actual and budgeted prices) to the *ex post* difference between actual and standard values, and the indicator of volume change, $V(p^0, p^1, q^0, q^1)$, is similarly interpreted as the contribution of quantity change (between actual and budgeted quantities). Variance analysis can be traced back to the early accounting and industrial engineering literature; see Whitmore (1908, 1931), Harrison (1918),[5] and Solomons (1968: 46–47) for the early history.

5. *Changes in Consumer Surplus.* In this application, the values are the expenditures of a consumer or household on *N* commodities during two periods. The task is to decompose the change in consumer expenditures over the two periods into a price change component $I(p^0, p^1, q^0, q^1)$ and a quantity change component $V(p^0, p^1, q^0, q^1)$, which can be interpreted as a constant dollar measure of real utility change. This line of research was started by Marshall (1890) and Bennet (1920). Other early contributors include Hotelling

(1938: 253–254) and Hicks (1941–1942: 134, 1945–1946: 73, 1946: 330–333).[6]

With the above preliminary material disposed of, we turn our attention to the contributions of Bennet.[7]

II

Bennet's Indicator of Price Change

> The fundamental idea is that in a short period the rate of increase of expenditure of a family can be divided into two parts, x and ℓ, where x measures the increase due to change of prices and ℓ measures the increase due to increase of consumption . . .
>
> T. L. Bennet (1920: 455)

Bennet (1920: 457) proposed the following decomposition of a value change:

$$\begin{aligned} p^1 \cdot q^1 - p^0 \cdot q^0 &= (1/2)(q^0 + q^1) \cdot (p^1 - p^0) \\ &\quad + (1/2)(p^0 + p^1) \cdot (q^1 - q^0) \\ &= \sum_{n=1}^{N} (1/2)(q_n^0 + q_n^1)(p_n^1 - p_n^0) \\ &\quad + \sum_{n=1}^{N} (1/2)(p_n^0 + p_n^1)(q_n^1 - q_n^0). \end{aligned} \quad (7)$$

That Equation (7) is true follows simply by multiplication and cancellation of terms. Thus the Bennet indicators of price and volume change are defined as follows:

$$I^B(p^0, p^1, q^0, q^1) \equiv (1/2)(q^0 + q^1) \cdot (p^1 - p^0); \quad (8)$$

$$V^B(p^0, p^1, q^0, q^1) \equiv (1/2)(p^0 + p^1) \cdot (q^0 - q^1). \quad (9)$$

Bennet (1920: 456–457) justified his volume indicator as a linear approximation to the area under a demand curve and his price indicator as a linear approximation to an area under an inverse demand curve. Hence, Bennet was following in Marshall's (1890) partial equilibrium consumer surplus footsteps. However, it is possible to derive Bennet's indicators by an alternative line of reasoning, which we now explain.

In the early industrial engineering literature, Harrison (1918: 393) made the following decomposition of a cost change into a price variation plus an efficiency variation:

$$p^1 \cdot q^1 - p^0 \cdot q^0 = q^1 \cdot (p^1 - p^0) + p^0 \cdot (q^1 - q^0). \tag{10}$$

Again, the proof that Equation (10) is true follows by straightforward arithmetic. The reader familiar with index number theory will recognize that Harrison's indicator of price change, $q^1 \cdot (p^1 - p^0)$, is the difference counterpart to the Paasche price index $p^1 \cdot q^1 / p^0 \cdot q^1$. Similarly, Harrison's indicator of quantity or efficiency change, $p^0 \cdot (q^1 - q^0)$, is the difference counterpart to the Laspeyres quantity index $p^0 \cdot q^1 / p^0 \cdot q^0$. Thus we define the Paasche indicator of price change I^P and the Laspeyres indicator of quantity change V^L as follows:

$$I^P(p^0, p^1, q^0, q^1) \equiv q^1 \cdot (p^1 - p^0); \tag{11}$$

$$V^L(p^0, p^1, q^0, q^1) \equiv p^0 \cdot (q^1 - q^0). \tag{12}$$

More recently in the accounting literature,[8] it was recognized that the traditional variance analysis decomposition of a value change, Equation (10) above, may not be as appropriate as the following decomposition:

$$p^1 \cdot q^1 - p^0 \cdot q^0 = q^0 \cdot (p^1 - p^0) + p^1 \cdot (q^1 - q^0). \tag{13}$$

The reason why the decomposition in Equation (13) may be preferable to Equation (10) in the context of comparing actual performance to "standard" performance is that in the case of exogenous prices, the firm manager will have an incentive to maximize profits $p^1 \cdot q^1$ with respect to q^1 and thus the efficiency change term, $p^1 \cdot (q^1 - q^0)$ in Equation (13), is consistent with profit maximizing behavior. Again, the reader will recognize that the indicator of price change in Equation (13), $q^0 \cdot (p^1 - p^0)$, is the difference analogue to the Laspeyres price index, $p^1 \cdot q^0 / p^0 \cdot q^0$, and that the indicator of quantity change in Equation (13), $p^1 \cdot (q^1 \cdot q^0)$, is the difference counterpart to the Paasche quantity index, $p^1 \cdot q^1 / p^1 \cdot q^0$. Thus we define the Laspeyres and Paasche indicators of price and quantity change, respectively, as follows:

$$I^L(p^0, p^1, q^0, q^1) \equiv q^0 \cdot (p^1 - p^0); \tag{14}$$

$$V^P(p^0, p^1, q^0, q^1) \equiv p^1 \cdot (q^1 - q^0). \tag{15}$$

Now we can explain our alternative derivation of the Bennet indicators: the Bennet indicator of price (quantity) change is simply the arithmetic average of the Paasche and Laspeyres indicators of price (quantity) change; that is,

$$I^B(p^0, p^1, q^0, q^1) = (1/2)I^L(p^0, p^1, q^0, q^1) + (1/2)I^P(p^0, p^1, q^0, q^1); \quad (16)$$

$$V^B(p^0, p^1, q^0, q^1) = (1/2)V^L(p^0, p^1, q^0, q^1) + (1/2)V^P(p^0, p^1, q^0, q^1). \quad (17)$$

We will present a geometric interpretation due to Bennet (1920: 456) of his indicators in the one-commodity case in the next section, in which we discuss the work of Montgomery.

III

Montgomery's Indicator of Price Change

> One of the reasons why there has been so much controversy on the subject of the price index of a group of commodities is that writers have never agreed on a definition.
>
> J. K. Montgomery (1937: 1)

In a rather obscure paper, Montgomery (1929)[9] defined some interesting indicators of price and quantity change. We revert to the separable framework explained in Section I above where we first find indicators of price and volume change, I_n and V_n, for commodity n (recall Equation (5) above) and then the overall indicators of price and volume change are obtained by summing over the commodity-specific indicators (see Equation (6) above).

The Paasche, Laspeyres, and Bennet indicators of price and quantity change were well defined, irrespective of the signs of the individual prices and quantities p_n^t and q_n^t. However, in the present section, we shall restrict all prices and quantities to be positive since it will be necessary to take natural logarithms of the individual prices and quantities. The restriction that all prices and quantities be positive is not restrictive in the context of computing revenue and cost indicators. Obviously, a profit indicator can be defined as the difference between the revenue and cost indicators and so, even in this context, the postivity restrictions are not too restrictive.[10]

The Montgomery (1929: 5) indicators of price and volume change for the *n*th commodity are defined as follows:

$$I_n^M(p_n^0, p_n^1, q_n^0, q_n^1) \equiv \{[p_n^1 q_n^1 - p_n^0 q_n^0]/[(\ln(p_n^1 q_n^1) - \ln(p_n^0 q_n^0)]\} \ln[p_n^1/p_n^0]; \tag{18}$$

$$V_n^M(p_n^0, p_n^1, q_n^0, q_n^1) \equiv \{[p_n^1 q_n^1 - p_n^0 q_n^0]/[(\ln(p_n^1 q_n^1) - \ln(p_n^0 q_n^0)]\} \ln[p_n^1/p_n^0]. \tag{19}$$

Note that the functional form for V_n^M is the same as the functional form for I_n^M except that the roles of prices and quantities have been interchanged. Montgomery (1929: 3–9) also showed that

$$p_n^1 q_n^1 - p_n^0 q_n^0 = I_n^M(p_n^0, p_n^1, q_n^0, q_n^1) + V_n^M(p_n^0, p_n^1, q_n^0, q_n^1). \tag{20}$$

In order to understand Equations (18) and (19) better, the reader should note that $L(a, b) \equiv [a - b]/[\ln a - \ln b]$ where $a > 0$, $b > 0$ is known in the economics literature as the *Vartia* (1976a, 1976b) *mean* and in the mathematics literature as the *logarithmic mean.*[11] It can be shown that L(a, b) is a linearly homogeneous symmetric mean.[12] In Equations (18) and (19), $a \equiv p_n^1 q_n^1$ and $b \equiv p_n^0 q_n^0$.

Montgomery (1929: 7–9) derived his indicators by using a very interesting argument (which parallels that of Bennet 1920) that we shall repeat since it shows how a large number of "reasonable" price and quantity indicators can be derived. Suppose that q^n is functionally related to p_n by a "supply" function:

$$q_n = s_n(p_n). \tag{21}$$

Note that the "supply" function s_n is a partial equilibrium supply function since only the price of the *n*th good appears in Equation (21) as an argument of the function. Montgomery (1929: 7) assumed the following functional form for s_n:

$$s_n(p_n) = \alpha_n p_n^{\beta_n}, \quad \alpha_n > 0, \quad \beta_n \neq 0. \tag{22}$$

Now define a theoretical price change indicator as the area under the "supply" curve going from p_n^0 to p_n^1:

$$P_n^*(p_n^0, p_n^1, s_n) \equiv \int_{p_n^0}^{p_n^1} s_n(p)dp \tag{23}$$

$$= \int_{p_n^0}^{p_n^1} \alpha_n(p^{\beta_n})dp \quad \text{using Equation (22)}$$

$$= \alpha_n(1+\beta_n)^{-1}p^{1+\beta_n})_{p_n^0}^{p_n^1} \quad \text{assuming } \beta_n \neq -1$$

$$= \alpha_n(1+\beta_n)^{-1}\left[(p_n^1)^{1+\beta_n} - (p_n^0)^{1+\beta_n}\right]. \tag{24}$$

The unknown parameters α_n and β_n that appear in Equation (24) can be determined by assuming that the two data points (p_n^0, q_n^0) and (p_n^1, q_n^1) are on the "supply" function defined by Equation (22). Thus we have

$$q_n^0 = \alpha_n(p_n^0)^{\beta_n} \quad \text{and} \quad q_n^1 = \alpha_n(p_n^1)^{\beta_n} \quad \text{or} \tag{25}$$

$$q_n^0/\alpha_n = (p_n^0)^{\beta_n} \quad \text{and} \quad q_n^1/\alpha_n = (p_n^1)^{\beta_n} \quad \text{or} \tag{26}$$

$$p_n^0 q_n^0/\alpha_n = (p_n^0)^{1+\beta_n} \quad \text{and} \quad p_n^1 q_n^1/\alpha_n = (p_n^1)^{1+\beta_n}. \tag{27}$$

By taking ratios in Equation (25), we can also deduce that

$$[q_n^1/q_n^0] = [p_n^1/p_n^0]^{\beta_n} \quad \text{or} \tag{28}$$

$$\beta_n = \ln[q_n^1/q_n^0]/\ln[p_n^1/p_n^0] \quad \text{or}$$

$$1+\beta_n = \{\ln[p_n^1/p_n^0] + \ln[q_n^1/q_n^0]\}/\ln[p_n^1/p_n^0]$$

$$= \{\ln[p_n^1 q_n^1] = \ln[p_n^0 q_n^0]\}/\ln[p_n^1/p_n^0]. \tag{29}$$

Now substitute Equation (27) into Equation (24) to get

$$P_n^*(p_n^0, p_n^1, s_n) = (1+\beta_n)^{-1}[p_n^1 q_n^1 - p_n^0 q_n^0]$$

$$= \ln[p_n^1/p_n^0][p_n^1 q_n^1 - p_n^0 q_n^0]/\{\ln[p_n^1 q_n^1] - \ln[p_n^0 q_n^0]\}$$

$$\text{using (29)}$$

$$= I_n^M(p_n^0, p_n^1, q_n^0, q_n^1), \tag{30}$$

where the Montgomery indicator of price change for good *n*, I_n^M, was defined by Equation (18).

Montgomery (following Bennet 1920: 456) also defined the theoretical indicator of quantity change going from q_n^0 to q_n^1 as the area under the *inverse* "supply" curve S_n where $p_n = S_n(q_n)$; that is, defined

$$Q_n^*(q_n^0, q_n^1, S_n) \equiv \int_{q_n^0}^{q_n^1} S_n(q)dp. \tag{31}$$

If the "supply" function s_n is defined by Equation (22), then the corresponding inverse "supply" function has the same functional form; thus, we have

$$p_n = S_n(q_n) = [q_n/\alpha_n]^{1/\beta_n} \equiv \gamma_n q_n^{\delta_n}, \tag{32}$$

where $\delta_n \equiv 1/\beta_n$; hence we require $\beta_n \neq 0$ and $\gamma_n \equiv (1/\alpha_n)^{1/\beta_n}$; hence we require $\alpha_n \neq 0$. Thus the same argument that we used to derive Equation (30) can be adapted to prove that if S_n is defined by Equation (32) or equivalently if s_n is defined by Equation (22), then

$$Q_n^*(q_n^0, q_n^1, S_n) = V_n^M(p_n^0, p_n^1, q_n^0, q_n^1), \tag{33}$$

where V_n^M is the Montgomery indicator of quantity change defined by Equation (19).

Montgomery (1929: 13) gave a nice geometric interpretation of his method for the case in which $0 < p_n^0 < p_n^1$ and $0 < q_n^0 < q_n^1$ that we repeat in Figure 1.

Figure 1

Montgomery's decomposition of a value change.

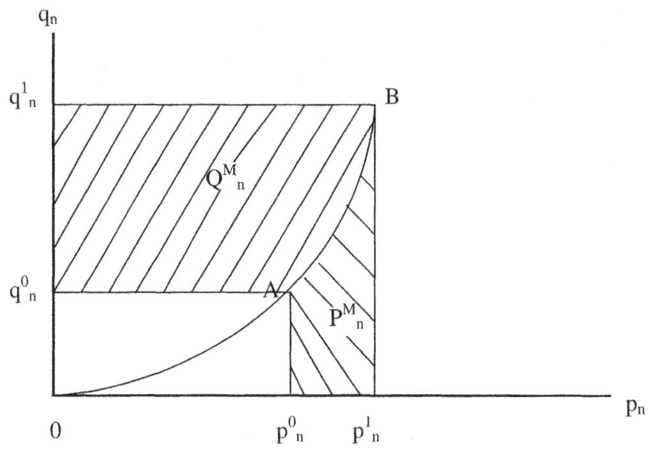

The line 0AB is the curve defined by $q_n = \alpha_n p_n^{\beta_n}$ that passes through the observed points A and B. The period 1 value, $p_n^1 q_n^1$, can be interpreted as the area of the big rectangle $0q_n^1Bp_n^1$, while the period 0 value, $p_n^0 q_n^0$, can be interpreted as the area of the small rectangle $0q_n^0Ap_n^0$. The part of the value change that is due to price change, I_n^M, is the shaded area below the curve AB (the area enclosed by $p_n^0ABp_n^1$) and the part of the value change that is due to quantity change, V_n^M, is the shaded area to the left of AB (the area enclosed by $q_n^0q_n^1BA$).

It is easy to see how Montgomery's idea could be generalized. Instead of using the constant elasticity functional form defined by Equations (22) or (32) to join the parts A and B, *any* monotonic curve could be used to join A and B and the corresponding indicators of price and quantity change can be defined by Equations (23) and (31).

In fact, Montgomery (1929: 9–11) considered an alternative curve. He repeated his analysis assuming that the "supply" function had the following *linear functional form*:

$$s_n(p_n) \equiv a_n + b_n p_n. \tag{34}$$

For the linear "supply" function defined by Equation (34), the area under the curve definition of the price change indicator yields:

$$\begin{aligned} P_n^*(p_n^0, p_n^1, s_n) &\equiv \int_{p_n^0}^{p_n^1} [a_n + b_n p]dp \\ &= a_n p + (1/2)b_n p^2 \Big]_{p_n^0}^{p_n^1} \\ &= a_n[p_n^1 - p_n^0] + (1/2)b_n\left[(p_n^1)^2 - (p_n^0)^2\right]. \end{aligned} \tag{35}$$

As usual, we determine the unknown parameters a_n and b_n in Equation (35) by assuming that the observed points (p_n^0, q_n^0) and (p_n^1, q_n^1) lie on the curve defined by Equation (34). Thus we have:

$$q_n^0 = a_n + b_n p_n^0; \quad q_n^1 = a_n + b_n p_n^1. \tag{36}$$

Assuming that $p_n^0 \neq p_n^1$, we find that

$$a_n = [p_n^1 q_n^0 - p_n^0 q_n^1]/[p_n^1 - p_n^0] \quad \text{and} \tag{37}$$

$$b_n = [q_n^1 - q_n^0]/[p_n^1 - p_n^0]. \tag{38}$$

Substituting Equations (37) and (38) into Equation (35) yields

$$P_n^*(p_n^0, p_n^1, s_n) = (1/2)(q_n^0 + q_n^1)(p_n^1 - p_n^0) \equiv I_n^B(p_n^0, p_n^1, q_n^0, q_n^1); \quad (39)$$

in other words, the theoretical indicator of price change $P_n^*(p_n^0, p_n^1, s_n)$, under the assumption that s_n is the linear "supply" function defined by Equation (34), turns out to equal the Bennet (1920) indicator of price change, $I_n^B(p_n^0, p_n^1, y_n^0, y_n^1)$, for commodity *n*.

The inverse "supply" function that corresponds to Equation (34) is:

$$p_n = S_n(q_n) \equiv -(a_n/b_n) + (1/b_n)q_n \equiv c_n + d_n q_n, \quad (40)$$

where $c_n \equiv -a_n/b_n$ and $d_n \equiv 1/b_n$ (assuming $b_n \neq 0$). The functional form for the inverse "supply" function defined by Equation (40) is linear, and so we can simply adapt the above argument that we used when the direct "supply" function s_n was linear. Thus if Equation (34) or (40) holds, then

$$Q_n^*(q_n^0, q_n^1, S_n) \equiv \int_{q_n^0}^{p_n^1} S_n(q)dq \quad (41)$$

$$= (1/2)(p_n^0 + p_n^1)(q_n^1 - q_n^0)$$

$$\equiv V_n^B(p_n^0, p_n^1, q_n^0, q_n^1), \quad (42)$$

where $V_n^B(p_n^0, p_n^1, q_n^0, q_n^1)$ is the Bennet quantity change indicator for commodity *n*.

The geometry of the linear "supply" function is given in Figure 2.

Figure 2

Bennet's decomposition of a value change.

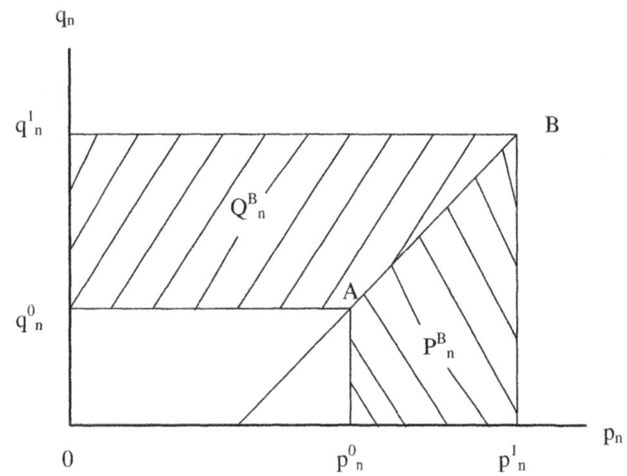

Montgomery (1929: 14) preferred the indicators I_n^M and $V_n^M V_n^M$ over the Bennet (1920) indicators I_n^B and V_n^B because the constant elasticity "supply" curve defined by Equation (22) passes through the origin, whereas the linear "supply" curve defined by Equation (34) will not generally pass through the origin (unless $p_n^1/p_n^0 = q_n^1/q_n^0$ so that the price change is equal to the quantity change in proportional terms). However, Bennet (1920: 457) argued that the straight line joining A and B was the simplest hypothesis to use in the absence of other information. Moreover, Montgomery's model, which has a "supply" curve going through the origin, is not appropriate in the context of a consumer demand for commodities model or a producer's demand for inputs model in which a negatively sloped "demand" curve (which would not pass through the origin) would be more appropriate. Bennet's framework is perfectly valid in the demand context, whereas Montgomery's model breaks down.[13]

Referring to Figure 2, the Laspeyres I_N^L indicator of price change can be represented as the area of the rectangle $q_n^0(p_n^1 - p_n^0)$, while the Paasche indicator I_n^P can be represented as the area of the larger rectangle $q_n^1(p_n^1 - p_n^0)$. It can be seen that the Bennet indicator I_n^B is the average of these two rectangles.

The above analysis shows that there are a large number of possible measures of price and quantity change, I_n and V_n, that satisfy Equation (5). Which measure should we use in empirical applications? In the following section, we suggest an axiomatic or test approach to the determination of the functional form for I_n and V_n while in Section V we suggest an economic approach.

IV

The Test Approach for Indicators of Price and Quantity Change

> How is this (increase in value) to be apportioned between the increase in price . . . and the increase in value due to the increase in quantity? . . . Again we note that if there is an increase in price, but no increase in quantity, the whole of the increase in value is due to the increase in price. . . . Conversely, if there is an increase in quantity, but no increase in price, the whole of the increase in value is due to the increase in quantity.
>
> J. K. Montgomery (1929: 3)

We consider axioms for the commodity *n* price change indicator, $I_n(p_n^0, p_n^1, q_n^0, q_n^1)$. We assume that the commodity *n* volume change indicator $V_n(p_n^0, p_n^1, q_n^0, q_n^1)$ is determined by Equation (5) once I_n has been determined. We also assume that all of the scalar prices and quantities $p_n^0, p_n^1, q_n^0, q_n^1$ are positive.

The tests and axioms that we propose are, for the most part, analogies to the tests that Diewert (1992b) used to characterize the Fisher (1922) ideal price index.

We assume that I_n and V_n satisfy the identity in Equation (5). Thus if I_n is defined, the corresponding V_n is implicitly defined by:

$$V_n(p_n^0, p_n^1, q_n^0, q_n^1) = p_n^1 q_n^1 - p_n^0 q_n^0 - I_n(p_n^0, p_n^1, q_n^0, q_n^1). \qquad (43)$$

Thus tests or properties of the quantity change indicator V_n can be imposed on the price change indicator I_n using Equation (43).

The first property we wish to consider for our price indicator I_n is the property of continuity.

A1 $I_n(p_n^0, p_n^1, q_n^0, q_n^1)$ is defined for $p_n^0 > 0$, $p_n^1 > 0$, $q_n^0 > 0$, $q_n^1 > 0$ and is a *continuous* function over this domain of definition.

The following two tests were first proposed by Montgomery (1929: 3). If prices remain unchanged during the two periods, then we want our indicator of price change to equal zero; if quantities remain unchanged during the two periods, then we want our indicator of quantity change to equal zero.

A2 *Identity Test for Prices*: $I_n(p_n, p_n, q_n^0, q_n^1) = 0$.
A3 *Identity Test for Quantities*: $I(p_n^0, p_n^1, q_n, q_n) = (p_n^1 - p_n^0)q_n$.

We derived the test A3 using Equation (43). From Equation (43), we have

$$V_n(p_n^0, p_n^1, q_n, q_n) = p_n^1 q_n - p_n^0 q_n - I(p_n^0, p_n^1, q_n, q_n) = 0 \qquad (44)$$

and the second equation in Equation (44) is equivalent to the equation in A3.

Recall the Paasche and Laspeyres price indicators defined in the previous section, $I_n^P(p_n^0, p_n^1, q_n^0, q_n^1) \equiv (p_n^1 - p_n^0)q_n^1$ and $I_n^L(p_n^0, p_n^1, q_n^0, q_n^1) \equiv (p_n^1 - p_n^0)q_n^0$. From the perspective of the Montgomery approach presented in the previous section, it can be seen that the Paasche and Laspeyres price indicators give the most extreme results that could be considered acceptable. Hence it seems reasonable to require that $I_n(p_n^0, p_n^1, q_n^0, q_n^1)$ lie between these two "extreme" indicators.

A4 *Bounding Test*: $\min\{(p_n^1 - p_n^0)q_n^0, (p_n^1 - p_n^0)q_n^1\} \leq I(p_n^0, p_n^1, q_n^0, q_n^1) \leq \max\{(p_n^1 - p_n^0)q_n^0, (p_n^1 - p_n^0)q_n^1\}$.

It can be shown that if I_n satisfies A4, then the corresponding V_n defined by Equation (43) satisfies:

$$\begin{aligned}\min\{(q_n^1 - q_n^0)p_n^0, (q_n^1 - q_n^0)p_n^1\} &\leq V_n(p_n^0, p_n^1, q_n^0, q_n^1)\\ &\leq \max\{(q_n^1 - q_n^0)p_n^0, (q_n^1 - q_n^0)p_n^1\}.\end{aligned} \tag{45}$$

Our next four tests are monotonicity properties for I_n and V_n.

A5 *Monotonicity in Period 1 Prices*: $I_n(p_n^0, p_n^1, q_n^0, q_n^1) < I_n(p_n^0, p_n, q_n^0, q_n^1)$ if $p_n^1 < p_n$.

If the period 1 price increases from p_n^1 to p_n, then the indicator of price change should also increase.

A6 *Monotonicity in Period 0 Prices*: $I_n(p_n^0, p_n^1, q_n^0, q_n^1) > I_n(p_n, p_n^1, q_n^0, q_n^1)$ if $p_n^0 < p_n$.

If the period 0 price increases from p_n^0 to p_n, then the indicator of price change should decrease.

A7 *Monotonicity in Period 1 Quantities*: $p_n^1 q_n^1 - p_n^0 q_n^0 - I_n(p_n^0, p_n^1, q_n^0, q_n^1) < p_n^1 q_n - p_n^0 q_n^0 - I_n(p_n^0, p_n^1, q_n^0, q_n)$ if $q_n^1 < q_n$.

Thus if the period 1 quantity increases from q_n^1 to q_n, the implicit indicator of quantity change V_n defined by Equation (43) should also increase; that is, A7 is equivalent to

$$V_n(p_n^0, p_n^1, q_n^0, q_n^1) < V_n(p_n^0, p_n^1, q_n^0, q_n) \quad \text{if} \quad q_n^1 < q_n. \tag{46}$$

A8 *Monotonicity in Period 0 Quantities*: $p_n^1 q_n^1 - p_n^0 q_n^0 - I_n(p_n^0, p_n^1, q_n^0, q_n^1) > p_n^1 q_n^1 - p_n^0 q_n - I_n(p_n^0, p_n^1, q_n, q_n^1)$ if $q_n^0 < q_n$.

Thus, if period 1 quantity increases from q_n^0 to q_n, the implicit indicator of quantity change V_n defined by Equation (43) should decrease; that is, A8 is equivalent to

$$V_n(p_n^0, p_n^1, q_n^0, q_n^1) V_n(p_n^0, p_n^1, q_n, q_n^1) \quad \text{if} \quad q_n^0 < q_n. \tag{47}$$

The following four tests are postivity (or negativity) tests that are somewhat weaker than the previous four monotonicity tests. It can be shown that A2 and A5 imply A9; A2 and A6 imply A10; A3 and A7 imply A11; and A3 and A8 imply A12.

A9 *Positivity of Price Change if the Period 1 Price Exceeds the Period 0 Price*: $I_n(p_n^0, p_n^1, q_n^0, q_n^1) > 0$ if $p_n^1 > p_n^0$.

A10 *Negativity of Price Change if the Period 0 Price Exceeds the Period 1 Price*: $I_n(p_n^0, p_n^1, q_n^0, q_n^1) < 0$ if $p_n^0 > p_n^1$.

A11 *Positivity of Quantity Change if the Period 1 Quantity Exceeds the Period 0 Quantity*: $p_n^1q_n^1 - p_n^0q_n^0 - I_n(p_n^0, p_n^1, q_n^0, q_n^1) > 0$ if $q_n^1 > q_n^0$.

Of course, using Equation (43), the inequality in A11 is equivalent to

$$V_n(p_n^0, p_n^1, q_n^0, q_n^1) > 0 \quad \text{if} \quad q_n^1 > q_n^0. \tag{48}$$

A12 *Negativity of Quantity Change if the Period 0 Quantity Exceeds the Period 1 Quantity*: $p_n^1q_n^1 - p_n^0q_n^0 - I_n(p_n^0, p_n^1, q_n^0, q_n^1) < 0$ if $q_n^0 > q_n^1$.

Using Equation (43), the inequality in A12 is equivalent to:

$$V_n(p_n^0, p_n^1, q_n^0, q_n^1) < 0 \quad \text{if} \quad q_n^0 > q_n^1. \tag{49}$$

In index number theory, we generally require our price and quantity indexes to be invariant to changes in the units of measurement. It seems reasonable to impose this invariance property in the present context.

A13 *Invariance to Changes in the Units of Measurement*: $I_n(p_n^0, p_n^1, q_n^0, q_n^1) = In(\lambda p_n^0, \lambda p_n^1, \lambda^{-1}q_n^0, \lambda^{-1}q_n^1)$ where $\lambda > 0$.

There are also the following two linear homogeneity properties that we can impose on *P*.

A14 *Linear Homogeneity in Prices*: $I_n(\lambda p_n^0, \lambda p_n^1, q_n^0, q_n^1) = \lambda I_n(p_n^0, p_n^1, q_n^0, q_n^1)$ for all $\lambda > 0$.

A15 *Linear Homogeneity in Quantities*: $I_n(p_n^0, p_n^1, \mu q_n^0, \mu q_n^1) = \mu I(p_n^0, p_n^1, q_n^0, q_n^1)$ for all $\mu > 0$.

Note that the price homogeneity axioms A14 and A15 differ from their index number counterparts; in other words, the prices in *both* periods are scaled up by the multiplicative factor λ in A14 and A15.

Note that if A14 holds, we have $I_n(p_n^0, p_n^1, q_n^0, q_n^1) = p_n^0 I_n(1, p_n^1/p_n^0, q_n^0, q_n^1)$ (let $\lambda = 1/p_n^0$) and if A15 holds, we have $I_n(p_n^0, p_n^1, q_n^0, q_n^1) = q_n^0\, I(p_n^0, p_n^1, 1, q_n^1/q_n^0)$ (let $\mu = 1/q_n^0$). If both A14 and A15 hold, then we have A13 and moreover:

$$I_n(p_n^0, p_n^1, q_n^0, q_n^1) = p_n^0 q_n^0 I_n(1, p_n^1/p_n^0, 1, q_n^1/q_n^0). \tag{50}$$

Our final three tests are symmetry tests.

A16 *Time Reversal*: $I_n(p_n^0, p_n^1, q_n^0, q_n^1) = -I_n(p_n^0, p_n^1, q_n^0, q_n^1)$: in other words, if we interchange prices and quantities for the two periods, then the price indicator function should change sign. Put another way, the price change going from period 0 to 1 plus the price change going from period 1 back to period 0 should sum to zero; that is, $I_n(p_n^0, p_n^1, q_n^0, q_n^1) + I_n(p_n^1, p_n^0, q_n^1, q_n^0) = 0$.

A17 *Quantity Weights Symmetry*: $I_n(p_n^0, p_n^1, q_n^0, q_n^1) = I_n(p_n^0, p_n^1, q_n^1, q_n^0)$.

Thus if (A17) holds, we can interchange the role of quantities in the two periods and the indicator of price change remains unchanged. This implies that the quantities q_n^0 and q_n^1 enter into the price indicator formula in a symmetric manner.

A18 *Price Weights Symmetry*: $p_n^1 q_n^1 - p_n^0 q_n^0 - I_n(p_n^0, p_n^1, q_n^0, q_n^1) = p_n^0 q_n^1 - p_n^1 q_n^0 - I_n(p_n^1, p_n^0, q_n^0, q_n^1)$.

Making use of Equation (43), A18 is equivalent to:

$$V_n(p_n^0, p_n^1, q_n^0, q_n^1) = V_n(p_n^1, p_n^0, q_n^0, q_n^1): \tag{51}$$

that is, if we interchange prices in the indicator of quantity change, this indicator of quantity change remains unchanged. Thus p_n^0 and p_n^1 enter into the quantity indicator formula in a symmetric fashion.

It turns out that the Bennet price and quantity indicators

$$I_n^B(p^0, p^1, q^0, q^1) \equiv 1/2\,(q_n^0 + q_n^1)(p_n^1 - p_n^0); \tag{52}$$

$$V_n^B(p^0, p^1, q^0, q^1) \equiv 1/2\,(p_n^0 + p_n^1)(q_n^1 - q_n^0) \tag{53}$$

satisfy all 18 of the above tests and in fact are uniquely characterized by the above tests.

Proposition 1: If I_n satisfies the three symmetry tests A16, A17, and A18, then $I_n = I_n^B$ where I_n^B is defined by Equation (52).

See Appendix 1 for proofs of propositions.

Proposition 2: I_n^B defined by Equation (52) satisfies tests A1–A18.

What tests does the Montgomery price change indicator I_n^M defined by Equation (18) satisfy?

Proposition 3: $I_n^M(p_n^0, p_n^1, q_n^0, q_n^1)$ defined by Equation (18) satisfies all of the tests except the monotonicity tests A5, A6, A7, and A8 and the symmetry tests A17 and A18.

It should be mentioned that Montgomery (1929: 3) also proposed the following symmetry test, which is a counterpart to Fisher's (1921: 53, 1922: 72) factor reversal test in index number theory:

A19 $V_n(p_n^0, p_n^1, q_n^0, q_n^1) = I_n(q_n^0, q_n^1, p_n^0, p_n^1)$: that is, the volume indicator is equal to the price indicator when the role of prices and quantities is interchanged in the latter function.[14] Montgomery (1929: 11) noted that both the Bennet and Montgomery indicators satisfied the factor reversal axiom (A19) and that he could not find any other simple formula that satisfied this axiom. However, it is easy to adapt Fisher's (1922: 142)[15] crossing of factor antitheses approach to rectify any given indicator of price change $I_n(p_n^0, p_n^1, q_n^0, q_n^1)$ into an indicator $I_n^r(p_n^0, p_n^1, q_n^0, q_n^1)$ that satisfies the factor reversal test A19. We show how this can be done.

Let $I_n(p_n^0, p_n^1, q_n^0, q_n^1)$ be an arbitrary indicator of price change that perhaps does not satisfy A19. Define the *factor antithesis* I_n^f to I_n as follows:

$$I_n^f(p_n^0, p_n^1, q_n^0, q_n^1) \equiv p_n^1 q_n^1 - p_n^0 q_n^0 - I_n(q_n^0, q_n^1, p_n^0, p_n^1). \qquad (54)$$

Define the *factor rectified indicator* I_n^{fr} as the arithmetic average of I_n and I_n^f:

$$I_n^{fr}(p_n^0, p_n^1, q_n^0, q_n^1) \equiv (1/2)I_n(p_n^0, p_n^1, q_n^0, q_n^1) + (1/2)I_n^f(p_n^0, p_n^1, q_n^0, q_n^1). \qquad (55)$$

Proposition 4: The factor rectified indicator of price change I_n^{fr} defined by Equation (55) satisfies the factor reversal test A19; that is, we have

$$I_n^{fr}(p_n^0, p_n^1, q_n^0, q_n^1) + I_n^{fr}(q_n^0, q_n^1, p_n^0, p_n^1) = p_n^1 q_n^1 - p_n^0 q_n^0. \qquad (56)$$

It is also easy to modify Fisher's (1922: 140) time rectification procedure, which will allow us to transform an arbitrary indicator of price change $I_n(p_n^0, p_n^1, q_n^0, q_n^1)$ that perhaps does not satisfy the time reversal test A16 into one that does. Define the *time antithesis* I_n^t to I_n as follows:

$$I_n^t(p_n^0, p_n^1, q_n^0, q_n^1) \equiv -I_n(p_n^1, p_n^0, q_n^1, q_n^0). \qquad (57)$$

Define the *time rectified indicator* I_n^{tr} as the arithmetic mean of I_n and I_n^t:

$$I_n^{tr}(p_n^0, p_n^1, q_n^0, q_n^1) \equiv (1/2)I_n(p_n^0, p_n^1, q_n^0, q_n^1) + (1/2)I_n^t(p_n^0, p_n^1, q_n^0, q_n^1). \qquad (58)$$

Proposition 5: The time rectified indicator of price change I_n^{tr} defined by Equation (58) satisfies the time reversal test A16; that is, we have

$$I_n^{tr}(p_n^0, p_n^1, q_n^0, q_n^1) = -I_n^{tr}(p_n^1, p_n^0, q_n^1, q_n^0). \qquad (59)$$

The above propositions show that there are many parallels between the test approach to index numbers and the test approach to indicators of price change. The Fisher (1921, 1922) ideal price index (the geometric mean of the Paasche and Laspeyres price indexes) appears to be "best" from the viewpoint of the test approach,[16] while the Bennet indicator of price change (the arithmetic average of the Paasche and Laspeyres price indicators) appears to be "best" from the viewpoint of the test approach to indicators of price change.

We note that the Paasche and Laspeyres indicators of price change, I^P and I^L, defined by Equations (11) and (14), respectively, have rather good axiomatic properties, as is indicated in the following result:

Proposition 6: The Paasche and Laspeyres indicators of price change defined by Equations (11) and (14) satisfy all of the above axioms except the symmetry axioms, (A16), (A17), (A18), and (A19).

The reader may have noticed that we did not strongly endorse the factor symmetry test A19; it is not a particularly compelling test.[17] The weight symmetry tests (A17) and (A18) are also not tests that simply must hold. However, the time reversal test is an important test that we definitely will want to impose in any context in which the data from the two periods is symmetric. With respect to the five applications (outlined in Section I) where indicators of price and quantity change might be useful, all of these applications would seem to require a symmetric treatment of the data, with the exception of variance analysis, where the data are not symmetric. Thus the failure of the Paasche and Laspeyres price indicators I_n^P and I_N^L to satisfy the time reversal test A16 means that we should be cautious in using these indicators. The failure of the Montgomery indicator of price change I_n^M to satisfy the monotonicity tests A5–A8 means that we should be cautious in using it as well. This leaves the Bennet indicator of price change, I_n^B, as the "best'" from the viewpoint of the test approach.

We now turn our attention to economic approaches to the measurement of price and quantity change.

V

The Economic Approach to Indicators of Price and Quantity Change

> Therefore the problem of constructing a true index of the cost of living is inseparably bound up with the general problem of establishing a func tional relation between consumption and prices.
>
> A. A. Könus ([1924] 1939: 12)

In the economic approach to index number theory, prices and quantities are no longer regarded as being completely independent variables: prices are regarded as exogenous, but quantities are determined as solutions to optimization problems. For example, in the consumer context, it is assumed that a consumer maximizes a utility function f(q) subject to a budget constraint or, alternatively, the consumer minimizes the cost of achieving a given utility level. Following Samuelson and Swamy (1974) and Diewert (1976b), we assume that the utility function is homogeneous of degree one, in which case the consumer's cost or expenditure function C, defined as

$$C(u, p) \equiv \min_q \{p \cdot q : f(q) \geq u\}, \qquad (60)$$

has the following decomposition:

$$C(u, p) \equiv uC(1, p) \equiv uc(p), \tag{61}$$

where $c(p) \equiv C(1, p)$ is the consumer's unit cost function.[18]

In this case, where preferences are homothetic, the observed price and quantity data for period t, p^t and q^t, satisfy:

$$p^t \cdot q^t = f(q^t)c(p^t); \quad t = 0, 1. \tag{62}$$

Thus taking ratios, Equation (62) implies

$$p^1 \cdot q^1/p^0 \cdot q^0 = [c(p^1)/c(p^0)][f(q^1)/f(q^0)]. \tag{63}$$

For certain specific functional forms for the unit cost function c, we can find an index number formula, $P(p^0, p^1, q^0, q^1)$, such that the unit cost ratio is equal to this price index; that is, for such an index, we have

$$P(p^0, p^1, q^0, q^1) = c(p^1)/c(p^0). \tag{64}$$

Associated with such an exact price index P is the quantity index Q that satisfies Equation (2) above. Using Equations (2), (63), and (64), for such a Q, we have

$$Q(p^0, p^1, q^0, q^1) = f(q^1)/f(q^0). \tag{65}$$

This is a brief outline of the theory of exact index number formulae that is discussed by Pollak (1989: 22–32), Samuelson and Swamy (1974), and Diewert (1976b).

A particular example of Equation (64) that is used frequently in empirical applications is the Fisher (1922) ideal index P_F defined as:

$$P_F(p^0, p^1, q^0, q^1) \equiv [p^1 \cdot q^0 p^1 \cdot q^1/p^0 \cdot q^0 p^0 \cdot q^1]^{1/2}, \tag{66}$$

which is exact for the homogeneous quadratic unit cost function $c(p) = (p \cdot Bp)^{1/2}$ where B is a symmetric matrix of constants.[19] Another example is the Törnqvist[20] price index P_T defined as

$$\ln P_T(p^0, p^1, q^0, q^1) \equiv \sum_{n=1}^{M} (1/2)(s_n^0 + s_n^1)\ln(p_n^1/p_n^0), \tag{67}$$

where the period t expenditure share on commodity n, s_n^t, is defined as $p_n^t q_n^t/p^t \cdot q^t$ for $n = 1, \ldots,$ N and $t = 0, 1$. This index is exact for a translog unit cost function.[21]

Now return to the case of a generic exact price index P satisfying

Equation (64), along with its partner *Q* satisfying Equations (2) and (65). We can write the difference in consumer expenditures between periods 0 and 1 as follows:

$$
\begin{aligned}
p^1 \cdot q^1 - p^0 \cdot q^0 &= p^0 \cdot q^0[(p^1 \cdot q^1/p^0 \cdot q^0) - 1] \\
&= p^0 \cdot q^0[PQ - 1] \quad \text{using Equation (2)} \\
&= p^0 \cdot q^0[(1/2)(1 + Q)(P - 1) + (1/2)(1 + P)(Q - 1)] \qquad (68)
\end{aligned}
$$

where Equation (68) follows from the line above using the Bennet identity:

$$PQ - 1 = (1/2)(1 + Q)(P - 1) + (1/2)(1 + P)(Q - 1). \qquad (69)$$

Now from Equation (68) we see that the value change has been decomposed into an "economic" price change (the term involving P − 1) and an "economic" quantity change (the term involving Q − 1). Thus for our generic exact economic price and quantity indexes P and Q satisfying Equation (2), we define the following economic indicators of price and volume change:

$$
\begin{aligned}
&I_E(p^0, p^1, q^0, q^1) \\
&\quad \equiv (1/2)p^0 \cdot q^0[1 + Q(p^0, p^1, q^0, q^1)][P(p^0, p^1, q^0, q^1) - 1]; \qquad (70)
\end{aligned}
$$

$$
\begin{aligned}
&V_E(p^0, p^1, q^0, q^1) \\
&\quad = (1/2)p^0 \cdot q^0[1 + P(p^0, p^1, q^0, q^1)][Q(p^0, p^1, q^0, q^1) - 1]. \qquad (71)
\end{aligned}
$$

Proposition 7: If the exact price and quantity indexes *P* and *Q* satisfy Equations (2), (64), and (65) and there is cost minimizing behavior in the two periods under consideration so that Equation (62) holds, then the economic price and quantity indicators defined by Equations (70) and (71) satisfy the following equations:

$$
\begin{aligned}
I_E(p^0, p^1, q^0, q^1) &= (1/2)c(p^0)f(q^0)[1 + f(q^1)/f(q^0)][\{c(p^1)/c(p^0)\} - 1] \qquad (72) \\
&= (1/2)f(q^0)[c(p^1) - c(p^0)] - (1/2)f(q^1)[c(p^0) - c(p^1)] \qquad (73) \\
&= (1/2)[f(q^0) + f(q^1)][c(p^1) - c(p^0)]; \qquad (74) \\
V_E(p^0, p^1, q^0, q^1) &= (1/2)c(p^0)f(q^0)[1 + c(p^1)/c(p^0)][\{f(q^1)/f(q^0)\} - 1] \qquad (75) \\
&= (1/2)c(p^0)[f(q^0) - f(q^0)] - (1/2)c(p^1)[f(q^0) - f(q^1)] \qquad (76) \\
&= (1/2)[c(p^0) + c(p^1)][f(q^1) - f(q^0)]. \qquad (77)
\end{aligned}
$$

Equation (72) is a straightforward translation of Equation (70) using the exactness of the indexes *P* and *Q*. Equation (73) is a symmetric rearrangement of Equation (72); it shows that the overall price change can be written as the arithmetic average of the period 0 to 1 price change $c(p^1) - c(p^0)$ weighted by the period 0 aggregate quantity $f(q^0)$ and the negative of the period 1 to 0 price change $c(p^0) - c(p^1)$ weighted by the period 1 aggregate quantity $f(q^1)$. Equation (74) is the familiar Bennet price change decomposition, treating $c(p^0)$ and $c(p^1)$ as aggregate prices for periods 0 and 1 and $f(q^0)$ and $f(q^1)$ as aggregate quantities for periods 0 and 1. Note that the left-hand side of Equations (72), (73), or (74) is $I_E(p^0, p^1, q^0, q^1)$, which can be readily calculated if *P* and *Q* are given, whereas the right-hand side of Equations (72), (73), or (74) involves the unobserved aggregates $c(p^t)$ and $f(q^t)$.

It is useful to obtain an alternative formula for the economic indicator of price change I_E defined by Equation (70). Rearranging the right-hand side of Equation (70) yields

$$\begin{aligned} &I_E(p^0, p^1, q^0, q^1) \\ &\quad = (1/2)p^0 \cdot q^0[P - 1] + (1/2)p^0 \cdot q^0 Q[P - 1] \\ &\quad = (1/2)p^0 \cdot q^0[P - 1] + (1/2)p^0 \cdot q^0[p^1 \cdot q^1/p^0 \cdot q^0 P][P - 1] \\ &\qquad \text{using (2)} \\ &\quad = (1/2)p^0 \cdot q^0[P(p^0, p^1, q^0, q^1) - 1] \\ &\qquad - (1/2)p^1 \cdot q^1[\{1/P(p^0, p^1, q^0, q^1)\} - 1]. \end{aligned} \tag{78}$$

Equation (78) can be used to establish the following result.

Proposition 8: If *P* satisfies the time reversal test for price indexes (i.e., $P(p^1, p^0, q^1, q^0) = 1/P(p^0, p^1, q^0, q^1)$), then the corresponding economic indicator of price change I_E defined by Equations (70) or (78) satisfies a version of the time reversal test for price indicators, A16.

Obviously, there are other relationships between the axiomatic properties of the price index *P* and the axiomatic properties of the resulting economic price indicator I_E defined in Equation (78). For example, if *P* satisfies the identity test for price indexes ($P(p, p, q^0, q^1) = 1$), then the corresponding I_E will satisfy a version of the identity test A2; if *P* satisfies the invariance to changes in the units of measurement test for price indexes, then the corresponding price indicator I_E will satisfy a version of the test A13, and so on.

Which I_E defined by Equation (78) is "best" from the viewpoint of the economic approach? To answer this question, we must pick the "best" formula for the underlying economic price index *P* from the viewpoint of the economic approach. Unfortunately, there is no single "best" price index *P* from the viewpoint of the economic approach. However, there is a class of price indexes *P* that are considered "best" from the viewpoint of the economic approach: namely, those indexes *P* that are exact for a flexible functional form for *c* or *f*. Such indexes *P* were called superlative by Diewert (1976b: 117).[22] Hence if the price index formula *P* in Equation (78) is superlative, we will call the induced indicator of price change I_E superlative as well. Since the Fisher index P_F and the Törnqvist index P_T defined by Equations (66) and (67) above are superlative, the associated economic indicators of price change I_E^F and I_E^T are also superlative indicators. Thus from the viewpoint of the economic approach to price indicators, any superlative price indicator could be considered "best."

VI

Which Indicator of Price Change Should Be Used in Practice?

> It is worth emphasizing that these theorems hold *without* the assumption of optimizing behavior on the part of economic agents; i.e., they are theorems in numerical analysis rather than economics.
>
> W. E. Diewert (1978: 889)

From the viewpoint of the test or axiomatic approach to indicators of price change, the results of Section IV above suggest that the Bennet indicator I^B defined by Equation (8) is "best." From the viewpoint of an economic approach to indicators of price change, the results of Section V suggest that a superlative indicator of price change such as I_E^F (replace *P* in Equation (78) by P_F defined by Equation (66) above) or I_E^T (replace *P* in Equation (78) by P_T defined by Equation (67) above) is "best." Which of these "best" indicators should we use in empirical applications? The result below suggest that it will not matter much in practice which of these three indicators of price change is used.

Proposition 9: The Bennet indicator of price change approximates any superlative indicator (such as the Fisher or Törnqvist indicators) to the second order at any point where the two price vectors are equal (i.e., $p^0 = p^1$) and where the two quantity vectors are equal (i.e., $q^0 = q^1$).

The proof of the above proposition rests on analogous results for superlative price indexes: every known superlative price index $P(p^0, p^1, q^0, q^1)$ has the same levels, vectors of first-order partial derivative, and matrices of second-order partial derivatives when evaluated at an equal price (i.e., $p^0 = p^1$) and quantity (i.e., $q^0 = q^1$) point.[23]

Somewhat surprisingly, the Montgomery indicator of price change, $I^M(p^0, p^1, q^0, q^1) \equiv \Sigma_{n=1}^{N} I_n^M(p_n^0, p_n^1, q_n^0, q_n^1)$ where the I_n^M are defined by Equation (18), also approximates the indicators described in Proposition 9 to the second order around an equal price and quantity point.

Proposition 10: The Montgomery indicator of price change, $I^M(p^0, p^1, q^0, q^1)$, approximates the Bennet indicator $I^B(p^0, p^1, q^0, q^1)$ to the second order at any point where $p^0 = p^1$ and $q^0 = q^1$.

We require all prices and quantities to be positive in Proposition 10. All prices must be positive in Proposition 9, but the requirement that the quantity vectors be strictly positive can be relaxed provided that the superlative $P(p^0, p^1, q^0, q^1)$ is still well defined.

Proposition 10 appears to be the indicator counterpart to Theorem 3 in Diewert (1978: 887), who showed that the Vartia I (1976a: 124–125, 1976b: 122) price index approximated any superlative price index to the second order around an equal price and quantity point. However, it should be noted that Montgomery (1937: 35) actually came up with the formula for the Vartia I price index many years before Vartia's derivation.[24] The formula for the Montgomery-Vartia I index is:

$$\ln P_M(p^0, p^1, q^0, q^1) = \sum_{n=1}^{N} w_n \ln(p_n^1/p_n^0), \tag{79}$$

where the weights w_n are defined, using the logarithmic mean L, as follows:

$$w_n \equiv L(p_n^1 q_n^1, p_n^0, q_n^0)/L(p^1 \cdot q^1, p^0 \cdot q^0); \quad n = 1, \ldots, N. \tag{80}$$

Thus the Montgomery price indicator function I^M plays the same role in Proposition 10 above as the Montgomery-Vartia price index P_M played in Theorem 10 of Diewert (1978).

In order to check the accuracy of Propositions 9 and 10 above, we calculated the Paasche and Laspeyres indicators of price change, I^P and I^L defined by Equations (11) and (14) above, the Bennet indicator I^B defined by Equation (8), the superlative Fisher and Tornqvist indicators I_E^F and I_E^T, and the Montgomery indicator I^M using the price and quantity data on 36 primary commodities in the United States for the years 1913–1918 that are tabled in Fisher (1922: 489–490). We calculated the chain links for each year; that is, we calculated $I(p^{t-1}, p^t, q^{t-1}, q^t)$ for $t = 1914, \ldots, 1918$. We also calculated the Fisher and Törnqvist chain links $P_F(p^{t-1}, p^t, q^{t-1}, q^t)$ and $P_T(p^{t-1}, p^t, q^{t-1}, q^t)$ to show the year-over-year inflation rates. The results of these computations can be found in Table 1.

As can be seen from the table, there does appear to be a fairly close correspondence between the Bennet, Fisher, Törnqvist, and Montgomery indicators of price change, I^B, I^F, I^T, and I^M, respectively. Note also that the Paasche and Laspeyres indicators of price change, I^P and I^L, are rather different from each other and the other superlative and pseudo-superlative indicators.[25]

VII

Conclusion

> Today's dollar is, then, a totally different unit from the dollar of 1897. As the general price level fluctuates, the dollar is bound to become a unit of different magnitude. To mix these units is like mixing inches and centimeters or measuring a field with a rubber tape-line.
>
> Livingston Middleditch (1918: 114–115)

The above quotation alerts us to a potential problem with our treatment of value changes; namely, if there is a great change in the general purchasing power of money between the two periods being compared, then our indicators of volume change may be "excessively" heavily weighted by the prices of the period with the highest general price level. Put another way, the units that quantities are measured in do not require any comparisons with other quantities, but the dollar

Table 1

Comparison of Various Indicators of Price Change

Year	P_F	P_T	I^P	I^L	I^B	I^F	I^T	I^M
1914	1.00124	1.00118	41.3	−9.0	16.1	16.2	16.1	16.8
1915	1.00106	1.00117	1.9	26.0	13.9	14.5	13.9	14.7
1916	1.14060	1.14238	2,245.9	1,952.6	2,099.3	2,100.4	2,099.3	2,104.9
1917	1.41907	1.41974	7,337.8	7,599.4	7,468.6	7,447.2	7,468.6	7,445.1
1918	1.10023	1.09905	2,683.5	2,499.5	2,591.5	2,592.0	2,591.5	2,592.4
Average	1.1324	1.1327	2,462.1	2,413.7	2,437.9	2,434.1	2,435.3	2,434.8

price of a quantity is the valuation of a unit of a commodity *relative to a numeraire commodity, money.* Thus the indicators of price change that we have discussed in this paper encompass both *general changes* in the purchasing power of money as well as *changes in inflation-adjusted* prices. Thus if there is high inflation between periods 0 and 1 and quantities have increased, then the use of symmetric in prices and quantities indicators (like the Bennet and Montgomery indicators) will shift some of the inflationary increase in values over to the indicator of volume change. This problem can be cured as follows. If the general inflation rate going from period 0 to 1 is *i*, define the period 1 inflation adjusted price vector p^{1*} as $(1 + i)^{-1}p^1$. Then the value change going from period 0 to 1 is first decomposed into a value change due to general inflation, $p^1 \cdot q^1 - p^{1*} \cdot q^1$, and we use our "best" indicator of (inflation-adjusted) price change, $I(p^0, p^{1*}, q^0, q^1)$, along with the corresponding indicator of volume change, $V(p^0, p^{1*}, q^0, q^1)$, where the inflation-adjusted period 1 prices p^{1*} are used in the indicators of price and volume change rather than the inflation-contaminated prices p^1. Using this inflation-adjusted methodology, the actual value change has the following decomposition:

$$p^1 \cdot q^1 - p^0 \cdot q^0 = p^1 \cdot q^1 - p^{1*} \cdot q^1 + I(p^0, p^{1*}, q^0, q^1) + V(p^0, p^{1*}, q^0, q^1). \tag{81}$$

Why are decompositions of value changes like Equation (81) not more common in financial and cost accounting? The basic problem is that it is difficult to construct unit values and the corresponding total quantities by commodity when the firm may be producing thousands of outputs and utilizing hundreds or thousands of inputs. However, as the computer revolution spreads through the business world, decompositions of the type in Equations (3) or (81) become increasingly feasible.

Another problem that limits the usefulness of value change decompositions is the *new goods problem.* Our methodological approach assumed that the list of *N* commodities remained fixed over the two periods, but in the real world the list of inputs and outputs does not remain fixed from period to period. New products and new services are constantly being developed, and so the problem arises of what price do we use for a new commodity in the period prior to its introduction? Hicks (1940: 114) provided a theoretical solution to this problem, but it is difficult to implement. Thus the new goods problems has also limited the use of value decompositions.

A nice feature of the Bennet indicators of price and volume change is their additive over commodities property, which gives them a big advantage over the superlative indicators of price and volume change, which are inherently nonadditive over commodities. The Montgomery indicators of price and volume change are also additive over commodities but the axiomatic properties of the Montgomery indicators are not as attractive as those of the Bennet indicators.

APPENDIX 1

Proofs of Propositions

Proof of Proposition 1: Rearranging A18, we have

$$
\begin{aligned}
&(q_n^0 + q_n^1)(p_n^1 - p_n^0)\\
&\quad = I_n(p_n^0, p_n^1, q_n^0, q_n^1) - I_n(p_n^1, p_n^0, q_n^0, q_n^1)\\
&\quad = I_n(p_n^0, p_n^1, q_n^0, q_n^1) - I_n(p_n^1, p_n^0, q_n^1, q_n^0) \quad \text{using A17}\\
&\quad = I_n(p_n^0, p_n^1, q_n^0, q_n^1) + I_n(p_n^0, p_n^1, q_n^0, q_n^1) \quad \text{using A16}\\
&\quad = 2I_n(p_n^0, p_n^1, q_n^0, q_n^1)\\
&\quad = 2I_N^B(p_n^0, p_n^1, q_n^0, q_n^1) \quad \text{using definition in Equation (52).}
\end{aligned}
$$

Proof of Proposition 2: Routine computations.

Proof of Proposition 3: The proof of A4 follows from the definition of the Montgomery indicators of price and volume change as integrals. An algebraic proof procedes as follows. Define $\overline{q}_n \equiv \max\{q_n^0, q_n^1\}$ and assume that $p_n^1 > p_n^0$. Using the definition of the Montgomery indicator in Equation (18) and the fact that the logarithmic mean L(a, b) is nondecreasing and homogeneous in its arguments, we have:

$$
\begin{aligned}
I_n^M(p_n^0, p_n^1, q_n^0, q_n^1) &= L(p_n^1 q_n^1, p_n^0 q_n^0)\ln(p_n^1/p_n^0)\\
&\le L(p_n^1 q_n, p_n^0, q_n)\ln(p_n^1/p_n^0)\\
&= \overline{q}_n L(p_n^1, p_n^0)\ln(p_n^1/p_n^0)\\
&= \overline{q}_n\{[p_n^1 - p_n^0]/[\ln p_n^1 - \ln p_n^0]\}\{\ln p_n^1 - \ln p_n^0\}\\
&= [p_n^1 - p_n^0]q_n\\
&= \max\{[p_n^1 - p_n^0]q_n^0, [p_n^1 - p_n^0]q_n^1\}. \qquad (82)
\end{aligned}
$$

If $p_n^1 < p_n^0$, then the inequality in Equation (82) is reversed and we deduce:

$$I_n^M(p_n^0, p_n^1, q_n^0, q_n^1) \geq [p_n^1 - p_n^0]\bar{q}_n = \max\{[p_n^1 - p_n^0]q_n^0, [p_n^1 - p_n^0]q_n^1\}. \tag{83}$$

Now rework Equations (82) and (83), letting $\bar{q}_n \equiv \min\{q_n^0, q_n^1\}$.

To show that the monotonicity test A5 does not hold, differentiate $I_n^M(p_n^0, p_n^1, q_n^0, q_n^1)$ defined by Equation (18) with respect to p_n^1 and evaluate the derivative at a point where

$$p_n^0 q_n^0 = p_n^1 q_n^1. \tag{84}$$

L'Hospital's rule for differentiation can be used to show that $\partial L(a, b)/\partial b = 1/2$ if $a = b$ where $L(a, b)$ is the logarithmic mean of *a* and *b*. Using this result, we have

$$\begin{aligned}
&\partial I_n^M(p_n^0, p_n^1, q_n^0, q_n^1)/\partial p_n^1 \\
&\quad = (1/2)\{\partial[p_n^1 q_n^1]/\partial p_n^1\}\ln[p_n^1/p_n^0] + L(p_n^0, q_n^0, p_n^1 q_n^1)(p_n^1)^{-1} \\
&\quad = (1/2)q_n^1 \ln[p_n^1/p_n^0] + p_n^1 q_n^1/p_n^1 \quad \text{using Equation (84)} \\
&\quad = (1/2)q_n^1\{\ln[p_n^1/p_n^0] + 2) \\
&\quad < 0
\end{aligned}$$

if $\ln[p_n^1/p_n^0] + 2 < 0$. Thus if we choose p_n^1/p_n^0 small enough so that $\ln[p_n^1/p_n^0] < -2$ while simultaneously choosing q_n^1/q_n^0 to satisfy Equation (84), then we violate the monotonicity axiom A5. Proofs of violations for the axioms A6, A7, and A8 follow in an analogous manner.

Proof of Proposition 4: Substitute Equation (54) into Equation (55) to obtain the following formula for I_n^{fr} in terms of the original indicator I_n:

$$\begin{aligned}
&I_n^{fr}(p_n^0, p_n^1, q_n^0, q_n^1) \\
&\quad = (1/2)[p_n^1 q_n^1 - p_n^0 q_n^0] - (1/2)I_n(q_n^0, q_n^1, p_n^0, p_n^1) \\
&\qquad + (1/2)I_n(p_n^0, p_n^1, q_n^0, q_n^1).
\end{aligned} \tag{85}$$

Using Equation (85) for I_n^{fr}, a simple calculation shows that I_n^{fr} satisfies Equation (56).

Proof of Proposition 5: Substitute Equation (57) into Equation (58) to obtain the following formula for I_n^{tr} in terms of the original indicator I_n:

$$I_n^{fr}(p_n^0, p_n^1, q_n^0, q_n^1) = (1/2)I_n(p_n^0, p_n^1, q_n^0, q_n^1) - (1/2)I_n(p_n^1, p_n^0, q_n^1, q_n^0). \tag{86}$$

Using Equation (86) for I_n^{tr}, a simple calculation shows that I_n^{tr} satisfies Equation (59).

Proof of Proposition 6: Straightfoward computations.

Proof of Proposition 7: Replace *P* and *Q* in Equations (70) and (71) by the right-hand sides of Equations (64) and (65), respectively, and simplify.

Proof of Proposition 8: Replace the term $1/P(p^0, p^1, q^0, q^1)$ in Equation (78) by $P(p^1, p^0, q^1, q^0)$, and we obtain the following formula for the economic indicator I_E:

$$\begin{aligned} I_E(p^0, p^1, q^0, q^1) \\ = (1/2)p^0 \cdot q^0[P(p^0, p^1, q^0, q^1) - 1] \\ - (1/2)p^1 \cdot q^1[P(p^1, p^0, q^1, q^0) - 1]. \end{aligned} \tag{87}$$

Using Equation (87) for I_E, verify that I_E satisfies the following time reversal test:

$$I_E(p^0, p^1, q^0, q^1) + I_E(p^1, p^0, q^1, q^0) = 0. \tag{88}$$

Proof of Proposition 9: Routine computations show that the vectors of first-order partial derivatives of the Bennet indicator of price change $I_B(p^0, p^1, q^0, q^1)$, evaluated at a point where $p^0 = p^1 = p$ and $q^0 = q^1 = q$, are:

$$\nabla_p^0 I^B = -q; \tag{89}$$

$$\nabla_p^1 I^B = q; \tag{90}$$

$$\nabla_p^0 I^B = 0_N; \tag{91}$$

$$\nabla_p^1 I^B = 0_N. \tag{92}$$

More routine computations show that the matrices of second-order partial derivatives of $I^B(p^0, p^1, q^0, q^1)$ evaluated at $p^0 = p^1 = p$ and $q^0 = q^1 = q$ are:

$$\nabla_{p_0^2 p^0} I^B = O_{N\times N}; \tag{93}$$

$$\nabla_{p_0^2 p^1} I^B = O_{N\times N}; \tag{94}$$

$$\nabla_{p_0^2 p^0} I^B = -(1/2)I_N; \tag{95}$$

$$\nabla_{p_0^2 q^1} I^B = -(1/2) I_N; \tag{96}$$

$$\nabla_{p_1^2 p^1} I^B = O_{N\times N}; \tag{97}$$

$$\nabla_{p_1^2 q^0} I^B = (1/2) I_N; \tag{98}$$

$$\nabla_{p_1^2 q^1} I^B = (1/2) I_N; \tag{99}$$

$$\nabla_{p_0^2 q^0} I^B = O_{N\times N}; \tag{100}$$

$$\nabla_{p_0^2 q^1} I^B = O_{N\times N}; \tag{101}$$

$$\nabla_{p_1^2 q^1} I^B = O_{N\times N}. \tag{102}$$

By differentiating the formula for a superlative price index *P* (such as the Fisher ideal index), we can calculate the vectors of first-order partial derivatives and the matrices of second-order partial derivatives of a superlative price index evaluated at $p^0 = p^1$ and $q^0 = q^1$. Now calculate the first- and second-order partial derivatives of $I_E(p^0, p^1, q^0, q^1)$ defined by Equation (78) and evaluate these derivatives at $p^0 = p^1$ and $q^0 = q^1$.

Proof of Proposition 10: More routine computations. We need to use L'Hospital's rule to show that $\partial L(a, b)/\partial a = 1/2$ when $a = b > 0$.

APPENDIX 2

Generalized Bennet Indicators of Price Change

The Bennet indicator of price change has the form

$$I^{GB}(p^0, p^1, q^0, q^1) = \sum_{n=1}^{N} M(q_n^0, q_n^1)[p_n^1 - p_n^0], \tag{103}$$

where $M(q_n^0, q_n^1)$, is the *arithmetic mean* of the period 0 and period 1 quantities for commodity *n*, $(1/2)q_n^0 + (1/2)q_n^1$. We call an indicator I^{GB} of the type defined by Equation (103), where M(a, b) is a *general homogeneous symmetric mean* of the positive quantities *a* and *b*, a *generalized Bennet indicator* of price change.

An interesting special case of a homogeneous symmetric mean is the mean of order *r*, M_r, defined as follows:

$$M_r(a, b) \equiv [(1/2)a^r + (1/2)b^r]^{1/r}; \quad r \neq 0; \tag{104}$$

$$M_0(a, b) = a^{1/2} b^{1/2}. \tag{105}$$

Means of the *r*th order (for *r* a positive or negative integer) were defined by Schlömilch (1858: 303), who showed that $M_r(a, b)$ increased as *r* increased if a ≠ b. Dunkel (1909: 27) showed that M_r could be defined by Equations (104) and (105) for all real numbers *r*, and he showed that M_r increased as *r* increased if a ≠ b. The term "mean of order *r*" was used by Darmois (1928: 31), who also allowed for general positive weights p_i summing to one to replace the equal weights 1/2 in Equations (104) and (105). The properties of means of order *r* are documented in Hardy, Littlewood, and Pòlya (134: 12–21).

If we replace the general mean *M* in Equation (103) by the mean of order *r*, M_r, defined by Equations (104) and (105), we obtain the *mean of order r generalized Bennet indicator* of price change I^{GBr}:

$$I^{GBr}(p^0, p^1, q^0, q^1) \equiv \sum_{n=1}^{N} I_n^{GBr}(p_n^0, p_n^1, q_n^0, q_n^1), \tag{106}$$

where the indicator of price change for commodity *n*, I_n^{GBr}, is defined as:

$$I_n^{GBr}(p_n^0, p_n^1, q_n^0, q_n^1) \equiv M_r(q_n^0, q_n^1)[p_n^1 - p_n^0]. \tag{107}$$

What are the axiomatic properties of the indicator of price change I_n^{GBr}?

Proposition 11: $I_n^{GBr}(p_n^0, p_n^1, q_n^0, q_n^1)$ defined by Equation (107) satisfies all of the tests listed in Section IV above if $r = 1$ but fails the monotonicity tests A7 and A8, the price weights symmetry test (A18) and the factor reversal test (A19) if $r \neq 1$.

Proof of A3: Use $M_r(q_n, q_n) = q_n$.
Proof of A4: Use $\min\{q_n^0, q_n^1\} \leq M_R(q_n^0, q_n^1) \leq \max\{q_n^0, q_n^1\}$.
Proof of A5 and A6: Use $M_r(q_n^0, q_n^1) > 0$ if $q_n^0 > 0$, $q_n^1 > 0$.
Proof of A7: Define the corresponding volume indicator $V^{GBR}{}_n$ by:

$$V_n^{GBR}(p_n^0, p_n^1, q_n^0, q_n^1) = p_n^1 q_n^1 - p_n^0 q_n^0 - I_n^{GBR}(p_n^0, p_n^1, q_n^0, q_n^1). \tag{108}$$

For A7 to be true, we require that $\partial V^{GBR}{}_n(p_n^0, p_n^1, q_n^0, q_n^1)/\partial q_n^1 > 0$, except possibly at isolated points. Using Equations (107) and (108), this inequality becomes:

$$p_n^1 - (p_n^1 - p_n^0)\partial M_r(q_n^0, q_n^1)/\partial q_n^1 > 0. \tag{109}$$

Letting p_n^0 tend to zero, Equation (109) becomes

$$p_n^1[1 - \partial M_r(q_n^0, q_n^1)/\partial q_n^1] > 0. \tag{110}$$

Using $p_n^1 > 0$ and performing the differentiation of M_r assuming that $r \neq 0$ and $r \neq 1$, Equation (110) is equivalent to

$$\left[(1/2)(q_n^0, q_n^1)^r + (1/2)\right]^{(1-r)/r} < 2, \tag{111}$$

which is not true for all positive q_n^0 and q_n^1. For $r = 0$, (110) is equivalent to

$$(q_n^0/q_n^1)^{1/2} < 2, \tag{112}$$

which again is not true for all positive q_n^0 and q_n^1. Of course, if $r = 1$, Equation (110) becomes $p_n^1[1 - (1/2)] > 0$, which is true.

Proof of A8: Similar to the proof of A7.
Proof of A9: Follows from A2 and A5.
Proof of A10: Follows from A2 and A6.
Proof of A11: By assumption, $q_n^1 > q_n^0$. Hence, by the properties of M_r:

$$q_n^0 < M_r(q_n^0, q_n^1) < q_n^1 \quad \text{or} \tag{113}$$

$$-q_n^1 < -M_r(q_n^0, q_n^1) < -q_n^0. \tag{114}$$

If $p_n^1 = p_n^0$, the desired inequality follows immediately. Now consider the case where:

$$p_n^1 > p_n^0. \tag{115}$$

We have:

$$\begin{aligned}
&p_n^1 q_n^1 - p_n^0 q_n^0 - M_r(q_n^0, q_n^1)(p_n^1 - p_n^0) \\
&> p_n^1 q_n^1 - p_n^0 q_n^0 - q_n^1(p_n^1 - p_n^0) \quad \text{using Equations (114) and (115)} \\
&= p_n^0(q_n^1 - q_n^0) \\
&> 0 \quad \text{using} \quad p_n^0 > 0 \quad \text{and} \quad q_n^1 - q_n^0 > 0,
\end{aligned}$$

which is the desired inequality. Now consider the case where:

$$p_n^1 < p_n^0. \tag{116}$$

We have:

$$p_n^1 q_n^1 - p_n^0 q_n^0 - M_r(q_n^0, q_n^1)(p_n^1 - p_n^0)$$
$$> p_n^1 q_n^1 - p_n^0 q_n^0 - q_n^1(p_n^1 - p_n^0) \quad \text{using Equations (113) and (116)}$$
$$= p_n^0(q_n^1 - q_n^0)$$
$$> 0 \quad \text{using} \quad p_n^1 > 0 \quad \text{and} \quad q_n^1 - q_n^0 > 0,$$

which is the desired inequality.

Proof of A12: Similar to the proof of A11.
Proof of A13: Use $M_r(\lambda q_n^0, \lambda q_n^1) = \lambda M_r(q_n^0, q_n^1)$.
Proof of A15: Use $M_r(\lambda q_n^0, \lambda q_n^1) = \lambda M_r(q_n^0, q_n^1)$.
Proof of A16: Use $M_r(q_n^0, q_n^1) = M_r(q_n^1, q_n^0)$.
Proof of A17: Use $M_r(q_n^0, q_n^1) = M_r(q_n^1, q_n^0)$.
Q.E.D.

The above proposition shows that the mean of order *r* generalized Bennet indicators of price change, $I^{GBr}(p^0, p^1, q^0, q^1)$ have fairly good axiomatic properties. The failure of the price weights symmetry test A18 and the factor reversal test A19 is not particularly bothersome, but the failure of the two quantity monotonicity tests A7 and A8 when $r \neq 1$ is troublesome. However, the failure of I^{GBr} to satisfy A7 and A8 for $r \neq 1$ highlights the superiority of the Bennet indicator $I^B(= I^{GB1})$, which does satisfy these important monotonicity tests.

The following proposition shows that the mean of order *r* generalized Bennet indicators of price change are pseudo-superlative.

Proposition 12: The mean of order *r* generalized Bennet indicators of price change $I^{GBr}(p^0, p^1, q^0, q^1)$ approximate the Bennet indicator $I^B(p^0, p^1, q^0, q^1)$ and the superlative indicators of price change to the second order at any point where $p^0 = p^1$ and $q^0 = q^1$.

Proof: Straightforward computations.

Instead of using a mean of order *r*, $M_r(q_n^0, q_n^1)$, to replace the general homogeneous symmetric mean *M* in the definition of the family of generalized Bennet indicators of price change, Equation (103) above, we could use the logarithmic mean, $L(q_n^0, q_n^1)$. Thus we define the *logarithmic mean generalized Bennet indicator* of price change I^{GBL} as follows:

$$I^{GBL}(p^0, p^1, q^0, q^1) \equiv \sum_{n=1}^{N} I_n^{GBL}(p_n^0, p_n^1, q_n^0, q_n^1), \tag{117}$$

where the indicator of price change for commodity *n* is defined as:

$$I_n^{GBL}(p_n^0, p_n^1, q_n^0, q_n^1) \equiv L(q_n^0, q_n^1)[p_n^1 - p_n^0]. \tag{118}$$

Perhaps somewhat surprisingly, the logarithmic mean generalized Bennet indicator of price change, I^{GBL}, has almost the same axiomatic properties as the mean of order *r* generalized Bennet indicators of price change, I^{GBr}, for $r \neq 1$.

Proposition 13: $I^{GBL}{}_n(p_n^0, p_n^1, q_n^0, q_n^1)$ defined by Equation (118) satisfies all of the tests listed in Section IV above except the price weights symmetry test A18 and the factor reversal test A19.

Proof: Except for A7 and A8, the proof is analogous to the corresponding proofs of Proposition 11.

Proof of A7: We need to show that the following counterpart to Equation (110) is true:

$$p_n^1[1 - \partial L(q_n^0, q_n^1)/\partial q_n^1] > 0, \tag{119}$$

except possibly at isolated points. Performing the differentiation in Equation (119) and using $p_n^1 > 0$, we see that Equation (119) is equivalent to:

$$[-\ln(q_n^0/q_n^1) + (q_n^0/q_n^1) - 1]/[\ln(q_n^0/q_n^1)]^2 < 1, \tag{120}$$

provided that $q_n^0 \neq q_n^1$. Letting $x \equiv q_n^0/q_n^1$, Equation (120) is equivalent to

$$f(x) \equiv [\ln x]^2 + \ln x - x + 1 > 0. \tag{130}$$

Using calculus, we find that f(x) attains a strict global minimum over x > 0 at x = 1 where f(1) = 0. Thus Equation (130) is true except at the single point x = 1 and hence Equation (120) is true if $q_n^0 > 0$, $q_n^1 > 0$ and $q_n^0 \neq q_n^1$.

Proof of A8: The counterpart to Equation (119) that we need to show is true is

$$-p_n^0[1 - \partial L(q_n^0, q_n^1)/\partial q_n^0] < 0. \tag{131}$$

Assuming that $q_n^0 \neq q_n^1$, Equation (131) is equivalent to

$$\partial L(q_n^0, q_n^1)/\partial q_n^0 = [\ln(q_n^0/q_n^1) - 1 + (q_n^1/q_n^0)]/[\ln(q_n^0/q_n^1)]^2 < 1. \tag{132}$$

Letting $x = q_n^0/q_n^1$, Equation (132) is equivalent to

$$g(x) \equiv [\ln x]^2 - \ln x + 1 - x^{-1} > 0. \tag{133}$$

Again using calculus, we find that g(x) attains a strict global minimum over $x > 0$ at $x = 1$ where $g(1) = 0$. Thus Equation (131) is true if $q_n^0 \neq q_n^1$ and A8 follows.

Note that the proof of the above proposition shows that the derivatives of the logarithmic mean L(a, b) with respect to *a* or *b* are between 0 and 1. It is this boundedness property that allows I^{GBL} to satisfy A7 and A8, whereas the unbounded nature of the derivatives of $M_r(a, b)$ causes I^{GBr} to fail A7 and A8 for $r \neq 1$.

Since the tests A18 and A19 are not very important, Proposition 13 tells us that the logarithmic mean generalized Bennet indicator of price change I^{GBL} has almost the same excellent axiomatic properties as the Bennet indicator, I^B. The following proposition shows that I^{GBL} is also a pseudosuperlative indicator of price change.

Proposition 14: The logarithmic mean generalized Bennet indicator of price change $I^{GBL}(p^0, p^1, q^0, q^1)$ approximates the Bennet indicator $I^B(p^0, p^1, q^0, q^1)$ and the superlative indicators of price change to the second order at any point where $p^0 = p^1$ and $q^0 = q^1$.

Proof: Straightforward computations.

Recall that the Montgomery and Bennet indicators of price change for commodity *n* could be obtained by integrating under the "supply" curve $s_n(p_n)$ using Equation (23), where s_n was defined by Equations (22) and (32), respectively. It turns out that the commodity *n* logarithmic mean generalized Bennet indicator defined by Equation (118) can be given a similar interpretation. Thus we define the following exponential "supply" curve as follows:

$$s_n(p_n) \equiv \alpha_n e^{\beta_n p_n}; \quad n = 1, 2, \ldots, N, \tag{134}$$

where the α_n and β_n are constants. If s_n is defined by Equation (134), then it can be verified that

$$\int_{p_n^0}^{p_n^1} s_n(p)dp = I_n^{GBL}(p_n^0, p_n^1, q_n^0, q_n^1); \quad n = 1, \ldots, N, \tag{135}$$

where q_n^0 and q_n^1 are defined by

$$q_n^0 \equiv \alpha_n e^{\beta_n p_n^0}; \, q_n^1 = \alpha_n e^{\beta_n p_n^1}. \tag{136}$$

Note that $q_n^1/q_n^0 = \exp[\beta_n(p_n^1 - p_n^0)]$ and thus if $p_n^0 \neq p_n^1$, then β_n can be determined from the data as

$$\beta_n \equiv [\ln q_n^1 - \ln q_n^0]/1[p_n^1 - p_n^0]. \tag{137}$$

Once β_n has been determined, α_n can be determined using Equation (136).

We conclude this appendix by tabling a few of the mean of order *r* generalized Bennet indicators (for $r = 0$, 1/2, 1 and 2) and the logarithmic mean generalized Bennet indicator I^{GBL} using the Fisher (1922) data that we used earlier.

Note that the average I^{GBr} increases as *r* increases. This result *must* hold if all of the period-to-period price increases are positive, since the mean of order *r* quantity weights $M_r(q_n^0, q_n^1)$ increase as *r* increases (by the Schlömilch-Dunkel inequalities). Note also that the logarithmic mean generalized Bennet indicators of price change are between the corresponding mean of order *r* indicators for $r = 0$ and $r = 1/2$.

Table 2

Comparison of Mean of Order *r* and Logarithmic GB Indicator

Year	I^{GBO}	I^{GBL}	$I^{GBl/2}$	$I^{GB1} = I^B$	I^{GB2}
1914	17.3	16.9	16.7	16.1	15.0
1915	13.4	13.6	13.7	13.9	14.5
1916	2,088.5	2,092.1	2,093.9	2,099.3	2,109.8
1917	7,450.8	7,456.8	7,459.7	7,468.6	7,486.3
1918	2,587.3	2,588.7	2,589.4	2,591.5	2,595.7
Average	2,431.5	2,433.6	2,434.7	2,437.9	2,444.3

Again, if all price changes are positive, this result must hold since Diewert (1978: 898) showed that the logarithmic mean L(a, b) was bounded from below by $M_0(a, b)$ and from above by $M_{1/3}(a, b)$.

We turn now to generalizations of the Montgomery indicator of price change.

APPENDIX 3

Generalized Montgomery Indicators of Price Change

Generalized Montgomery indicators of price change have the form

$$I^{GM}(p^0, p^1, q^0, q^1) \equiv \sum_{n=1}^{N} M(p_n^0, q_n^0, p_n^1, q_n^1)\ln(p_n^1/p_n^0), \qquad (138)$$

where *M* is a general homogeneous symmetric mean. Of course, Montgomery chose the general mean *M* to be the logarithmic mean *L*. In the present appendix, we will replace the general mean *M* that appears in Equation (138) by the mean of order *r* defined by Equations (104) and (105). Thus we define the mean of order *r* generalized Montgomery indicator of price change as

$$I^{GMr}(p^0, p^1, q^0, q^1) \equiv \sum_{n=1}^{N} I_n^{GMr}(p_n^0, p_n^1, q_n^0, q_n^1), \qquad (139)$$

where the indicator of price change for commodity *n*, I_n^{GMr} is defined as

$$I^{GMr}(p_n^0, p_n^1, q_n^0, q_n^1) \equiv M_r(p_n^0 q_n^0, p_n^1 q_n^1)\ln(p_n^1/p_n^0). \qquad (140)$$

What are the axiomatic properties of the indicator of price change I_n^{GMr}? The following proposition answers this question.

Proposition 15: $I^{GMR}{}_n(p_n^0, p_n^1, q_n^0, q_n^1)$ defined by Equation (140) fails tests A3–A8, A17–A19, and at least one of tests A11 and A12. I_n^{GMr} passes the remaining tests listed in Section IV above.

Proof of A3: Note that if $p_n^1 \neq p_n^0$, then

$$I_n^{GMr}(p_n^0, p_n^1, q_n, q_n) = M_r(p_n^0, p_n^1)q_n \ln(p_n^1/p_n^0) \neq (p_n^1 - p_n^0)q_n. \qquad (141)$$

In order for equality to hold in Equation (141), we would require that $M_r(p_n^0, p_n^1) = (p_n^1 - p_n^0)/\ln(p_n^1/p_n^0)$; that is, we would require that

$M_r(p_n^0, p_n^1)$ equals the logarithmic mean, $L(p_n^0, p_n^1)$, which is not possible for any *r*.

Proof of A4: Note the A4 reduces to A3 when $q_n^0 - q_n^1$. Since A3 fails, so does A4.

Proof of A5–A8: Similar to the proof of A5–A8 in Proposition 3.

Proof of A11 and A12: From Equation (141), when $q_n^0 = q_n^1$, we have

$$p_n^1 q_n^1 - p_n^0 q_n^0 - M_r(p_n^0, q_n^0, p_n^1, q_n^1)\ln(p_n^1/p_n^0) \neq 0. \qquad (142)$$

Hence by the continuity of M_r, for $q_n^0 \neq q_n^1$ but q_n^0 close to q_n^1, Equation (142) will still hold. Hence one of the tests A11 and A12 will fail to hold.

Q.E.D.

Proposition 15 shows that the axiomatic properties of the mean of order *r* generalized Montgomery indicators, $I^{GMr}(p^0, p^1, q^0, q^1)$, are not good. In particular, the failure of the quantity identity test A3 is devastating to the usefulness of these indexes in practice. Nevertheless, from a numerical point of view, the indicator I^{GMr} is pseudosuperlative, as the following proposition shows.

Proposition 16: The mean of order *r* generalized Montgomery indicators $I^{GMr}(p^0, p^1, q^0, q^1)$ approximate the Bennet indicator $I^D(p^0, p^1, q^0, q^1)$ and the superlative indicators of price change to the second order at any point where $p^0 = p^1$ and $q^0 = q^1$.

Proof: Routine computations.

The results in Appendices 2 and 3 solidify the position of the Bennet indicator of price change I^B as being the best (against the competitors we have considered) from the axiomatic point of view. The logarithmic mean generalized Bennet indicator I^{GBL} considered in Appendix 2 above is a close runner-up in the axiomatic sweepstakes, failing only the rather unimportant tests A18 and A19. However, the geometric interpretation for the Bennet indicator I^B (recall Figure 2 above), which rests on the assumption of partial equilibrium linear "supply" functions in Equation (34), is more attractive than the nonlinear exponential "supply" functions of Equation (134), which in turn provide a geometric interpretation for the logarithmic indicator I^{GBL}. Thus the Bennet indicator I^{B} appears to be a worthy "ideal" indicator counterpart to the Fisher "ideal" index P_F.

Notes

1. Diewert (1993a: 43, 1993c: 24) mentions Bennet's approach and Balk (1996: 358) explains one of Montgomery's (1937) main results. However, there are some more recent papers that are related to our topic, including those of Vartia (1976a, 1976b), Törnqvist, Vartia, and Vartia (1985), and Balk (1996).

2. See, for example, Diewert (1995: 20–23) and Hill (1996: 43). Balk (1998) considered the axiomatic properties of a unit value price index.

3. Index number theorists, from the very beginning of the subject, have repeatedly emphasized that the construction of index numbers cannot be divorced from their ultimate purpose. Consider the following quotations:

> The answer to the question what is the *Mean* of a given set of magnitudes cannot in general be found, unless there is given also the object for the sake of which a mean value is required. (F. Y. Edgeworth 1988: 347)
>
> What index numbers are "best"? Naturally much depends on the purpose in view. (Fisher 1921: 533)
>
> In constructing an index number by which to measure the change of prices between two dates there are, in general, four chief problems:
>
> (1) To decide on the exact *field* of items to be covered, implying specifically:
> (a) A group of *prices* (p's) to be indexed and
> (b) A group of *quantities* (q's) to be used in forming weights expressing the relative importance of the respective items in the included field;
> (2) To select, from this whole field of items, the best *sample* to represent it;
> (3) To select the best *formula* to be used;
> (4) To select the best *base*, or system of bases . . .
>
> The first problem, that of delimiting the field, is one the solution of which depends eminently on the purpose in view. (Fisher 1927: 419–420)
>
> Once the question has been refined, the development of a measure that would answer the question is a technical task. To be sure, the formulation of indexing objectives is by far the most difficult task, and it is not entirely an economic one. (Jack E. Triplett 1983: 476)

4. Miller (1984: 146) describes the net income and productivity analysis system used by AT&T as an example of a firm that uses a profit change decomposition as a performance evaluation tool. The price change term is called "price recovery" and the quantity change term is called "productivity." Compensation committees of boards of directors should also find profit change decompositions useful when determining bonuses for management.

5. The (cost) system should provide for showing daily, weekly, or monthly, as desired, increases or decreases in cost:

> Resulting from variations in the purchase price of material,
>
> Resulting from variations in the efficiency of the use of material . . . (G. Chester Harrison 1918: 275)

6. More recent contributors include Harberger (1971) and Diewert (1976a, 1992a).

7. Bennet was a civil servant in the Ministry of Finance in Cairo in 1920.

8. See Mensah (1982), Marcinko and Petri (1984), and Darrough (1986). Barlev and Callen (1986) contrast the ratio approach to the measurement of efficiency change (the economist's traditional productivity measurement approach) with the difference approach (the accountant's variance analysis approach).

9. Bert Balk found this paper in the Statistics Netherlands library. It was privately printed and circulated by Montgomery who was at that time the Chief of Section in the Bureau of Economic Social Studies of the International Institute of Agriculture in Rome. Later, he expanded this paper into the book, Montgomery (1937), where he notes that he was a member of the Econometric Society and had an MA and MSc. Unfortunately, only Diewert (1993c: 24) seems to have referred to Montgomery (1929), and only Diewert (1993c: 24) and Balk (1995: 73, 1996: 358) have referred to Montgomery (1937).

10. However, situations where a commodity changes from being an input in one period to an output in the other period cannot be modeled by Montgomery type indicators.

11. Cisbani (1938: 24) refers to a family of generalized means for two variables introduced by L. Galvani in 1927 that includes the logarithmic mean. Dodd (1941: 422) refers to the work of Cisbani and uses the term "logarithmic mean." For a generalization of the logarithmic mean to *N* variables, see Pittenger (1985). For more accessible discussions of the logarithmic mean, see Carlson (1972) or Lorenzen (1990).

12. $M(x_1, \ldots, x_N)$ is a homogeneous symmetric mean if *M* is a continuous, increasing, symmetric, and (positively) homogeneous of degree one function over its domain of definition; see Diewert (1993b: 361–364).

13. Bennet (1920: 456) used a diagram similar to Figure 2 except he had a negatively sloped demand curve join the points A and B.

14. Montgomery (1929: 3) described this test as follows: "The formula which represents Vq_1 must be the same as the formula which represents Vp_1 with the factors p and q reversed." Montgomery's (1929: 4) last major test was the following one: if $q_n^1/q_n^0 = (p_n^1/p_n^0)$, then $V_n(p_n^0, p_n^1, q_n^0, q_n^1)/I_n(p_n^0, p_n^1, q_n^0, q_n^1) = a$.

15. Actually, this technique is due to Walsh (1921b: 541–542) who discovered it when discussing Fisher (1921).

16. See Diewert (1992b).

17. Many index number theorists objected to Fisher's (1922) factor reversal test. Samuelson and Swamy (1974: 575) commented on this test as follows: "A man and his wife should be properly matched; but that does not mean I should marry my identical twin!"

18. The consumer theory application that we are outlining in this section is isomorphic to the producer's problem of minimizing cost subject to a production function constraint. In this case, interpret c(p) as the producer's unit cost function, q as a vector of inputs, and f(q) as output. A similar reinterpretation of the results of this section is possible for the case of a producer maximizing revenue subject to an aggregate input constraint. In this case, c(p) is a unit input revenue function, q is a vector of outputs, *min* is replaced by *max*, and f is an input requirements function. Finally, our results can also be reinterpreted in a profit-maximization model. In this case, we assume that the producer's period t profit function has the form $\alpha^t\pi(p^t)$, $t = 0, 1$, where α^t is interpreted as a period t efficiency factor. In this case, $c(p^t)$ is $\pi(p^t)$ and $f(q^t)$ is replaced by the efficiency factor α^t.

19. See Diewert (1976b: 130–134).

20. Törnqvist (1936) does not have Equation (67) explicitly, but Törnqvist and Törnqvist (1937: 18) does have Equation (67), where it is termed the "geometric ideal." This index first appeared as Formula 123 in Fisher (1922: 473). Fisher (1922: 265) listed it as one of his best 29 formulae. Walsh (1921a: 97) used the geometric average of the weights s^0_n and s^1_n in place of the arithmetic average in Equation (67). Finally, Persons (1928: 21–22) recommended Equation (67) and eight other indexes as being "best" from the viewpoint of his test approach.

21. See Diewert (1976b: 121).

22. Fisher (1922: 247) was the first to use the term *superlative* to describe price indexes P that were numerically close to his ideal index P^F defined by Equation (66). Diewert (1976b, 1992a: 578) exhibits several entire families of superlative indexes.

23. See Diewert (1978: 887–888, 1992a: 578).

24. Montgomery (1937: 40–48) also established a version of Vartia's (1976a: 134, 1976b: 24–25) results on the consistency in aggregation of the Vartia I price index.

25. We shall call an indicator *pseudo-superlative* if it has the same first and second partial derivatives as a superlative indicator around an equal price and quantity point. Thus the Bennet and Montgomery indicators, I^B and I^M, are pseudo-superlative. We note that the Paasche and Laspeyres indicators, I^P and I^L, only approximate superlative (and pseudo-superlative) indexes to the first order around an equal price and quantity point.

References

Balk, B. M. (1995). "Axiomatic Price Index Theory: A Survey." *International Statistical Review* 63: 69–93.

——. (1996). "Consistency in Aggregation and Stuvel Indices." *Review of Income and Wealth* 42: 353–363.

——. (1998). *On the Use of Unit Value Indices as Consumer Price Subindices.* Voorburg, the Netherlands: Division of Research and Development, Statistics Netherlands.

Barlev, B., and J. L. Callen. (1986). "Total Factor Productivity and Cost Variances: Survey and Analysis." *Journal of Accounting Literature* 5: 35–56.

Bennet, T. L. (1920). "The Theory of Measurement of Changes in Cost of Living." *Journal of the Royal Statistics Society* 83: 455–462.

Carlson, B. C. (1972). "The Logarithmic Mean." *American Mathematical Monthly* 79: 615–618.

Cisbani, R. (1938). "Contributi alla teoria delle medie." *Metron* 13(2): 23–59.

Darmois, G. (1928). *Statistique Mathematique.* Paris: Gaston Doin.

Darrough, M. N. (1986). "Variance Analysis: A Unifying Cost Function Approach." *Contemporary Accounting Research* 5: 199–221.

Davies, G. R. (1924). "The Problem of a Standard Index Number Formula." *Journal of the American Statistical Association* 19: 180–188.

——. (1932). "Index Numbers in Mathematical Economics." *Journal of the American Statistical Association* 27: 58–64.

Diewert, W. E. (1976a). "Harberger's Welfare Indicator and Revealed Preference Theory." *American Economic Review* 66: 143–152.

——. (1976b). "Exact and Superlative Index Numbers." *Journal of Econometrics* 4: 114–145.

——. (1978). "Superlative Index Numbers and Consistency in Aggregation." *Econometrica* 46: 883–900.

. (1992a). "Exact and Superlative Welfare Change Indicators." *Economic Inquiry* 30: 565–582.

——. (1992b). "Fisher Ideal Output, Input and Productivity Indexes Revisited." *Journal of Productivity Analysis* 3: 211–248.

——. (1993a). "The Early History of Price Index Research." In *Essasys in Index Number Theory*, Vol. 1. Eds. W. E. Diewert and A. O. Nakamura. Amsterdam: North-Holland.

——. (1993b). "Symmetric Means and Choice Under Uncertainty." In *Essasys in Index Number Theory*, Vol. 1. Eds. W. E. Diewert and A. O. Nakamura. Amsterdam: North-Holland.

——. (1993c). "Overview of Volume I." In *Essasys in Index Number Theory*, Vol. 1. Eds. W. E. Diewert and A. O. Nakamura. Amsterdam: North-Holland.

——. (1995). *Axiomatic and Economic Approaches to Elementary Price Indexes.* Discussion Paper No. 95-01. Vancouver, Canada: Department of Economics, University of British Columbia.

Dodd, E. L. (1941). "Some Generalization of the Logarithmic Mean and of Similar Means of Two Variables Which Become Indeterminate When the Two Variates Are Equal." *Annals of Mathematical Statistics* 12: 422–428.

Dunkel, O. (1909). "Genearlized Geometric Means and Algebraic Equations." *Annals of Mathematics* 10(4): 21–32.

Edgeworth, F. Y. (1888). "Some New Methods of Measuring Variation in General Prices." *Journal of the Royal Statistical Society* 51: 346–368.

Fisher, I. (1911). *The Purchasing Power of Money.* London: Macmillan.

——. (1921). "The Best Form of Index Number." *Journal of the American Statistical Association* 17: 533–537.

——. (1922). *The Making of Index Numbers.* Boston: Houghton-Mifflin.

——. (1927). "The 'Total Value Criterion': A New Principle in Index Number Construction." *Journal of the American Statistical Association* 22: 419–441.

——. (1933). "Statistics in Service of Economics." *Journal of the American Statistical Association* 28: 1–13.

Harberger, A. C. (1971). "Basic Postulates for Applied Welfare Economics: An Interpretive Essay." *Journal of Economic Literature* 9: 785–797.

Hardy, G. H., J. E. Littlewood, and G. Polya. (1934). *Inequalities.* Cambridge: Cambridge University Press.

Harrison, G. C. (1918). "Cost Accounting to Aid Production." *Industrial Management* 56(Part I, II, and III): 273–282, 391–398, 456–463.

Hicks, J. R. (1940). "The Valuation of the Social Income." *Economica* 7: 105–140.

——. (1941–1942). "Consumers' Surplus and Index Numbers." *Review of Economic Studies* 9: 126–137.

——. (1945–1946). "The Generalized Theory of Consumers' Surplus." *Review of Economic Studies* 13: 68–74.

——. (1946). *Value and Capital.* 2nd ed. Oxford: Claredon Press.

Hill, P. (1996). *Inflation Accounting.* Paris: OECD.

Hotelling, H. (1938). "The General Welfare in Relation to Problems of Taxation and of Railway and Utility Rates." *Econometrica* 6: 242–269.

Konüs, A. A. ([1924] 1939). "The Problem of the True Index of the Cost of Living." Trans. *Econometrica* 7: 10–29.

Lorenzen, G. (1990). "A Unified Approach to the Calculation of Growth Rates." *American Statistician* 44: 148–150.

Marcinko, D., and E. Petri. (1984). "Use of the Production Function in Calculation of Standard Cost Variances—An Extension." *Accounting Review* 59: 488–495.

Marshall, A. (1890). *Principles of Economics.* London: Macmillan Co.

Mensah, Y. M. (1982). "A Dynamic Approach to the Evaluation of Input-Variable Cost Center Performance." *Accounting Review* 57: 681–700.

Middleditch, L. (1918). "Should Accounts Reflect the Changing Value of the Dollar?" *Journal of Accountancy* 25: 114–120.

Miller, D. M. (1984). "Profitability Equals Productivity Plus Price Recovery." *Harvard Business Review* 62(3): 145–153.

Montgomery, J. K. (1929). "Is There a Theoretically Correct Price Index of a Group of Commodities?" Rome: Roma L'Universale Tipogr. Poliglotta (privately printed paper).

——. (1937). *The Mathematical Problem of the Price Index.* Orchard House, Westminster: P.S. King & Son.

Persons, W. M. (1928). *The Construction of Index Numbers.* Cambridge, MA: Riverside Press.

Pittenger, A. O. (1985). "The Logarithmic Mean in n Variables." *American Mathematical Monthly* 92: 99–104.

Pollak, R. A. (1989). *The Theory of the Cost-of-Living Index.* Oxford: Oxford University Press.

Samuleson, P. A., and S. Swamy. (1974). "Invariant Economic Index Numbers and Canonical Duality: Survey and Synthesis." *American Economic Review* 64: 566–593.

Schlömilch, O. (1858). "Uber Mittelgrössen verschiedener Ordnungen." *Zeitschrift für Mathematick und Physik* 3: 303–308.

Solomons, D. (1968). "The Historical Development of Costing." In *Studies in Cost Analysis.* Ed. D. Solomons. Homewood, IL: Richard D. Irwin.

Törnqvist, L. (1936). "The Bank of Finland's Consumption Price Index." *Bank of Finland Monthly Bulletin* 10: 1–8.

Törnqvist, L., and E. Törnqvist. (1937). "Vilket är förhällandet mellan finska markens och svenska kronans köpkraft?" *Ekonomiska Samfundets Tidskrift* 39: 1–39. Rpt. in (1981) *Collected Scientific Papers of Leo Törnqvist.* Helsinki: Research Institute of the Finnish Economy.

Törnqvist, L., P. Vartia, and Y. O. Vartia. (1985). "How Should Relative Changes Be Measured?" *American Statistician* 39: 43–6.

Triplett, J. E. (1983). "Escalation Measures: What Is the Answer? What Is the Question?" In *Price Level Measurement.* Eds. W. E. Diewert and C. Montmarquette. Ottawa: Statistics Canada.

Vartia, Y. O. (1976a). *Relative Changes and Index Numbers.* Helsinki: Research Institute of the Finnish Economy.

——. (1976b). "Ideal Log-Change Index Numbers." *Scandinavian Journal of Statistics* 3: 121–126.

Walsh, C. M. (1901). *The Measurement of General Exchange Value.* New York: Macmillan and Co.

——. (1921a). *The Problem of Estimation.* London: P.S. King & Son.

——. (1921b). "Discussion of the Best Form of Index Number." *Journal of the American Statistical Association* 17: 537–544.

Whitmore, J. (1908). "Shoe Factory Accounts." *Journal of Accountancy* 6: 12–25.

——. (1931). "Poverty and Riches of 'Standard Costs.'" *Journal of Accountancy* 51: 9–23.

Comment on W. Erwin Diewert's, "Index Number Theory Using Differences Rather Than Ratios"

By MATTHEW D. SHAPIRO*

ABSTRACT. A comment on the article by W. Erwin Diewert in this volume.

I

Fisher

A SUBSTANTIAL FRACTION of what we know about how to construct measurements that are good approximations to the change in the cost of living owes to Irving Fisher. His Ideal price index was invented to address the vexing, although fairly narrowly defined, question of how to measure changes in the purchasing power of money. Fisher's thinking about index numbers is based on economics rather than accounting, based on prices and quantities rather than prices alone, and based, perhaps most critically, on multiplication rather than addition. Fisher's index is becoming incorporated in many aspects of the statistical system.

- As of the last major benchmark revision of the National Income and Product Accounts, the Bureau of Economic Analysis has adopted a feasible approximation of Fisher's Ideal index for measuring both the change in price and quantity. This major switch away from double deflation means that—at least for broad aggregates—the national statistics correctly account for the reaction of supply and demand to relative prices.

*Matthew D. Shapiro is Professor of Economics and Research Professor in the Survey Research Center at the University of Michigan. He received B.A. and M.A. degrees from Yale and a Ph.D. from M.I.T. In 1993–1994, he was a senior economist at the Council of Economic Advisers. Shapiro was co-editor of the *American Economic Review* from 1997 to 2000. Prior to joining Michigan's faculty in 1989, Shapiro was an Assistant Professor of Economics at Yale.

The American Journal of Economics and Sociology, Vol. 64, No. 1 (January, 2005).

- Fisher's ideas about how to construct elementary price indexes, in other words, how to average individual observations on the price of bread to obtain a price index for bread, are also gaining currency. Despite stern warnings in Fisher's writings, the Bureau of Labor Statistics has used an arithmetic rather than a geometric average. In the face of growing evidence supporting Fisher's views, the Bureau of Labor Statistics (BLS) experimented with a geometric index and announced its intention to use it for parts of the Consumer Price Index.

Effective January 1999, the BLS began using the geometric formula to aggregate elementary price observations for approximately two-thirds of the items in the CPI. This change should reduce the rate of growth in the CPI by approximately 0.2 percentage points per year.

The Fisherian program for economic measurement does have some features that only an economist could love. For example, C + I + G does not equal Y in quantity or real terms in the National Income and Product Accounts. For some components of demand, the arithmetic is even more startling. For example, the implied level of real spending on computers actually exceeds the total of the subcomponent of investment including computers for some time periods. The Fisherian procedure alerts us to the effect of dramatic changes in relative prices that get swept under the rug by more mechanical procedures.

Fisher's method for calculating price indexes is in the tradition of the Econometric Society and the Cowles Foundation. Researchers in the program of the Econometric Society and Cowles have been willing to push the methodological frontier far ahead of what is practical for current analysis owing to limitations of computing power or data availability. In the case of Fisher's Ideal index and its superlative cousins, the indexes depend on current and historical data on both price and expenditure. The use of base-period expenditure weights in the CPI, for example, is a pragmatic response to having infrequent data on expenditures. More frequent expenditure data are now available. The statistical system has been slow to incorporate these data, especially in the CPI.[1] Moreover, with the growing amount of data available electronically—from scanners or other computerized transactions—there is the possibility for computing Fisher Ideal indexes virtually in real time.

II

Diewert

WHILE IT SHOULD NOT surprise us, it is not apparent on its face that Fisher's Ideal index performs far better than a number of seemingly plausible alternatives. We owe this knowledge to the extremely important work of Erwin Diewert (1976), who proved that under suitable assumptions, it was a second-order approximation to the true cost of living. Since his seminal paper in 1976, Diewert has continued an important program of expanding and systematizing what we know about index numbers.

The paper for today's session is classic Diewert. In asking how to construct indexes that decompose revenue changes into real and nominal components, it poses a classic question. It then goes on to tell us that a classic question typically has been addressed in a forgotten literature. I doubt that Diewert's present exertions will succeed in elevating Montgomery and Bennet to the index number pantheon that contains Fisher, Törnqvist, and Konüs, but Diewert's elegant resurrection of their work is characteristic of his papers. Indeed, in a literature that perhaps some find prosaic, Diewert's papers stand out for their wit and charm as well as their scholarship.

This paper provides an interesting framework for studying the "supply" curve, that is, the locus traced out by exogenous variation in prices. The approach is to fit exactly (thorough two points) a curve in price-quantity space. Different functional forms of the curve give rise to different exact index formulas for price and quantity. For a given change in revenue, the price effect is the increment to the revenue over the curve. The quantity effect is the increment to revenue under the curve. The different index number formulas give different answers because they make different assumptions about the shape of the curve. These differences are illustrated in Figure 1 and Figure 2 of Diewert's paper. Quantitatively, the difference between the indexes depends on the elasticity of this "supply" curve—not just at a point, but averaged over the region of price and quantity change.

These results are very revealing about how the price and quantity indexes operate. The paper also provides a useful graphical illustration of superlative indicators of price and quantity. Nonetheless, these illustrations have only limited applicability because they rest on the assumption of exogenous price movements. This remark applies to similar exercises with standard index numbers. It should come as no surprise to an audience with its roots in the Cowles Commission that it is impossible to infer changes in economic fundamentals from observations on price and quantity alone in practical applications where changes in revenue arise from a mixture of shifts of supply and demand. There might, however, be circumstances when auxiliary information might permit a shift in revenue to be identified as arriving from a shift in supply. This auxiliary information would be isomorphic to identifying restrictions in the econometric context.

A major limitation of the indexes presented in Diewert's paper relates to what they have to say about inflation. Fisher invented his index numbers to quantify the changes in the purchasing power of money. The results of the paper cannot be applied to measuring inflation, which is inherently multiplicative. Indeed, the framework of the paper applies most naturally to relative prices, as in Section VII of the paper. There is no aggregate analogue to the microeconomic supply-and-demand framework that rationalizes the use of the indexes that Diewert studies.

III

Fisher Again

MOST—IF NOT ALL—of the serious, unsolved problems with price measurement relate to the instability of the economic environment over time. The analytic framework that studies the maximization of time-invariant, additively-separable-across-time utility or profit function abstracts from many of the important changes in the economic environment that should be taken into account in price measurement.

One of the most underdeveloped areas of price and cost-of-living measurement is health care. Consideration of health care demand requires an explicitly intertemporal and lifetime view. Hence, the

Fisher of Ideal indexes needs that framework of the Fisher of the *Theory of Interest,* perhaps with the kibitzing of the Fisher of jogging and wheat germ.

Consider several examples in which the standard question asked in cost-of-living analysis—comparing expenditure needed to deliver base-period utility at current period prices—is completely inadequate.

First, the purchase of life-extending procedures renders endogenous whether the current and subsequent periods of life even enter the calculation for an individual. While exogenous technological advance may be driving price change, it is important to understand how the endogenous response to lower price leads to the purchase of more life-extending and life-enhancing procedures.

Second, changes in the price of health care have a significant impact on the timing of treatment in the course of a disease. For example, the drop in the cost and patient burden of cataract extraction has led to the operation being carried out at decreasing thresholds of visual impairment (see Shapiro, Shapiro, and Wilcox 2001). Hence, though it appears that the flow benefit immediately following surgery has fallen, an appropriate calculation of the benefits of surgery needs to account for the durability of the treatment and the possibility that an early treatment preempts a period of declining health. Although these issues with the purchase of health care have been related to the problem of purchase of a durable good, the mechanics of analyzing durable goods purchases do not apply straightforwardly owing to the time-, age-, or state-of-health-contingency of demand.

Hence, there remain many interesting economic problems to be tackled by Diewert and other students of Fisher's work.

Note

1. It is also possible to get very good approximations of superlative indexes in real time where expenditure data are available only a year or two after the price data are collected. See Shapiro and Wilcox (1997).

References

Diewert, W. Erwin. (1976). "Exact and Superlative Index Numbers." *Journal of Econometrics* 4: 114–145.

Shapiro, Irving, Matthew D. Shapiro, and David W. Wilcox. (2001). "Measuring the Value of Cataract Surgery." In *Medical Care Output and Productivity.* Eds. David M. Cutler and Ernst R. Berndt. Chicago: University of Chicago Press.

Shapiro, Matthew D., and David W. Wilcox. (1997). "Alternative Strategies for Aggregating Prices in the CPI." *Federal Reserve Bank of St. Louis Review* 79 (May/June): 113–125.

Irving Fisher and the Contribution of Improved Longevity to Living Standards

By WILLIAM D. NORDHAUS*

ABSTRACT. It is not widely recognized that conventional measures of national income and output exclude the value of improvements in the health status of the population. The present study discusses the theory of the measurement of national income, proposes a new concept called "health income" that can be used to incorporate improvements in health status, and applies the theory to data for the United States over the 20th century. It concludes that accounting for improvements in the health status would, over the twentieth century in the United States, make a substantial difference to our measures of economic welfare.

I

Introduction

AMONG IRVING FISHER'S many contributions to economics, one that is little noted and scarcely remembered is his emphasis on the economic importance of health. For the most part, his concern was in promoting healthy lifestyles. In addition, he made an early (perhaps the earliest) estimate of the impact of mortality and morbidity on national output.

This essay considers the question of how measures of economic welfare might change if they included measures of health status as well as of conventional consumption. The surprising finding is that

*William D. Nordhaus is Sterling Professor of Economics at Yale University. He is a member of the National Academy of Sciences, a Fellow of the American Academy of Arts and Sciences, and is on the research staffs of the Cowles Foundation and of the National Bureau of Economic Research. He serves on the Congressional Budget Office Panel of Economic Experts and is Chair of the Advisory Committee for the Bureau of Economic Analysis. From 1977 to 1979, he was a member of the President's Council of Economic Advisers, and from 1986 to 1988 he served as the Provost of Yale University. The present research was supported by the National Science Foundation. The author is grateful for research support of Joseph Boyer and for helpful comments from William Brainard, David Cutler, Angus Deaton, Robert Gordon, and T. N. Srinivasan.

The American Journal of Economics and Sociology, Vol. 64, No. 1 (January, 2005).

inclusion of improvements in health status would, over the 20th century in the United States, make a substantial difference to our measures of economic welfare. While Fisher thought and cared deeply about index numbers, measurement of income, utility theory, and health, he never connected these different concepts. On the other hand, he must have had an intuitive understanding of the importance, as suggested by the following passage:

> A large part of our subjective income is due to our conditions of health or disease. . . . [A] healthy body is absolutely essential for receiving and enjoying the income from external wealth. . . . Economists, by fixing attention exclusively on physical phenomena, leave out the most essential element of all, the vigor of human life. The true "wealth of nations" is the health of its individuals. (Barber 1997, Vol. 2: 204)

In the sections that follow, I begin with a brief discussion of Fisher's writings on health. I then provide an analysis of how traditional measures of income might be modified to incorporate changes in mortality and life expectancy. Finally, I make preliminary estimates of the quantitative impact of adjusting national-income measures for mortality.

II

Fisher on Health

FISHER'S CAMPAIGN FOR healthful living today seems quirky. Its origins came when he contracted tuberculosis in the summer of 1898, shortly after having been promoted to full Professor of Political Economy at Yale at the age of 31. As Fisher explained in 1917, it was this experience that opened his eyes to the importance of health:

> I feel a little ashamed to admit that as an economist and as a student of society I had been blind, as the average man or woman of today is blind, to what heath conservation means. Suddenly I discovered I had tuberculosis and took a long enforced vacation. When after three years I went back to Yale, I was unable for two years to do even half a man's work. . . . At length by dint of conscientious application of a dozen or more specific points of hygiene, not only did I succeed in winning back my previous working power, but acquired more than I had ever dreamed of acquiring. (Barber 1997, Vol. 13: 83)

As with all Fisher's passions, he set about studying and proselytizing with enormous vigor. Among his most notable contributions were the establishment of the Life Extension Institute and a book, jointly written with Dr. Eugene Fisk, which stressed rules on individual hygiene (Fisher and Fisk 1915). In this field, as in so many others, Fisher was decades ahead of his time, emphasizing the importance of individual lifestyles. He laid out the Fifteen Rules of Health (see Table 1). Fisher was open—some might say, too open—to every new nostrum, and it is easy to poke fun at them. Among more entertaining rules were "Ventilate your clothes while they are on you," "Eat slowly," and "Eat some hard foods." However, he also emphasized the importance of weight, abstinence from tobacco, alcohol, and drugs, and vigorous exercise. All these sound commonsensical today, but it is striking that the Fisher-Fisk volume was the first important pamphlet emphasizing the importance of lifestyles in addition to antimicrobial health care.

III

Including Health Status in Measures National Income

A. Current Approaches to Measuring the Contribution of Health in the National Accounts

While the GDP and the rest of the National Income and Product Accounts (NIPA) may seem to be arcane concepts, they are truly among the great inventions of the 20th century. Nevertheless, since the beginning, there have been concerns that the accounts are incomplete and misleading because they omit most nonmarket activity. To meet this criticism, private scholars as well as official statistical agencies have begun extending the national accounts to include several nonmarket sectors, including national resources, the environment, transportation, leisure time, and unpaid work.[1]

One question that has been virtually ignored in attempts to extend the national accounts is the need to account adequately for improvements in human health. It is little understood outside the priesthood of national accountants that there is no serious attempt to measure the "real output" of the health care industry. The techniques used to measure the price and quantity of health care are highly defective, and there are *no* attempts to account for improvements in the length of life into current national accounts.

Table 1

Fisher's Fifteen Rules of Health*

The book summarizes in fifteen rules the ways in which the individual has it within his own power to add to his efficiency. These rules are under four heads: Air, Food, Poisons, Activity.

Under Air There Are Five Rules:

1. Ventilate every room you occupy.
2. Ventilate your own clothes while they are on you. In other words, select light, and loose, and porous materials for your clothing. The skin needs the air contact.
3. Live out of doors as much as you can. Seek outdoor avocations and recreations. . . .
4. Sleep out of doors, if it is possible. We do not yet understand what that great sense of well-being is which comes after sleeping out-of-doors, but it is very real.
5. Breathe deeply. Take some long breaths every day systematically. One doctor advises his patients to take 100 long breaths every day. In India, rhythmic deep breathing is a part of the religious system.

Under Food the Four Rules Are:

6. Avoid overeating and overweight. This rule becomes especially important soon after you graduate from college, and therefore it is important before you graduate. It is the rich, overfed sedentary man or woman who later becomes the prey of the wear-and-tear diseases.
7. Avoid overeating of nitrogenous or protein foods. Consequently this rule practically means to avoid overeating of meat and eggs. Such indulgence is really the great dietetic sin of Americans, and one of the chief reasons, I believe, for the fact that in America certain degenerative diseases are more common than in other countries. We eat so excessively of meat, partly because we can afford it, party because of an abnormal appetite coming from the hurry habit. Therefore we who hurry

Table 1 *Continued*

so are heavier meat eaters than the people of Europe and other countries and we pay for that indulgence in high blood pressure and diseases of the kidney.

8. Eat some hard foods, some raw foods and some bulky foods every day. Hard foods exercise the teeth.
9. Eat slowly. The hurry habit is responsible for many evils.

Under Poisons the Four Rules Are:

10. Evacuate thoroughly, regularly and frequently, to avoid "auto intoxication."
11. Stand, sit and walk erect for the same purpose; for bad posture is largely responsible for constipation.
12. Do not allow poisons and infections to enter the body. Among other things this rule means total abstinence from alcoholic beverages and from the use of tobacco.
13. Keep the teeth, gums and tongue clean. Primitive people have perfect sets of teeth without the use of the toothbrush.

Under Activity, There Are Two Rules:

14. Work, play, rest and sleep in moderation and in due relation to each other.
15. Keep a healthful mental attitude, for it is worry rather than work which kills.

*From Barber 1997, Vol. 13. They have been renumbered for this table.

It might be thought that including health status is some radical, far-out, and woolly-headed attempt to incorporate intangible, non-economic, and sociological measures into our social accounts. This argument is wrong; health care expenditures are already included in measures of national income and output. Indeed, they are a growing fraction of GDP—the fraction of personal consumption expenditures devoted to medical care rose from 5.1% in 1959 to 16.7% in 2003. While inclusion of health care is not radical, it is radical to suggest that we should make a serious attempt to measure the *output* of the health care sector and to *value* this output correctly.

Recent economic studies suggest that there is little connection between medical spending and the measured economic value of health-status improvements. At a commonsense level, the lack of connection comes because "real" medical care spending in fact measures spending on inputs rather than on health outcomes. The current approach is to measure health output primarily by the number of physician-visits, the number of hospital days, and similar measures, rather than the actual delivery of services or changes in health status. It may come as a surprise to most non-economists that improvements coming from new products, such as the discovery of antibiotics or the substitution of drugs for invasive surgery, are completely omitted in current measures of real output.

Attempts to measure improvements in the health status of the population—including everything from vaccinations, microsurgery, and new drugs to airbags, exercise, and anti-cigarette advertising—pose a new and difficult challenge to measuring national income. Recently, economists have begun providing better outcome-oriented estimates of the prices and outputs in the health-care sector. One of the most striking findings comes from a study by Cutler, McClellan, Newhouse, and Remler (1998), who estimated that a true price index for the treatment of heart attacks would rise about 5.5% per year more slowly than the corresponding component of the CPI. Similar results were found in studies of treatment for glaucoma by Shapiro and Wilcox and for cataract surgery by Shapiro, Shapiro, and Wilcox.[2]

Given the likelihood that we are dramatically mismeasuring, and almost certainly underestimating, the contribution of improvements in health care to economic welfare, this raises the question of how to proceed to obtain better estimates. One approach would be to continue the approach just described, of constructing better measures of output and prices. This approach was adopted by the Boskin Commission and is the thrust of much current research on health economics.[3]

Another quite different approach, which is used in the present study, is to obtain direct measures of health status, weight them with appropriate prices, and then estimate the value of improvements in health status. This approach is actually much simpler than "fixing" price and output indexes because measures of health status are generally much better than data on the impacts of particular technologies on health status. We will see that following this path has radical impacts on our measures of real income and output.

B. Alternative Measures of National Income

Before proposing alternative concepts, it will be useful to describe different approaches to measuring national income. The concepts of social income and national income go back centuries. They are largely based on the analogous definitions of individual income with appropriate adjustments for aggregation and national boundaries. We can distinguish two fundamentally different approaches to measuring income—one based on production and one based on utility. The former is the basis of modern national-income accounting while the latter is more appropriate when considering sustainable income and the contribution of improvement in health status.

1. *Production-Based Measures (Hicksian Income)*

The modern treatment of social income dates from the writings of J. R. Hicks. When economists and accountants measure national income, they have almost universally relied upon the Hicksian definition. The discussion of social income in *Value and Capital* states: "The purpose of income calculations in practical affairs is to give people an indication of the amount which they can consume without impoverishing themselves" (Hicks 1939: 172). Hicks then goes on to provide his first definition of social income:

> *Income No. 1* is thus the maximum amount which can be spent during a period if there is to be an expectation of maintaining intact the capital value of prospective returns; it equals Consumption plus Capital accumulation. (Hicks 1939: 173, 178, emphasis added)[4]

This definition is what is called "Hicksian income"—the maximum amount that can be consumed while leaving capital intact. In practice, income equals consumption plus a generalized measure of capital accumulation.

The Hicksian concept is the standard definition of net national or domestic product used in the national-income accounts of virtually all nations today. It is *production based* in the sense that it attempts to measure the rate of production at a given time. Such measures are not concerned with the health status of the population or whether people are enjoying that production for a longer lifespan.

2. *Utility-Based Measures (Fisherian Income)*

While standard concepts of income are useful tools for measuring current production, they are not equivalent to economic welfare. The shortcoming of the traditional approach is clear when we consider situations in which technologies are improving or people are living longer. An economy in which people have a per capita income of $20,000 with lives that are nasty, brutish, and short would be ranked as equivalent to one with the same per capita income and lives that are healthy, civilized, and long. In the context of health, the key point is that the same *annual* income with a long and healthy life has a higher living standard than that income with a short and diseased life. Including health status in income is particularly important when a large and growing fraction of our economy is devoted to health care.

An alternative approach is to define income as utility-equivalent consumption.[5] I denote this "Fisherian income" after Irving Fisher, who defined income as the flow of consumption that could be harvested from the nation's capital stock.[6] Under this approach, income is defined as the level of consumption that would give the equivalent level of utility from consumption and other determinants of utility in different situations. This definition has been used to define the level of "sustainable income" in situations in which there is a tug of war between resource exhaustion and technological change.[7] In cases in which lifetimes are fixed, this is equivalent to defining income as the maximum that can be consumed with current assets and current and future incomes.

For concreteness, call this "utility national income" and define it as follows:

> *Definition. Utility national income* is the maximum amount that a nation can consume while ensuring that members of all future generations can have lifetime utility that is at least as high as that of the current generation.

If life expectancy is unchanging, income is the maximum real consumption annuity that a nation can spend out of its resource endowment. The major difference in analyzing living standards with variable lifetimes is to recognize that people are better off when they live longer, and that this fact should be reflected in measures of their incomes and living standards. This approach measures the increased income from longer life expectancies by the consumption equivalent of the utility or value of the health or longevity improvements.

IV

Integrating Health Status into Income Measures

CONSUMPTION AND INCOME are traditionally measured as flows of goods and services (or utilities) during a given period of time. Changes in an individual's health status pose no terribly deep issues of measurement, for we can treat these as new or improved "goods and services" that can be appropriately priced and included in the consumption basket.

Incorporating changes in lifetimes, by contrast, poses qualitatively different problems of measurement. I begin this section by considering a simple life-cycle model of consumption in which there are tradeoffs between life and consumption. I then show how this approach might be used to construct a framework for measuring income.

A. A Life-Cycle Model with Variable Lifetime

We want to examine the gain in "real income" from improved health and life expectancy. We do this in the context of the life-cycle model of consumption. An individual is assumed to value consumption and health according to a lifetime utility function:[8]

$$V[c_t; \theta, \rho, \mu_t] = \int_{\theta}^{\infty} u(c_t) e^{-\rho(t-\theta)} S[\mu_t] dt, \tag{1}$$

where $V[c_t; \theta, \rho, \mu_t]$ is the value at time t of the consumption stream now and in the future faced by an individual of age θ; $u(c_t)$ is the stream of instantaneous utility or felicity of consumption; ρ is the pure rate of individual time preference; $S[u_t]$ is the set of survival probabilities; and μ_t is the set of mortality rates. The key assumption here is that utility is a function of the utility of consumption weighted by the probability of survival. As we will see, the utility function has a natural semi-cardinal interpretation as the value of life extension.

We begin with a simple and tractable assumption about mortality to show the basic relationships; when developing the empirical estimates in later sections we will use more realistic life tables. Consider the simple case in which the survival function is exponential. Equation (1) then becomes:

$$V[c_t;\, \theta,\, \rho,\, \mu_t] = \int_{\theta}^{\infty} u(c_t)e^{-(\rho-\mu)(t-\theta)}dt. \tag{2}$$

We assume that each individual has a given endowment of expected labor income and can buy full-value real annuities with any desired trajectory. We can further simplify for computational purposes (to be relaxed later) by assuming that the real interest rate faced by the individual is equal to the mortality adjusted rate of time preference, $(\rho + \mu)$. Given these assumptions, the individual will choose a consumption annuity that yields constant consumption during the individual's lifetime, $c_t = c^*$. Integrating Equation (2) yields a particularly simple outcome:

$$V[c_t;\, \theta,\, \rho,\, \mu] = u(c^*)/(\rho + \mu). \tag{3}$$

Equation (3) shows that the total utility value of consumption is the utility of the flow of constant consumption discounted by a discount rate that equals the sum of the force of impatience and the force of mortality.

An individual will often face a tradeoff between "health and wealth." What would be the tradeoff given by Equation (3)? At age θ, changes in consumption and health yield:

$$\begin{cases} dV/dc^* = u'(c^*)/(\rho + \mu) \\ dV/d\mu = -u(c^*)/(\rho + \mu)^2. \end{cases} \tag{4}$$

Hence the relative value of consumption and mortality is:

$$dc^*/d\mu = -u(c^*)/[u'(c^*)(\rho + \mu)]. \tag{5}$$

We make two normalizations that will simplify the discussion without loss of generality. First, we simplify by selecting a goods-metric utility function. This gives us a metric in which utility is measured in terms of goods at the equilibrium, which implies that $u'(c^*) = 1$. Second, we chose the units so that zero is the utility at which the individual is indifferent between life and death. This implies that there is zero utility after death.

Given these assumptions, Equation (5) reduces to:

$$dc^*/d\mu = -u(c^*)/(\rho + \mu) \tag{6}$$

or, without discounting:

$$dc^*/d\mu = -Tu(c^*) \tag{7}$$

where T is life expectancy and equal to $1/\mu$ in the exponential case. The interpretation here is that a uniform change in mortality rates at every age will produce a welfare change equal to the number of years of life (T) times the goods value of life, given by $u(c^*)$.

The major difficulty in applying this approach is determining the value of life. We can consider this question in the simple model sketched above. Suppose that the mortality rate declines by an amount Δ for one period. Then the survival rate is higher by e^{Δ} at the end of the period. Discounted utility evaluated at age $\theta \geq K$ is then

$$V(\theta) = e^{\Delta}u(c^*)/(\rho + \mu) \tag{8}$$

Hence, using this simple mortality assumption, the tradeoff between current risk and current consumption is approximately $dc/d\mu(\theta) = u(c^*)$.

From this discussion we see that it is generally not correct to adjust for changes in health status by calculating lifetime consumption, which would be c^*T in the present example. This approach is only correct when $u(c) = 1$. Our numerical estimates below indicate that this approach will generally undervalue improvements in life expectancy.

B. *Valuation of Life*

Measuring utility income with health improvement requires finding appropriate "prices" to use to value health status. There is a voluminous literature on the value of fatalities prevented.[9] It is generally accepted that the "willingness to pay" to reduce risk is the appropriate approach for valuing risk reductions. Studies of this fall into three general categories: labor market studies, which examine the risk-wage tradeoff; consumer purchase decisions (such as for smoke detectors), which examine the price-risk tradeoff; and contingent valuation studies, which attempt to determine preferences from a systematic examination of an individual's stated preferences.

The most weight is generally put on labor market studies because these reflect actual behavior, because labor force decisions are repeated, and because there are dozens of studies from different periods, countries, occupations, and samples. It is important to note that the tradeoff examined is a *current risk-current income* ($dc/d\mu$) choice between current occupational risks and current wages. From these tradeoffs (which involve comparing income per year against mortality risk per year) we derive an implicit dollar cost per unit mortality risk. Because the risks are relatively small (around between 1/100,000 per year to 50/100,000 per year), we interpret these prices as the marginal valuation of risk changes.

Not surprisingly, there is great variation in the implicit price of risk (or price of a statistical life). The serious estimates from a recent survey range from $0.6 million to $13.5 million per fatality prevented. The U.S. Environmental Protection Agency uses the relatively high figure of $4.8 million per fatality prevented in its cost-benefit study of the value of clear air.[10] Tolley, Kenkel, and Fabian (1994) recommend a value of $2.0 million per fatality prevented for use in health care decisions. In this study, I settle on $3.0 million per fatality prevented in 2000 prices and 1990 income levels as a reasonable choice, but the figures are easily modified to reflect different assumptions.

In our analysis above, we calculated the increment to sustainable consumption of an additional life-year, LY. There is some confusion but little solid evidence on how to measure the value of an added life-year. Most studies derive LY values from the studies of the value of reduced mortality.

To convert the value of mortality reduction to the value of a life-year requires further assumptions about timing and discounting. Many of the studies underlying the value of mortality reduction concern labor market decisions of working men. Assume for simplicity that the representative worker is aged 40 and that the mortality rate is a constant 2.5% per year. To convert these into value per life-year requires assuming a utility discount rate, which we alternatively take to be 0, 1, and 2.5% per year. With no discounting and the $3 million life value, the population-weighted value of a life-year is $210,000 and the annuity value of an additional life-year is about $5,000 per year. Again using the simplified mortality assumption and a discount rate of 2.5% per year, a life-year has value of $625,000 and the annuity value is $31,000 per year. These numbers appear somewhat high relative to other estimates. Tolley et al. (1994) recommend a central present value of $100,000 per LY from their studies (see also the discussion in Viscusi 1993).

In the estimates presented below, we use actual survival functions rather than the theoretical ones analyzed above. Using the equilibrium 1950 population distribution and 1980 mortality rates, the value of a LY varies from $152,000 at a zero discount rate to $376,000 at a 2.5% discount rate. The associated consumption annuities are $2,200 per year and $11,400 per year per additional LY, respectively (all scaled to 1990 income levels in 2000 prices).

C. Measuring Income with Variable Lifetimes

Next we turn to the issue of measuring income or consumption. For this purpose, we take the utility-based measure of income. We begin with the simplest case of utility-based income with fixed and certain lifetime. Assume that the consumption discount rate is a constant, *r*. Once we know the entire path of consumption, given by C(s) for s ≥ t, we can easily calculate utility income at time *t*, denoted by **C**(t), as

$$\mathbf{C}(t) = r\left[\int_t^{\infty} C(s)\exp[-r(s-t)]ds\right].$$

Note that **C**(t) measures the *constant* consumption annuity available at time *t*. This definition shows that measures of utility income or sustainable income are inherently wealthlike measures, as was emphasized by Irving Fisher and Paul Samuelson.[11]

The utility definition of income is a natural springboard for considering the measurement of income with varying lifetimes. Begin by extending the definition of income and consumption to uncertain, variable, and endogenous lifetimes. To begin with, consider the traditional definition of income. For example, say that in lifetime situation "Short" individuals consume 100 units per year each and live for 50 years, while in situation "Long" individuals consume 100 units per year and live for 60 years. Under the standard flow definition of consumption, there would be no difference in economic welfare or living standards between Short and Long. This is clearly defective to the extent that people prefer to live longer.

An alternative and preferable approach is to convert the consumption trajectory and survival function into the equivalent utility with a benchmark survival function and consumption. Take the Short lifetime situation as the benchmark. Using the example of the last paragraph, we ask what consumption annuity using the life expectancy of situation Short would give individuals the same utility as the consumption and life expectancy of situation Long. An individual might consider situation Long (with a constant consumption of 100 and a lifetime of 60 years) to be equivalent to, or have equivalent utility with, a constant consumption annuity of 110 units per year with the life expectancy of situation Short. We would then say that (using situation Short as the benchmark) the income in situation Long was 110 compared to that of 100 in situation Short.

Using the notation of the last section, define S = Short and L = Long. Then let $V[c_t^S; \theta, \rho, \mu_t^S]$ be the utility of consumption stream c_t^S and age-specific mortality rate μ_t^S while $V[c_t^L; \theta, \rho, \mu_t^L]$ is the utility of consumption stream c_t^L and age-specific mortality rate μ_t^L. We define income $c^*(L, \mu^S)$ as the constant consumption stream that would go with mortality rates in Short, which yields the equivalent utility as the consumption stream and mortality rates in situation Long. That is, $V[c^*(L, \mu^S); \theta, \rho, \mu_t^S] = V[c_t^L; \theta, \rho, \mu_t^L]$.

We then compare incomes in different situations by estimating the constant equivalent consumption annuity with a benchmark mortality function. Say we use mortality rates from situation S as the benchmark. We can then compare situations S and L by comparing $c^*(S, \mu^S)$ and $c^*(L, \mu^S)$, such that $V[c^*(S, \mu^S); \theta, \rho, \mu_t^S] = V[c_t^S; \theta, \rho, \mu_t^S]$

and $c^*(L, \mu^S)$ such that $V[c^*(L, \mu^S); \theta, \rho, \mu_t^S] = V[c_t^L; \theta, \rho, \mu_t^L]$. There will be the usual index-number problems involved in these comparisons because the definitions will differ depending on whether we use the mortality rates of situation S or L.

Because this tangle of algebra is somewhat forbidding, it will be useful to summarize the major points. Traditional income accounting looks at the flows of consumption and income in measuring living standards—consumption of food, purchases of electricity and apparel, airline travel, and so forth. These measures do not consider the length of life or the quality of the population's health. The alternative proposed here corrects for mortality by asking how much consumption the individual would be willing to pay to trade off for health. If, for example, an individual would pay 2% of consumption each year to gain an additional life-year, then we use that number to say that an additional life-year is equivalent to a 2% increase in annual income. In the estimates below, we use this technique only to adjust for changes in life expectancy, although they could also be used to adjust for changes in morbidity.

V

The Impact of Improved Life Expectancy on Economic Welfare in the United States, 1900–1995

A. Previous Studies

The literature on estimating the economic value of improved health is surprisingly sparse. Dan Usher (1973, 1980) considered the issue as part of a more general study of the adequacy of conventional national output measures, but his approach was highly stylized. A number of indexes incorporate life expectancy, particularly the United Nations Development Program's Human Development Index (HDI).[12] The technique for incorporating health in the HDI is, however, completely arbitrary. Economic historians have begun to compile systematic indicators on various health-related measures, such as height and the body-mass index, and these tend to move with other measures of health status, but it is difficult to put a price tag on these indexes.[13] Important additions to the literature are studies by David Cutler and Elizabeth Richardson (1997), which are discussed below, and the contribution of Kevin Murphy and Robert Topel (2002).

B. Methods

We now implement the ideas in earlier sections using data for the United States. The calculations here estimate the value of the health component of utility income, or the value of improvements in health status, which we call "health income." The fundamental data for the United States are shown in Figures 1 through 4. Figure 1 shows per capita disposable income for the United States from 1900 to 2000. The data are from the Commerce Department for the period 1929–2000 and from various private scholars for 1900–1929. The Commerce Department figures are in chained indexes converted to 2000 price levels. Earlier estimates are in constant prices.

Figure 1

Disposable income per capita, 2000 prices.

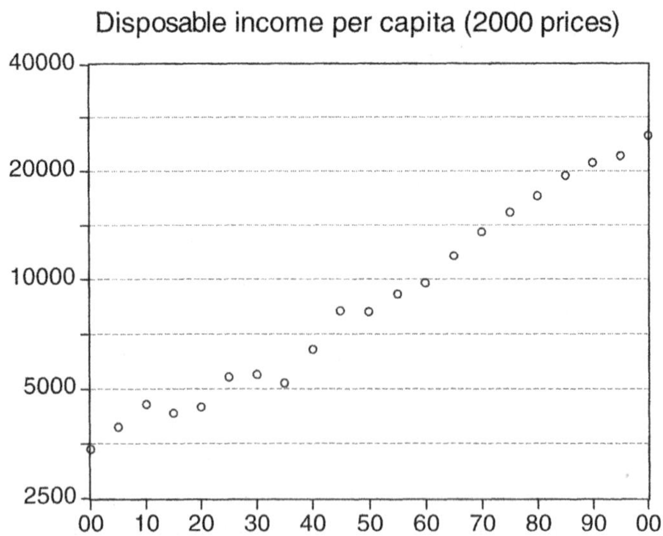

Source: Bureau of Economic Analysis.

Figure 2 shows the survival rates for three years: 1900, 1950, and 2000. The most dramatic change came in the early part of this century—the probability of surviving the first year rose from 85% in 1900 to 97% in 1950. Figure 3 shows life expectancy at different ages. Figure 4 shows the change in life expectancy at different ages over the last century. Gains in life expectancy have been substantial throughout the entire century.

To calculate the value of improved health status, we use the *life-years approach* outlined above (an alternative, using the mortality approach, can also be done and gives similar answers). Under the life-years approach, the economic value of improved health is equal to the increase in life expectancy times the value of an additional life-year. The estimates are weighted by the share of the population that

Figure 2

Survival probabilities by age, 1900, 1950, 2000.

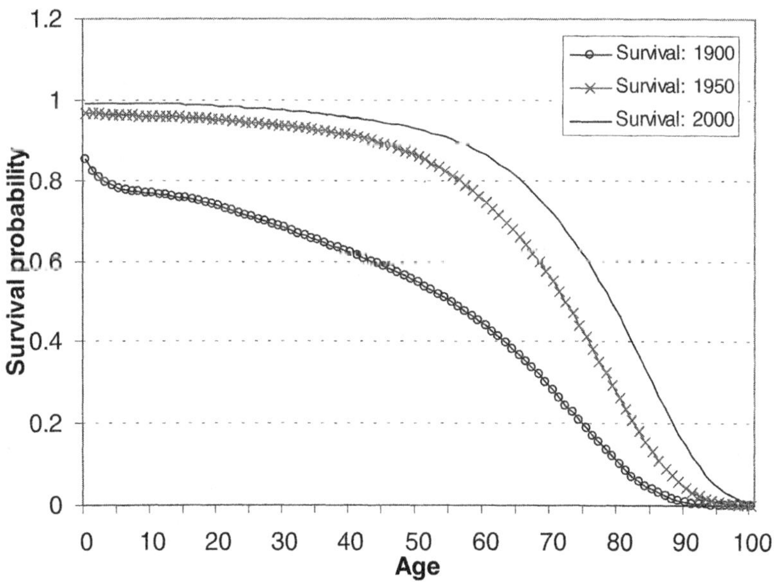

Source: Department of the Census and Social Security Administration.

Figure 3

Life expectancy at different ages, 1900–2000.

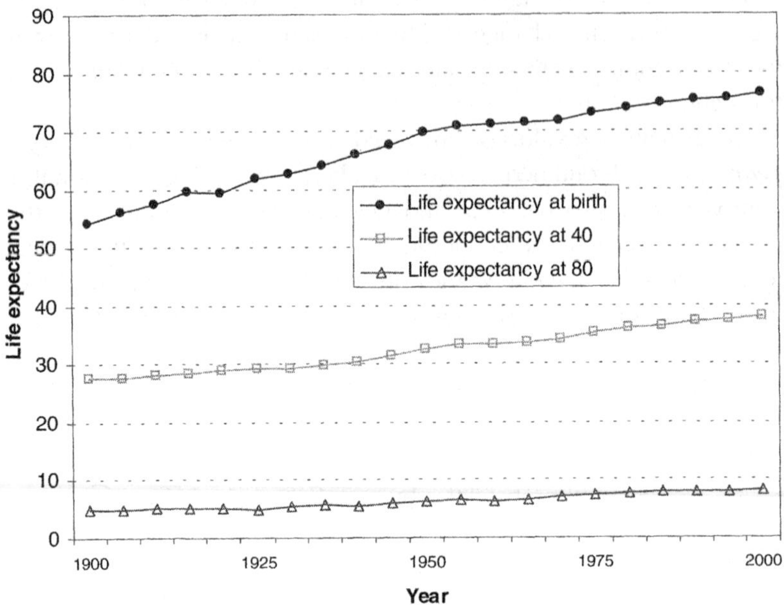

Source: Constructed from data in Figure 2.

is experiencing the greater life expectancy, where we use the 1950 equilibrium population weights for all years.

C. Simple Calculations

It may be helpful to work through a simple example to illustrate the methodology. For the period 1975 through 2000, the undiscounted increase in weighted life-years was 2.53 years. Raising life expectancy by one LY is estimated to be the equivalent of raising the consumption annuity at each age by 10.3% of income. Therefore, the gains over that quarter-century were equal to $2.53 \times 10.3 = 26.1\%$, or 1.05% per year. Per capita real income grew by 1.98% per year over that

Figure 4

Change in life expectancy at different ages, 1900–2000.

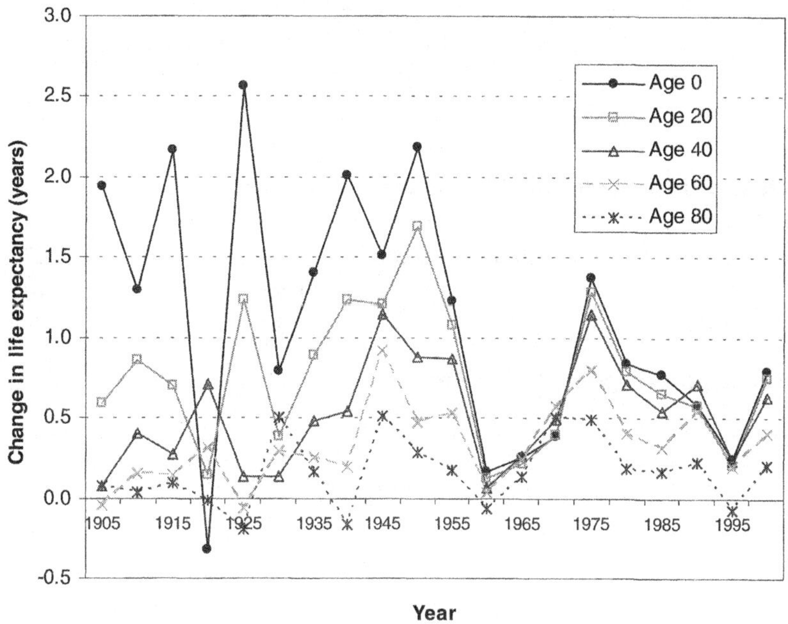

period, so the value of health increases was 53% as the growth in conventional measured per capita real income.

D. Actual Calculations

The central results of this paper, showing calculations on the economic contribution of health and nonhealth consumption, are shown in Table 2 and Figure 5. For these estimates, we use only estimates based on changes in life expectancy. These estimates differ from the simple calculations in the last section because they use actual survival rates and population distributions rather than the simplified ones assumed above.

The major result that comes through using all techniques is that the value of improvements in life expectancy improvements is about as

Table 2

Health Income Improvements and Growth in Per Capita Income

	Growth Rates (Percent per Year)				
	1900–1925	1925–1950	1950–1975	1975–2000	1900–2000
Health improvements (as fraction of income)					
Discount rate					
0.0%	1.0%	1.6%	1.1%	1.0%	1.2%
1.0%	1.4%	2.3%	1.5%	1.4%	1.6%
2.5%	2.2%	3.6%	2.3%	2.1%	2.5%
Per capita disposable income					
	1.8%	1.7%	2.5%	2.0%	2.0%

Gains in consumption from improvements in health have been the same order of magnitude as conventionally measured income. Results are sensitive to the discount rate.
Source: See discussion in text.

large as the value of all other consumption goods and services put together. For example, over the two decades from 1975 to 2000, conventionally measured per capita income grew at an average rate of 2.0% per year. Over this period, the annual average improvements in life expectancy had an economic value between 1.0 and 2.1% of income, depending upon the discount rate.[14] Over the entire period from 1900 to 2000, the value of improved health or health income grew at between 1.2 and 2.5% of consumption, whereas income grew at a rate of about 2.0% of consumption.

Looking at the entire 20th century, the contribution of the increase in life expectancy was between 59% and 126% of the contribution of income from all sources combined.

E. Qualifications

How robust are the estimates provided here? The underlying mortality data are among the most reliable of our social statistics. The most

Figure 5

Growth in health income and conventional income, 1900–2000.

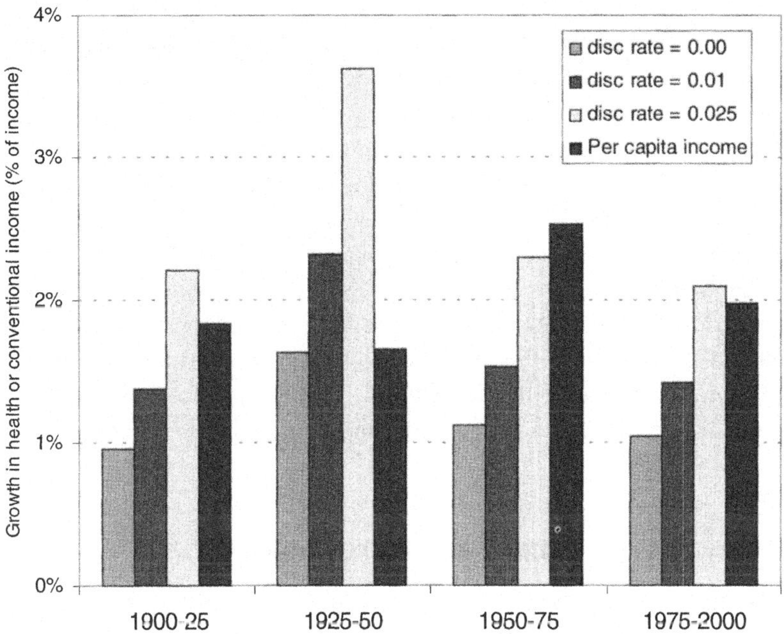

Growth in health income is change in health income divided by income and is shown for three different discount rates. See text for discussion.

fragile estimates concern mortality and life-year valuation, as discussed above. One assumption on which there is little evidence is that the premium on reduced mortality is a constant fraction of per capita consumption over the entire period. More precisely, we assume that the value of a reduction in the mortality rate of 0.001 per year is $3,000 at 1990 income levels and in 2000 prices, and we scale that value over time to the ratio of the given year's per capita income to 1990 per capita income. There are no comprehensive studies of the mortality premium over time, although movements in the wage of risky occupations (such as coal mining) are consistent with this assumption. I suspect, however, that the premium has risen over time. This would be consistent with the rising share of health care expenditures in total consumption. If the premium were indeed increasing over time, then the contribution of health to economic welfare would be relatively smaller in the earlier period and relatively larger in the later period.

A few other assumptions are significant but will not affect the major results. One important issue is whether people should be weighted the same at every age. Many health care professionals and some survey evidence suggest that the value of a life-year is higher in the middle of the life span (between 20 and 40 years) than at either end.[15] Most surveys indicate, for example, that infant mortality would receive a lower weight than adult mortality.

Another major omission from this study is the value of reduced morbidity. The data on morbidity is less comprehensive and more difficult to value. One study indicates that including morbidity might add another 5% or so to the value of health improvements estimates here, although that number seems suspiciously low.[16]

VI

Discussion and Conclusion

THIS PAPER CONTRIBUTES to a new view of the economics of health. This new view is that improvements in health status have been a major contributor to economic welfare over the 20th century. To a first approximation, the economic value of increases in longevity in the last 100 years is about as large as the value of measured growth in nonhealth goods and services. This conclusion validates the view of Irving Fisher in 1906:

> [T]he devices of modern hygiene, sanitation, and preventive medicine . . . are of greater economic import than many of the luxurious and enervating devices commonly connoted by "wealth." (Barber 1997, Vol. 2: 204)

The first question one should ask is whether this finding is plausible. One way of considering the question is to consider the health equivalent of the Sears-catalogue question:

> Consider the improvements to both health and nonhealth technologies over the last half century (say from 1950 to 2000). Health technologies include a variety of changes such as the Salk polio vaccine, new pharmaceuticals, joint replacement, improved sanitation, improved automobile

> safety, smoke-free workplaces, etc. Over this period, life expectancy at birth increased from a little under 70 years to a little more than 76 years. Nonhealth technologies were wide-ranging and include the jet plane, television, superhighways, VCRs, and computers.
>
> Now consider the following choice. You must forgo either the health improvements over the last half-century or the nonhealth improvements. That is, you must choose either (a) 1950 health conditions and 2000 non-health living standards or (b) 2000 health conditions and 1950 nonhealth living standards. Which would you choose?

If you would either choose (b) or find it a difficult choice, then you would agree with the results of this paper.

There are many questions left open by the present findings. It is important to note that we cannot attribute the growth in health income to particular investments or expenditures. Such a task, which would apply the techniques of growth accounting to health improvements, is especially challenging.[17] It is also necessary if we are to recognize not only the historical sources of improved health but also those investments that may best contribute to future improvements.

Another particularly important question is the extent to which improvements arise from improved basic knowledge (such as the germ theory of disease, the discovery of antibiotics, or the DNA revolution) or investments in improved health capital and infrastructure (such as larger investments in health education or improvements in emergency response services). A second issue, particularly relevant for the contribution of basic knowledge, is the extent to which improvements in knowledge were domestically generated or imported. It seems likely, for example, that most of the major medical discoveries in the first part of the period covered here arose in Europe, while America was increasingly the source of increases in medical knowledge in the last few decades.[18] To the extent that improvements in health income are due to imported technologies, this emphasizes one of the gains from trade that is largely overlooked in traditional measures of the economic impacts of international trade.

Of course, health is more than doctors and hospitals. It encompasses other parts of national output, such as pollution control and highway safety spending, and reflects individual lifestyles, such as decisions about smoking, drinking, driving, drugs, and exercise.

Moreover, medical knowledge is a global public good, which is increased by efforts in many countries. Because we cannot tally the totality of costs on health care, we cannot say for sure whether we are getting one-half or twice or thrice the return on health dollars that we are on nonhealth dollars. And it is surely the case that health care expenditures are often misallocated and wasteful. However, notwithstanding the complexity and bureaucracy, improvements in health status in the United States have yielded major increases in economic welfare, and those are not captured in our present national accounting systems.

Notes

1. See Eisner (1989). A recent review of environmental and other aspects of nonmarket accounting is contained in National Research Council (1999).

2. See Shapiro and Wilcox (1997) and Shapiro, Shapiro, and Wilcox (1999).

3. See Advisory Commission (1996) and Murray and Lopez (1996).

4. This discussion ignores the subtlety of Hicks's discussion of price changes, interest rate effects, the difference between *ex ante* and *ex post* capital, and a number of other factors.

5. This approach is used in an analogous manner in the theory of measuring the cost of living.

6. See Nordhaus (1994, 2000) for a discussion.

7. See Nordhaus (1994).

8. An early treatment of this issue is contained in Shepard and Zeckhauser (1984). A detailed treatment of the value of life with extensions is contained in Rosen in Tolley et al. (1994).

9. See Viscusi (1993) and Unsworth, Neumann, and Browne (1992) for a comprehensive review of the economics literature. The monumental study edited by Murray and Lopez (1996) is a particularly useful analysis of the issue in the context of health care.

10. This was based on the survey by Unsworth, Neumann, and Browne (1992).

11. Irving Fisher's discussion dates from 1910–1914 and is contained in Fisher (1997). Paul Samuelson's approach is contained in Samuelson (1961).

12. See UNDP (1997) for a discussion and the numbers.

13. A useful review of the economic history literature is contained in Costa and Steckel (1995).

14. Because there is no natural denominator for measuring improvements in health care, we use the same denominator for calculating growth as we

do for income. This allows us to compare the relative importance of income and improvements in health status, whereas there is no obvious way to measure the value of the level of health status.

15. A particularly interesting discussion is contained in Murray and Lopez (1996).

16. See Cutler and Richardson (1997), discussed below.

17. One of the most comprehensive studies of growth accounting is Denison (1961).

18. A nontechnical history is contained in Porter (1997).

References

Advisory Commission. (1996). *Toward a More Accurate Measure of the Cost of Living: The Final Report of the Advisory Commission to Study the Consumer Price Index.* December 4 (updated version).

Barber, William J. Ed. (1997). *The Works of Irving Fisher.* London: Pickering and Chatto.

Costa, Dora L., and Richard H. Steckel. (1995). *Long-Term Health Trends in Health, Welfare, and Economic Growth in the United States.* NBER Historical Working Paper 76. Cambridge, MA: National Bureau of Economic Research.

Cutler, David, Mark B. McClellan, Joseph Newhouse, and Dahlia Remler. (1998). "Are Medical Care Prices Declining?" *Quarterly Journal of Economics*, vol. 113, no. 4, 991–1024.

Cutler, David, and Elizabeth Richardson. (1997). "Measuring the Health of the U.S. Population." *Brookings Papers on Economic Activity: Microeconomics* 217–271.

Denison, Edward. (1961). *The Sources of Economic Growth in the United States.* New York: Committee for Economic Development.

Eisner, Robert. (1989). *The Total Incomes System of Accounts.* Chicago: University of Chicago Press.

Hicks, J. R. (1939). *Value and Capital.* 2nd ed. Oxford: Clarendon Press.

Murphy, Kevin M., and Robert H. Topel. (2002). "The Economic Value of Medical Research." In *Measuring the Gains from Medical Research: An Economic Approach.* Eds. Kevin M. Murphy and Robert H. Topel. Chicago: University of Chicago Press.

Murray, Christopher, J. L. Murray, and Alan D. Lopez. Eds. (1996). *The Global Burden of Disease.* Cambridge, MA: Harvard School of Public Health.

National Research Council. (1999). *Nature's Numbers: Expanding the National Economic Accounts to Include the Environment.* Eds. William D. Nordhaus and Edward Kokkelenberg. Washington, DC: National Academy Press.

Nordhaus, William D. (1994). "Reflections on the Concept of Sustainable

Economic Growth." In *Economic Growth and the Structure of Long-Term Development.* Eds. Luigi L. Pasinetti and Robert M. Solow. Oxford: Oxford University Press.

——. (2000). "New Directions in National Economic Accounting." *AEA Papers and Proceedings* vol. 90, no. 2, May: 259–63.

Samuelson, Paul A. (1961). "The Evaluation of 'Social Income.'" In *The Theory of Capital.* Eds. F. A. Lutz and D. C. Haig. London: Macmillan.

Shapiro, Irving, Matthew Shapiro, and David Wilcox. (1998). "Measuring the Value of Cataract Surgery." In *Medical Care, Output, and Productivity.* Eds. E. Berndt and D. Cutler. NBER/CRIW conference.

Shapiro, Matthew, and David Wilcox. (1997). "Mismeasurement in Consumer Price Index: An Evaluation." NBER *Macroeconomics Annual* 11: 93–142.

Shepard, Donald S., and Richard J. Zeckhauser. (1984). "Survival Versus Consumption." *Management Science* 30(4): 423–39.

Tolley, George S., Donald Scott Kenkel, and Robert Fabian. Eds. (1994). *Valuing Health for Policy.* Chicago: University of Chicago Press.

United Nations Development Programme. (1997). *Human Development Report, 1997.* New York: Oxford University Press.

Unsworth, Robert, James Neumann, and W. Eric Browne. (1992). *Review of Existing Value of Life Estimates: Valuation Document.* Background document prepared for Section 812 Analysis, Industrial Economics Incorporated, Cambridge, MA, November 6.

Usher, Dan. (1973). "An Imputation to the Measurement of Economic Growth for Changes in Life Expectancy." In *The Measurement of Economic and Social Performance.* Ed. Milton Moss. New York: Columbia University Press.

——. (1980). *The Measurement of Economic Growth.* New York: Columbia University Press.

Viscusi, W. Kip. (1993). "The Value of Risks to Health and Life." *Journal of Economic Literature* 31: 1912–1946.

Comments on William D. Nordhaus's, "Irving Fisher and the Contribution of Improved Longevity to Living Standards"

By ROBERT W. DIMAND*

ABSTRACT. This essay discusses Fisher's contributions to life extension and to human capital theory.

Bill Nordhaus's paper would, I think, have greatly pleased Irving Fisher. It brings together two major themes of Fisher's career: the economic value of improving the health of the population, and the measurement of economic quantities. After his recovery from tuberculosis, Fisher was a prolific writer on health issues, warning against alcohol, tobacco, stress, lack of exercise, and poor diet, sanitation, and hygiene as preventable causes of illness and death. He published more than 60 articles and pamphlets on health from 1910 to 1915 alone, not counting a dozen specifically on tuberculosis (Allen 1993: 139). The first 19 editions of Fisher's *How to Live*, written jointly with Dr. Eugene Lyman Fisk and first published in 1915, sold more than 400,000 copies in the United States by 1937, and the book was translated into Spanish, German, French, Polish, Russian, Italian, Swedish, Norwegian, Chinese, and Japanese (Sudela 1937: 443). In addition, Metropolitan Life distributed between 12 and 15 million copies of a pamphlet condensation of *How to Live* (Allen 1993: 140). Fisher donated all his royalties from this phenomenal bestseller to his Life Extension Institute.

In his opening paragraph, Nordhaus mentions that Fisher "made an early (perhaps the earliest) estimate of the impact of mortality and morbidity on national output." This was in *National Vitality, Its Wastes and Conservation, Report of the National Conservation Commission*, completed in November 1908 and published as a U.S. Senate

*The author is at the Department of Economics, Brock University, St. Catharines, Ontario L2S 3A1, Canada.

The American Journal of Economics and Sociology, Vol. 64, No. 1 (January, 2005).

Document in 1909 (the report's summary is reprinted in Fisher 1997, Vol. 13: 21–40). Fisher wrote this report, paralleling reports drafted by other commission members on waste and conservation of natural resources. In Chapter XII, "The Money Value of Increased Vitality," Fisher estimated the economic value of life as the present discounted value of likely future earnings after subtracting the cost of maintenance, an approach that he attributed to the British statistician and public health official William Farr. Assuming $700 per year as average earnings in middle life and three-quarters of Americans of working age as income earners or housekeepers, Fisher found that

> the average value of a person now living in the United States is $2,900, and the average value of the lives now sacrificed by preventable deaths is $1,700. The latter is smaller than the former because the age of the dying is greater than the age of the living. Applying the $2,900 to the population of eighty-five and a half millions, we find that our population may be valued as assets at more than $250,000,000,000; and since the number of preventable deaths is estimated at 630,000, the annual waste from preventable deaths is 630,000 times $1,700, or about $1,000,000,000. This represents the annual preventable loss of potential earnings. (Fisher 1997, Vol. 13: 38)

Fisher estimated that the annual loss from preventable illness was at least another half-billion dollars. In 1930 in *The Theory of Interest*, Fisher reported that Louis I. Dublin (head of the statistical department of Metropolitan Life) "computes the total value of the 'human capital' of the United States to be 1,500 billion dollars, or about five times the value of all other capital" (Fisher 1997, Vol. 9: 72n).

Fisher's innovation was in quantifying the annual preventable loss of potential earnings through illness and death, rather than in valuing human capital. In *Verbiem Sapienti and on the Value of People*, written around 1665, Sir William Petty estimated the total stock of England and Wales at £250 million (144 million in land, 30 million in houses, 3 million in ships, 36 million in livestock, 6 million in money, 31 million in durable goods) and the interest rate at 6% per annum, so that the annual return on stock accounted for 15 million of an annual expenditure of £40 million. Taking the remaining £25 million per year as the return to labor, and discounting at 6% per annum, Petty valued the total human stock of England and Wales at £416.66 million sterling, and cited auction prices of young adult slaves in confirmation of his per capita estimate (see Olson 1993: 64–65).

Nordhaus mentions that "[w]hile Fisher thought and cared deeply about index numbers, measurement of income, utility theory, and health, he never connected these different concepts together," whereas Nordhaus begins his analysis of the valuation of life expectancy with a lifetime utility function. It is striking that, when Fisher estimated the loss from preventable death and illness or the benefits of Prohibition, he did so in terms of earnings and production, not in terms of the utility analysis of his 1892 *Mathematical Investigations in the Theory of Value and Prices* (Fisher 1997, Vol. 1), a landmark in the use of indifference curves. Utility theory is conspicuous by its absence from some other works of Fisher. In particular, *The Making of Index Numbers* (1922; Fisher 1997, Vol. 7) concerns statistical tests that an "ideal" index number formula should satisfy, in contrast to the work of A. A. Könus in the 1920s on the economic theory of "exact" index numbers that correspond to an underlying utility function (see my introduction and postscript to Fisher 1997, Vol. 7). The most important appearances of utility in the work of Fisher's maturity (apart from his *Elementary Principles of Economics*) are the role of impatience in his interest theory, represented by the indifference curves of his two-period consumption diagram (*The Rate of Interest*, 1907: 409; Fisher 1997, Vol. 3), and, rather isolated from the main lines of Fisher's research, a 1927 essay on "A Statistical Method for Measuring 'Marginal Utility' and Testing the Justice of a Progressive Income Tax" (Fisher 1997, Vol. 12).

When Fisher (1926: 162) estimated the economic value of Prohibition, and hence what cost would be worth paying to enforce Prohibition, he assumed that the productivity gain from Prohibition increased wages and profits by 5%, a gain of $6 billion a year in U.S. output (cf. Fisher 1997, Vol. 13: 126–129, testimony to the Senate Judiciary Committee). As John Kenneth Galbraith (1977: 192) phrases it, Fisher "argued, no doubt correctly, that men were more productive when off the sauce" (but Warburton 1932 failed to find statistical evidence that Prohibition significantly improved efficiency or even reduced spending on alcoholic beverages). Since Fisher did not frame his analysis in terms of utility, he did not have to treat utility derived from drinking (or smoking) as an offsetting item, to be balanced against the effect on productivity. Fisher (1926: 138n) did, however, acknowledge "a eugenic argument against Prohibition. The work of Karl Pearson, Dr. Stockard, and Dr. Pearl indicates that alcohol is a selective agent for killing off the unfit, while leaving the fit relatively unharmed. . . . This is the old argument, in a new and improved form, that alcohol is a good fool-killer." This eugenic argument clearly did not rest on a concern for individual utility. (Cf. Viscusi 1998: 120 for an estimate of the net benefit to American society per pack of cigarettes smoked, because premature death reduces pension, Social Security, and nursing home expenditures by more than it increases such costs as medical care.) Beyond doubting that rational choice applies to addictive substances, Fisher was uneasy about utility maximization interpreted as pleasure seeking. Especially after his recovery from tuberculosis, he disdained mere pleasure as a goal, and this presumably influenced the casting of his analyses of health and of Prohibition in terms of potential earnings or productivity rather than utility.

"At present the United States has the unenviable distinction of being the only great industrial nation without compulsory health insurance," stated Fisher (1917: 9) in his December 1916 presidential address to the American Association for Labor Legislation on "The Need for Health Insurance." His observation remains relevant today, and so does his concern with the loss in present discounted value of potential earnings due to preventable illness and death. Bill Nordhaus's interesting and valuable exercise in quantifying the contribution of improved longevity to economic welfare is a worthy part of a celebration of Irving Fisher's intellectual legacy.

References

Allen, Robert Loring. (1993). *Irving Fisher: A Biography.* Cambridge, MA: Blackwell.

Fisher, Irving. (1917). "The Need for Health Insurance." *American Labor Legislation Review* 7(1): 9–23. Rpt. in in Fisher (1997). *The Works of Irving Fisher.* Vol. 13. Ed.William J. Barber. London: Pickering & Chatto.

——. (1926). *Prohibition at Its Worst.* New York: Macmillan.

——. (1997). *The Works of Irving Fisher.* 14 vols. Ed.William J. Barber. London: Pickering & Chatto.

Galbraith, John Kenneth. (1977). *The Age of Uncertainty*. Boston: Houghton Mifflin.

Olson, Richard. (1993). *The Emergence of the Social Sciences, 1642–1792*. New York: Twayne.

Sudela, Amelia G. (1937). "Appendix: Biographical Sketch of Irving Fisher." In *The Lessons of Monetary Experience: Essays in Honor of Irving Fisher*. Ed. Arthur D. Gayer. New York: Farrar & Rinehart.

Viscusi, W. Kip (1998). *Rational Risk Policy*. Oxford: Clarendon Press.

Warburton, Clark. ([1932] 1968). *The Economic Results of Prohibition*. New York: AMS Press.

Comments on William D. Nordhaus's, "Irving Fisher and the Contribution of Improved Longevity to Living Standards"

By T. N. SRINIVASAN*

ABSTRACT. A comment on the article by William D. Nordhaus in this volume.

I very much enjoyed reading William Nordhaus's paper. Being utterly ignorant of the health economics literature, I learned a lot about it from the paper. In reading it, a number of questions came to my mind. Let me state them in the expectation that Nordhaus and others will respond.

Nordhaus considers several interrelated issues: to wit, tradeoff between "health and wealth," as he puts it, in an individual's intertemporal consumption optimization decisions; valuation of life; measurement of income given that the length of life is uncertain; and lastly, adequacy of conventional national income measures and associated growth accounting exercises in reflecting improvements in health and longevity of the population.

*T. N. Srinivasan, Ph.D., is the Samuel C. Park, Jr. Professor of Economics at Yale University. Formerly a Professor, and later Research Professor, at the Indian Statistical Institute, Delhi (1964–1977), he has taught at numerous universities in the United States. His research interests include international trade, development, agricultural economics, and microeconomic theory. He recently authored *Reintegrating India with the World Economy* with Suresh D. Tendulkar (Washington: Institute for International Economics, 2003) and edited *Trade, Finance and Investment in South Asia* (New Delhi: Social Science Press, 2001). He is also the author of *Developing Countries and the Multilateral Trading System* (Boulder, CO: Westview Press, 1998). He is a Fellow of the American Philosophical Society, the Econometric Society, and the American Academy of Arts and Sciences, and a Foreign Associate of the National Academy of Sciences. He was named Distinguished Fellow of the American Economic Association in 2003. This paper was originally presented at a conference celebrating Irving Fisher held at Yale in May 1998.

The American Journal of Economics and Sociology, Vol. 64, No. 1 (January, 2005).

Taking the last issue, the health sector is no different from service sectors such as education for which national accounts data measure the out-of-pocket cost of inputs but do not include other costs such as the opportunity cost of time spent away from work while being educated. The opportunity cost of time while receiving health care is the analogy of the value of time spent by students in educational institutions. These costs do not necessarily equal the value of the services to the users.

Health expenditures are in part like expenditures on repair and maintenance of capital, and in part like investment expenditures that yield their returns over the future. In principle, health maintenance expenditures are no different from economic depreciation of equipment (except that maintaining (or failing to maintain) an individual's health may have externalities) and should be netted out in calculating income as, of course, Irving Fisher had proposed. Now, some of the returns to investment in an individual's health do not accrue to the individual, and some are not in the form of marked outputs. For this reason, the cost of inputs associated with the investment component of health expenditures need not be the same as the present value of future of total returns (market and nonmarket, individual, and social) from the investment. Once again, this is analo-gous to the investment component of educational expenditures. For example, the estimates of Jorgenson and Fraumeni (1995) of the output of the education sector, measured as the present value of increments in lifetime labor incomes (including nonmarket incomes), are considerably larger than the estimates based on cost of education by Kendrik (1976).

Nordhaus has long been critical of the fact that conventional measures of national income at constant prices do not correctly reflect productivity gains, and I agree with him. This criticism applies also to the contribution of the health sector.

Nordhaus estimates the value of improved health using two alternative approaches. In the first, he estimates the number of deaths (per person in the population) prevented by reductions in mortality rates arising from improved health care and then multiplies them by an estimated value of a life. The product yields the value of health improvement per person. In the second, the value of improved health is the product of the increase in life expectancy times the value of an additional life-year. Both methods yield similar estimates for the value of health improvements. While recognizing the wide variations in the estimates for the value of life based on labor market studies of mortality risk versus wage tradeoff, he settles on $3 million per death prevented. This he identifies with the current risk-current income trade-off parameter in his model of individual intertemporal welfare maximization. By the same token, this $3 million also implies a value of an additional life-year as a function of the discount rate. I am not entirely persuaded by this procedure, mainly because it seems to equate the mortality-consumption tradeoff of a single representative agent of the model, in which mortality is represented by a constant instantaneous probability of death regardless of age, with the corresponding tradeoff for an average individual (in terms of mortality experience) in a changing population of heterogeneous individuals.

Nordhaus nicely sets out an individual's intertemporal welfare optimization problem. In doing so, he makes many assumptions that seem much too strong and implausible to me. Let me list them. First, he assumes that the probability of death of an individual at *any instant* dt is an exogenous constant μdt. This ensures that the probability $s(t,\theta)$ of any individual aged θ surviving up to $t > \theta$ is:

$$s(t, \theta) = e^{-\mu(t-\theta)}. \tag{1}$$

It is obviously much too strong an assumption—it implies that the probability of surviving a *further* Δ unit of time is the same regardless of the person's age or health status. Since an individual has some influence over his or her own survival probability through choice (e.g., lifestyle), treating μ as an exogenous constant is again strong. One could in principle recognize an exogenous component arising from, say, public expenditures on health, hygiene, environment, and medical research, as well as an endogenous component in mortality probability. Nicola Spatafora (1997), in his Yale dissertation, showed that this distinction matters: if both public and private expenditures on improved health and nutrition reduce mortality, there may not be a positive growth effect of public expenditure if there is sufficiently strong substitution between private and public expenditures

Second, Nordhaus writes the expected welfare of an individual aged θ as:

$$V(\theta, \rho, \mu) = \int_{\theta}^{\infty} \left[\int_{\theta}^{t} e^{-\rho(\tau-\theta)} u(c(\tau)) d\tau \right] h(t, \theta) dt, \tag{2}$$

where $u(c(\tau))$ is the instantaneous felicity of consumption $c(\tau)$ at τ and $h(t,\theta)$ is the hazard rate at t, that is, $h(t, \theta) = -\frac{\partial s}{\partial t}$. With $s(t,\theta)$ being $e^{-\mu(t-\theta)}$, $V(\theta,\rho,\mu)$ can be simplified to:

$$V(\theta, \rho, \mu) = \int_{\theta}^{\infty} u(c(t+\theta)) e^{-(\rho+\mu)t} dt. \tag{3}$$

Two very strong assumptions underlying Equation (3) should be noted. First, the instantaneous felicity $u[c(t)]$ is independent of age or health status of the individual. Second, the felicity, if I may infelicitously use the word, of death is zero. If $u(\ )$ could be treated as a von Neumann-Morgenstern utility function, so that its origin and scale of measurement is arbitrary, setting felicity of death at zero would be a harmless normalization of the felicity function. I am not sure that $u(\ )$ could be treated this way. In any case, the individual is choosing among consumption paths of uncertain length and scale. Treating all feasible paths as if they are of equal length, but substituting zero for consumption in the periods after death in such paths, is no solution, since it simply restates the problem, in other words, it treats a person who consumes nothing as no different from a dead person. In any case, even if one rules out bequests, one can imagine an individual anticipating the impact of her death on her children and reflecting it in her postdeath felicity. It is also possible that a person suffering from an incurable and painful disease might view death as relief from pain. For such a person, felicity after death could be higher than felicity before death.

I will explore below the implications of setting felicity of death as a constant negative number, although it should depend on age of death and predeath health status. This is analogous to what is often done in the health economics literature, where the utility of a worker with wage w while healthy $U(w)$ is distinguished from his or her utility $V(w)$ if she is injured. Before I do that, let me point out another assumption made by Nordhaus.

Nordhaus maximizes Equation (2) subject to a lifetime budget constraint:

$$\int_0^{\infty} c(t+\theta)e^{-rt}dt \leq W(\theta), \tag{4}$$

where $W(\theta)$ is the wealth of the individual at age θ and r is the interest rate. By assuming $r = \rho + \mu$, Nordhaus ensures that along the optimal path consumption will be a constant c^*. This assumption is easily seen to be very strong—while r can be reasonably assumed to be the same for all individuals, neither ρ nor μ need be, particularly if μ is not an exogenous constant.

Let me now turn to the implications of assuming the felicity of death as $-D$ where $D > 0$. Then:

$$\begin{aligned} V &= \int_{\theta}^{\infty}\left[\int_{\theta}^{t} e^{-\rho(\tau-\theta)}u(c(\tau))d\tau - e^{-\rho(t-\theta)}D\right]h(t,\theta)d\theta \\ &= \int_0^{\infty} u(c(t+\theta))e^{-(\rho+\mu)t}dt - \frac{D\mu}{\rho+\mu}. \end{aligned} \tag{5}$$

Maximizing Equation (5) subject to Equation (3), assuming $r = \rho + \mu$, leads to:

$$V = \frac{u(c^*) - D\mu}{\rho + \mu} \tag{6}$$

and

$$c^* = (\rho + \mu)W(\theta). \tag{7}$$

Nordhaus defines the tradeoff between "health and wealth" as $\frac{dc^*}{d\mu}$. I do not think this is correct. It should be defined as the marginal rate of substitution $-\frac{\partial V}{\partial \mu}\Big/\frac{\partial V}{\partial W}$ between μ and W along a V indifference curve. Now:

$$\frac{\partial V}{\partial \mu} = \frac{-[u(c^*) - D\mu]}{(\rho + \mu)^2} + \frac{[u'(c^*)W - D]}{(\rho + \mu)} = \frac{u'(c^*)W - V - D}{\rho + \mu} \tag{8}$$

$$\frac{\partial V}{\partial W} = u'(c^*) \tag{9}$$

$$-\frac{\partial V}{\partial \mu} \Big/ \frac{\partial V}{\partial W} = \frac{-[u'(c^*)W - V - D]}{(\rho + \mu)u'(c^*)} \quad \text{or} \quad = \frac{u(c^*) + D\rho - u'(c^*)c^*}{(\rho + \mu)^2 u'(c^*)}. \tag{10}$$

It is clear that the value of D does affect this tradeoff. With u concave in c and $D > 0$, it follows from Equation (10) that the marginal rate of substitution is positive, that is, at the margin an increase in mortality probability μ needs to be compensated by an increase in wealth W for the individual to remain on the same V indifference curve.

Lastly, let me suggest a possible approach to introducing age and health status into the felicity function. Suppose one can somehow define an individual's most preferred age and health status as $\bar{\theta}$ and $\bar{h}$. Let $u(c, \bar{\theta}, \bar{h})$ be her felicity when consuming c at her most preferred age and health status. Then the felicity u that a person age θ and health status h derives from consuming the same c could be defined as follows:

$$u(c, \theta, h) = u(cf(\theta, h), \bar{\theta}, \bar{h}). \tag{11}$$

The idea underlying Equation (11) is that the individual has to be compensated for not being at her most preferred age and health status through adjustments in c. $f(\theta,h)$ represents the compensation function. This is the approach used by Helpman (1981) to represent utility derived from consuming differentiated products when an individual has her most preferred variety and has to be compensated were she to consume any other variety, the compensation depending on how close that variety is to her most preferred variety.

References

Helpman, E. (1981). "International Trade in the Presence of Product Differentiation, Economies of Scale and Monopolistic Competition: A Chamberlin-Heckscher-Ohlin Approach." *Journal of International Economics* 11(3): 305–340.

Jorgenson, D., and B. M. Fraumeni. (1995). "The Accumulation of Human and Nonhuman Capital, 1948–84." In *Productivity, Volume 1: Postwar U.S. Economic Growth.* Ed. Dale W. Jorgenson. Cambridge: MIT Press.
Kendrik, J. (1976). *The Formation and Stocks of Total Capital.* New York: Columbia University Press.
Spatafora, N. (1997). *Essays on Growth, Development, and International Trade.* Ph.D. diss., Yale University.

Health, Government, and Irving Fisher

By Victor R. Fuchs*

Abstract. This paper provides a few historical notes on government involvement in health, followed by a summary of the theoretical arguments that economists offer in its support. Irving Fisher's views and recommendations about health are examined in the light of today's perceptions concerning health, health economics, and health policy. The wide variety of roles that the U.S. and other governments currently play in health is reviewed, and the ability of economics to explain these roles is assessed. The consequences of government involvement for the health of populations, for expenditures on health care, and for political and social stability are examined. The paper concludes with an overview of new worldwide trends in health policy and some probable explanations for these trends.

In the 50 years since the death of Irving Fisher, the U.S. government's role in health has expanded enormously. Fisher would have approved; indeed, he devoted an enormous amount of time and energy to advocating such expansion. His perceptions and recommendations about health were often on the mark, but some strayed from the theoretical and empirical rigor one would expect from the foremost American economist of his time. Some of his writings about health can serve as an object lesson of what can go wrong when a brilliant analyst and keen observer becomes a crusading social reformer. This paper also illustrates the strengths and the limitations of economics in explaining such a complex phenomenon as government's role in health.

I begin with a few historical notes on government involvement, followed by a summary of the theoretical arguments that economists offer in its support. I then consider several of Fisher's health-related

*The author is Henry J. Kaiser Jr. Professor Emeritus, Stanford University, and Research Associate at the National Bureau of Economic Research. Thanks are due to the Robert Wood Johnson and Andrew W. Mellon Foundations for financial support of this work.

The American Journal of Economics and Sociology, Vol. 64, No. 1 (January, 2005).

"enthusiasms" in the light of today's perceptions concerning health, health economics, and health policy. The wide variety of roles that the U.S. and other governments currently play in health is reviewed, and the ability of economics to explain these roles is assessed. This is followed by an examination of the consequences of government involvement for the health of populations, for expenditures on health care, and for political and social stability. The paper concludes with an overview of new worldwide trends in health policy and some probable explanations for these trends.

I

Historical Notes

ALTHOUGH GOVERNMENT INVOLVEMENT IN HEALTH ON A LARGE SCALE is largely a 20th-century phenomenon, some precursers can be traced back for thousands of years. One of the earliest interventions for which we have written record is the Mosaic prohibition on the eating of pork and shellfish. There are also references to the construction of hospitals in India by an emperor who ruled three centuries before the birth of Christ. In the Western world prior to the rise of nation-states, religious institutions tended to dominate health-related activities, especially the construction of hospitals to provide the poor with a place to die.

In the 17th century the king of Sweden built several hospitals to house soldiers returning from European wars. Many of these soldiers had contracted the "French disease," as syphilis was commonly known. (In France it was referred to as the "Italian disease.") Inasmuch as there was no effective cure for syphilis at that time, one possible motivation was the state's desire to isolate these soldiers from the rest of the Swedish population. A similar goal may have motivated one of the first major forays of the U.S. government into health, namely, the construction of merchant marine hospitals in major ports in the early 19th century.

In the mid-19th century there was a strong public health movement in England led by Sir Edwin Chadwick, a follower of Jeremy Bentham. Chadwick, along with Nassau W. Senior, produced a report in 1834 that led to increased government supervision over health and safety.

Throughout his life, Chadwick gave particular emphasis to improvements in sanitary conditions and other reforms designed to reduce the toll of communicable diseases. Although not an economist, he welcomed the application of economics to problems of health policy, writing: "When the moralist and the sentimentalist fails, he will have as a last resource to call on the aid of the economist."

In the late 19th century, Bismarck introduced national health insurance to Germany. Although this event is much celebrated today among enthusiasts for national health insurance, it was not Bismarck's original legislative objective, and he thought so little of it that he failed to mention it in his autobiography. Bismarck's original objective was insurance for workers who were injured and disabled in industrial accidents. He was frustrated in this attempt by a coalition of liberals (free market advocates), conservatives, and organizations that were already in the business of selling such insurance. As an alternative, he accepted health insurance even though there was little reason to think that medical care had much to offer the population at that time in terms of improved health. Several years earlier, a prominent American physician had asserted that if the entire pharmacopaeia were sent to the bottom of the sea, it would be so much the better for mankind and so much the worse for the fishes. Indeed, most medical historians believe that at the time of Bismarck's initiative and for several decades thereafter, a random patient with a random disease consulting a random physician had no better than a 50-50 chance of benefitting from the encounter.

Two political imperatives undoubtedly fueled Bismarck's desire to achieve some kind of social legislation. First, he was continually trying to consolidate allegiance to the German nation-state, which he had created out of an array of smaller kingdoms, principalities, duchys, and other political units. Second, he wished to blunt the political appeal of the socialist and working-class parties that were regaining strength after the abortive uprisings in the middle of the 19th century.

In 1911 Japan suddenly entered the health scene when the emperor created a sick fund for the poor; this was followed by the construction of a hospital in 1912 (Ikegami 1998). The precipitating event appears to have been the discovery in 1910 of a plot to assassinate the emperor. This discovery had a profound effect on the Japanese ruling classes; it reflected deep unrest among the mass of workers who were being brought into a newly industrializing, urban society.

Subsequent historical highlights include the introduction of compulsory health insurance for workers by Lloyd George in England in 1912, a Soviet system of national health insurance introduced by Lenin after the Bolshevik Revolution, the British National Health Service initiated by Beveridge and Bevan in 1945, the Canadian federal-provincial plans (hospital care in the late 1950s and physician services in the late 1960s), and the U.S. programs of Medicare and Medicaid enacted in 1965. In nearly all cases, these plans built on previous systems of medical organization and finance that reflected particular national traditions, values, and circumstances (Abel-Smith 1964).

In reviewing these interventions it is apparent that the earlier ones were dominated by concern about externalities, especially the desire to prevent the spread of communicable infectious diseases. Beginning with Germany in the late 19th century and for most of the 20th century, the primary emphasis shifted to ensuring access to medical care, the provision of which is seen to be politically and socially important, independent of its effects on health.

II

Economists' Rationales

ECONOMICS PROVIDES SEVERAL THEORETICAL RATIONALES for government intervention in health, mostly under the general rubric of "market failure." The concept that is most frequently invoked is "externalities." First and foremost are the externalities associated with communicable infectious diseases, which were the major source of mortality and morbidity until well into the 20th century. Most of the important early government interventions were aimed at reducing the spread of these diseases. These interventions could be justified without assuming any interdependent utilities among individuals. When my health depends upon my neighbor's health, I have a strong interest in his staying well, even if I would be otherwise indifferent about his well-being.

With the decline in importance of infectious diseases and the rise of heart disease, cancer, and stroke as the major causes of mortality and morbidity, the traditional rationale of externalities became less compelling. Even economists who are strong supporters of national health insurance do not rely on the externality argument. Lester Thurow (1974), for instance, has noted: "Once a society gets beyond public health measures and communicable diseases, medical care does not generate externalities." Although governments did not abandon public health measures, the emphasis of intervention changed to providing access to personal medical care. The rationale for collective provision draws in part on the idea of "philanthropic externalities" (Pauly 1971). It assumes some interdependence of utilities—that is, individuals derive utility from knowing that other (sick) individuals are receiving medical care. Voluntary philanthropy is likely to be less than socially optimal because each individual's giving tends to be based on his or her private satisfaction, ignoring the effects on others. The solution may be compulsory philanthropy, that is, government programs.

When discussing market imperfections in health, it is useful to distinguish between the market for health insurance and the market for medical care itself. Neither market experiences major problems from monopoly or monopsony, but that may change as a result of the current wave of mergers (Fuchs 1997). Both markets suffer extensively from problems of information. In the insurance market the buyer typically has more information than the seller; this can lead to adverse selection and the breakdown of the market (Rothschild and Stiglitz 1976). In health care the asymmetry is reversed, with the seller typically having more information than the buyer. This has led to reliance on professional norms (Arrow 1963) and to government regulation.

Efficiency considerations are not the only ones offered by economists in support of government involvement in health. Redistributive objectives also play a role (Poterba 1996). While income determines access to most goods and services, it is often argued that income should not determine access to life itself. Although most health care does not involve life or death, this argument still carries considerable weight, partly because it is often difficult to determine with certainty which care will extend life and which will not.

Redistribution tied to particular commodities (such as health care) is often criticized by economists as less efficient than redistribution of income, but an efficiency argument can be made for redistribution tied to health care along the following lines. Assume that an economy is in a state of equilibrium with regard to redistribution. Then someone gets sick, and society may wish to redistribute additional resources to that individual. But in order to do so by a cash transfer, there would first have to be a determination as to how sick the person is and how much redistribution would restore the equilibrium. Thus, two parallel medical care systems would be needed, one to establish the amount of money and the other to deliver whatever care the individual chose to purchase. Furthermore, it is usually difficult to determine at the onset of a disease how much redistribution would be appropriate, so this process would have to continue on an iterative basis.

Some economists offer a paternalistic rationale in support of government health programs such as national health insurance. Lester Thurow (1974: 193), for example, has argued that if society desires to raise each family up to some minimum level of real welfare, it may be more efficient to do this through in-kind transfers than through cash grants because many individuals may not be competent to make such allocation decisions on their own.

The conventional view of paternalism involves at least two individuals; for example, Jones thinks that he has a better understanding of what is in Smith's best interest than Smith does. There is another variation, however, which involves only one individual who is concerned about bad decisions that he might make in the future. In this two-self model, Jones at time t wishes to precommit in order to prevent Jones at time $t + n$ from making poor choices. Support for health insurance and other government interventions can be viewed as a form of precommitment.

III

Fisher on Health

AFTER HIS SEVERAL-YEAR BOUT WITH TUBERCULOSIS at the age of 31, Fisher developed a life-long interest in health and health policy. His illness also led to his becoming a "partaker in public movements for the betterment of mankind" as a complement to his theoretical work (Fisher 1925). His concern with health problems and health policy was expressed in many forms, including publications, letters, speeches, testimony, and active leadership of several groups dedicated to policy reforms. His principal enthusiasms included expansion of public health programs, a vegetarian diet, annual physical exams, national health insurance, prohibition of alcohol, and eugenics.

A. Public Health

In his advocacy of an expanded public health effort and systematic collection of vital statistics, Fisher was on the side of the angels. At the time he began his public health crusade (1907), impure milk and milk products were especially dangerous to infants and young children. Improper handling of garbage and the transmission of disease by insects and vermin posed major health problems for the population. Unlike many European countries, the United States had no accurate birth statistics and less than half the population lived in states with registration of deaths. Fisher argued (correctly, I believe) that the absence of timely, reliable statistics impeded attempts to improve the health of the population. Although he thought that industrial child labor imperiled children's health, he did not favor its abolition at the time. Showing the economist's appreciation of tradeoffs, he judged it to do less harm than the alternative—exposure to hookworm disease on polluted farms (Fisher 1909).

B. Diet

Fisher's advice about diet provides a good example of being right for the wrong reason. Although not an uncompromising vegetarian, he believed that "flesh-abstainers" were much healthier than "flesh-eaters," and he conducted experiments with Yale undergraduates as subjects to prove the point. The essence of his dietary theory was that carbohydrates were good for health and proteins were bad. Thus he favored vegetables and grains over animal products. Today, most nutrition experts endorse complex carbohydrates (but not simple ones), and many urge a reduction in consumption of animal products. Their opposition to animal products, however, is not because they are protein-rich, but because many of them contain a high percentage of fat. Excess consumption of fat is believed to increase the risk of heart disease, cancer, and possibly other diseases.

A curious omission in Fisher's discussion of changes in diet and other health-related behaviors is the fact that the costs and benefits of these investments in health usually occur at different points in time. The theorist who pioneered in the analysis of intertemporal choice, the economist who eagerly accepted the concept of "living capital" (an early version of "human capital") and argued that it was five times as important as physical capital showed little inclination to inquire systematically about rates of return to investment in health relative to other forms of investment.

C. Annual Physical Exams

One area where Fisher did make some claim for "cost effectiveness" for his recommendation was in the advocacy of annual physical examinations. He believed that life insurance companies could profit by providing such exams to their policyholders. It is possible that Fisher was correct at the time, although the subsequent failure of this recommendation to catch on in a sustained way suggests that it did not meet the market test. Today, many health experts question the value of general annual physical exams. Some specialized screenings, however, such as mammograms or Pap smears, are deemed cost effective for appropriate populations at appropriate intervals.

D. National Health Insurance

Irving Fisher was one of the first prominent Americans to advocate national health insurance (NHI). The arguments he advanced in support of NHI illustrate the strengths and weaknesses of this complex man. Fisher readily appreciated the fact that the market for individual insurance would tend to be inefficient and unstable; thus, he recommended compulsory universal coverage. He believed—and subsequent experience tends to support his view—that national health insurance would result in substantial savings in administrative and sales costs.

More dubious was his belief that the great virtue of NHI would lie in the prevention of illness. One must also question his assumption that the portions of the premium paid by the employer or by government would not be at the expense of the workers through effects on wages, prices, or taxes. This assumption, unfortunately, was still alive and well during the debate over the Clinton health plan (Fuchs 1994), although decisively rejected by health economists and economic theorists (Fuchs 1996).

While Fisher was quick to appreciate the theoretical points that supported NHI, he apparently never considered the dead-weight loss that might be expected from reducing the marginal cost of health care to zero. Or, if he did consider it, he decided not to confront the issue. In addition to theoretical lapses, Fisher was particularly weak in his attempt to muster empirical (historical) support for NHI. Consider his reading of the blessings Germany was supposed to have realized from national health insurance after its introduction by Bismarck in 1883: "Her wonderful industrial progress since that time, her comparative freedom from poverty, reduction in the death rate, advancement in hygiene, and the physical preparedness of her soldiery, are presumably due, in considerable measure, to health insurance" (Fisher 1917). It would be difficult to find convincing support for any one of those claims; taken as a whole, the statement would hardly warrant inclusion in a speech by a politician, let alone in a publication by a distinguished social scientist.

E. Prohibition of Alcohol

If alcohol is viewed purely as a health problem, Fisher's lifelong crusade against drinking had and still has strong empirical support. At present, excess consumption of alcohol is a major contributor to morbidity and mortality in the United States. Fisher probably went too far, however, in asserting that alcohol was an unequivocal evil that had no benefits. He says he reached this conclusion after a "thoroughly disinterested study" on the basis of statistics and physiology (Fisher 1912). Most health experts see no harm from moderate consumption of alcohol, and many now believe there may be some positive effects on health, especially from wine. Advocating abstention from alcohol is one thing; Fisher's enthusiastic embrace of Prohibition before its enactment and his endorsement of its effects afterward is another. In testimony before a Senate subcommittee in 1926, Fisher stated: "In my opinion, the good done by Prohibition greatly overbalances the harm, not because I underestimate the harm done—at least I do not think I do—but simply because the good is so great. Moreover, the harm should be only temporary, while we are adjusting ourselves to the revolutionary change. The good should last forever" (Fisher 1926).

In reaching this conclusion, one wonders how much weight Fisher gave to the fact that Prohibition denied millions of Americans a source of pleasure, and turned millions of others into lawbreakers? How much weight did he give to the corruption and violent crime induced by Prohibition? And how did he compare the good (better health, less absenteeism, etc.) with the harm to reach his conclusion? We know that reasonable men and women with access to the same facts urged repeal of Prohibition, presumably because they weighted good and harm differently; in short, because they had different values. In failing to make his values explicit, and in failing to show how his values interacted with his analyses to reach policy conclusions, Fisher was doing what many leading economists before and after him have done, but that does not make it right.

F. Eugenics

In my judgment the least commendable of Fisher's health "enthusiasms" (perhaps "passions" would be more accurate) is his embrace of eugenics. His writings on this subject are a curious mixture of mysticism, pseudoscience, and policy. Fisher (1913) believed that "eugenics is hygiene raised to the highest power" and that in the future it would be "the essential foundation of ethics." He also wrote that "we shall realize the dream of the founder of this science, Sir Francis Galton, and will link up eugenics with religion." Fisher held at times a Lamarckian view of evolution. He believed that changes in conditions of living could lead to what he called "racial degeneration," and he asserted: "It is easily practical to alter and improve the human race, and to do so in a very short time."

Fisher was particularly eager to apply his beliefs about eugenics to immigration policy. He wrote: "The generally higher intelligence of recent immigrants from Northern and Western Europe is definitely established, as is the fact that the immigrants who have been coming during the past few decades, mostly Southern and Eastern Europeans, have been steadily deteriorating in intelligence." He concluded: "It is high time for the American people to put a stop to such degradation of American citizenship, and such a wrecking of the future American race."

In his defense, it must be said that Fisher was far from alone in holding these views. Indeed, leading scholars in many fields reached similar conclusions and advocated similar policies. With the benefit of hindsight, however, we can see that the reasoning borders on the irrational, the scientific underpinnings were deeply flawed, and the policy recommendations misguided.

IV

Government Involvement in Health: What? Why?

TWO THEMES DOMINATE THE STORY of government and health in the 20th century. First and foremost, government involvement in health has *expanded* greatly in every industrialized nation. Countries may embrace free markets, may privatize some industries and deregulate others, but when it comes to health insurance and health care, governments in these same countries own facilities, provide care, subsidize insurance, regulate drugs, license personnel, promote health, and more. Even in the United States, which is virtually alone in not having national health insurance, government pays directly for almost half of all medical care and subsidizes private purchase of care through favorable tax treatment.

Second, the *form* of government intervention in health varies greatly from country to country. Some finance medical care out of general tax revenue, others use earmarked taxes, still others rely on mandates and/or subsidies for health insurance plans. Ownership of hospitals is public in one country and private in another; private hospitals may be nonprofit (religious or secular) or for-profit. Physicians may be government employees or in private practice and, if the latter, may be compensated fee-for-service, by salary, or by some form of capitation. U.S. health care is particularly rich in diversity; the institutional arrangements for financing, organizing, and reimbursing care include virtually all of the possibilities evident in countries across the world.

How well have economists explained the great expansion of government in health? The answer, unfortunately, is "hardly at all." Some economists, such as Milton Friedman, have argued that the expansion is all a vast policy mistake. But George Stigler (1975) has noted: "If an economic policy has been adopted by many communities, or if it is persistently pursued by society over a long span of time, it is fruitful to assume that the real effects were known and desired." Twenty years ago I proposed a menu of possible explanations, including the ever-increasing complexity of modern life, an increase in psychological externalities resulting from urbanization and improvements in communications, the declining importance of family and church as providers of insurance and regulators of behavior, and the pressure for a more egalitarian society (Fuchs 1978). The last point was made earlier by British economists Sylvia and John Jewkes when they wrote that the driving force behind the creation of the British National Health Service was not a search for efficiency so much as a surging national desire to share something equally (Jewkes and Jewkes 1963).

With respect to explaining the diversity of institutional arrangements for government in health, James Poterba's review of the "choice of instrument problem" suggests that economists have barely scratched the surface (Poterba 1996). He believes redistributive concerns have been important in U.S. government health policy, but the use of tax breaks as a major instrument seems inconsistent with such a goal. Also, a recent study by McClellan and Skinner (1997) concludes that the benefits of Medicare are positively correlated with income. In his comment on the Poterba paper, Richard Zeckhauser (1996) agrees with the general conclusion that economics does a poor job of explaining intercountry and intertemporal variation in social policy. He argues that if economists wish to make more of an impact they will need "an improved knowledge of the real game, including both empirical realities and matters of institutional design and politics."

As an example of how a narrow application of economics can fall short of explicating a policy choice, consider a country choosing between two plans for financing health care. The first plan relies on a proportional payroll tax earmarked for health care. The second relies on a mandated contribution to a health insurance fund, also proportional to payroll. Most economists would see no difference between the plans, but the public might view them very differently because the tax would be collected and administered by the department of finance (e.g., the Treasury), while the mandated contribution would be received and administered by the department of social insurance (e.g., the Department of Health and Human Services). The public might (correctly) believe that the two departments differed markedly in efficiency, honesty, and ability to withstand partisan political pressure. Moreover, the perceived differences might lead to favoring the first plan in one country and the second in another.

V

Consequences of Government Involvement

PUBLIC HEALTH EFFORTS BY GOVERNMENT have undoubtedly done a great deal to improve health. Immunization programs have led to the eradication of many serious communicable diseases; cleaner water and air have reduced morbidity and mortality. Some public health efforts undoubtedly overreach, and some health progress would have occurred as a corollary of rising real income, but the gains in health recorded in the late 19th and early 20th centuries were primarily attributable to public health programs. Even today, no country seriously considers turning over all public health activities to the interplay of demand and supply in a free market that would ignore externalities.

The effect of national health insurance programs on health levels is less clear. Proponents argue that NHI improves the health of the population by increasing access to medical care. Critics argue that it worsens health by rationing the introduction of new technology and by constraining the behavior of physicians and hospitals. The effect of national health insurance on health depends on the product of two elasticities: (a) the responsiveness of the quantity of medical care to national health insurance and (b) the responsiveness of health to changes in the quantity of medical care. In my judgment, in developed countries the product of these two terms is quite small.

Apart from the effects of NHI on average health levels, one might ask whether it has done much to reduce socioeconomic differentials in mortality and morbidity within a country. A reduction in such differentials was one of the principal arguments used to support the introduction of NHI in England and other countries. Here the evidence is more compelling: universal coverage does not eliminate or even substantially reduce differentials across socioeconomic groups. In England, for instance, infant mortality in the lowest socioeconomic class is double the rate of the highest class, just as it was prior to the introduction of national health insurance (Townsend and Davidson 1982). The relatively homogeneous populations of Scandinavia not only enjoy universal coverage for health care but also have many other egalitarian social programs. Nevertheless, life expectancy varies considerably across occupations; the age-standardized mortality ratio for male hotel, restaurant, and food service workers is double that for teachers and technical workers (Andersen 1991). A study of age-standardized death rates in Sweden among employed men ages 45–64 found substantial differences across occupations in 1966–1970, and slightly greater differentials in 1976–1980 (Calltorp 1989).

NHI does reduce differentials in access to care, and that could be a highly valued social objective, even if it does not reduce differentials in health outcomes. Physicians and other health professionals can offer caring, sympathy, and support. Many patients want physicians to assume responsibility for a difficult decision or to provide validation for a course of action. A government that ensures access wins support from large segments of the population. When refugees from the Soviet Union were interviewed in western Europe after World War II, they invariably praised the West and disparaged life in Russia—with one notable exception. They said they sorely missed the comprehensive health insurance provided by the Soviet state (Field

1967). Conservative politicians, when they come to power, are loath to retreat from national health insurance, although British Prime Minister Thatcher did push through some market-oriented reforms in the organization of the National Health Service.

The consequences of NHI for health care expenditures appear to have been the opposite of expectations. Because insured patients face no financial barrier to the utilization of care, economic theory predicts that the quantity demanded should increase. Perhaps it does, but this does not translate into greater expenditures. Countries with universal health insurance uniformly spend much less on medical care than does the United States. It is clear that countries with universal coverage find other methods to contain health care spending, methods that apparently are more effective than financial constraints on patients. No one knows what the optimal level of expenditures is; thus no claim can be made that NHI is, in the economist's sense, more efficient. Countries with national health insurance contain expenditures in part by using their monopsony power to squeeze down the prices of resources, especially drugs and physicians' services. They also rely heavily on "upstream resource allocation"; in other words, control over capital investment and facilities and equipment, specialty mix of physicians, and the development and diffusion of high-cost new technology. The price paid for such controls is delay or inconvenience in receiving high-tech services, or sometimes not receiving such services at all. Whether such delays or denials have a significant effect on the health of the population is not known with certainty; the available evidence suggests that they do not.

For many countries, NHI is viewed as more than just a device for holding down the growth of health care expenditures. It is valued for its contribution to political stability and social solidarity. This objective is stated most explicitly in the Scandinavian countries, but I believe it is implicit in the support for NHI in other countries as well. Symbols and institutions have always played an important role in providing cohesion for nation-states. In earlier times religion was a major force, but today many people find a white coat more reassuring than a black one, a medical center more impressive than a cathedral.

VI

New Trends in Health Policy

HEALTH POLICY IS IN A STATE OF FERMENT in nearly all industrialized nations. Rising expenditures for health care, driven primarily by technological and demographic changes, are forcing governments to reexamine and modify long-standing arrangements for financing and delivering care.

One new trend features attempts to place the practice of medicine on a more scientific footing. These attempts appear under different names: "evidence-based medicine," "outcomes research," "clinical guidelines," "the new technology assessment" (Fuchs and Garber 1990). Whatever the name, the idea is the same. Although the practice of medicine will always be partly an art, new information technology, new analytical techniques such as "meta-analysis," and the presence of health professionals who combine clinical and quantitative skills make it possible to improve substantially the scientific basis for medical practice.

The pressure behind these attempts is coming primarily from governments and private payors of health care. They suspect that much of current medical practice will not stand up to scientific scrutiny; this kind of research is expected to save money. The results, however, are likely to prove problematical. Some current practice will prove to be ineffective. The new research, however, will also reveal that a great deal of care doesn't do the patient harm and, at considerable cost, may do some good. Public and private health insurance plans that promise to deliver "all necessary care" will then have to explicitly face very difficult choices regarding the care to be made available.

A second new trend that is closely related to the first is explicit priority setting. The State of Oregon, for example, implemented a plan that specifies services and technologies that are available to Medicaid patients and those that are not. The latter list includes many that are clearly effective, at least for some patients, but do not meet the standard of cost-effectiveness as determined by experts and the public. Another indication of this trend is the sponsorship by Sweden, Norway, Finland, the World Health Organization, and the European

Union of the First International Conference on Priorities in Health Care in Stockholm in 1996. Participants came from more than 50 countries and from every continent except Antarctica. Difficult choices regarding the allocation of resources are becoming more pressing every day. These choices include the allocation of resources between health care and other goods and services, between extending life and improving the quality of life, between individuals at different levels of income, between individuals at different stages of the lifecycle, and between extending life (at great cost) for patients with low probability of survival and preventive interventions (at lower cost per year of life extended) for individuals who have a high probability of survival. Explicit priority setting, however, is likely to move very slowly because it is politically explosive.

Another new development, possibly temporary, is a reversal of the long-term trend toward greater equality in health care. The emergence of so-called two-tier medical care is evident not only in the United States but also in other countries that nominally provide the same care to all through national health insurance. In fact, these countries have "escape valves" for those who are willing and able to purchase more than the general standard. Indeed, it may be that the new systems that are emerging might properly be described as "*n*-tiered." Nations probably will concentrate on providing a basic package of care for all; beyond that, some individuals will purchase more, and some a great deal more, depending upon their circumstances. The argument that income should not determine "who shall live and who shall die" will carry less force than in the past for two reasons. First, it is becoming increasingly clear that life expectancy depends on many factors other than medical care, including occupation, diet, housing, and auto safety, and that individuals with higher income can clearly opt for life-extending choices in those areas. Second, an increasing proportion of medical care expenditures is likely to be directed toward improving the quality of life rather than increasing its length.

* * * *

As a concomitant of economic development, government involvement in health has been growing for several hundred years and has accelerated in the 20th century. Most of the earlier interventions were public health measures designed to prevent or limit the spread of infectious diseases. Subsequently, the emphasis shifted to broadening access to personal medical care. Economic theory provides numerous rationales for government involvement in health. Most of them address elimination of inefficiencies resulting from "market failures." In addition, proponents of government involvement frequently invoke redistributive objectives.

Irving Fisher's writings about health policy exhibit a curious range from prescient and judicious recommendations to policy proposals that lack secure theoretical and empirical grounding. The crusading social reformer in Fisher sometimes overwhelmed the brilliant social scientist. As George Stigler (1966) has noted, a scholar "ought to be tolerably open-minded, unemotional and rational. A reformer must promise paradise if his reform is adopted. Reform and research seldom march arm in arm."

Apart from theoretical speculations, economists have not contributed much to the explanation of government involvement in health or of the wide variation in the forms that such involvement takes. To make progress on these questions, economists' traditional theoretical and empirical approaches must be combined with research that focuses on history and institutions. The newest trends in health policy—quantitative analysis of medical practice, explicit priority setting, and a reversal of long-term egalitarian trends—present additional challenges to the study of the role of government in health.

References

Abel-Smith, Brian. (1964). "Major Patterns of Financing and Organization of Medical Care in Countries Other Than the United States." *Bulletin of the New York Academy of Medicine* 40 (2nd series).

Andersen, O. (1991). "Occupational Impacts on Mortality Declines in the Nordic Countries." In *Future Demographic Trends in Europe and North America*. Ed. W. Lutz. New York: Academic Press, Harcourt-Brace-Jovanovich.

Arrow, Kenneth. (1963). "Uncertainty and the Welfare Economics of Medical Care." *American Economic Review* 53(5): 941–973.

Barber, William. Ed. (1997). *The Works of Irving Fisher.* London: Pickering and Chatto.

Calltorp, J. (1989). "The 'Swedish Model' Under Pressure: How to Maintain Equity and Develop Quality." *Quality Assurance in Health Care* 1(1): 13–22.

Field, Mark G. (1967). *Soviet Socialized Medicine 14.*

Fisher, Irving. (1909). "Summary." In *National Vitality, Its Waste and Conservation, Report of the National Conservation Commission: Vol. 3, Senate Document 676.* 60th Congress, 2nd Session.

——. (1912). "Testimony on the Sale of Intoxicating Liquors Before a Subcommittee on Excise and Liquor Legislation of the Committee on the District of Columbia, U.S. Senate, March 7." In *The Works of Irving Fisher,* Vol. 13: 98.

——. (1913). "Eugenics." *Good Health Magazine* 48(11). (Quoted in Barber, *The Works of Irving Fisher,* Vol. 13: 161.)

——. (1917). "The Need for Health Insurance." *American Labor Legislation Review* March.

——. (1925). In William Barber, *The Works of Irving Fisher,* Vol. 1: 8. Ed. W. Barber, London: Pickenng and Chatto. (This quote from Fisher is an extract from copy prepared in February 1925 for *Political Economics in Autobiographies.*)

——. (1926). "Testimony on the National Prohibition Law Before the Subcommittee of the Committee on the Judiciary, U.S. Senate, 69:1, April 5: 1015–1031." In *The Works of Irving Fisher,* Vol. 13: 116. Ed. W. Barber, London: Pickenng and Chatto.

Fuchs, Victor R. (1978). "Economics, Health, and Post-Industrial Society." The E. S. Woodward Lectures in Economics, presented at the University of British Columbia, Nov. 1–2.

——. (1994). "The Clinton Plan: A Researcher Examines Reform." *Health Affairs* 13(1): 102–114.

——. (1996). "Economics, Values, and Health Care Reform." *American Economic Review* 86(1): 1–24.

——. (1997). "Managed Care and Merger Mania." *Journal of the American Medical Association* 277(11): 920–921.

Fuchs, Victor R., and Alan M. Garber. (1990). "The New Technology Assessment." *New England Journal of Medicine* 323(10): 673–677.

Ikegami, Naoki. (1998). Personal communication.

Jewkes, John, and Sylvia Jewkes. (1963). *Value for Money in Medicine 60.*

McClellan, Mark, and Jonathan Skinner. (1997). *The Incidence of Medicare.* Mimeo.

Pauly, Mark V. (1971). *Medical Care at Public Expense: A Study in Applied Welfare Economics.* New York: Praeger.

Poterba, James M. (1996). "Government Intervention in the Markets for

Education and Health Care: How and Why?" In *Individual and Social Responsibility: Child Care, Education, Medical Care, and Long-Term Care in America*. Ed. Victor R. Fuchs. Chicago: University of Chicago Press.

Rothschild, M., and J. Stiglitz. (1976). "Equilibrium and Competitive Insurance Markets: An Essay on the Economics of Imperfect Information." *Quarterly Journal of Economics* 90: 629–649.

Stigler, George J. (1966). *Chicago Today*. Winter: 30.

——. (1975). *The Citizen and the State: Essays on Regulation*. Chicago: University of Chicago Press.

Thurow, Lester C. (1974). "Cash Versus In-Kind Transfers." *American Economic Review* 64(2): 190–195.

Townsend, P., and N. Davidson. Eds. (1982). *Inequalities in Health: The Black Report*. Hartmondsworth, UK: Penguin Books.

Zeckhauser, Richard. (1996). "Comment on James M. Poterba, 'Government Intervention in the Markets for Education and Health Care: How and Why?'" In *Individual and Social Responsibility: Child Care, Education, Medical Care, and Long-Term Care in America*. Ed. Victor R. Fuchs. Chicago: University of Chicago Press.

Does "Health Promotion" Really Promote Health?

By Alvan R. Feinstein*

Abstract. In his comment on Victor Fuch's essay, the late Alvan Feinstein raised the question of whether government-sponsored programs of "health promotion" are always good for well-being.

Like many other discussions of the government's role in "health promotion," Victor Fuchs' excellent paper[1] makes the assumption that "promotion" is a well-established entity, so that the main job now is to disseminate it to everyone, at reasonable cost. Since the history of medicine and public health contains many splendid triumphs that followed a long array of errors and blunders, it is always important, in any era of medicine, to consider the possibility that the establishment beliefs are not always correct.[2]

The idea of "promotion" is itself relataively new. Health and health care have always involved various forms of personal or societal interventions, but the idea of "promotion" usually refers to many new types of prevention, administered to apparently healthy people, that will help retain health and thwart illness. Until about 1920,

*Alvan R. Feinstein, M.D., HS '54, Sterling Professor of Medicine and Epidemiology, died October 24, 2001. A native of Philadelphia, Feinstein received his bachelor's degree, a master's degree in mathematics, and his doctor of medicine degree from the University of Chicago. He completed his clinical training in internal medicine at Yale and his research training at Rockefeller Institute. Feinstein joined the Yale faculty in 1962 and became the founding director of the Robert Wood Johnson Clinical Scholars Program at Yale in 1964. Under his direction, the program became recognized as one of the leading sites for training in the methods of clinical research. He was also the director of the clinical examination course and created a course in quantitative clinical epidemiology that was imitated throughout the country. Because of his work on the statistical analysis of clinical signs and symptoms of real patients—rather than on the historically nonclinical methods of pure statistics—Feinstein was a key figure in the establishment of the field of clinical epidemiology. His approaches and methods were reported in three books: *Clinical Judgment*, *Clinical Epidemiology*, and *Clinimetrics*. His approaches to quantitative data were presented in three other books: *Clinical Biostatistics*, *Multivariable Analysis*, and *Principles of Medical Statistics*.

The American Journal of Economics and Sociology, Vol. 64, No. 1 (January, 2005).

preventive interventions were usually aimed at infectious diseases, and were given to society or individuals. The societal activities involved mainly sanitation, arranged in pertinent community settings, to remove or exclude bacterial contaminants from water, sewage, milk, meat, and other foods. The treatments given to individual persons were vaccinations against such diseases as smallpox and diphtheria.

These individual prophylactic treatments, which began late in the 19th century, were intended to prevent or delay the appearance of a target that has not yet occurred. The prophylactic treatments were a striking departure from the then-traditional medical practice of remedial therapy, which was intended to eliminate or ameliorate a target that already existed. Examples of remedial therapy are the use of an analgesic such as aspirin for headache, an antibiotic for infection, or blood transfusion for anemia.

I

Expanded Spectrum of "Prevention"

With the success of sanitation and vaccination in the first quarter of the 20th century, attention was turned to other forms of prevention aimed at noninfectious or chronic diseases, such as cancer or cardiovascular disease. These activities, some of which became today's "health promotion," have vastly expanded the spectrum of prophylactic therapy for both individuals and society. Individually, prevention has been subclassified into primary, secondary, and tertiary activities. The primary activities include not only the old "one-shot" types of vaccination, but the short-term use of antibiotics in healthy persons, such as college students, to prevent the spread of small epidemics, such as meningitis.

Almost all other types of prophylaxis today involve daily or repeated long-term activities, often continued for life. In primary prophylaxis, individual healthy persons are encouraged to eliminate or reduce "risk factors" in diet, smoking, or physical sloth. Secondary prophylaxis involves efforts to reduce an asymptomatic physiologic abnormality, such as an elevated blood pressure or serum cholesterol, to prevent future diseases such as heart attacks or stroke. Tertiary prophylaxis, for diseases that already exist, is given with the hope of keeping them from getting worse. Thus, efforts are made to prevent recurrent attacks of asthma, rheumatic fever, epilepsy, or myocardial infarction. Whenever death is the outcome to be prevented, the treatment of cancer or coronary disease constitutes tertiary prophylaxis. A special new form of tertiary prophylaxis involves "screening." It is intended to find things like cancer in an "early" stage, and to treat it successfully before it spreads or does other harm.

Beyond these complex activities in prophylactic interventions for individuals, an expanded spectrum of prevention has developed for society. We now have the following public-health activities: campaigns against smoking, alcohol, and violence; efforts to prevent accidents, occupational injuries, and environmental pollution; procedures to improve maternal and child health; and tactics that bring greater safety to sex, contraception, and illicit use of intravenous needles.

These diverse activities in prophylaxis are all motivated by the old aphorism that "an ounce of prevention is worth a pound of cure." Prevention of disease certainly seems cheaper than having to give remedial therapy afterward. And everyone recognizes intuitively the unmeasurable individual value of remaining alive and healthy.

II

Problems Associated with Expanded "Prevention"

NEVERTHELESS, THE NEW ACTIVITIES in prevention have brought an array of problems in the altered ethos of the doctor-patient relationship, in medicalization of the public, in the enthusiastic advocacy of strategies that have not yet been fully evaluated or proved, and in costs of all the preventive activities.

In relationships with patients, doctors of the past used mainly remedial therapy in carrying out the old maxim that the physician's job is to cure occasionally, relieve often, and comfort always. This Samaritan role has often changed to something more like that of a nanny or scold, as doctors badger patients who otherwise feel well to change diet, exercise more, and take prophylactic medications more faithfully. A prominent objection to this approach came from H. L. Mencken, who said: "The problem with our society is the corruption of medicine by morality. The purpose of medicine is not to make men virtuous, but . . . to rescue them from the consequences of their vices."

As annual checkups and other medical examinations often became imposed on people who had no medical complaints, various "risk factors" or other "abnormalities" might be detected and might lead to various unsolicited medical intrusions. A prominent dissent against this tactic was delivered by Henry David Thoreau, who said: "If I knew there were coming to my home, univited and unbidden, someone who had the express intention of doing me good, I would run for my life."

The medicalization of the public has eliminated serenity from many people who formerly led a doctor-free existence. The old medical question, "How are you?" had long ago entered common usage as a social greeting, but an increasingly common social question today is: "What's your cholesterol number?" There have also been two kinds of adverse effects, on psyche and soma. The psychic effect is the "labeling" that occurs as people begin worrying about their blood pressure, or about being designated as "hypertensive." The somatic effects have occurred as side reactions—such as fatigue, insomnia, or impotence—arising from the pharmaceutical agents used to treat elevations in blood pressure or blood lipids (such as cholesterol).

For example, I remember being shocked in the early 1970s when I visited the office of the Dean of the Johns Hopkins School of Public Health. He was chain-smoking and had an ashtray filled with cigarette butts. Noting my reaction, he said: "Yes, I smoke. I started again because when I stopped I was making myself and my family too miserable. My life may be shorter, but they and I will enjoy it much more."

The advocates of the public health measures have often been so scientifically zealous that they were unconcerned about anything other than preventing mortality. In the mid-1970s, I attended a discussion and planning session for a large-scale clinical project called the Multiple Risk Factor Intervention Trial.[3] It contained long-term dietary, pharmaceutical, and exercise interventions for asymptomatic people with the appropriate risk factors. When I asked what efforts would be made to appraise the personal distress of patients trying, perhaps unsuccessfully, to maintain those interventions, the answer from a leading American biostatistician was: "The endpoint will be death. We don't want any of that quality of life s—t."

During the zealous pursuit of prophylaxis, unintended adverse consequences were neglected at both psychic and somatic levels. For example, earlier in this century, people wanting to marry were required to take and pass a Wassermann blood test for syphilis. The procedure may have helped prevent the spread of syphilis, but the test often produced false positive results. Unfortunately, the fact that they were falsely positive did not become known until many years later. The persons with the positive tests were all regarded as having syphilis and were treated accordingly. Many lives were ruined by the erroneous diagnosis as people were denied marriage and jobs, as well as being regarded as liars when they denied any pertinent exposures to syphilis. A new set of psychic problems has been produced in the past few years for women who had false positive results in a screening mammogram for cancer of the breast and who were not effectively reassured by subsequent tests showing the absence of breast cancer.

One of the more striking adverse effects of prevention was an epidemic of retrolental fibroplasias that occurred in premature babies during 1946–1954.[4] The disease developed as scarred membranes behind the lens of the eyes and produced permanent blindness in about 10,000 children. The disease was caused by the prophylactic administration of high doses of oxygen given in the hope of preventing the respiratory distress syndrome that sometimes occurred in premature babies. The motivating belief was that anything so beneficial to the lungs as oxygen could not be harmful elsewhere. The event has sometimes been called the "academic epidemic," because only the high-tech academic institutions had the special incubators needed to deliver the high-dose oxygen.

A separate problem in screening activities is the uncertain evidence of their effectiveness. Randomized trials have shown that more of the target disease is found, as expected, in the screened group, but the subsequent benefits have been equivocal. The rate of death attributed to the target disease has been lower in the screened group, but the total death rates have usually been the same in the screened and unscreened groups. For example, in a trial where about 153,000 persons were screened and appropriately treated for colorectal cancer in the United Kingdom,[5] the follow-up results about eight years later showed a slightly lower death rate for colorectal cancer (about 6 per 1,000) in the screened group than in the unscreened group (about 7 per 1,000). The total death rates in the two groups, however, were essentially the same, at 211 and 210, respectively, per 10,000.

III

Sources of Problems

THE MAIN SOURCES OF these problems are unrestrained advocacy, inadequate data, unsatisfactory scientific policy, and misleading economic calculations. People in the world of medicine and public health sometimes become carried away by the obvious rightness or righteousness of their cause. The result is often vigorous advocacy rather than objective science. For example, the "Love Canal" region of New York State is still regarded as dangerous despite several subsequent demonstrations of gross error in the original "indictment" of allegedly adverse effects of ground pollution. A high-ranking public official recently confessed his blunder more than a decade ago in ordering the total evacuation, homes and all, of about 2,000 residents of a Missouri town where the ground had been found "polluted" by dioxin.

Vigorous advocacy is sometimes accompanied or followed by sublime neglect of contradictory evidence. For example, the value of intervening against "multiple risk factors" was supposed to be definitively resolved by the MRFIT study[3] and by several other large randomized trials. That the results of those "definitive" studies showed no substantial benefit for the interventions, however, has been generally ignored or left unpublicized as the advocates continue their calls for action.

The problem of inadequate data arises because the cancers, arteriosclerosis, and other asymptomatic ailments found by screening are almost always promptly treated. We know that many instances of cancer or arteriosclerosis are found at autopsy of people who died of other conditions, but we have no information about what would happen if the ailments discovered by screening during life were left untreated. Furthermore, the statistics regarding "cure" of the asymptomatic diseases are misleading, because the patients are classified only according to their morphologic (anatomic) abnormalities, not for their functional status as asymptomatic "screenees." Despite the same morphologic category of disease, the symptomatic and asymptomatic patients can have major differences in subsequent survival or other outcomes.

The problems are partly caused and are certainly increased by the constrained scientific policy of the National Institutes of Health (NIH). The NIH gives vigorous support to the "basic science" research that develops molecular and other explanations for the mechanisms involved in biologic and medical phenomena, but the NIH has given almost no support or attention to the different kind of "basic science" needed to evaluate prophylactic and therapeutic interventions. Instead, the NIH has supported an array of mathematical approaches and models (randomized trials, quantitative decision analysis, multi-item psychometric instruments) that are unsatisfactory for answering the most cogent questions. The overall merit of many prophylactic programs could be sharply increased, and the overall costs greatly reduced, if the programs were suitably evaluated and then appropriately curtailed or eliminated. These evaluations have not been done, however, because the appropriate basic scientific methods have not yet been developed for the appraisals.

A final cause of problems is the abuse of economic data when screening programs are zealously advocated. A particular program may seem to be inexpensive when it is reported as costing only $3 per person. Nevertheless, if the program is applied to 10,000,000 persons, the total cost is $30,000,000. Furthermore, the reported costs almost never include the additional technologic costs of the diagnostic "work-ups" that follow a positive result in a screening test, the time lost from work during those additional tests, and the adverse effects of false positive results.

IV

Conclusions

CERTAIN ACTS OF "health promotion" seem unequivocally worthwhile when they involve preventing infectious diseases by a simple vaccination, and the prevention of phenomena such as violence, trauma, alcoholism, and recurrent episodes of established diseases such as asthma, epilepsy, or rheumatic fever. Many other long-term preventive activities (and major changes in lifestyle), however, have not yet been suitably confirmed in randomized trials or other appropriate evaluations.

Programs of screening and prevention for chronic disease are currently justified by their "prudence," not by unequivocal evidence of their efficacy and their freedom from adverse physical and psychic effects. Nevertheless, the general public has been conditioned to approve and expect these activities; and physicians comply with the current "zeitgeist" because they too believe the programs are worthwhile or, even if skeptical, they fear the lawsuits that might follow failure to recommend the activities.

In a thoughtful book that appeared almost 15 years ago, Louise B. Russell[6] pointed out, in an essentially economic analysis, that preventive measures seldom reduce medical expenditures, and that what is offered essentially is "better health" at additional cost. At a different level of analysis and discussion, however, clinical and scientific questions can also be raised about whether the allegedly "better health" is truly better. With either or both types of analysis, the main policy issue today, bereft of suitable evidence to provide a definitive answer, is whether a pound of prevention is worth an ounce of cure.

Notes

1. Fuchs, V. (1998). "Promoting the Population's Health: The Role of Government." *American Journal of Economics and Sociology.*

2. Feinstein, A. R. (1997). "The Santayana Syndrome I: Errors in Getting and Interpreting Evidence; and II: Problems in Reasoning and Learning about Error." *Perspect. Biol. Med.* 41: 45–57, 73–85.

3. MRFIT Research Group. (1982). "Multiple Risk Factor Intervention Trial." *Journal of the American Medical Association* 248: 1465–1477.

4. Jacobson, R. M., and A. R. Feinstein. (1992). "Oxygen as a Cause of Blindness in Premature Infants: 'Autopsy' of a Decade of Errors in Clinical Epidemiologic Research." *Journal of Clinical Epidemiology* 45: 1265–1287.

5. Hardcastle, J. D., J. O. Chamberlain, M. H. Robinson, S. M. Moss, S. S., Amar, T. W. Balfour, P. D. James, and C. M. Mangham, J. O. (1996). Randomised Controlled Trial of Faecal-Occult-Blood Screening For Colorectal Cancer. *Lancet* 348: 1472–1477.

6. Russell, L. B. (1986). *Is Prevention Better than Cure?* Washington, DC: Brookings Institution.

Irving Fisher, Victor Fuchs, and the Health-Government Tangle

By Richard Zeckhauser

Abstract. A comment on the article by Victor Fuchs in this volume.

Victor Fuchs alerts the modern world to Irving Fisher's deep and abiding interests in health. To most of us trained in Fisherian models of money, index numbers, and capital markets, this will be a revelation (see Barber 1997). But disappointment will be just a step behind. As Fuchs points out in this volume, Fisher seems to have set his economics aside when approaching health issues. His tubercular condition, more than economists' marginal conditions, appears to have spurred Fisher's health interests. In sharp contrast to the leading health economists of the modern era, whose health commentaries derive from their professional expertise, Fisher was a social crusader on health issues, who happened to be an economist. Fisher's reluctance or inability to apply his extraordinary economic logic is most telling in his failure to capture health promotion as an investment problem with a significant time dimension, an area where his contributions to economics endure.[1]

Irving Fisher endorsed active government participation in the health sector. The government should be a public health scold and enforcer

*Richard J. Zeckhauser is the Frank Plumpton Ramsey Professor of Political Economy at Harvard University's John F. Kennedy School of Government. Zeckhauser pursues a mix of conceptual and applied research. The primary challenge facing society, he believes, is to allocate resources in accordance with the preferences of the citizenry. Much of his conceptual work examines possibilities for democratic, decentralized allocation procedures. His ongoing policy investigations explore ways to promote the health of human beings, to help labor and financial markets operate more efficiently, and to foster informed and appropriate choices by individuals and government agencies. Zeckhauser's current major research addresses the performance of institutions confronted with inadequate commitment capabilities, incomplete information flow, and human participants who fail to behave in accordance with models of rationality (for example, by engaging in herd behavior). Financial markets and health risks are the subjects of his major empirical investigations. He thanks Miriam Avins, David Cutler, and Victor Fuchs for helpful conversations.

The American Journal of Economics and Sociology, Vol. 64, No. 1 (January, 2005).

(prohibiting alcohol, for example) and a provider of national health care insurance. And Fisher had strong views of how health might be promoted, ranging from diet to eugenics. Fuchs, though a kind man, is not kind to Fisher's analysis of health issues. The explanation, I believe, is that Fisher's approach to health promotion is about as far from Fuchs's as one could imagine. Fuchs is a data man who takes delight in drawing straightforward empirical insights about what works and what does not. And the delight is redoubled when the insights diverge sharply, as they often do, from the conventional wisdom. Fisher, by contrast, though believing himself driven by evidence and urging the development of better health data, often eschews empirical analysis of health issues but makes pronouncements nevertheless. Fuchs the careful researcher, it seems, is offended.

I

The Health-Government Tangle

FISHER'S ATTENTION TO the government's role in health spurs much of Fuchs's analysis. Were brevity not a concern, I would urge Fuchs to retitle his paper "Health and Government, and the Prescriptions of Irving Fisher." Fuchs, in his usual deft manner, identifies simple truths about the distinctive role of government in support of health. Fuchs is a devout economist, and he shows the discipline's explanatory powers. But he is also a realistic economist, and he makes it painfully clear that in the real world many of the government's actions regarding health have little to do with the information asymmetries, redistributional efficiencies, and physical externalities that comprise so much econobabble about why health and government are linked.

My commentary looks at the central issue that Fuchs addresses: the health-government tangle. I chose the word tangle for two reasons. First, there are a dozen strands to the government's involvement in health care, from subsidizing the training of medical students (a rapidly declining subsidy), to supporting biomedical research (an area of rapid growth), to operating veterans hospitals, to running and significantly supporting health insurance systems for the poor and elderly. Second, the nature of government involvement, at least to the eyes of an economist, is more tangled than neat.

Fuchs mentions a number of economic justifications for government participation in health care. I shall mention some others. But however many are included, Fuchs is correct that economics is not able to explain most of the variation over time and space in the way governments support health care. For example, if the purchase of drugs by the elderly merits government support in the year 2005, as a number of current policy initiatives seem to suggest, why did it not in 1990? Psychology and politics—more specifically prospect theory and the 2000 and 2004 presidential elections—both explain the "rapid escalation in costs, government must do something" rationale and the program that Bush put in place. Economics can only contribute that risk spreading has become more important. But if risk spreading were the major factor underlying insurance provision, our nation, much less the developed world, would hardly have so much first-dollar coverage for health care.

Why is so much government assistance delivered in the form of health care, as opposed to cash transfers? (Our nation spends roughly eight times as much on Medicaid, a program paying for health care for the poor, as on welfare.) James Tobin (1970), our fellow participant in this celebration, alas, now deceased, provided much of the economist's rationale for in-kind transfers in a famed essay now reaching its 35th birthday. What follows adds to Tobin's classic array some arguments that are particularly germane to government-supported health services. Despite their substantial normative merit, I recognize that much of what happens in health care is not explained by such factors.

II

Economic Rationales for Government Involvement in Health

Market failures are where economists start when considering a role for government policy. Informational asymmetries play a major role in health care. The agency problem, moral hazard, and adverse selection are three asymmetry-related problems that plague health care. Government policy can do little in the first area and a modest amount in the second; a range of government insurance-related policies can help with adverse selection.

The agency problem is hardly new in the health care realm. As Plato presented the faithful doctor: "No physician insofar as he is a physician, considers his own good in what he prescribes, but the good of his patient; for the true physician is also a ruler having the human body as a subject, and is not a mere moneymaker" (Plato, *The Republic*, Book 1: 342-D). Alas, many doctors, at least in the modern era, are not perfectly faithful to their patients' needs, and the rise of third-party payers has made the agency problem much worse in health care. Such payers trace a new route of accountability, from provider agents back to insurance plan principals. These insurance plans, whether for profit or nonprofit, have a responsibility to their insureds to constrain costs, but this pathway is often ignored. Recently, the government, the preeminent third-party payer in America, has squeezed the health care system. In response, many doctors have struggled to maintain their incomes; hospitals to stay afloat. For some, Mammon has competed effectively against Hippocrates as a figure to guide action.

Moral hazard means those whose care is paid for by a third party demand more care; and those whose services are paid for by a third party provide more services, assuming the price exceeds the marginal cost. The government, where it is the payer, has dealt with moral hazard, at least by providers, in precisely the manner economists would prescribe. It uses the contingent claims approach. When a Medicare recipient gets sick, the hospital is paid a fixed amount, independent of the service delivered. The danger is that the hospital may skimp. However, the fact that the physician is the predominant decisionmaker, and that the patient is quite interested in his or her own welfare, diminishes this danger.

In a book preoccupied with love and adventure, Lord Byron addressed adverse selection: "Tis said that people living on annuities/Are longer lived than others" (Lord Byron, *Don Juan*). The potential for adverse selection—high-risk individuals selecting more generous and expensive coverage—creates a prospect for government activity. Government can provide insurance directly, as it does with Medicare; standardize insurance or make it mandatory, two cornerstones of the Clinton health plan; or subsidize insurance sufficiently to induce purchase by virtually all parties, as it does by not taxing employer-paid premiums.

Surprisingly, many of Fisher's arguments for a public role in health care revolve around asymmetric information, but none deal with these three classic arguments. As Fuchs points out, Fisher simply thought he had better ideas about such areas as diet, physical exams, and the prohibition of alcohol, happily relying on his own assessments of causal relationships, a number of which proved unreliable. Moreover, though he recognized the tradeoffs implicit in policies in each of these areas, he prescribed numerous policies, using his own weights to make tradeoffs within and across individuals. Fisher deserves credit for identifying the importance of lifestyle on health, an area explored much more systematically subsequently by Fuchs ([1974] 1998), but should be chastised for severe overconfidence and for tossing aside the methods of his own discipline.

Turning from informational asymmetries, government's role in funding public goods helps explain why we have an NIH budget, and why its burgeoning collaborative programs with the pharmaceutical industry make sense. It also suggests that it is worthwhile to have a government-supported effort to assess best practices in medicine. Traditional externalities, such as limiting the spread of contagious diseases, explain little of modern government involvement with health. Even in the AIDS epidemic, apart from exhortation, government—with a strong and contemporary concern for privacy and civil liberties—is doing little to control the disease's spread.

Fiscal externalities come next. An individual's income provides a fiscal externality to the government; as he or she earns more, the government collects more taxes. Thus, the government, acting for us all, has an incentive to keep the individual healthy. This provides a justification for government-subsidized health care, at least for potential workers.[2] At the margin, the government is a 40% beneficiary from our richest citizens' incomes, and a 15% beneficiary from less affluent taxpayers. Efficiency demands that a party that shares in the benefits should share in the costs as well. But this fiscal externality principle, though meriting extra credit on public finance exams, is not part of the political debate; indeed it is rarely discussed anywhere, and assuredly does not explain the government's significant policies in the health arena. Risk spreading provides another potential explanation for a government role. But since most insurance plans cover initial or early dollar coverage, where the financial risks to the insured are small, this explanation is not convincing.

Paternalism does help explain why our redistributional policies focus on health. We do not trust the poor to spend their money wisely, on medicines, say, rather than lottery tickets. A complementary argument applies in this realm: Redistributing health dollars rather than green dollars makes the donors feel better. That is, there is a good-specific externality. Health care is a red flag for conscience. If poor people lack health care, the whole system seems unjust. From the donors' standpoint, and frequently all of us are donors as citizens, better the poor person receive a vaccination than a VCR, a mobile checkup than a mobile phone. His lack of Sonys and Nokias doesn't bother us; it doesn't trumpet the inequities of our society. Sometimes the issue is less how the money is spent than in who gets to spend the money. Target efficiency is lost if Grandma gets a general support check, which is cashed and used to pay for a family trip to the movies; it is preserved if her health checkup is paid for by Medicare.

These economic arguments about the rationales for government-supported health care make for lively debate about the appropriate role of government, but primarily among economists. Economists just see these issues differently than the world at large. They tend to see little special about health care, apart from its economic properties, whereas many policymakers and citizens believe that health care, unlike even housing, is a right, something God-given. And what God gives, it seems, in a form of double provision, the government must pay for. (Many agnostics and atheists concerned with a just society also feel the government should pay for health care.)

Whatever the rationale for government involvement in health care, the natural question arises about what happened between Irving Fisher's time and today that so many developed nations today believe that government should simply pay for the bulk of health care. Fisher was well ahead of his time in two respects: identifying national health insurance as a priority, and reaching this conclusion on the basis of limited economic analysis.

III

Appropriate Government Roles in Health Care

THE BACK PORTION of Fuchs's essay looks at the causes and consequences of government involvement. Though we all know there should be a government role in health care, it is much less clear what the role should be. Three decades ago, government policy increased the number of medical specialists and hospital beds. But today it pushes in the opposite direction, in part because we think underutilized resources create their own demand, rather than fostering competition that reduces prices.

Medical technology has marched smartly forward in this era with strong support from government. Though theory suggests improved technologies may save monies on net, they have not. The burgeoning NIH budget must therefore be justified for the knowledge it brings, for the cures of Alzheimer's and cancer that may be just around the corner. In assessing the potential contributions of emerging medical technologies to both health and cost control, Fuchs has often been a sober voice. I am more Pollyannaish. The pathways to production of new medical technologies are much more complex than economists have imagined. Anti-angiogenesis provides an intriguing example. It is a technology that seeks to starve malignant tumors by shutting down their ability to stimulate new blood supplies. Dr. Judah Folkman conceived of this approach 35 years ago and received initial support from the nonprofit American Cancer Society in the late 1960s. Subsequently he received some support from the government. Now the technology is on the brink of a test in humans, and it is commercial biotech and pharmaceutical firms that will be conducting the work. If the results are promising, the government will step in again, to decide whether to let the anti-angiogenesis agents on the market, and for which patients. And the government-run patent system will at all times be in the background, spurring new medical developments by protecting intellectual property, but perhaps discouraging their spread by allowing monopoly pricing.[3]

Even when the goals are clear, what the government should do is not. Consider tobacco regulation. Whatever the role of Joe Camel, neither the government nor the tobacco companies know how to effectively curb tobacco use, beyond raising the price through taxation.[4] But since cigarettes are disproportionately purchased by the poor, using price as a discouragement works against distributional goals. And leaving distributional considerations aside, should we set the tobacco tax way above the fiscal externalities tobacco imposes?[5] Moral arguments and great pots of money appear to be motivating our nation's tobacco policies, not analytic thought. As a perusal of Fisher's arguments against alcohol make clear, strong moral views do not always lead to sensible policies.[6] Fuchs aptly cites Stigler on the dangers of linking reform and research.

IV

Conclusion

Irving Fisher has been more than discovered as a health economist. He has been dissected by Victor Fuchs, a master anatomist. One of Fisher's greatest contributions is his systematic thought about time and the future. On health issues, he was assuredly future-minded. His emphasis on personal habits, as opposed to health care, as contributors to well-being appears prescient. His strong support for national health insurance was well ahead of his time. Will government begin to emphasize individuals' responsibilities for their own health? Will the U.S. government initiate national health insurance for significant new groups? The answer to these questions will emerge primarily from political considerations. To recognize that policy reality is not to welcome it. The discussion will be less well informed, our health policies less sensible if the economic foundations are not understood.

Irving Fisher was no role model with his analysis of health policy, long on self-assurance, short on economic reasoning. Economists seeking sustenance on health issues should look elsewhere in his works. Fisher bequeathed them a substantial legacy in his pioneering studies at the core of economics, ranging from optimal capital accumulation to the construction of index numbers. On such solid foundations—the first on dynamics, the second on evaluation—sound economics and wise policies in health will be anchored.

Notes

1. See Nordhaus in this volume for an exemplary application of economic logic to the analysis of health.

2. Of course, if health care enables the individual to live longer, to collect more Social Security and Medicare benefits, that creates a fiscal externality cutting in the opposite direction.

3. Economists have a neat solution to this problem. When important technologies become available, have the government buy the patent and make the technology available at marginal cost. This recommendation only holds sway in public finance classes.

4. Recent studies found that the highly regarded, well-established, and widely employed D.A.R.E. Program, intended to curb drug use by the young, is not effectual (*Boston Globe*, August 2, 1999: 1.)

5. Manning et al. (1989) estimated the net fiscal externality of smoking to be roughly zero at a 3% discount rate. The cigarette taxes just covered the difference between smokers' increased medical costs and lower expected Social Security payments, which is below current taxation levels, much less levels that are being contemplated.

6. See Phillips and Zeckhauser (1996) for an assessment of the value of the cardiovascular benefits of moderate alcohol consumption. Should government publicize such benefits, at the risk of increasing problem drinking?

References

Barber, William (ed.). (1997). *The Works of Irving Fisher.* London: Pickering and Chatto.

Fuchs, Victor R. ([1974] 1998). *Who Shall Live? Health, Economics, and Social Choice—Expanded Edition.* Singapore: World Scientific Publishing Company.

Manning, Willard G., Emmett B. Keeler, Joseph P. Newhouse, Elizabeth M. Sloss, and Jeffrey Wasserman. (1989). "The Taxes of Sin: Do Smokers and Drinkers Pay Their Way?" *JAMA* 261: 1604–1609.

Phillips, Carl V., and Richard Zeckhauser. (1996). "Communicating the Health Effects of Consumer Products: The Case of Moderate Alcohol Consumption and Coronary Heart Disease." *Managerial and Decision Economics* 17: 459–470.

Tobin, James. (1970). "On Limiting the Domain of Inequality." *Journal of Law and Economics* 13: 263–277.

Index

for

CELEBRATING IRVING FISHER: THE LEGACY OF A GREAT ECONOMIST

9 781405 133074